CATASTROPHIC HISTORICISM

IDIOM INVENTING WRITING THEORY

Jacques Lezra and Paul North, series editors

CATASTROPHIC HISTORICISM

READING JULIA DE BURGOS DANGEROUSLY

RONALD MENDOZA-DE JESÚS

Fordham University Press *New York*   *2023*

Copyright © 2023 Fordham University Press

All rights reserved. No part of this publication may be reproduced, stored in a retrieval system, or transmitted in any form or by any means—electronic, mechanical, photocopy, recording, or any other—except for brief quotations in printed reviews, without the prior permission of the publisher.

Fordham University Press has no responsibility for the persistence or accuracy of URLs for external or third-party Internet websites referred to in this publication and does not guarantee that any content on such websites is, or will remain, accurate or appropriate.

Fordham University Press also publishes its books in a variety of electronic formats. Some content that appears in print may not be available in electronic books.

Visit us online at www.fordhampress.com.

Library of Congress Cataloging-in-Publication Data available online at https://catalog.loc.gov.

Printed in the United States of America

25 24 23   5 4 3 2 1

First edition

CONTENTS

Introduction: Reading Danger   1

Part I. Catastrophic Traditions: Reading the Image of Julia de Burgos, *Dangerously*   23

Part II. The Closure of Historicism; or, History in Deconstruction   98

Part III. Reading Now: The Catastrophic Modernity of Julia de Burgos   154

Epilogue. After Sovereignty?   273

    Acknowledgments   *277*

    Notes   *283*

    Index   *325*

CATASTROPHIC HISTORICISM

Leave the possible to those who love it.
—Georges Bataille

INTRODUCTION: READING DANGER

§0. DESEDIMENTING HISTORICISM: A PROBLEM FOR THOUGHT

After enjoying a somewhat lengthy reign as the default methodology of literary studies in the North American academy, historicism has again come under fire in ways perhaps not seen since the heyday of "high theory" and the Yale School.[1] Challenges to historicism's hegemony have been launched recently from multiple disciplinary fronts by scholars committed to addressing historicism's faulty ontological assumptions and epistemological impasses, countering its ethical and political blind spots, and undoing the damaging effects of its hold on the institutional framework of humanistic disciplines. Not only has the demand that the past be narrated *wie es eigentlich gewesen* ("as it really happened") been charged with reducing humanistic methods of inquiry to an antiquarian concern with the gathering of facts—in what amounts to a far more damning indictment, historicism's reputed reduction of historical *significance* to positive or empirical *evidence* has opened it to the accusation of endorsing the violence that has made history by obfuscating entrenched power inequities and erasing the gaps that trouble the smooth unfolding of historical narratives, thereby condemning the silences that haunt historical archives to further illegibility.

While offering a provisional endorsement of these critiques, *Reading Danger* resets the terms of the ongoing debate about historicism, redefining in the process the conditions that would have to be met for a *nonhistoricist concept of history* to be theorized and practiced. Fittingly, this book's transformative work begins with the term *historicism*, which I argue stands in dire need of interrogation. Asking the question of historicism anew has become necessary in light of the overly sedimented ways this word is used in the humanities today, where a mere mention of "empiricism" or "positivism," accompanied by a perfunctory reference to Ludwig von Ranke's motto *wie es eigentlich gewesen*,[2] are often all that is required not only to use this term "correctly" but also to give an adequate description of this concept. By taking a "step back" from this tradition in order to question some of its key conceptual and historical presuppositions, *Reading Danger* makes the case that the inherited definitions of historicism as a realism, empiricism, or positivism of historical facts are *theoretically insufficient, historically dubious*, and *strategically ineffective*:[3] These definitions are theoretically insufficient because they do not give an appropriate account of what historicism *is*. They are historically dubious because they do not allow us to locate the genesis of historicism within the admittedly longer history of Western and non-Western historiographical practices, nor do they help us understand why historicism has become virtually coextensive with the field of historical representation in general, if not even with history itself. And they are strategically ineffective because they fail to present a compelling case for why challenging historicism's claim to have saturated the field of possibilities of historical representation remains an urgent matter.

In this respect, *Reading Danger* joins contemporary efforts to criticize and displace historicism within and beyond literary studies, but it does so first and foremost by addressing the *somnambulism* at work in the ongoing debates about historicism. I borrow the term "somnambulism" from Jacques Derrida, who relies on the figure of the sleepwalker to describe the specific mode of inheritance that ensures the stable replication of a tradition through acts of reactivation that appear wholly programmed by the explicit terms set through the institution of that tradition or by its unstated or implicit assumptive logic.[4] Understood in this way, somnambulism designates a threshold of indistinction in which the process of historical transmission is suspended between activity and passivity, conscious response and reflexive action, scholarly vigilance and intellectual laxity. This book is written in the conviction that the concept of historicism has fallen prey to this sleepwalking form of historical transmission, which bears some affinities with that mode of tradition that Walter Benjamin describes as "catastrophe."[5] The scholarly consensus regarding the fact that historicism is the historical variant of empiricism or positivism is sufficient proof of this somnambulism. Contemporary critics of historicism within literary theory may think they're laying claim to the most solid of scholarly grounds from the moment they repeat as a ready-made answer to the question "What is historicism?" the definitions crafted by historicism's first major opponents (a notable club that includes figures such as Ralph Waldo Emerson, Friedrich Nietzsche, and, perhaps most crucially, Edmund Husserl) or their successors (a group that counts figures such as Martin Heidegger, Walter Benjamin, Michel Foucault, Paul de Man, Jacques Derrida, and Hayden White). But the solidity of this conceptual ground and the prestige of the names associated with it should not be taken prima facie as an indication of its reliability. To put it plainly, my claim is that the stability of these conceptual grounds rests not on the fact that they express the truth about historicism's essence; rather, these grounds are stable as a result of a decades-long process of sedimentation that has successfully lent the reductive description of historicism as a realism, positivism, or empiricism of historical facts the veneer of a truism.[6] Among other byproducts, this sedimentation has served to insulate both contemporary critics and their authoritative sources from any serious theoretical inquiry regarding the sufficiency of the concept of historicism they have instituted or inherited. By sleepwalking on these compacted grounds, scholars in the contemporary antihistoricist camp within literary studies and the broader theoretical humanities continue to foreclose the chance of posing the *question* of historicism in earnest. To counter this foreclosure, *Catastrophic Historicism* carries out a *de*sedimentation of these compacted conceptual grounds for the sake of posing the question of historicism anew. To do so, this book lays the groundwork for an inquiry into the conceptual bases of historicism deep enough to force the conflation of historicism with realism to appear *as* the reductive and unwarranted conflation it is. Only then, to borrow Nahum D. Chandler's felicitous expression, historicism may become again a "problem for thought."[7]

§1. TRANSCENDENTAL HISTORICISM; OR, HISTORY'S COSMO-POETICS

If historicism is not reducible to a realism (let alone to an empiricist or positivist approach to historical facts), then what is it? Sketching an answer to this question is the central task of Part II, "The Closure of Historicism; or, History in Deconstruction." The reader here will encounter an attempt at conceptual reconstruction that seeks to transform not only the shape and structure of the received, realist concept of historicism but also the philosophical problem in relation to which historicism's first critics crafted this concept as well as what Gilles Deleuze and Félix Guattari call the "field," "plane," or "ground" in which this concept was initially constructed.[8] Rather than offer a detailed road map of the analyses that I carry out in Part II, I want to provide a more general account of the philosophical work that I accomplish there by addressing each of the three insufficiencies of the realist concept of historicism I have just outlined.

The first of these was of a *theoretical* order. Reducing historicism to realism produces an unwarranted restriction of the scope of this concept, depriving us of the chance to experience historicism as a *problem* by making it possible to declare any methodological approach to historical facts that purportedly breaks with realism as already nonhistoricist. To be sure, historicism could not have been conceived without a realist moment or element, but, as I contend in this book, the realist motif that was *necessary* for its emergence and institutionalization is not *sufficient* to ground its essence and existence. This assumption explains why, despite sharing the view that a positivistic attitude to the past is detrimental to our historical imagination, I nonetheless reject the very grounds on which that judgment of historical positivism rests. This ambivalence regarding the established terms of the critique of historicism explains the idiosyncratic task that this book takes up: to reaffirm the necessity and urgency of this critical task while crafting a concept of historicism that, unlike the realist straw man, may be better able to convey the threat that its hegemony poses to humanistic scholarship and to our experience of ourselves as historical beings.

At the most general level, this book redefines historicism as the sense-configuration within the history of history that instituted the *possibility* of historical *appropriation* by endowing the historian with the power to transform the past in general into a possible onto-phenomenological region or site through its re-presentation within historical *narratives*. Such a definition captures the gist of Frank Ankersmit's recent defense of historicism in *Meaning, Truth, and Reference in Historical Representation*, which could be summarized with the following phrase: "The historian's breath permeates the past as presented by him, in much the same way that the pantheist God is present in His creation."[9] Despite the theological overtones of Ankersmit's characterization of the historicist historian, this description does not suggest a complete lapse into pre-Kantian metaphysical dogmatism; rather, it provides a rigorous, metaphorical expression of the specifically post-Kantian type of *transcendental correlationism* that constitutes the formal core of historicism.

On the basis of the first part of this highly schematic definition we can already begin to glean some of the reasons why this book rejects the conflation of historicism with realism as reductionist. For if historicism is concerned above all with a *possibility*, and if, furthermore, this possibility is neither an onticized possibility (say, a possible *x*) nor the possibility (in an ontological sense) of any given historical *thing* or *object* but what *possibilitates* the specific mode of *correlation* through which alone our *access* to historical phenomena *in general* has been first secured, then it is clear that any definition of historicism as a realism would have failed to take into consideration the *transcendental* argument that attended the genesis and consolidation of historicism as *the* ontology of history. Historicism does contain a realist moment within its structure, but the *possibility* of historicism does not rest on the ascription of any substantial properties to the past as a reality or a thing "in itself," that is, to the past posited outside the correlational space in which alone it *appears* and *is for the historian*. Any critique of historicism that centers the untenability of historicism's realism misses the chance to attack historicism at its very roots by failing to target the *metaphysical concept of possibility* that gave rise to historicism, which, I argue, coincides with what the late Derrida calls "ipseity," a modal category that foregrounds the structural indissociability of *power* and *possibility*, of *mastery* and *potentiality*.[10]

Since the metaphysical concept of possibility or ipseity will be examined later, I want to now unpack the second major part of the definition I have given, namely, historicism's *narrative* or *poetic* component. These two aspects are deeply interrelated. For, as Ankersmit's description suggests, historicism could not have emerged without the investment in the historian's *presentational* faculties of the power to constitute the phenomenal reality of the past. And the medium in which the past attains presentation is precisely the *representations* of the historian. Those representations, in turn, can only deliver historical cognition of historical objects through their synthetic integration within a narrative. As Hans Michael Baumgartner, a major exponent of the transcendental approach to historiography, puts it:

> The formation of history proves to be a narrative construction, a construction that institutes sense-contexts and sense-formations on top of the fundamental structures of the human life-world, which are schematized in narrative-intentions. What it produces is an originary narrative synthesis, an a priori schema for histories, which underlies concrete histories and the empirical historical object as its condition of possibility.[11]

To appreciate both the generality of Baumgartner's statement and its centrality for the constitution of historicism does not require entering into—let alone settling—the thorny debate about the validity of Louis O. Mink's claim that "stories are not lived, but told: Life has no beginnings, middles, or ends; there are meetings, but the start of an affair belongs to the story we tell later, and there are partings, but final partings only in the story."[12] For both Mink's view—including any of its variations in Paul Ricœur or Hayden White—and the "narrative self" thesis embraced by Alasdair MacIntyre or David Carr leave untouched the core of Baumgartner's transcendental argument. Whether the view of historical cognition as essentially narrative based is grounded in a view of the *life-world* as always already narratively schematized (call this *ontological* historicism), justified on the basis of the belief that the historian's *self* is already *in itself* constituted as a narrative (call this *phenomenological* or *transcendental psychological* historicism), or held as valid for us in spite of the fact that historical events are not already composed as stories *in themselves* (call this *epistemological* historicism) does not alter the essential fact that narrative *form* constitutes the a priori schema for the experience of historical cognition—and, by extension, determines the core of historicism.[13]

There is, however, a crucial element missing from this account. If narrative is at the basis of the *possibility* of history, then the question remains as to how this possibility *actualizes itself*. Do *all* narratives evince the requisite formal conditions required for narrative to fulfill its function as history's transcendental? The answer to this question constitutes one of the main theoretical claims of *Catastrophic Historicism*, since it is both decisive for its redefinition of historicism and, by extension, for the nonhistoricist concept of historicity this book projects. Bluntly speaking, this book answers this question negatively: Not all forms of narrative could conform to the metaphysical strictures of historicism's transcendental grounding of historical objectivities. In thus answering this question, I am making a case for the centrality of Ankersmit's "narrative idealism" and his recent retrieval of the German historicist concept of the "historical idea" as theoretical proposals that *suffice* to characterize the specific form of historicism with which this book seeks to break. As will become clear in Part II, Ankersmit's defense of historicism is dependent upon a claim that this book rejects as unduly metaphysical, indeed dogmatic, namely, the belief that the space of historical narration is akin to a Leibnizian *world*—a cosmic *plenum* in which there are no gaps. Far from being a fundamentally realist ontology that would presume a correspondence between the world of historical realities or facts and the *harmonious* world of narration, historicism is a transcendental narrative-idealism that requires grounding the possibility of historical knowledge in the *cosmo-poietic* power of historians, which is, in turn, actualized in the composition of historical narratives. It is only in the worldly space of historical narration that the past in general becomes *ontologically available* as an object of re-presentation for a historicist historian who, like the Leibnizian God, calculates with compossibilities in order to decide on the best possible plot in which to represent the past "as it *properly* happened."

§2. HISTORICISM IN THE HISTORY OF METAPHYSICS: ELEMENTS FOR A DECONSTRUCTIVE GENEALOGY

I now want to address the second of the charges I laid before the realist concept of historicism, namely, its historical dubiousness. In the process, I will clarify how my efforts to theorize and practice a nonhistoricist literary history entail engaging with the more general task of a *deconstructive genealogy* of historicism.

To do so, I want to briefly go over an aspect of the description of historicism that I gave earlier, namely, its status as a "sense-configuration within the history of history." My use of the Husserlian motif of *Sinngebilde*, or "sense-configuration,"[14] and the doubling of the noun *history* are part of an attempt to thematize the *historical* status of historicism. Historicism's emergence and consolidation are "part" of the history of history, a broader sense-configuration that encompasses the tradition of historiographical practices in general. Even this broader tradition should ultimately be seen as "part" of a *general history* whose empirical boundaries are difficult to establish for essential reasons. If, following Husserl, we describe the *form* of this general history as "the living movement of the coexistence and the interweaving of originary sense-formation [*urspüng-licher Sinnbildung*] and sense-sedimentations [*Sinnsedimentierungen*]," then the *history* of historicism would have to be approached similarly, namely, as an institution whose historical fabric is composed of the inseparable intertwining of sense-formation and sense-sedimentations.[15]

Taking a cue from Husserl, this book claims that the *realist* definition of historicism is a sedimented result produced by historicism's formative process. As such, realist historicism necessarily dissimulates the living movement of its genesis, covering over the historicity of historicism's history by obfuscating the transcendental motif that alone ensured its institutionalization as the privileged ontology of history. This dissimulation, in turn, extends beyond the history of historicism to the history of history itself, which results in the realist determination of the very idea of history in general, which Ethan Kleinberg has aptly characterized in his definition of the ontological realism of normative historians as "a commitment to history as an endeavor concerned with events assigned to a specific location in space and time that are in principle observable and as such are regarded as fixed and immutable."[16] A deconstructive genealogy desediments the realist concept of historicism in order to retell its history on the basis of a concept of historicity that no longer takes historicism, whether in its narrow realist form or in its broader transcendental version, for granted.

That said, since the term *deconstructive* in the phrase "deconstructive genealogy of historicism" refers not only to Husserl's method of *Abbau* or Heidegger's *Destruktion* but, above all, to Derrida's *déconstruction*, the utility of Husserl's approach to historical sedimentation (or, for that matter, of Heidegger's history of being) for this genealogy must be qualified. One of the hallmarks of Derridean deconstruction is the insistence that the formation of sense cannot be regarded as originary with regards to its sedimentation precisely because the formation and the sedimentation of sense are indeed as imbricated (or, as Derrida would put it, *contaminated*) as Husserl himself claims. Put otherwise, if Derrida asks in his 1953–1954 mémoire (akin to an MA thesis) on Husserl, "why must we always begin with the constituted or the derivative product to then go back to the constituting source?," by the time his philosophical thinking gives way to the thought of *différance*, the directionality of this movement is put under erasure.[17] Accordingly, the attempt to desediment historicism must abandon the double presumption that the *genesis* of historicism coincides with the *originary* institution of its sense and that this sense could be reactivated without sedimented residues through a historical *Rückfrage* or "questioning-back." A deconstructive genealogy of historicism would have to take at its point of departure historicism's constituted sense and engage in a historical mode of inquiry that is not merely empiricist but that has also abandoned the safety of an uncomplicated recourse to a transcendental, constituting instance that is not *at the same time* saddled with historical sedimentations constituted a priori by the very history it appears to inaugurate. As a result of this generalizable contamination, any moment of historical inauguration or sense-institution turns out to be necessarily inhabited or haunted by prior instances of already-configured senses that endanger not only its *life*—that is, its self-presence to itself in its temporal self-immanence—but also its claim to having the power of instituting an *absolutely new* sense-configuration. The text of history is thereby radically reconfigured: Rather than appearing as the unfolding of a *cyclical line* that moves unidirectionally from its point of departure in the originary vitality of sense-formation, to the moment of crisis and negativity that ensues when the life of history is endangered by sedimentation, to the mediated recuperation of that lost vitality via the appropriative reactivation of the originary intuitions and experiences that grounded the process of sense-formation, the life of history is entirely dissolved in its open-ended textualization, in such a way that history itself appears now in the guise of a Borgesian labyrinth. Foucault perhaps gave the most lapidary version of this insight when he stated that "behind history, there is always history."[18] This is the quasi-transcendental commitment required to enter into *the scene of historical reading*.

Where could we turn to begin such a reading? How should we enter the historicist labyrinth? If we must begin with the constituted or sedimented sense of historicism, then it stands to reason that the texts of self-proclaimed historicists might provide a good point of departure for this genealogy. In this respect, I take Frederick Beiser's closing remarks in the introduction to his monumental *The German Historicist Tradition* as a helpful index to begin this desedimentation. Turning to the question of the causes of historicism's decline (note that *historicism* is here understood in the narrowest possible sense, that is, as a philosophical movement with more or less discrete spatiotemporal boundaries), Beiser formulates an argument that is equal parts dubious and insightful: According to Beiser, since "the original project behind historicism" was "to have history recognized as a science," its very success spelled its end: "Having achieved what it set out to do, historicism did not need to exist anymore."[19] But in a dialectical reversal more evocative of the phoenix-like movement of Hegelian historicism than of its Rankean counterpart, the death of historicism gives way to its new and higher form of life: "Historicism was not an abject failure but an astonishing success. Indeed, since it continues to exercise such enormous influence, it never really died at all. It continues to live in all of us, and it is fair to say that, as heirs of Meinecke's revolution, *we are all historicists today.*"[20] A similar though more modest statement can be found near the beginning of Ankersmit's *Meaning, Truth, and Reference in Historical Representation*, where Ankersmit writes that "no historian can avoid subscribing to historicism. For what could possibly be the purpose of his activity if he rejected the historicist claim that a thing's nature or identity lies in its past? Without it, there would be no sense or meaning to the historian's efforts."[21] Reading these two passages with and against each other, a picture of historicism's historical institutionalization and sedimentation emerges with relative clarity. That the historian cannot avoid being a historicist is itself a historical fact grounded in the generalization of historicism, in the fact that "we are all historicists today." The advent of historicism (in the narrow or empirico-historical sense of the term) facilitated the institutionalization and sedimentation of what is now a habitual attitude of wide swaths of humanity, namely, that specific mode of cognitive comportment toward beings that leads to the location of their *ground* or *essence* in their *history*, that posits identity or nature as something constituted in the past. In this respect, it is not just the historian who can't avoid being historicist; even those of us who are not professional historians and who might be interested in theorizing alternative models of historicization *have never not been historicists.*

But if historicism has become coextensive with the historical in general, then there is no easily available position outside its sense-configuration, no easy standpoint within the broader history of history from which one could precisely locate its emergence and anticipate its end. It is from this *Faktum*, at once historical and transcendental, that a deconstructive genealogy of historicism ought to begin. The becoming-science of history provides a crucial entry point into historicism's history because it is this most metaphysical of achievements that has contributed the most to the obfuscation—if not outright obliteration—of historicism's historicity. Historicism's success in turning history into a science (in the broader sense of a *Wissenschaft* or an academic discipline) retroactively occupies the position of the hidden normative *telos* of the entire "history of history," which is thereby implicitly constructed as slowly marching from its stillborn Aristotelian inception to its eventual constitution as a science. Retracing the steps of this march, which always entails the risk of tacitly endorsing this teleological narrative, is a prerequisite for this deconstructive genealogy. Its preliminary task is to re-present, in a sui generis narrative form, how the becoming-science of historical representation marked the completion of a long process whereby historical time—for centuries regarded as ontology's *no man's land*—progressively came in the service of ontology and historical representation became increasingly available for Western metaphysics. In other words, its task is to remain within the historicist sense-configuration while reinscribing (indeed rewriting) the history of that formation as a key rearticulation of the totality of the *history of metaphysics*, that is, as another instantiation of the transhistorical determination of being *as* presence. Only then could we attain the position from which Derrida's claim in *La voix et le phénomène* that " 'history' has never meant anything but this: the presentation (*Gegenwärtigung*) of being, the production and gathering of beings within presence, as knowledge and mastery"[22] appears as a truism. At the same time, it is only after delimiting, as rigorously as possible, historicism's *closure* that we may begin the difficult task of prying open the history of history in order to *resituate*, as well as possible, the *genesis* of historicism within the broader historical field of historical representation, which it would no longer dominate.

§3. A DANGEROUS HISTORICITY; OR, UNSETTLING HISTORICAL IPSEITY: ON THE IM-POSSIBLE

The restitution of historicism's transcendental cosmo-poetics and the attempt to sketch its historical closure are only two aspects of *Catastrophic Historicism*'s threefold attempt to address the insufficiencies of the dominant approach to historicism. The third aspect requires articulating *another* concept of *historicity*, one that would no longer be entirely dominated by historicism—now understood as the ontology of history that instituted the figure of the historian as the *ipse* or the "self itself" who, as sovereign history-teller, lords over the past. Such conceptual effort is required if we are to counter the sleepwalking that has characterized historicism's deeply sedimented, almost naturalized transmission, which has resulted in a situation in which, as Beiser puts it, *we are all historicists*.

In this paragraph, I would like to lay out what is arguably the most crucial aspect of this book's theoretical strategy and make the case for its expediency, explaining in the process what I meant earlier when I charged critiques of historicism that center on its realism with being strategically ineffective. As will become clear in what follows, this book's strategy requires a conceptual effort pitched at a philosophical scale that is properly speaking *transcendental*. At stake, in other words, is the necessity of clarifying the concept of *possibility* that provided the historico-metaphysical conditions of possibility for the genesis and institutionalization of historicism. This task is a prerequisite for elaborating a nonhistoricist concept of *historicity*. Although this concept will not totally sever all ties with transcendentalism, it departs from the *metaphysical* determination of *modal* categories that characterizes not just transcendental philosophy since Kant but philosophy since Parmenides's separation of the paths of being and nonbeing.[23] This metaphysics of modality finds expression in the traditional privilege of actuality (*energeia, actualitas, Wirklichkeit*)—and thus of reality—over possibility (*dunamis, potentia, Möglichkeit*) and, more profoundly still, in the *near-absolute privilege of the possible over the impossible*.

In challenging this privilege, this book unfolds within a "logical" space profoundly altered by the fundamental ontology of Heidegger's *Sein und Zeit* (*Being and Time*), which undoes the two "modal" privileges outlined earlier. For the existential analytic of *Dasein* not only shows that "possibility stands higher than actuality"; it also demonstrates that the privilege of possibility over actuality is itself grounded in and can only be phenomenologically attested by the *proper* experience of *my own death*, whose essence presents a modality that can be described only in terms of "the possibility of the measureless impossibility of existence."[24] Since it is only *out of* this limit, extreme modality, out of the limit experience of "running ahead" to my own nothingness, that all "my" possibilities are first *possibilitated*, opened up and instituted *as* possibilities, Heidegger's thinking breaches the Parmenidean fortress, granting a concept of possibility that is no longer determined by the privilege of being over nonbeing or of the possible over the impossible.

Still, despite his centrality for this book, it is not to Heidegger but to Benjamin and Derrida that I ultimately turn in order to craft a nonhistoricist concept of historicity, understood in (quasi-)modal terms. I do so by retrieving two conceptual motifs that play a crucial role in their thinking, namely, *ipseity* and *danger*. Derrida's engagement with the category of ipseity is paramount for this book for a very simple reason: Unlike so many other contemporary continental thinkers writing in the wake of Husserl and Heidegger, Derrida does not take ipseity to be that very essence which philosophical thinking must restore to its ontological or ethical purity by rescuing the self from its "inauthentic" or "vulgar" fallenness or by restoring a *proper* experience of appropriation or selfhood that would be *toto cælo* different from the reified language of property and self-possession. Rather, as will become clearer in Part II, Derrida's work on the category of ipseity insists on the indissociability of *possibility*, *selfhood*, *self-referentiality*, and *power*, with the result that *being-possible* and *being-oneself* become contaminated with *mastery* and *sovereignty* from the get-go. Derrida's conception of ipseity sheds light on the specific valence that this word has in the definition of historicism I provided earlier. Historicism presupposes a concept of possibility that boils down to *ipseity* as Derrida understands it. History *after* historicism becomes another fortress from which the self is able to consolidate its boundaries by appropriating the past through its narrative-poetic powers, thereby domesticating its contingency and neutralizing the chance of an *event*, of something that might exceed the narrative self and its power to anticipate and integrate happenings within the totality of what Wilhelm von Dilthey calls the "life-nexus."[25] Historicism lives off this metaphysical determination of possibility; indeed, it only attained closure and secured its institutionalization by extending the form of *ipseity* to all historical phenomena—and especially to the historian. Historicism thus emerges as a defensive system that safeguards the belief in the historian's power to resurrect the past through historical narratives that preclude any possibilities that may not exhibit the form of ipseity.

Only if we approach historicism as a metaphysical prophylaxis can we begin to grasp the reasons why *danger* constitutes for Benjamin a sine qua non of any critique of historicism. Danger names the affective and modal quality of a historical experience in which the past does not appear as a secure possession of the historian but manifests itself in the mode of radical contingency. In other words, if historicity entails an experience of danger, if the past is only historical when its very occurrence remains in question, then danger holds the key to a notion of historicity that goes against the grain of historicism's metaphysical investment in ipseity. Danger *endangers* the link between possibility and mastery that enabled the historicist and their cosmo-poetic narratives to declare themselves the ground of the historicity of the past. And if historicism relies on a metaphysical poetics of historical *writing* that forces historical events into a compositional mold characterized by continuity, linearity, and in some cases, causality, then *reading danger* names a historical practice that interrupts historicism by reintroducing contingency and nonlinearity into the text of history.

§4. AN EXCEPTIONAL LIFE: JULIA DE BURGOS

But *Catastrophic Historicism* does not simply intervene in debates about the *theory* of history. As its subtitle, *Reading Julia de Burgos Dangerously*, suggests, this book also enters the *practical* arena of literary history by reexamining the historical constitution of the *image* of Julia de Burgos (1914–1953), the most iconic figure in Puerto Rican letters.

Born on February 17, 1914, in the Barrio Santa Cruz, a rural neighborhood in the city of Carolina, Puerto Rico, de Burgos (née Julia Constanza Burgos García) was the firstborn child of Francisco Burgos Hance (best known as Francisco Burgos Hans) and Paula García de Burgos (née García Marcano).[26] Besides de Burgos, the couple had twelve more children—six of whom died in childhood. Factual information about the socioeconomic background of the Burgos-García family is scarce, but most biographers of the poet agree that de Burgos grew up in a household marked by poverty. Identified as a farmer on the poet's birth certificate, Francisco Burgos Hance also seems to have worked for the island's National Guard;[27] he was, by all accounts, a Don Juan type who loved literature, horseback riding, and alcohol, introducing de Burgos to a bohemian lifestyle from an early age.[28] As if counterbalancing Francisco Burgos's carefree existence, Paula García seems to have played a stabilizing role in the poet's childhood, anchoring a family that would be forced by economic circumstances to move with relative frequency. Having excelled early at school, de Burgos left the family home in 1925 to attend "Grammar School" in what was then the town of Carolina, living with one of her schoolteachers during those years. In 1927, her entire family moved with her to the city of Río Piedras, where she attended the University High School, subsequently gaining admission to the Normal School of the University of Puerto Rico, from which she graduated in 1933. In a portentous coincidence, the commencement address at UPR that year was delivered by 1945's Nobel Prize winner Gabriela Mistral—a poet who occupies a position in the cultural memory of her natal Chile that is in many ways analogous to de Burgos's place in Puerto Rican life.

Over the course of the 1930s, de Burgos's career as a poet and political activist saw a meteoric rise, laying the foundations for her posthumous incorporation into the pantheon of "national poets." During this decade, widely regarded as the most decisive period in Puerto Rican modern history, de Burgos emerged not only as an "organic poet" of sorts of the Nationalist movement, publishing at least ten political poems in the pages of journals affiliated with the party (such as *Renovación* and *La Acción*); she also became a prominent leader of different initiatives affiliated with numerous political and civil causes, from the Frente Unido Femenino Pro Convención Constituyente de la República de Puerto Rico (United Women's Front Pro Constitutional Convention of the Republic of Puerto Rico) to the Congreso Nacional Pro Liberación de los Presos Políticos (National Congress Pro Liberation of Political Prisoners). Toward the end of the decade, and with most of the leadership of the Nationalist Party serving sentences for sedition in prisons around the United States, her poetry began to step beyond the limits of *Nacionalista* ideological orthodoxy. Whereas the Nationalist Party became increasingly dominated by its conservative, Catholic, bourgeois wing, de Burgos began to rehearse other political imaginaries in her poetry, which now featured the island's peasantry as a revolutionary, political class in its own right, declared unconditional support to the cause of the Second Spanish Republic (an issue that deeply divided ideologically the Nationalist movement), and denounced the misery accumulating in the Puerto Rican slums as waves of peasants displaced by industrialization came to the island's urban centers searching for work. Around this time, de Burgos also began to rehearse a plurality of lyric voices quite distant from the combative voice for which she had been known until then, ranging from the intimist erotic lyricism that will be on full display in her second poetry volume, *Canción de la verdad sencilla* (*Song of the Simple Truth*, San Juan, Puerto Rico, 1939)—which won the top literary prize for poetry awarded by the Instituto de Literatura Puertorriqueña in 1940—to the ironic detachment of the protofeminist speaker that voices her first poetry volume, *Poema en 20 surcos* (*Poem in 20 Furrows*, San Juan, Puerto Rico, 1938).

By the time de Burgos left Puerto Rico in late 1939 to follow her new lover, the Dominican politician, intellectual, and anti-Trujillo activist Juan Isidro Jimenes Grullón, she was already an established figure in San Juan's lettered city. A list of de Burgos's interlocutors at that time would look like a veritable Who's Who in Puerto Rican and Caribbean cultural life and would include figures like Luis

Lloréns Torres, widely regarded as the foundational figure in Puerto Rican literary modernism; Antonio S. Quiñones and Vicente Géigel Polanco, who played key roles in the foundation of the Partido Popular Democrático (Popular Democratic Party), which ruled Puerto Rican politics until 1968; the literary critic Nilita Vientós Gastón, who lamented the "propagandistic" tone of some of her poems even as she praised de Burgos on her lyric accomplishments; the leading suffragette and Catholic Nationalist Trina Padilla de Sanz, who openly gave her blessing to de Burgos's antipatriarchal poetics even as she herself pursued a feminism of respectability and advocated against divorce laws; the future socialist president of the Dominican Republic, Juan Bosch, who praised her poetry on both aesthetics and political grounds and who, a year later, would be instrumental in staging de Burgos's encounter with Pablo Neruda in La Habana, Cuba, where Bosch, Jimenes Grullón, and other anti-Trujillo revolutionaries in exile founded the Partido Revolucionario Dominicano (Dominican Revolutionary Party); and Dr. José Lanauze Rolón, a Howard University graduate who was one of the leading figures of the Puerto Rican Communist Party. Over the course of six years of intense intellectual and political activity, and despite her humble background, de Burgos managed to cement her standing as one of the leading voices in Puerto Rican letters, even as rumors about her supposed sexual promiscuity and her alcoholism began to circulate more widely within the very elite cultural and intellectual circles that embraced both her poetry and her political militancy.

After Jimenes Grullón decided to end their relationship in 1942 at the behest of his parents, who presumably refused to entertain the idea that their son would marry a bohemian, alcoholic divorcée, de Burgos settled in New York City. She remained in the city until her untimely death eleven years later, barring a brief period in the mid-1940s where she lived in Washington, DC, after being hired as a clerk at Nelson Rockefeller's Office on Inter-American Affairs, a position from which she was fired after the FBI opened a Hatch Act investigation into her literary and political engagement with *Pueblos Hispanos*, a socialist New York–based Spanish publication. Although de Burgos would continue to write poetry until the very end of her life, her dreams of becoming a professional poet never materialized. She spent the last years of her life going from hospital to hospital, living in abject poverty and facing homelessness until she collapsed on July 5, 1953, near the corner of 106th Street and Fifth Avenue, and died a day later. She was buried as a Jane Doe until her relatives finally identified her remains, and, after a moving funeral in New York, she received the burial of a cultural icon in her natal Puerto Rico.

§5. A CATASTROPHIC TRADITION: THE TOTEMIC HISTORICISM OF JULIA DE BURGOS'S RECEPTION

Given de Burgos's background as the *mestiza* daughter of poor peasants, her early militancy in Puerto Rico's nationalist movement and her lifelong support for the island's independence, her status as a divorcée and her position as a forerunner of antipatriarchal feminism in Latin America, her lifelong political engagement in the cause of antifascism, and her tragic and premature death after an adulthood marked by poverty and alcoholism in her self-imposed New York exile, it is not surprising that her biography has provided fodder for all kinds of historical, if not even mythological, appropriations. This ongoing mythomania explains why de Burgos's historical reception provides fertile ground for my effort to reorient the critique of historicism away from the ongoing concerns with historical positivism that continue to preoccupy literary theorists and heterodox historians alike. The consolidation of de Burgos as a privileged institution within Puerto Rican historicity is as far removed as possible from the modes of objectivization that characterize what Hayden White calls the "historical past," that is, the past constituted by professional historians, who are generally speaking the community most invested in defending historical realism.[29] Remaining almost exclusively within the limits of what White calls the "practical past," the construction of de Burgos as a historical figure has been instead largely driven by the goal of enshrining the poet in Puerto Rico's pantheon of "national treasures."[30] To do so, her critics and historians have relied on a monumental grammar of historical memorialization, thereby reducing her historical image to the status of a *totemic figure*. More than any other Puerto Rican writer, de Burgos functions both as an emblem of group identification as well as a depository of imaginary projections and ego-idealizations that are ultimately grounded in what we may describe as a collective, ethnonationalist narcissism—exacerbated no doubt by the singularities of Puerto Rico's troubled, colonially intervened process of nation formation.

The redefinition of historicism in terms of ipseity and appropriation allows me to expose the often-unconscious aims that have animated de Burgos's historical reception. Her totemization positions de Burgos's life and works as the idealized past that contains the model for the future constitution of a specifically (though not exclusively) Puerto Rican modality of postcolonial ipseity. Within the strictures of this historicist reception, reading de Burgos's poetry becomes another ritual of historical reappropriation: Her textual corpus is the privileged mirror in which her Puerto Rican readers encounter the *imago* of their long-awaited yet still elusive sovereignty. The paradoxical result of this sedimented protocol of specular legibility is that de Burgos's image becomes more historically illegible the more her totem circulates and the fame of her proper name expands.

Since the totemic reception of de Burgos is so deeply sedimented in Puerto Rican historicity, Part I, "Catastrophic Traditions: Reading the Image of Julia de Burgos, *Dangerously*" is concerned primarily with laying the foundations for a *dangerous reading* of de Burgos. To do so, I draw from Benjamin's notion of *catastrophic tradition* and Edmund Husserl's concept of *sedimentation* in order to sketch out a critical desedimentation of the key stages in the process that led to de Burgos's posthumous institution as a privileged totemic figure within Puerto Rican historicity, where she symbolizes multiple competing, though always idealized, scripts of Puertoricanness. To do so, I center on two critical events that I argue consolidated two alternative regimes of totemization: The first of these events was a eulogy delivered by José Emilio González on September 8, 1953, at an homage for the poet held at the Ateneo Puertorriqueño just two days after her burial in Carolina, Puerto Rico. My claim is that in this speech, aptly titled "Julia: Intensa, siempre viva," ("Julia: Intense, Always Alive") González instituted the telos that has bound together generations of de Burgos's readers, establishing the reenactment of de Burgos's reputed sacrifice in the name of the joint causes of Puerto Rican nationalism and humanistic authenticity as the goal that animates normative readings of her life and works. In the wake of González's critical intervention, to read de Burgos unavoidably entails taking part in a devotional practice that I call *imitatio Iuliæ* (Imitation of Julia), by analogy with the Christian devotional practice of the *imitatio Christi* (Imitation of Christ).

Forty years later, another critical event took place that has altered, at least on the surface, the nature of this tradition, namely, the publication of Juan Gelpí's essay "El sujeto nómada en la poesía de Julia de Burgos" ("The Nomadic Subject in the Poetry of Julia de Burgos"). Claiming for de Burgos the status of a Deleuzian-Braidottian nomadic subject, Gelpí's essay erected a different totem out of her poetry by turning de Burgos into a perennial "line of flight" from the conservative, patriarchal, Hispanophilic cultural nationalism that took shape around the time of de Burgos's poetic debut—and that remains dominant even today. As Lena Burgos-Lafuente has argued, this essay "marked a watershed [*un antes y un después*] in the criticism on de Burgos's work."[31] That being said, I contend that Gelpí's text retains this privilege because it consolidates a hermeneutic countertradition that had been taking shape since the 1970s and that modified significantly the *content* for which de Burgos ought to be enshrined in the Puerto Rican pantheon. Rather than standing as the emblem of human authenticity in an inhuman, inauthentic world or emerging as the voice of Puerto Rico's anticolonial struggles, this tradition allowed *other* readers whose lives occupy minoritarian modes of Puertoricanness to recognize themselves in de Burgos by reading her writings and her life as *symbolizing* the political struggles of minoritarian subjectivities and other counterhegemonic formations within Puerto Rican historicity.

Although this alternative tradition presents itself as engaged in an open ideological conflict with the hegemonic, sedimented traditional reading of de Burgos that crystallized most intensively in González's eulogical intervention, this supposedly counterhegemonic reading shares the same monumental-symbolic grammar of historicization as its adversary. Indeed, both modes of reception are ultimately engaged in maintaining and safeguarding de Burgos's status as the privileged totemic figure of Puertoricanness, regardless of how it may be defined. In other words, I argue that these two modes of reception constitute different version of the *same* catastrophic tradition that has produced a situation in which de Burgos's poetry and life is increasingly illegible other than in the symbolic terms sanctioned by her monumental-totemic reception.

By tracing the historical outline of this catastrophic tradition, Part I clears the ground for a different protocol of historical reading of de Burgos, for which I take Benjamin's concept of the *dialectical image* as my model. What Benjamin calls the dialectical image provides a different schema for the construction of a historical object, one that breaks with historicism insofar as it understands the task of "rescuing the phenomena" of history as necessarily entailing their *endangerment*.[32] Benjamin puts it thus in an entry from *Das Passagen-Werk* that contains the most thorough account of his concept of the image: "The image *that is read*, that is to say, the image in the now of knowability, bears to the highest degree the stamp of the *critical, dangerous* moment that underlies all reading."[33] To rescue de Burgos from her catastrophic tradition requires subtracting her image from the traditional continuum that has turned her life and her works into a monument and a myth, producing a situation in which the historical possibilities that her afterlife may yet afford us are systematically narrowed down to those aspects that enable and support the different identity-formations that vie for cultural hegemony within Puerto Rican history. Deconstructing her totem figure is thus a prerequisite for the dangerous possibility that de Burgos's life and works may give themselves to our legibility *now*, that is, may attain the form of nonhistoricist objectivity that the image affords. Only then could the space-time for another history open itself, one in which de Burgos's historicity would no longer be determined by our desire to recognize ourselves in her paradigmatic ipseity.

§6. CATASTROPHE AND MODERNITY: JULIA DE BURGOS, THE POET OF (PUERTO RICAN) MODERN LIFE

Part III of this book, "Reading Now: The Catastrophic Modernity of Julia de Burgos," takes a step further in the direction of a nonhistoricist literary history by building on the critical work of Parts I and II and offering a novel interpretation of *Poema en 20 surcos* (*Poem in 20 Furrows*; San Juan, Puerto Rico, 1938), the first poetry volume de Burgos published. One of the most visible indices of the illegibility mentioned earlier is the relative lack of any sustained *historical reading* of *Poema en 20 surcos*, especially in light of both the privileged place it occupies in her reception and the privileged role that the 1930s play in Puerto Rican historiography, where it is usually regarded as the decade that marked the onset of modern Puerto Rican life. Like Part I, Part III is also concerned with another attempt to experience de Burgos as a historical phenomenon by constructing her historicity in terms of Benjamin's notion of the dialectical image. Taking a page, again, from Benjamin—this time from his reading of Charles Baudelaire—I argue that the historicity of *Poema* may attain legibility for us *now* only if the volume is situated within the constellation of *modernity*. Rather than understanding this term as the proper name for a historical context or period, I treat modernity as an allegorical title (*allos* + *agoreuō*, a literal rendition of which would be *otherspeak*) for historico-metaphysical processes whose minimal semantic core could be characterized in terms of Bolívar Echevarría's *formal* definition of modernity as the historical process whereby a "life-world" is transformed.[34] My claim is that the unity of de Burgos's *Poema* can only be ascertained if we understand its twenty poems as different attempts to allow her own experience of Puerto Rican modernization to crystallize in all its catastrophic ambivalence.

My reading of *Poema* is structured by the hypothesis that de Burgos's ambivalent response to modernity finds its clearest articulation in her attempt to transform the space of the lyric into the site for the constitution of an *embodied/ gendered ipseity*, safeguarding auto-affection from the alienating forces of modernity. But for the speaker of *Poema* to turn her immanent embodiment into the unassailable refuge for the possibility of an experience of intimacy—an *ownness* or a *mineness*—that no historical event could ever dislocate or expropriate, the self that emerges in de Burgos's volume had to put in place a process akin to a phenomenological reduction with the goal of separating, in quasi-dualistic terms, the *proper* experience of the body as a gendered-whitened *soma* from the body's *impropriety*. Tellingly, the old name that the latter receives in *Poema* is *la carne* or *the flesh*, and its three major allegorical incarnations are (1) the poet herself, or rather, the person who bears the *proper name* "Julia de Burgos" and who stands as the emblem of the submissive, patriarchalized woman whose self-relation and indeed desire are thoroughly shaped by the desire of Man/men; (2) the figure of *Man/men*, the speaker's main antagonist throughout the volume; and (3) an emblematic figure of Black femininity who I argue functions as an instance of what Zakiyyah Iman Jackson calls the "Black *mater*," since she is assigned the task of birthing the *mestizo* race by mothering White men's children.[35] The *ipseity* that speaks and thus bodies herself forth throughout the text of *Poema* must unleash the violence of her political utopia against these three major emblems of what Alexander Weheliye calls a "fleshy surplus" if she is to present herself as the phenomenological embodiment of a *form-of-life* that already lies beyond the modern humanism of Man/men.[36]

To what extent *Catastrophic Historicism* provides a preliminary example of a literary history *after* historicism can only be grasped after situating de Burgos's *Poema* within the constellation of modernity. Part III shows yet again that historicism's catastrophic mode of traditionalization remains untouched so long as it is understood as a positivism or an empiricism. For historicism has not shaped the reception of *Poema* by turning this text into a depository of historical facts about a specific historical epoch. (As a matter of fact, given the intense degree of specular identifications that still mediate her reception, an increase in both the availability of empirical data about de Burgos's life and historico-hermeneutic rigor about her corpus might not be the worst thing that could happen to the critical study of her legacy.) Rather, historicism works here by pre-positioning de Burgos's inheritors within a catastrophic tradition whose unity and continuity is secured by the sedimented telos of reactivating her totem, of paying homage to de Burgos as the *imago* of Puertoricanness. In ensuring that the link that binds the readers who instituted this sedimentation and her future inheritors remains unbroken, this tradition also serves as the medium for the historical self-appropriation of her readers, who inscribe themselves in the pages of the book of Puerto Rican historicity by inheriting her in an appropriate, that is, totemic, manner, thereby ensuring the re-constitution of a *historical ipseity*. My reading of *Poema* is thus animated by a double wager: on the one hand, that her catastrophic traditionalization provides one of the reasons why the historicity of *Poema* has remained largely illegible to this day. Indeed, this tradition of Puertoricanness ensures its replication through the a priori deselection of any possible reading that might attend to the violence that the speaker of *Poema* had to unleash in order to give herself a properly *excarnated* body and, in particular, of any reading that may attempt to reckon with the historico-metaphysical script of anti-Blackness that determines de Burgos's sarxophobic somatophilia. For the goal that animates this tradition is that of upholding her poetics of ipseity as the ego-ideal that provides a mirror in which we should all look at ourselves, not to question, let alone "stain," that idealized formation by paying attention to the process of abjecting and disavowal that ensured that ipseity's constitution. On the other hand, this tradition, made in and of history, is not natural and can be interrupted and transformed both from without and from within. *Catastrophic Historicism* aims to take a step in the direction of such transformation.

§7. TOWARD A DECONSTRUCTION OF HISTORY

In spite their thematic divergence, the three parts that compose *Catastrophic Historicism* all converge toward a single insight, namely, that to the extent that we continue to live in a world that has been decisively shaped by historicism in ways that exceed the limits of the practice of historiography, a *deconstruction of history* is urgently needed. By reducing the problem of historicism to a debate about the methodology of the study of literature or of culture writ large, critics of historicism have missed the chance to carry out a more thorough delimitation of this historical ontology, thereby misconstruing the threat that historicism continues to pose to our own historical experience. Such threats are not primarily epistemological in nature. Historicism remains a problem for thought because, *pace* Reinhart Kosselleck, it institutes an idea of history as necessarily determined by the phantasmatic desire to attain a *form of life* that would have finally *mastered time*[37]—a life for whom history primarily means the appropriation of the past through the domestication of temporal difference via the narrative mastering of contingency. By elaborating the concept of a dangerous historicity and attempting to restore legibility to the image of Julia de Burgos, *Catastrophic Historicism* hopes to set in motion, or at least facilitate, such a deconstruction, whose task is to demonstrate, *pace* Derrida himself, that *history* may yet mean something *other* than "the presentation (Gegenwärtigung) of being, the production and gathering of beings within presence, as *knowledge* and *mastery*."[38]

In truth, such a deconstruction is already underway; its historical indices can be read everywhere historicism is forced to bear witness to the reinscription of those dangerous possibilities that it had to violently exclude or disavow to secure its boundaries. These eminently historical dislocations in the historicist text are taking place both beyond the academy and inside its walls, by nonhistorians and even by members of the historical guild. Within the latter, Kleinberg's *Haunting History: For a Deconstructive Approach to the Past* marks a watershed in the self-deconstruction of the historical discipline; his claim that theorizing what historians do requires abandoning the belief that the past has *any* ontological status has been particularly important for this book.[39] But it is perhaps in the work of those scholars who have taken on the difficult task of thinking and writing about the historical afterlife of extreme forms of violence, domination, and genocide that we find the clearest index of this ongoing deconstruction of history within the university. When Marc Nichanian, writing about the denial of the Armenian genocide, diagnoses the perversion that structures historiography's demand for facts even in a genocidal context that entails "the very destruction of facts, of the notion of fact, of the factuality of fact";[40] when Cathy Caruth describes the historicity of trauma in terms of events that happen by erasing themselves;[41] when María del Rosario Acosta remarks that a different *grammar* is required that might restore audibility to "those lives designated as or constantly under the threat of being defined as *impossible* (as unbelievable) by traumatic and colonizing forms of violence";[42] or when Saidiya Hartman describes her practice of "critical fabulation" within the historicity of slavery's afterlife as an attempt "to tell an *impossible* story and to *amplify the impossibility of its telling*,"[43] historicism and its metaphysical poetics are being shaken to the core. By carrying out an apposite intervention within the fields of the theory of history and Puerto Rican studies, *Catastrophic Historicism* also strives to reopen the field of the historical beyond its historicist closure so that the dangerous historicity of the *im-possible* may stake its claim to legibility. To articulate the claims of a history *otherwise*—that is the in-finite task to which *Catastrophic Historicism* seeks to contribute.

From what are phenomena rescued? Not only and not so much from the disrepute and the disdain into which they have fallen as from the catastrophe in which a determined type of their tradition, their "enshrinement as heritage," often presents them. (They are rescued through the indication of their leap.) There is a tradition that is catastrophe.

To the process of rescue belongs the firm, seemingly brutal grasp.

Enshrinement or *apologia* strives to cover over the revolutionary moments in the historical process. What lies at its heart is the production of a continuity. It places value only on those elements of the work that have already entered into its reception. It misses the places where tradition breaks off and, with it, its rugged crags, which offer a hold to those who want to get out of it.

—Walter Benjamin

Part I

CATASTROPHIC TRADITIONS: READING THE IMAGE OF JULIA DE BURGOS, *DANGEROUSLY*

§8. AN UNTARNISHED HUMANITY

On Sunday June 28, 1953, the Puerto Rican poet Julia de Burgos wrote a letter to her closest sister, Consuelo Burgos, who lived on the island. Only a few weeks had passed since de Burgos had been discharged from the Goldwater Memorial Hospital, a clinic for patients with chronic diseases located right outside Manhattan on Welfare Island (now known as Roosevelt Island). De Burgos had been interned at Goldwater Memorial toward the beginning of 1953 after spending the last weeks of 1952 in New York City's infamous Bellevue Hospital, where she was treated for vocal papilloma and acute hepatic cirrhosis, the latter caused by alcoholism. It was during her stay at Bellevue that she resumed her correspondence with Consuelo after a conspicuous three-year hiatus in an otherwise steady epistolary exchange. Although the first letter that de Burgos wrote from Bellevue, dated November 20, 1952, makes clear that communication channels between the poet and her family back in Puerto Rico had not been interrupted during this hiatus in their written correspondence,[1] one can hardly avoid reading this resumption as indicative of de Burgos's awareness of her rapid deterioration, as if sensing death's proximity had led de Burgos to write again to her sister—the only stable source of affection throughout the poet's tumultuous and intense life. Here's the full text of the letter:

Central Harlem, N.Y.C.
Domingo 28 de junio de 1953
Mi adorada Consuelito:

No estás cada vez, ni cada minuto peor. Al contrario, cada contratiempo individual o colectivo te hace más grande en la faz del mundo, y en los ojos de mi corazón. *Sabes que estoy viva solamente por ti, porque representas la humanidad.*

No te desesperes por mí. Soy valiente como tú y me estoy portando bien, contra viento y marea. La Sociedad de Escritores y Periodistas a la cual pertenezco, me tiene el pasaje separado en una agencia, pero solamente te lo darán a ti. *Yo no voy para Puerto Rico.* Pero tú le dices a ellos que me llevas, te entregan el pasaje y todo se puede remediar. Tengo también mucha ropa recogida para Uds.

Tal vez yo vuelva al hospital, *pero no importa. Me sabré defender.* Lo más importante es que sigas luchando. No te pasará nada. Tan pronto llegues búscame por teléfono en casa de Augusto o por carta especial, o a esta dirección telefónica de Lolín Quintana, que está encargada de darte mi pasaje. Ella es enfermera, secretaria del doctor Janer. El teléfono del Dr es (103 West End Ave.) M02-0404.

La dirección de ella es 319 West 13 St. N.Y.

No te me pierdas en N.Y. Tenemos que hablar mucho.

Te adoro y tiene fe en ti, tu Julita. Abrazos a todos.[2]

Central Harlem, N.Y.C.
Sunday, June 28, 1953
My dear Consuelito:

You're not each time, nor each minute, worse off. On the contrary, each individual and collective setback makes you greater in the face of the world, and in my heart's eyes. *You know I'm alive only because of you, because you represent humanity.*

Do not despair of me. Like you, I am brave and I am behaving well, against all odds. The Society of Writers and Journalists to which I belong has my plane ticket reserved at an agency, but they will only give it to you. *I am not going to Puerto Rico.* But you can tell them that you're taking me, they will give you the ticket, and everything can be remedied. I also have gathered a lot of clothing for all of you.

Perhaps I will return to the hospital, *but it doesn't matter. I will know how to defend myself.* The most important thing is that you continue the struggle. Nothing will happen to you. As soon as you arrive reach me by phone at Augusto's home or via special courier, or try me at the phone number of Lolín Quintana, who is supposed to give you my ticket. She is a nurse and Dr. Janer's secretary. The Dr.'s phone is (103 West End Ave.) M02-0404.

Her address is 319 West 13 St. N.Y.

Don't get lost in N.Y. We have much talking to do.

I adore you and have faith in you, your Julita. Hugs to all.

Although, to my knowledge, there is no written testimony of Consuelo Burgos's reaction to this letter, I can't help but imagine that, upon reading it, she must have sensed that something was amiss. For when compared to the previous letters that de Burgos sent to her sister during the last round of hospitalizations, this one reads like a farewell note—an impression that becomes more palpable if we consider that this letter was written in anticipation of their awaited reencounter. As if de Burgos was greeting her sister by saying her goodbyes, a gesture foretelling of the fact that, although Consuelo did arrive in New York City in the summer of 1953 on a rescue mission to bring her sister back to Puerto Rico, the two sisters would not meet.

Even more striking than her indifference concerning the likelihood of being hospitalized again is de Burgos's lapidary rejection of her sister's plans to bring her back to Puerto Rico. This constitutes a noticeable shift from her previous letters, in which de Burgos appeared to be willing to return to the island. As a matter of fact, in a letter from May 17, 1953 de Burgos tells her sister that she wants to return to Puerto Rico with her, though only for a visit: "Quiero ir contigo a P.R. Pero como te dije, con mi pasaje de ida y vuelta" (I want to go with you to P.R. But, as I told you, with a return ticket.")[3] What could have brought about this sudden shift in de Burgos's attitude toward the prospect of returning home? Did she fear that, once her sister's plan to bring her back to Puerto Rico had been set in motion, she would not be allowed to return to New York City and would be forced to live under her sister's supervision? This question becomes more urgent if we keep in mind that de Burgos was aware that the difficulties she faced after leaving the hospital would most likely result in her being again interned against her will. Given how desperate her situation was, why not simply return to Puerto Rico to be among her people and, especially, alongside the very sister who, in her own words, embodied the idea(l) of an untarnished humanity and, as such, constituted her sole reason to keep on living?

As it turns out, the letter that de Burgos wrote on June 28, 1953, would be the last one she would write to her sister. On July 5, 1953, just eight days after writing this letter, de Burgos collapsed on the corner of Fifth Avenue and 106th Street and died a day later of pneumonia at Harlem Hospital. After her body remained unclaimed for several days, she was buried as "Jane Doe" at Hart's Island, where New York's potter's field is located. She lay there until her relatives were able to identify her corpse in early August. Arrangements were made for a wake to be held in the city she regarded as her "segunda casa" ("second home"), after which her remains were repatriated to Puerto Rico.[4] The week-long wake held at the Funeraria Ortiz in the Bronx brought together members of the Puerto Rican diaspora and of New York's Latin American leftist circles and was accompanied by the publication of obituaries in the city's major Spanish-language journals, such as *La Prensa* and *Pueblo* (the latter of these two was associated with the Puerto Rican Communist Party, in which Consuelo played an important role throughout the 1940s and 1950s). On September 6, 1953, de Burgos's remains arrived in her hometown of Carolina, Puerto Rico, where she was received as a national hero and given a proper burial. At the time of her death, she was thirty-nine years old.

Although in 1940 de Burgos wrote a letter to her sister in which she stated her intention to publish a poetry volume per year,[5] only two of her completed collections ever saw the light of day during her lifetime: *Poema en 20 surcos*, which appeared in 1938, and *Canción de la verdad sencilla (Song of the Simple Truth)*, which was published in 1939 and won the most prestigious literary prize for poetry in Puerto Rico in 1940. A previous poetry collection, *Poemas exactos a mí misma (Poems Exact to Myself)*, which de Burgos appears to have finished and circulated among her friends in 1937, is today lost, presumably because de Burgos judged it unworthy of publication. Although by 1941 de Burgos had already finished a version of *El mar y tú (The Sea and You)*—regarded by most critics as her masterpiece—this volume would only be published posthumously in 1954. Over the course of her short and intense life she conceived of several other poetry volumes, such as *Campo* (Countryside), *Autobiografía de una bala* (Autobiography of a Bullet), *El cielo de Julma* (The Sky of Julma), and a volume of "proletarian" poems, but these were never finished. At the time of her death, de Burgos had written more than two hundred poems, several scripts for radio, and dozens of essays and columns dealing with some of the most urgent political and social questions of her day, paying special emphasis to the cause of Puerto Rican independence, Pan-American solidarity, and the struggle for an international socialist revolution.

It is telling that the last thing that de Burgos wrote was a letter to her sister in which she reasserts two of the most persistent traits that marked both her life and her work: on the one hand, her unshakeable belief in the idea of an untarnished humanity (embodied, in this case, by her sister) and, on the other, her acute awareness that a redeemed humanity remains of the order of a promise that is seldom actualized. To the impossibility of living a properly human life within an all-too-(in)human society, which in the last months of her life took the painful shape of being submitted to the disciplinary power of the medical establishment, de Burgos responded the only way she knew how: by anticipating the need to defend herself again from the very inhumane forces to which she was nonetheless consigned—a task that she embraced with stoicism and sobriety.

§9. OVERLOOKED?

On May 2, 2018, the *New York Times* published an obituary for Julia de Burgos written by Maira García under the title "Overlooked No More: Julia de Burgos, a Poet Who Helped Shape Puerto Rico's Identity."[6] To readers familiar with the life and legacy of de Burgos, the obituary arrived late, almost sixty-five years too late to be precise. Given the considerable delay between de Burgos's death and the publication of this death notice, it is fair to wonder about the reasons why the *New York Times* decided to publish such a belated obituary for a figure who remains relatively unknown in North America. When it comes to obituary writing, the legal maxim "justice delayed is justice denied" also holds; an obituary that arrives too late to the scene of a life's end fails to fulfill its role as "the first station to canonization or more permanent memorialization" of that figure, thereby failing to do historical justice to that life.[7] All the more reason to ask: Why bother running an obituary of de Burgos *now*, more than half a century after her death?

This line of questioning, however, would seem unwarranted in light of the context in which the *New York Times* decided to pay such a delayed homage to de Burgos. As the titular phrase "Overlooked No More" indicates, this obituary is part of the Overlooked series, which the *New York Times* launched in March 2018 in an attempt to rectify its record of excluding from its obituary pages "remarkable people"—mostly women and people of color, and especially women of color—"who left indelible marks but were nonetheless overlooked" by the obituarists at the US paper of record.[8] A quick and very partial glance at the list of people featured in the series would seem to confirm this statement: Besides de Burgos, the Overlooked series has published obituaries for Charlotte Brontë, Homer Plessy, Ida B. Wells, Nella Larsen, Sylvia Plath, Valerie Solanas, and Ana Mendieta, to mention just a few of the figures featured in this initiative whose canonization certainly did not depend on a *New York Times* obituary, whether timely or untimely. Indeed, the marks left behind by these lives are as indelible today as they were at the moment of their deaths, if not more so. Which raises, again, the question of the pertinence of these obituaries. If the "marks" left by these "remarkable people" were nonetheless remarked in the absence of a *New York Times* obituary, what is the use of these belated eulogies?

But this question also seems unwarranted given the unevenness of de Burgos's reception, especially in the United States. Although no canonical Puerto Rican writer has achieved such iconic status within the island and its diasporas, de Burgos still remains somewhat unknown outside the Caribbean diasporic circles of New York City, the city in which she spent the last years of her adult life. To that extent, it is possible that this obituary, unlike Sylvia Plath's or Ida B. Wells's, might actually play a role in shaping de Burgos's reception on this side of the Atlantic. At the same time, the decision to include Julia de Burgos among the first lives to be belatedly obituarized in the Overlooked series is also a testament to the increasing visibility of de Burgos's legacy in New York City, as well as in other major urban centers across the United States. Cultural centers, schools, and parks bearing her name can be found all over Puerto Rico, as well as in New York City, Chicago, Cleveland, Lehigh, Willimantic, Tijuana, and Santo Domingo. Although this process of memorialization has been primarily spurred by generations of diasporic Puerto Ricans who continue to rally around her name as an emblem of national identity and of minoritarian struggles against gender-, racial-, and class-based forms of oppression, an incipient canonization of de Burgos has also been taking place within more mainstream, White-dominated institutions in the United States, whose milestones would include Leonard Bernstein's adaptation of the poem "A Julia de Burgos" for *Songfest* (1977), a Bicentenary commission that featured adaptations for voice and orchestra of works by canonical American poets such as Edgar Allan Poe, Walt Whitman, Gertrude Stein, Langston Hughes, and Frank O'Hara;[9] the establishment in 1989 of the Julia de Burgos Cultural Arts Center in Harlem, just a few blocks away from where she was found unconscious; the publication of her complete works in a bilingual edition translated and edited by Jack Agüeros under the title *Song of the Simple Truth* (1997, Curbstone Press); the renaming of East 106th Street between Fifth and First Avenues as "Julia de Burgos Boulevard" in 2006; the honoring of Julia de Burgos with a US Postal Service stamp in the context of National Hispanic Heritage Month in 2010; and the recent publication of the first English academic monograph on her life and poetry, Vanessa Pérez Rosario's *Becoming Julia de Burgos: The Making of a Puerto Rican Icon* (2014, University of Illinois Press). The *New York Times* obituary could thus be seen as the capstone of this initial phase in her process of North American reception, marking the moment in which the proper name Julia de Burgos would have finally crossed the threshold that separates invisibility from visibility, memory from oblivion, so that henceforth it can be said with confidence that she will be "overlooked no more." This crossing would be all the more significant in light of the fact that, according to her biographer Juan Antonio Rodríguez Pagán, when de Burgos was buried on Hart's Island she was given as sole identifier a number: P 149935—as if the obituary of the *New York*

Times marked the end of an allegory through which de Burgos finally recovered the proper name that she lost when she lost her life in the city.

Still, this allegory has other, more politically charged valences that are specific to the singularities of the actants in this scene of belated, posthumous tribute. By paying homage to a poet often described as the "national poet" of Puerto Rico alongside figures such as Ida B. Wells, Sylvia Plath, and Valerie Solanas, the *New York Times* is not merely offering a mea culpa for allowing de Burgos's life to go unremarked at the moment of her death. Nor is the paper only passing judgment on its own history of complicity with white supremacy and patriarchy, which determined which lives could be memorialized publicly and which lives could be ignored—however "indelible" their marks may still be. For, as the US paper of record, this gesture can also be read as an attempt to weigh in on the thorny issue of Puerto Rico–US relations. Indeed, the sheer fact of this obituary's existence strikes me as an implicit admission of a cultural fact that is as self-evident as it is easily and routinely ignored, namely, that after more than a century of Puerto Rican colonization and after massive waves of Puerto Rican migration into the major urban centers of the imperial "mainland," the very cultural "body-image" of the US body politic has "indelible" Puerto Rican "marks"— which de Burgos, as "The Poet Who Helped Shape Puerto Rico's Identity" is arguably in a better position to represent than any other historical figure from the island or its diaspora. Moreover, the fact that the US paper of record is also the major newspaper of the North American city whose identity and history has been more deeply marked by the presence of generations of Puerto Ricans adds an extra layer of political significance to this revisionist gesture of cultural inclusion. Indeed, if we keep in mind that de Burgos's death in 1953 happened while New York City was in the midst of the "Great Migration" (which led to Puerto Ricans constituting 12 percent of New York City's population by the 1970s), this obituary could also be seen as an attempt to redress New York City's record of anti–Puerto Rican discrimination, best captured by the harmful stereotypical depictions of Puerto Ricans in Leonard Bernstein and Stephen Sondheim's 1957 musical *West Side Story*.

But is it possible to settle historical debts—even "symbolic" ones—so easily? Especially when these are not just historical but also "colonial debts," as the Puerto Rican philosopher Rocío Zambrana has recently shown?[10] There is something about the title of the series, Overlooked, and especially about the title that accompanies each obituary, "Overlooked No More," that betrays a certain naive trust in the power of this gesture to settle matters finally. The perfective aspect of the simple past verb *overlooked*, amplified by the adverbial phrase *no more*, positions both the writers and the readers of these obituaries within a neat temporality in which the present death notice is presumed to establish a clean cut between the past and the future of both the life obituarized and of the *New York Times* itself. It is this decisive cut that would then serve as the referent of the title/declaration "Overlooked No More," thus justifying its validity. The credit that this declarative title gives to the actuality of this temporal break is further buttressed by an aspect of this title that emerges more clearly if we read it as a speech act. Although, at first sight, the phrase "Overlooked No More" appears to describe a reality, the reality to which it refers is produced through the utterances that compose each of the obituaries and that the title declaratively ratifies. A certain performativity, and the retrospective temporality of a self-fulfilling promise, thus hide themselves in what offers itself prima facie as a constative statement. And, as Derrida has alerted us, with performativity comes a certain *sovereignty*, namely, the erection or institution of a linguistic position that claims to have the power to utter a statement whose force, as if by fiat, produces the very thing to which it refers, in the process neutralizing the very chance of what Derrida calls "an event worthy of the name."[11] With this sovereign performance, we touch on a certain perversion at the heart of this entire endeavor. The editors of Overlooked may cast their series as a mea culpa, which might prompt us to add a tacit qualification to the title of each obituary so that "Overlooked No More" should actually be read as saying "Overlooked No More (by Us)." But the very fact of claiming the prerogative to be able to declare that a remarkable life is no longer overlooked because it has finally been included in the obituary pages of your newspaper exposes the limits of this display of institutional humility and ratifies the journal's self-positioning as the site that dispenses recognition, cultural relevance, and iconicity. It is as if the editors were saying, between the lines: "Your deeds might have been remarkable, but they will only be admitted *as such* once they are remarked by us."

If we now consider the colonial dimension that subtends this ironic performance of sovereign humility, the obituary and its mea culpa provide another occasion to explore what I would call the "quandary" of Puerto Rican colonization.[12] The obfuscation of Puerto Rico's colonial relation to the United States has only intensified since Hurricane María made landfall on the island in September 2017 and the botched federal response of the Trump administration reminded liberals that Puerto Ricans are "American citizens" and thus deserve the protection of the federal government—as if that citizenship were not the very linchpin of Puerto Ricans' ongoing colonial conscription into a polity to which they belong but of which they are not a part.[13] This more explicitly political reading of this obituary could be conducted along two different lines, both of which could be labeled under the heading of what Frank Wilderson calls "the politics of culture," in opposition to a "culture of politics."[14]

First, by treating de Burgos as a monument of cultural identification, the obituary reduces her afterlife to what Denise Ferreira da Silva might have called a "transparent" bearer of an equally transparent minoritarian cultural identity, readily available for easy consumption by a public eager to participate in what Gayatri Chakravorty Spivak describes as the "benevolent first-world appropriation and reinscription of the Third World as an Other."[15] Taking another cue from da Silva, we might say that the ultimate (though certainly unconscious) goal of this obituary is to facilitate a specifically Puerto Rican protocol of what she calls "racial emancipation," which "comes about when the (juridical and economic) *inclusion* of the racial others and their voices (historical and cultural representations) finally realizes *universality* in postmodern social configurations."[16] By being lauded as a poet "who helped shape Puerto Rican identity," de Burgos is implicitly positioned as paradigmatic of how the racialized subaltern may become what da Silva calls a *"transparent 'I,'"* a process whereby the racially marked are granted the capacity to re-present themselves as universal subjects capable of self-determination on the condition that they *become the bearers of cultural difference*.

Second, the sheer fact that the newspaper of record is paying homage to a poet who was a lifelong supporter of the cause of Puerto Rican independence— a fact nowhere mentioned in the obituary—only exposes the limits of the form of emancipation that cultural recognition can afford. As it turns to de Burgos in order to incorporate markers of Puerto Rican "identity" within the multicultural, "postmodern social configuration" of the United States, the ruse of the "politics of culture" obfuscates both the island's ongoing colonial subjugation and the racial basis of this colonial arrangement. To further substantiate this claim, we only have to recall that the juridical infrastructure of Puerto Rico's colonization by the United States was first established under the sign of raciality—with the most infamous of the Insular Cases, *Downes v. Bidwell*, justifying the Supreme Court's invention of the doctrine of territorial unincorporation on grounds that, since the island is "inhabited by alien races, differing from us in religion, customs, laws, methods of taxation and modes of thought, the administration of government and justice, according to Anglo-Saxon principles, may for a time be impossible."[17] Not only has this racial-juridical logic continuously been ratified by the US Supreme Court, but the effective dismantling of Puerto Rico's limited form of self-rule under the juridical framework established in 2016 by PROMESA

(Puerto Rico Oversight, Management, and Economic Stability Act) could be read as a perverse weaponizing of the island's debt crisis that ratifies the racial equation of self-government with Anglo-Saxonness and retroactively justifies the imperial, paternalistic logic that deferred granting political autonomy to the newly acquired colonies until the culture of White politics had taken sufficient hold in the "modes of thought" of the colonized.[18] It may seem to some as if we have strayed far from the terrain of symbolic debts, presumably the kind that the *New York Times* is trying to settle with de Burgos's afterlife through the publication of this belated obituary. But my point is precisely that only the reduction of a political culture through a politics of culture—and the compulsion to perform transparency entailed by such a reduction—can transform the willful ignorance of the colonial dynamics that undergird the publication of this obituary into a progressive display of minoritarian inclusion.

I have refrained from citing the text of the obituary not only because most of the information it contains will be discussed in the pages that follow but also because, in a way, what the obituary says matters less than the *fact* and *context* of its publication. That de Burgos was, as the obituary's title claims, "A Poet Who Helped Shape Puerto Rico's Identity" is at best an innocuous truism. At worst, it demonstrates a failure in judgment on the part of the editors of Overlooked, who do not seem even to entertain the question as to whether the inclusion of de Burgos should lead them to reconsider the status of the obituary and the pertinence of the recognitive homage it affords. Although there are other aspects of de Burgos's life that should have led the editors of the Overlooked series to question both the form and the pertinence of their obituary, I would like to close this section by highlighting a very famous moment from de Burgos's poetic corpus whose consideration should have led them to a similar question. Consider the last stanza of "20. Yo misma fui mi ruta" ("20. I myself was my own route"), the poem that brings to a close *Poema en 20 surcos*, her first published collection:

Yo quise ser como los hombres quisieron que yo fuese:	I wanted to be like men wanted me to be:
un intento de vida;	an attempt at life;
un juego al escondite con mi ser.	a game of hide-and-seek with my being.
Pero yo estaba hecha de presentes;	But I was made of presents;
cuando ya los heraldos me anunciaban en el regio desfile de los troncos viejos;	Already when the heralds announced me in the regal parade of the old trunks;
se me torció el deseo de seguir a los hombres	my desire to follow men was bent
y el homenaje se quedó esperándome.[19]	and the homage was left waiting for me.

Note that this stanza marks a before and after in the speaker's sense of both life and being, a shift indicated through the reemergence of the past perfect tenses after a succession of imperfect verbs. The event that separates this before and after is the bending of the speaker's "desire to follow men," which brings about a deviation in her trajectory: Rather than finding her appointed place within the "regal parade of the old trunks" to which "the heralds" are hailing her, the speaker disregards the calling of her name and flees from the scene of her homage, which is "left waiting" for her. As we will see in more detail in Part III, the force of de Burgos's literary modernism unfolds in poetic gestures such as these, which set in motion a *disidentification* so radical that it compromises the status of the proper name as a key technology of anthropogenesis and as the presumed site in which the lyrical "I" and the authorial figure coincide.

What kind of obituary might be able to inherit a poem such as "20. Yo misma fui mi ruta," as well as those other aspects of de Burgos's life and poetic corpus that militate against her ongoing reception as one of Puerto Rico's "national treasures," as a shaper of national identities? To *read* such a self-conflicted life, to recognize and even to honor the internal war that keeps this poetry and this life alive and constitutes the chance of their survival today, would require an*other* obituary.

§10. METHODOLOGICAL EXCURSUS: FAME, LEGIBILITY, AND THE CONSTRUCTION OF A *DIALECTICAL* IMAGE (BENJAMIN READING BAUDELAIRE'S READING)

The *New York Times*' insistence on the indelibility of de Burgos's life and works implicitly poses a question that we might label as *historical*, in a sense of this term that will become clearer as this book unfolds: If her achievements were so indelible, how can we explain that it is just *now* that her work seems to be attaining a wider audience, especially in the United States? In order to accentuate the historical stakes of this inquiry, we may invert the terms of this question and pose it again in the following way: Does the increased possibility of being touched by de Burgos's poetry and by the "legends" that have contributed to her transformation into a Puerto Rican icon tell us anything about the historicity of our *present*? What features of our current historical moment attain legibility in and through the expansion and intensification of de Burgos's fame?

Readers familiar with Benjamin's groundbreaking engagement with Charles Baudelaire might recognize in the questions I just posed the beginnings of an inquiry that resembles Benjamin's attempt to read in Baudelaire's poetry the historical constellation of late European modernity. Indeed, Benjamin's last essay on Baudelaire, "Über einige Motiven bei Baudelaire" ("On Some Motifs in Baudelaire"), begins by posing a similar question, prompted by what we may call the *historical paradox* of Baudelaire's fame: Since lyric poetry entered into a period of decline in Europe by the end of the nineteenth century, and since, by 1940 (the year Benjamin wrote the "Motifs" essay), the lyric had already lost its status as a mass cultural form in Europe, how could we explain that Baudelaire's fame continued to grow unabated after the publication of *Les fleurs du mal* (*Flowers of Evil*) in 1857?[20] Moreover, even a cursory glance at the first section of the "Motifs" essay would be enough to conclude that Benjamin's interest lies not so much in Baudelaire's fame per se but in what its unabated expansion under adverse conditions for the lyric might say about both the historicity of late European modernity and about his own (that is, Benjamin's) historicity. This raises the following question: How could Baudelaire's growing fame serve as a point of departure for a historical inquiry into both the historicity of modernity and the historicity of the historian who is attempting to write this modern literary history? And, accordingly, how could something similar obtain in the case of de Burgos's increasing fame? What kind of literary history might be able to transform such a seemingly empirical fact into a medium for a historical knowledge in which our own historicity may attain legibility?

This excursus is primarily concerned with presenting Benjamin's attempt to answer this question in the "Motifs" essay. Two main reasons could be adduced to justify the necessity of this excursus at this precise moment in this book's unfolding, which could be roughly categorized as thematic and methodological or, to borrow Eugen Fink's terminology, as *thematic* and *operative*.[21]

On the one hand, this excursus is necessary because Benjamin's engagement with Baudelaire's fame serves as an analogical model for my own engagement with the historicity of de Burgos's afterlife and its historical significance throughout this book. Indeed, just as Benjamin transforms Baudelaire's fame into a medium of historical knowledge, in the next section (see §11), I carry out an analogous inquiry into the historical significance of de Burgos's afterlife by centering her fame, taking it as an index to examine the fraught and paradoxical status of her corpus's historical *(il)legibility*. And just as Benjamin anchors in Baudelaire's fame his effort to transform this poet into the *text* that renders legible crucial dimensions of the historicity of European modernity, in Part III of this book I carry out an analogous historical inquiry with the goal of showing that de Burgos's *Poema en 20 surcos* should be read as *the poem of (Puerto Rican) modernity*.

On the other hand, tarrying with this crucial moment in Benjamin's intellectual itinerary will go a long way toward clarifying several aspects of this book's way of proceeding that will not always be explicitly thematized or rendered transparent to the reader.[22] Indeed, Benjamin's reading of Baudelaire provides a model for this book's engagement with de Burgos because I take this aspect of Benjamin's corpus as one of the few extant methodological prototypes or models for a *nonhistoricist* literary history that remains yet to come and to whose invention and institutionalization this book seeks to contribute. At the center of this model is Benjamin's concept of the dialectical image, which constitutes the cornerstone of his nonhistoricist theory of history and remains to this day one of the most elusive concepts in Benjamin's philosophy. For this reason, this excursus would be incomplete without a preliminary foray into this concept. This foray, however, will be mediated by Benjamin's engagement with the historical puzzle of Baudelaire's increasing fame. The objective of this preliminary exposition of the concept of the dialectical image will have been met if I can demonstrate that Benjamin's engagement with Baudelaire's fame is ultimately part of his broader effort to construct Baudelaire as a dialectical image, even if this concept is nowhere mentioned explicitly in the "Motifs" essay.

In doing so, my goal is to lay the theoretical groundwork for this book's attempt to achieve the analogous task of constructing Julia de Burgos as an *image*, in a Benjaminian sense of the term. If we recall Benjamin's remark in *Das Passagen-Werk* that the dialectical image is nothing but "the historical object ... constructed in the materialist presentation of history," the stakes of this exercise become clearer:[23] By clarifying *how* Baudelaire appeared to Benjamin's "eyes" in such a way that he could become a historical object in a *nonrealist*, indeed *nonhistoricist* sense of this term, I will at once shed light on how this book takes de Burgos's catastrophic fame and her unrecognized status as the poet of Puerto Rican modernity as the two main themes for an attempt to read de Burgos's *image*, and do so *dangerously*, thereby providing an intimation of what a literary history *after* historicism may be. In this respect, this excursus is not only an attempt to clarify Benjamin's concept of history; it is also an indirect effort at self-clarification.

Baudelaire, Bergson, and Their Readers: Positioning the Image

Let us return to Benjamin's reading of the historical significance of Baudelaire's fame. How does Benjamin intimate in the vicissitudes of this poet's afterlife an image that renders legible not only the historicity of modernity but also his own historicity? Benjamin's answer to this question begins, perhaps surprisingly, with

Baudelaire's "striking" decision to address his *Les fleurs du mal* to an improbable reader of lyric poetry:

> Baudelaire reckoned with readers to whom the reading of lyric poetry would present difficulties. The introductory poem of *Les fleurs du mal* is dedicated to this reader.... And this turned out to have been a far-sighted calculation. The reader for whom he was ready would be provided to him eventually.... This book, which counted on the least indulgent readers and at first only found a few indulgent ones, has, over the decades, become a classic—as well as one of the most widely printed.
>
> If conditions for the reception of lyric poetry have become less favorable, it is reasonable to assume that only in exceptional cases does lyric poetry maintain contact with the experience of its readers. This could be because their experience has been altered in its structure.[24]

According to Benjamin, if Baudelaire is the last European lyric poet to have become a popular classic, this is ostensibly because there is a correspondence between the structure of experience that finds articulation in Baudelaire's *Les fleurs du mal* and the structure of experience of his readers. By the end of the first section of the "Motifs" essay, this hypothesis will have been further substantiated when Benjamin draws an analogical comparison between Baudelaire and Henri Bergson, who stands here as the paradigmatic figure of the philosophical movement of *Lebensphilosophie*, or "Life-philosophy." The onus of this comparison is precisely to yield some insight into the *historicity* of the *structure* or of the *eidetic constitution* of *experience itself*, which amounts to an attempt to discover something like a *historical a priori*.

Bergson is well suited to draw this contrast because his philosophy constitutes in Benjamin's eyes the culmination of the project of *Lebensphilosophie*, which he characterizes as "a series of attempts to take possession of 'true' experience, as opposed to the experience that sediments itself in the normed, denatured existence of the civilized masses."[25] Given their antagonistic stance toward the vulgar, average, or fallen experience of "modern humanity," it is understandable that *Lebensphilosophen* such as Wilhelm von Dilthey, Ludwig Klages, and Carl Jung "did not take as their point of departure the existence of men in society," turning instead to "poetry," "nature," and to "mythical epochs" as potential sources for the retrieval of true or authentic experience.[26] And, to be sure, Bergson's thought does not constitute an exception to the ahistorical tendencies that Benjamin detects in this philosophical movement:

> Rising as a towering monument above this literature is Bergson's early work, *Matière et mémoire*. More than others in this field, it preserves links with exact research. It

is oriented toward biology. As its title suggests, it regards the structure of memory as decisive for the philosophical structure of experience. In fact [*In der Tat*], experience is a matter of tradition, in collective as in private life. It is formed less of individual facts strongly fixed in recollection [*Erinnerung*] than of accumulated and frequently unconscious data that flow together in memory [*Gedächtnis*]. To specify memory historically is obviously not Bergson's intention. On the contrary, he rejects any historical determination of experience. As a result, he essentially avoids getting close to that experience out of which his own philosophy emerged or rather against which it was summoned. It is the inhospitable, blinding experience of the age of large-scale industrialism.[27]

Bergson may be just as blind to the blinding historical and societal conditions that conditioned the very emergence of *Lebensphilosophie*, but he towers above Dilthey, Klages, and Jung for at least two interrelated reasons: First, because he avoids the aestheticizing (Dilthey), naturalistic (Klages), or mythological (Jung) shortcuts that characterized these predecessors, producing a philosophy of life whose vitalist spiritualism is asserted through a remarkably rigorous engagement with the natural sciences of his time, from psychology and evolutionary biology to quantum mechanics; and second, and most importantly, because Bergson's attempt to "take possession of 'true' experience" grounds the very possibility of such an experience on a distinction between what he calls *mémoire volontaire*—which we may designate in English as *recollection* and which is largely voluntary, conscious, and fixed—and a truer and deeper form of memory that is characterized by spontaneity, involuntariness, unconsciousness, and cumulativeness.[28] It is this aspect of Bergson's philosophy that resonates the most with Benjamin's own concerns. For, as the passage just quoted makes clear, Benjamin also assigns a crucial role within the structure of experience to an experience of memory that he designates with the German noun *Gedächtnis*, whose essence excludes the properties of consciousness and voluntariness that characterize memory as *recall* (for which he reserves the German term *Erinnerung*). Yet despite this convergence, there is a deeper divergence between Benjamin's and Bergson's conceptions of memory and experience. Whereas Bergson's commitment to pure memory as a largely unconscious process of continuous accumulation provides the ultimate justification for Life-Philosophy's blindness to its own historical and social basis, the opposite seems to be the case for Benjamin, for whom experience as such, and therefore memory in its spontaneity and involuntariness, is so charged with historicity that it must be seen as "a matter of tradition."

This divergence regarding the "historical determination of memory" cannot but raise the following question: Given his avoidance of history, how could comparing Bergson to Baudelaire yield any insight into the historicity of experience and clarify in the process how Baudelaire's fame can be taken as an index of said historicity? To understand why Benjamin seems to be unbothered by this question, we must turn to the moment in which he explicitly constructs the analogical comparison between Baudelaire and Bergson. Right after identifying the "inhospitable, blinding experience of the epoch of large-scale industrialism" as the experience against which Bergson's conception of spontaneous memory took shape, Benjamin adds the following:

> To the eye that shuts itself in the face of this experience appears an experience of a complementary type as, so to speak, its spontaneous afterimage [*Nachbild*]. Bergson's philosophy is an attempt to detail and fix this afterimage. It thus furnishes indirectly an indication of the experience that presented itself undistorted before Baudelaire's eyes in the figure of his reader.
>
> *Matière et mémoire* determines the essence of experience in *durée* [duration] in such a way that the reader must tell themselves: only a poet could be the adequate subject of such an experience.[29]

Bergson's blindness to the historicity of his own philosophy does not prevent Benjamin from taking his philosophy as a historical index because this blindness can be read as a symptom of the transformation in the very essence of experience brought about by industrialization and capitalist modernity. To do so, however, Bergson must be placed in an antagonistic relation with Baudelaire, each standing in as a metaphor, or better, as an *analogue* for the other's insight (or blindness) into the historicity of experience under modernity. As Elissa Marder writes, "Benjamin locates the imprint of history on Bergson's philosophy in the very gesture through which Bergson attempted to blot it out. . . . The trace of history that Bergson's philosophy records can only be seen when it is 'developed' through the gaze of the figure of Baudelaire's reader."[30]

That being said, the reasons why this analogical metaphor is necessary remain a bit puzzling. If Bergson's ahistorical philosophy of experience is but an "afterimage" that pales in comparison with Baudelaire's "undistorted" insight into the historicity of experience, then why is the recourse to Bergson at all necessary? Can this detour be explained simply as the result of Benjamin's commitment to the view that "method is detour"?[31] Or is Benjamin implicitly operating on the assumption that, although the experience of his readers appeared undistorted before Baudelaire, this experience is less directly available *to him* (and, perhaps by extension, *to us*) than the distorted version that lies at the basis of Bergson's philosophy?

Although I am inclined to answer the previous two questions in the affirmative, I would argue that Benjamin here is laying the groundwork for the construction of Baudelaire as a dialectical image. More specifically, my claim is that the comparison between Baudelaire and Bergson is grounded in the methodological strictures of this key concept of Benjamin's theory of history. To substantiate this claim, in what follows I will briefly unpack the passage that I just quoted in order to show how two key characteristics of the image—namely, its mode of access and its position within thought—structure this encounter between Baudelaire and Bergson.

To begin reconstructing the first of these two characteristics, we must not lose sight of a small but highly significant detail, namely, that Benjamin's historical characterization of Bergson's concepts of duration and spontaneous memory *are also mediated by the figure of his reader*: "*Matière et mémoire* determines the essence of experience in *durée* [duration] in such a way that the reader must tell themselves: only a poet could be the adequate subject of such an experience."[32] Rather than a mere comparison between these two historical figures, what we have here is a strikingly complex analogy. For to map the relationship between Baudelaire and Bergson's respective historicities we must measure the differential trajectories drawn out not only by their divergent relationships to the *same* average reader (who is presumably ill-suited to be an "ideal" reader not only of lyric poetry but also of philosophy) but also by how these readers would have read their writings. This emphasis on the figure of the reader is in keeping with Benjamin's identification in *Das Passagen-Werk* of *Lesbarkeit*, or "legibility," as the experiential medium in which the dialectical image can be constituted: "The image *that is read*, that is to say, the image in the now of knowability, bears to the highest degree the stamp of the *critical, dangerous* moment that underlies all reading."[33] My suggestion is that Benjamin begins his essay foregrounding both Baudelaire's decision to address his poetry volume to a reader apostrophized as "Hypocrite reader—, my likeness—, my brother!"[34] and inscribing the figure of Bergson's readers within this complex analogy precisely because he is attempting to take Baudelaire's fame as an index for the construction of Baudelaire as a dialectical image. This requires that Benjamin not only must *read* the constellation of legibility that links Baudelaire and his future readers and Bergson and his hypothetical readers but also that he himself must enter the terrain of reading and "read his own now" as it emerges in and through the encounter with this constellation.

Still, however convincing this suggestion may be, it does not yet suffice to explain why Benjamin chose Bergson as Baudelaire's antagonist. This is where the second key aspect of Benjamin's concept of the dialectical image comes in, namely, the site of its emergence within the movement of historical thinking. In an oft-quoted passage from *Das Passagen-Werk*, Benjamin characterizes the position of the dialectical image in the following way: "Where thinking comes to a standstill in a constellation saturated with tensions—there the dialectical image appears. It is the caesura in the movement of thought. Its position is naturally not an arbitrary one. It is to be found, in a word, where the tension between *dialectical opposites is greatest*."[35] In an earlier passage in *Das Passagen-Werk*, Benjamin gives a vivid illustration of this aspect of the image when he writes the following: "To encompass Breton and Le Corbusier—that would be to draw the spirit of contemporary France like a bow with which knowledge strikes the moment [*Augenblick*] straight at the heart." My suggestion is that Bergson, qua representative of *Lebensphilosophie*, functions precisely as such a dialectical antipode to Baudelaire; when held together in their opposition, they form the bow that allows Benjamin to strike at his own historical now and remove it from "the homogeneous course of history."[36] Hence, the construction of this image requires something more than relating to the appearance of Baudelaire and Bergson as legible phenomena—that is to say, *as* they appear to the "eyes" of their readers. For it is their very dialectical oppositionality that must manifest itself in their legible presentation if the dialectical image of Baudelaire is to take place at all.

And indeed, I would argue that this is precisely what becomes legible through Benjamin's reading of *how* Baudelaire and Bergson read their readers and attain their reader's legibility. To see this, we must pay attention to the ironic chiasmus that Benjamin draws between these figures, which complicates and intensifies the dialectical nature of their oppositionality. And to retrace this chiasmus, we should pay close attention to the previously quoted passage in which Benjamin evokes the figure of Bergson's reader. According to Benjamin, Bergson's reader must be driven to the conclusion that only a poet would be able to achieve the strenuous change in attitude that is required for us to experience ourselves in accordance with Bergson's concept of *durée*. To understand what this claim presupposes, a brief engagement with Bergson's concept of *durée* is in order. As Bergson puts it in the first definition that he gives of this concept in his groundbreaking *Essai sur les données immédiates de la conscience* (known in English as *Time and Free Will*), "pure duration is the form that the succession of our states of consciousness takes when *our self* [notre moi] *lets itself live*, when it abstains from establishing a separation between the present state and previous states."[37] To live our lives durationally requires a constant effort to avoid the *spatialization* of our lived time and memory. Nothing less than a transformation of our existence, of our lived experience of our own self-consciousness, would be required for us to restore our first-person existence to its proper essence, for us to experience our lives as an indecomposable totality constituted by states that are purely qualitative, nonspatializable, constantly blending into one another and retained by an equally pure memory that does not establish any discrete boundaries or separations between quantifiable, discrete, countable locations in our lived time. This is why, according to Benjamin, any average reader of Bergson ought to regard duration, and thus *true life*, as something only poets could achieve. Indeed, in the wake of Bergson, it would seem as if only poets are endowed with the power to restore their lives to its proper vivacity, or *Lebendigkeit*, since only someone like a poet would seem capable of securing an experience of their own selves in its true durational, qualitative, temporal purity.

Although I have only retraced one side of this chiasmus, we can already read the irony that informs this figure. For note that the poet and the philosopher here have exchanged places and identities: Whereas the philosophical voice summoned by Bergson's metaphysical prose appears to modern eyes as one of the last avatars of the poet as a barely secularized demigod endowed with exceptional powers of intuition and sensibility, more capable than the average human being of grasping things in their true and uncorrupted essence, both the lyric speaker of *Les fleurs du mal* (who figures himself as a poet) and the volume's author (who is a poet) are read by their modern readers as *nonpoetic* figures. If we take the implicit logic of Benjamin's chiasmus to its ultimate consequences, we should conclude that the continued growth of Baudelaire's fame even under conditions unfavorable for the massive diffusion of the lyric is a result of the fact that his readers don't recognize the experience that underlies *Les fleurs du mal* as *poetic*—whereas those same readers would presumably not fail to conclude that only a poet could have actually *lived* in accordance with the structure of experience laid out by Bergson in his philosophical texts. If *modernity* can serve as a catachrestic name for this alteration of the *structure* of experience itself, then we might say that Baudelaire's poetry, according to Benjamin, has served as a medium in which his readers, most likely without being explicitly aware of this, have encountered their own modernity. Benjamin appears to suggest as much when he uses the term *Kontakt*, or "contact," to designate the form of connection that Baudelaire's poetry has with his readers. *Les fleurs du mal* would have thus enabled Baudelaire's *modern* readers to *read themselves*, to maintain some form of contact with their own historicity—however damaged by the fungibilizing forces of capitalist modernization this historicity may be. But *Les fleurs du mal* could achieve this only because Baudelaire had already read the historicity of his own transformed experience in reading the transformed experience of those readers to whom he blindingly and calculatingly dedicated his improbable masterpiece.

We can now understand how Benjamin could have taken Baudelaire's fame as an *index* of a historical phenomenon whose phenomenality necessarily exceeds the realist, empiricist, or positivist realm of historical facts or objectivities, namely, the attunement or correspondence between the modernity of the structure of experience consigned in Baudelaire's poetry and the structure of experience of his readers. We are also now in a better position to understand why Bergson emerged as the dialectical antagonist through Benjamin's construction of the Baudelairean image. For the opposition at stake here runs deeper than the ultimately superficial distinction between an ahistorical Bergson and a historical Baudelaire, or a poetic philosopher of durational experience and a prosaic poet of the commodification of memory and the spatialization of time characteristic of modern life. Indeed, what attains legibility in this chiasmus is a conflict regarding the very constitution of history in its foundation and organization, that is, in its ground and telos. Bergson's seemingly ahistorical *Lebensphilosophie* actually harbors a philosophy of history that could be seen as the afterlife of the teleological tendencies that Benjamin saw as characteristic of both classicism and romanticism in the *Trauerspiel*. To be more specific, I would argue that Bergson's belief in the capacity of his method of intuition "to seek experience at its source, or rather above this decisive *turn* through which, inflecting itself in the direction of our *utility*, it becomes properly *human experience*"[38] reactivates the "theosophical" tendencies that, according to Benjamin, have animated the aestheticization of historicity since the advent of classicism and Romanticism.[39] If classicism was committed to "the apotheosis of existence in an individual who is fulfilled in not just an ethical sense," and if Romanticism situated "this fulfilled individual in a historical process that is, to be sure, infinite but nevertheless salvific, indeed sacred,"[40] Bergsonian vitalism intensifies this aestheticization by reauratizing and thus resacralizing not only "true human experience" but also the life of the cosmos through the extension of duration and pure memory beyond the confines of human consciousness, which finds mature expression in the Bergsonian concept of the *élan vital*, or "life impulse."[41] Put otherwise, by claiming that the possibility of restoring experience to its truly suprahuman essence lies *within our intuitive powers*, by positing that we can regain a sense of how life "lets itself live" *below* its utilitarian capture and *before* its historical determination by modernity, Bergson effectively posits such a pure life as the *arkhē* and telos of a history that can never truly touch, let alone alter life in its essence.

In Benjamin's dialectical image, the contrast between Baudelaire and Bergson renders legible the extent to which Bergson's faith in an immediate access to an untarnished life is a disavowal rather than a transcending of history. If there is such an untarnished life, access to it will not be granted by the freedom of the will through any method of intuition. Nor is such life the guaranteed outcome of the historical process. Instead, it could only be attained through a thoroughly historical struggle. And, as the famous allegory of the Angel of History suggests, to struggle with history for Benjamin means tarrying with both the continuity of catastrophe and our structural inability to overcome it once and for all.[42] This inability is a key aspect of Benjamin's historical messianism; indeed, it is the reason why the materialist or dialectical historian for Benjamin is endowed with a force that is "*weak* messianic."[43] Benjamin's construction of the image of Baudelaire does not restore or heal Baudelaire from his exposure to the corrosive forces of modernization. Instead, it answers to the claim that the past of Baudelaire has on Benjamin himself by *inheriting* that damaged experience, recognizing himself as intended or addressed by Baudelaire's own experience of a radical alteration of experience in its very essence. As Kevin Newmark writes: "By thus making available . . . the disruption of traditional modes of consciousness and understanding that occurs traumatically in the very experience of modernity, Baudelaire is finally able to appear at the end of Benjamin's essay, and in the words of Nietzsche, as a 'rarefied star' in the otherwise dreary sky of the Second Empire."[44] And if this experience is available to Benjamin (and, thanks to Benjamin, to us), this is arguably because, since the publication of *Les fleurs du mal*, the conditions unleashed by modernity upon the structure of experience and of being itself have intensified to such an extent that Benjamin could count himself among those readers for whom Baudelaire was ready and on whose own altered experience he counted.

This excursus through Benjamin's engagement with the historical paradox of Baudelaire's fame has yielded three insights that are as pertinent for this book's methodology as for its thematic interest in de Burgos's fame and in the catastrophic tradition that continues to drive its expansion (to which I will turn in the next section). The first of these concerns some of the basic requirements that must be met if the past is to be constructed as an image. The second concerns some of the aspects of Benjamin's theory of history—above all, his conception of messianism—which will remain in the background of this book but which nonetheless inform my approach to the problem and the concept of historicity, thus functioning as an *operative*, rather than thematic, concept for this book. The third insight has to do with the possibility of approaching de Burgos's modernity by taking Benjamin's dialectical opposition of Baudelaire and Bergson as a model. One of my arguments in Part III is that the singularity of de Burgos's ambivalent relationship to modernity could be understood, at least initially, by recourse to the two alternatives that Benjamin sees at work in these two figures. To be more specific, my reading of de Burgos's *Poema* suggests that we can begin to approach de Burgos's singular modernity if we read her poetics as encompassing both the Baudelairean and the Bergsonian responses to modern life: De Burgos's modernism both exposes and intensifies some of the radical changes in the experience of time, space, and, especially, sexuality and gender brought about by modernization even as her poetics reactivates a vitalistic, life-philosophical or life-phenomenological faith in the possibility of restoring life to its pure autoaffectivity.

To bring this excursus to a close, I want to flesh out further the first of these insights by giving a more explicitly philosophical account of Benjamin's concept of the dialectical image. Doing so will require a quick detour through other moments of Benjamin's corpus in which he's directly concerned with describing the structure of this concept. Obtaining some clarity on the kind of literary history to which Benjamin's thinking of the image gives rise to will lend some theoretical solidity to this book's attempt to read de Burgos's *image* and, in so doing, will furnish a preliminary example of that nonhistoricist literary history whose theoretical armature and methodological procedures remain still to come.

Index, Correlation, Constellation: The Dialectical Image as History's Transcendental

Earlier I mentioned that the thematic and methodological aspects of Benjamin's concern with Baudelaire's fame are *stricto sensu* inseparable, and we are now in a better position to see why this is the case. As I remarked earlier, Benjamin here treats fame as a "historical index" for an inquiry that is eminently *historical*, even if its scope and ends are both *transcendental* and *speculative* in nature.[45] To grasp this, we need to understand what exactly distinguishes Benjamin's thinking of the "historical index" from what we take this concept prima facie to mean. To do this, we should turn to the fourth sentence of entry N3,1 in *Das Passagen-Werk*, which contains Benjamin's most philosophically audacious, if still underexamined, exposition of the dialectical image: "To wit, the historical index of images not only says that they *belong* to a determined time, it says above all that they only *come to legibility* at a determined time."[46]

Note that Benjamin's concept of the historical index of the image retains the most general semantic determination of the historical as the region of entities that evince the form of *ta genomena* or *res gestæ*—that is, beings that have *really* happened and, as such, are localizable in a *determined* position within historical time-space. In keeping with the Leibnizian principle of the identity of indiscernibles, Benjamin's historical index thus maintains a reference to the *hic-et-nunc* ("here-and-now") character of historical entities as the source of historical individuation, which implies that if the "same" qualitative event were to happen on multiple occasions, the sheer *fact* of their spatiotemporal localization at *different* moments in historical space-time would be enough to guarantee their difference, so that the most we could say about these events is that they are *equal* to each other without constituting the *self-same* event.[47]

Because of his commitment to historical indexicality, Benjamin's concept of the dialectical image would appear to ratify the basic tenets of what Ethan Kleinberg calls ontological realism, "a commitment to history as an endeavor concerned with events assigned to a specific location in space and time that are in principle observable and as such are regarded as fixed and immutable."[48] Upon closer examination, however, this appearance turns out to be misleading. As a matter of fact, Benjamin's concept of the historical index challenges ontological realism by precisely denying that the spatiotemporal localization of an event— its *hic et nunc*—suffices on its own to lend reality, fixity, and individuation to historical phenomena. But to appreciate the radicality of Benjamin's theory, we must grasp how his concept of the historical index radically transforms the field of historical temporality. To do so, we must unpack the implications of Benjamin's discovery of a *complexity* at the heart of what is held to be most simple, namely, the *here and now* that serves as the ground for the traditional concept of indexicality as punctual and nonextended. Indeed, one of crucial theoretical innovations of Benjamin's concept of the image lies in his reconfiguration of the structure of historical indexicality, so that it is no longer understood on the basis of *simplicity*. Instead, indexicality, for Benjamin, is complicated from its very origin, to echo Derrida, since the structure of the index is composed of two irreducible moments in historical time: the determined time to which the image belongs and the determined time in which the image attains legibility. Several crucial consequences follow from this: Whereas in realist historicism a temporal index is treated as a brute fact (with the index pointing to the elemental or atomic fact that x event happened at y time), in Benjamin's theory of the image the index is the site of an originary synthesis insofar as the time of the legibility of an event is constitutive of the very *happening* of that event. As a result of this, for Benjamin an event cannot be established in its sheer immanence and self-immediacy without the intervention of a posterior *here and now* that thereby comes to inhabit or haunt from without the presumably indecomposable spatiality of the temporal index. We can understand now why Benjamin, in a conversation with Ernst Bloch, compared his theory of history "to the method of splitting the atom," since his concept of the image "unleashes the tremendous forces of history that lie bound in the 'Once upon a time' of classical history. The history that showed matters 'as they really had been,' was the strongest narcotic of the century."[49] Whereas realist historicism or ontological realism requires the belief in the atomic, indecomposable simplicity of the past, Benjamin's thinking of the index reveals the synthetic entanglement of temporal determinations that predates and enables the constitution of any historical object.

But Benjamin's concept of the index not only lays the groundwork for a theory of historical time that splits into two temporal moments the atomic punctuality of an event's here-and-now. To fully appreciate the audacity of Benjamin's thinking of historical indexicality and its challenge to historical realism, we must also take into account the *transcendental* dimension of the concept of the image. And doing so requires that we pay close attention to how Benjamin's rethinking of historical indexicality tacitly introduces the schema of an *a priori correlation* at the very heart of the historical index.

The correlation at stake in Benjamin's concept of the image can be helpfully illuminated if we compare it to both Kantian and Husserlian versions of a transcendental correlation. Regarding the first of these two versions, it must be noted that Benjamin himself is quite explicit about the post-Kantian roots of his concept of the image. Indeed, he even characterizes his theory of history elsewhere in *Das Passagen-Werk* as an attempt to bring about a "Copernican turn in historical intuition," which, like Kant's own,[50] would entail a "paradigm shift" in how we conceive of the relation between the known historical object and the knowing subject or the historian:

> The Copernican turn in historical intuition is this: Before, one held "what has been" as the fixed point and saw the present as struggling to lead knowledge tentatively to this fortress. Now, this relation must be inverted and what has been must become the dialectical reversal, the incursion of awakened consciousness. Politics maintains primacy over history. Facts become something that befall us just now; fixing them is the matter of memory.[51]

At first sight, this passage makes clear the extent to which Benjamin's Copernican turn entails the abandonment of any approach to historical reality that does not adhere to the minimal conditions of Kant's version of the transcendental argument, according to which "the conditions of the *possibility of experience* in general are at the same time conditions of the *possibility of the objects of experience*."[52] And yet, Benjamin's way of recasting the military metaphors that are present in the Kantian original passage on the Copernican revolution in metaphysics paradoxically obfuscates and underscores the idiosyncrasies of his transcendental gesture and the ways it departs from Kant's.[53] The inversion of the roles assigned to "what has been" and "the present" in this martial allegory where the past goes from being a fortress to an incursion may lead us to assume that the opposite holds for the present after Benjamin's Copernican turn, namely, that the present is now the fortress of knowledge that would then be raided by the past. Still, Benjamin's characterization of the past in terms of a "dialectical reversal" and the fact that the past's incursion is enacted by "awakened consciousness" suggests that the shift brought about by his Copernican turn in history should not be seen a simple transcendental inversion of the realist schema.[54]

To be more specific, I take Benjamin here to be doing something other than merely changing which term occupies the position of grounding knowledge while leaving the structure intact (with one term being fixed and the other mobile, one doing the grounding and the other being grounded). On the contrary, the fact that Benjamin describes the past as the incursion of awakened consciousness into the historian's "present" indicates that the past and the present are *absolutely* entangled in their very *genesis*, which implies that the present (and, by extension, the historian) should *not* be seen as now occupying the position of the fixed fortress of historical knowledge. Rather than being self-identical, discrete, already constituted temporal instances that then enter into an asymmetrical relationship for the sake of the constitution of historical objectivity (asymmetrical, since the present would have a constitutive role in the objectivation of the past without being submitted to a retroactive constitution by the past it constitutes), the past of awakened consciousness *is* none other than the consciousness of the historian's own present—and vice versa. This originary entanglement of temporal instances makes clear to what extent Benjamin's use of the term "*dialectical* reversal" is rigorously speculative, in a Hegelian sense of the term. Indeed, after Benjamin's Copernican turn, the *genesis* of both historical objectivity and subjectivity must be itself grasped as a form of the Absolute, that is, as "the identity of identity and non-identity," in which the "being opposed" and the "being one" of subject and object "are both together in it."[55] In the context of Benjamin's thinking of the image, this absolute dialectics takes the form of what Derrida describes, in a different (though intimately related) context, as "a certain *simultaneity* of the non-simultaneous,"[56] namely, the *at-*

the-same-timeness of two irreducible yet indissociable temporal determinations of the image's historical index: the time to which the image belongs and the time in which it attains legibility.

If, as I suggested in this book's Introduction, historicism is a correlationism that locates in the historian's ipseity the power to appropriate and constitute historical time, then this excursus through Benjamin's engagement with Kant allows us to understand that historicism is also a presentism. This explains why Benjamin's Copernican turn in history should not be simply characterized as the mere inversion of historical realism in favor of a historical idealism that would locate the very *reality* of history in the historian's consciousness and thus in their present. Instead, for Benjamin the historian's own present experience of the past must be seen as the result of a dialectical process that *generates*, in and through their mutual entanglement, both the present and the past, the time of historical experience and the objectivity that the historian experiences.

There is, however, another aspect of the type of correlationism at work in Benjamin's concept of the image's index whose unpacking requires that we set aside Kant's unspecified concept of experience and turn to what Husserl, in the *Krisis*, calls "the universal a priori of the correlation of objects of experience and *modes* of givenness."[57] Although the German idealist schema of the absolute can account for the formal conditions for the emergence of both the image and the historian and, above all, their a priori correlation, the specific mode of givenness of the image and hence the phenomenal concretization of this historical correlation can't be simply derived from such a formal absolute, whose content is solely the synthetic identity of the nonidentity of the subject of experience and the object as what is experienced. Instead, as I previously mentioned in my discussion of Benjamin's reading of Baudelaire, the two temporal moments that constitute the complex indexicality of the dialectical image relate to each other in the phenomenal medium that is determined by a very specific activity, namely, *reading*. As Stefano Marchesoni has recently put it, "its construction [of a dialectical image] as well as its epiphany are indissociable from reading. One does not *see* dialectical images, one can only *read* them."[58] The fact that the correlation that characterizes historical knowledge, indeed the very givenness of historical phenomena, can only obtain in the medium of legibility inflects all aspects of the dialectical structure of the image: Whereas the identity of the historical reader and the read image is established concretely at every moment of the historical correlation, their difference nonetheless appears to emerge through the fact that only one of the two moments that constitute the image's index is able to occupy the active position, that is, be the *reader* of the other moment. Moreover, this asymmetry within the structure of the image would confirm some of our most deeply held commonsense intuitions about history, beginning with the belief that only the present can know the past and, concomitantly, that the past can only be *known* by the present. But wouldn't this strong asymmetry reinscribe a more traditional, subjectivist position—one closer to the transcendental idealisms of Kant or of Husserl—at the level of that index's very constitution? By extension, wouldn't the theory of the image in fact boil down to a presentism that posits the historian's now as the site in which historical phenomena are constituted or, to be more precise, *read* by the historian? If, for Benjamin, the experiential condition of the concrete possibility of historical objectivity is the moment of reading, if the givenness of the historical or dialectical image lies in its legibility, doesn't this imply that only the historian-cum-reader is endowed with the power of historicization? Wouldn't this constitute an interruption of the dialectics of historical time and the installation of the same type of transcendentality that characterizes historicism, as discussed before (see §1)?

I would like to propose an answer to these questions that I believe does justice to several aspects of Benjamin's conception of history that are well known and often mentioned but haven't received sufficient theoretical attention. To understand why, despite his insistence on the necessity of reading for the constitution of historical objectivity, Benjamin's concept of the image is neither simply transcendental-idealist in a Kantian or Husserlian sense nor presentist, we need to turn briefly to another moment in the passage from *Das Passagen-Werk* that I quoted earlier, where Benjamin gives the most thorough exposition of the concept of the image. After introducing the concept of the image's historical index, Benjamin then offers a sketch of another of his main historical concepts, namely, the concept of the *Konstellation*, or "constellation":

> Each present is determined by those images that are synchronic with it: each now is the now of a determined knowability. In it, truth is charged with time to the point of bursting. . . . It is not that the past sheds its light on the present or the present on the past; rather, image is that in which what has been enters flashing into a constellation with the now. . . . The image *that is read*, that is to say, the image in the now of knowability, bears to the highest degree the stamp of the *critical, dangerous* moment that underlies all reading.[59]

For my purposes here, there are at least three moments in this passage that deserve close attention: In the first place, note that Benjamin does not characterize the present as a constitutive, transcendental instance that would have the power of historical determinacy; rather, the present or the now is determined by the images that it can know at that moment. This idea is further complicated dialectically by the concept of the "constellation," which, for Benjamin, constitutes the specific mode of "spatio-temporization" of the image. This concept affords a clearer picture into the *originary contamination* between the "now" and the "what has been" that characterizes Benjamin's thinking of historical time than Benjamin's passage on the Copernican turn in historical intuition that I examined earlier. The dialectical image may well configure historical knowledge as a mode of *reading* that is inevitably bound to the present, but it is neither the case that the present is the instance that *determines* the historical past by projecting its own needs, interests, and concerns over it, nor is it the case that historical knowledge, understood as the *reading of images*, obtains when the historical significance of the past overrides and determines the historicity of the present. Instead, the image and its constellation provide an a priori schema for a view of historical experience as constituted synthetically through the generation of two identical yet radically nonidentical "times"—the now that reads and the "what has been" that is read—within the space-time of the *Konstellation*, which thereby emerges as a catachrestic metaphor for *historical* time *as such*. Reconfigured by the metaphor of the constellation, historical time ceases to be re-presented *sub specie continuitatis*, that is, as a "flow" that runs in accordance with the schema of succession, becoming instead radically *spatialized* (this is even more salient in the German, where *Kon-stellation* could always be read literally as "placing with," *Kon-stellen*). And finally, note that Benjamin closes this passage by introducing the idea of *danger* as an affective modality that lies at the very ground of the time of reading, that is, of the now, which itself constitutes the *conditioned condition* of historical knowledge.

Since Benjamin's motif of *Gefahr*, "danger" or "peril," will be discussed more extensively in Part II, I want to close this discussion of Benjamin's dialectical image by clarifying why Benjamin's understanding of historical reading as the very essential activity in which historical experience is transcendentally constituted does not transform his theory of history into a subjectivist, transcendental idealism. The key to grasp this point is to register the fact that, although Benjamin does indeed conceive of the "now of knowability" (which coincides with the moment of reading) as a necessary condition for the constitution of historical knowledge, the dialectical image requires extending the originary contamination of "what has been" and "the now" not only to the time of historical legibility itself (that is, "the now") but to the reputed subject of that experience, that is, to the "substance" of that now (that is, "the historian"). As a consequence of this, the historian themself becomes radically desubstantialized and desubjectified, acquiring the status of a historical event, rather than an agent—and this despite the fact that the historian remains the reader and, thus, in a way, the subject of historical knowledge. The historian does *read* and, hence, *constitutes* the objectivity of the past, but the historian's reading of the past is first and foremost an attempt at *self-reading* in which what is at stake is not simply the historicity of the past but the historian's own historicity. What the Benjaminian historian must read first of all is not the image of the past, understood simply as a historical objectivity, but the image of the past as the instance that has first summoned the historian to the task of historical reading and thus harbors the very historicity of the historian. As a result, the historian and their now are not a priori endowed with the presential power of historical constitution; instead, it is this very weak force that the historian must first of all *read* and hence *discover*, if not even invent, through their engagement with a past that will also lack any substantiality if the historian cannot answer its call and enter the scene of reading.

One of the places where Benjamin formulated this insight most clearly is in a letter from March 7, 1931, written to Max Rychner, editor of the *Neue Schweizer Rundschau*, in response to a previous letter in which Rychner challenged Benjamin to situate himself within the field of "materialistic," or Marxist, literary criticism. As part of his response, Benjamin writes the following:

> That historical magnitude has an index [*Standindex*] by virtue of which any genuine knowledge of it becomes the historico-philosophical—not psychological— self-knowledge of the knower, that may be a very unmaterialistic formulation, but it is an experience that still connects me more to the outlandish and coarse analyzes of a Franz Mehring than to the most profound descriptions of the realm of ideas as they are emerging today from Heidegger's school.[60]

Note that this passage rearticulates not only Benjamin's basic insight that history has an indexical component but also his stronger claim that "genuine" (*echt*) historical knowledge of that indexical mark on historical magnitude or extension must necessarily give way to a form of self-knowledge that is both historical and philosophical *without being psychological*. Benjamin's explicitly antipsychologistic remark emphasizes a crucial quality of this self-knowledge, namely, the fact that it doesn't unfold as an internal, mental, or conscious process. This knowledge does not shed light on any aspect of the historian's "mind," let alone their historical personality, mentality, or identity; instead, the historico-philosophical quality of this self-knowledge suggests that what is *known* in this knowledge is the historian's very *genesis as historical reader*. Thus, historical knowledge, for Benjamin, does not unfold as the correlation between an indexical or empirical moment and a transcendental instance that enables and constitutes that empirical object in its objectivity. Rather, historical knowledge entails above all a speculative leap as a result of the fact that the messianic historian is determined by their transcendental destitution: Indeed, historians are those who must read the past in search of not only their historical identity and self-presence to themselves but also, and above all, their own *ability* to constitute historical phenomena. The historian's historicity—their self-knowledge or self-understanding as historical beings—is granted to them only through their engagement with a past that would have also remained unknown historically if the historian had not appeared on the scene of historical reading.

The ontological indigence that characterizes both historical phenomena and the historian in the wake of Benjamin's thinking of the image—since, properly speaking, it can't be said that there is any historical being except in the wake of the image's legibility—is further radicalized by Benjamin in his theses on history, which contains the last version of his thinking of historical indexicality but adds another essential component, namely, the *messianic*:

> The past carries with it a temporal index through which it is referred to redemption. There is a secret appointment between the generations that have been and ours. We have been awaited on the earth. Like every generation that came before us, a *weak* messianic force has been given to us on which the past has a claim. This claim cannot be settled cheaply. The historical materialist knows this.[61]

We are as far as possible from Frank Ankersmit's image of the historian as a "pantheist god" that breathes the past into existence through their historical representations.[62] The Benjaminian historian is a *self* that has lost or renounced *ipseity*, since the very possibility of their constitution as a historical selfhood is no longer guaranteed through that sheer form of self-speculation that would erect the historian into the secular substitute of the god of onto-theology. The force of historicization, the power of historicity itself, is "weak *messianic*" because what possibilitates and opens the historian to their historicity is not the actualization of an ability that would always already be within the historian's control. Instead, whatever power the historian has lies in their being claimed by the past. The "temporal index" is the name for what grounds that claim. But this claim is not self-actualizable either; the past's demand for redemption is radically dependent on the historian's response to that claim. The image of the "secret appointment" thus functions as another catachresis for Benjamin's "constellation"; it points to the spatialization of time that is required if the past is to meet up with the now, however close or far apart they may be on the "line" of time. It is only after this encounter, emerging out of the originary, contaminated synthesis of historical time, that, for Benjamin, we may speak of historical materialism.

Benjamin's theory of history entails a commitment to an a priori or transcendental correlation as the force field that renders the very possibility of history possible. But this correlation is *messianic*, hence *dangerous*, since its own constitution is *each time* exposed to its structural absence and failure. Another way of saying this is that the correlation in which alone historical objectivity and subjectivity are both constituted is, for Benjamin, a *historical* event in its own right and thus is something that *may always not have happened*. Benjamin's historical a priori—that is, the dialectical image—needs to happen *in* historical time for both object and subject to know themselves historically. In this respect, we might say that, for Benjamin, *the absolute is the messianic*, and its force renders even the most empowered transcendental-constitutive-subjective agent into an a priori weak reader that can only *read themselves historically* because the chance of their own historical legibility has been given to them by the past.

On the basis of this detailed excursus, we can now grasp the extent to which Benjamin's engagement with Baudelaire's fame could be seen as almost a strict application, if you will, of the schema of the dialectical image. Whereas the "empirical" or "factual" dimension of Baudelaire's undiminished fame functions as the *realist* moment within Benjamin's construction of the index of Baudelaire's image, Benjamin's figuration of the reader's responses to Baudelaire, triangulated by the analogous figuration of Bergson's legibility, marks the *transcendental* aspect of that index, that is, the moment in which Baudelaire's fame attains legibility not simply as a fact but as an essential component of that historical sense-formation that bears the poet's name. But, as Benjamin's use of Baudelaire's opening poem "Au lecteur" makes clear, Baudelaire's readers are in turn *read* by Baudelaire himself, and in such a way that they attain a higher degree of nonpsychologistic self-knowledge the more they enter into contact with what Baudelaire did not lose touch of, namely, the *historicity of modern experience itself*, the radical transformation of the very lifeworld that constitutes the ultimate source for the "secret appointment" between Baudelaire and his readers. Moreover, the time-space of this historical index—that is, the spatiality of the constellation—includes Benjamin, who is also reading his own *theory* of history as well as his own understanding of the historicity of modernity in and through the historical dynamics of Baudelaire's reception. But since what becomes legible in the crystallization of Baudelaire's historical image is modernity, understood not as a series of purely empirical processes that are regarded by a historical theory as constituting the "last instance of determination" of historical meaning but as a *historical a priori* in which what is at stake is a mutation in the structure of experience as such, Benjamin's construction of Baudelaire's image gives way to a mode of knowledge that is properly speaking *speculative* (not simply historicist, either in a realist-positivist or a transcendental-idealist sense of the term). Benjamin's attempt to read himself in Baudelaire's own self-reading as refracted through the eyes of his reader's constitutes an attempt "to read what was never written," which Benjamin qualifies as the task of a "true historian."[63] Baudelaire's image grants us access to a historical event that cannot have the character of an empirical event locatable in space-time, since it is the *event* through which the structure of experience itself—and thus the very constitution of space and time—underwent a radical *alteration*.[64]

I hope that this excursus has given the reader a better sense of the theoretical and practical implications of my decision to rely on Baudelaire's Benjamin as an analogical model for my reading of de Burgos. In the following section, I will return to the question with which I started this one in order to carry out a historical inquiry into the idiosyncratic "destiny" of de Burgos's fame. Since this inquiry is part of an attempt to construct the *image* of de Burgos, it must attempt to reconstruct the field of legibility in which her fame is inscribed. This will require a careful examination of *what* has been read in this image and *how* this reading has sedimented into a tradition. The ultimate goal of this exercise is to transform de Burgos's image into the historical "crystal" in which my own *refracted* historicity may attain some degree of clarification.[65]

But to do so in the case of de Burgos entails an added challenge. As we will see, the institutionalization of de Burgos as a key totem of Puertoricanness broadly construed has produced a paradoxical situation that will prevent us from taking her fame at face value as a means for a speculative, historical self-clarification. The paradox in question could be described as a curious form of *over*-reading in which the more de Burgos is "read"—that is, celebrated, paid homage as "a poet who helped shape Puerto Rican identity"—the less her image becomes available for a *historical reading* worthy of the name. As a result, the very historicity of the indices embedded in de Burgos's poetry remains, as it were, dormant. De Burgos's historical or dialectical image still awaits a reader who may be awoken to their own historicity through the sudden confrontation with precisely those historical elements of her image that have never been written in the official "Book of Puerto Rican Life" and remain in a state of latency, undigested by both dominant and alternative articulations of Puerto Rican historicity. It is to such a highly improbable—if not, strictly speaking, impossible—yet eminently *historical* task that this book's reading of de Burgos and her image is devoted. As Benjamin puts it when he introduces his historical version of the Copernican turn, the task is to articulate a literary-historical protocol in which the "facts" of de Burgos's life and the historical facticity condensed in her poetry may "become something that befall us just now"; only then would "politics maintain primacy over history."[66] And only then could we say that a literary history *after* historicism—that is, a mode of historical presentation that radically *alters* the *correlation* of the past and the present that pre-positions the historian as the *ipseity* that rules, like a secular god, over the totality of their historical narratives—may have taken place.

§11. OVER-READ? JULIA DE BURGOS'S CATASTROPHIC TRADITION

How, then, should we explain the fact that, decades after her abject and premature death, de Burgos's fame continues to spread unabated? What historical forces or processes attain expression through the fact that de Burgos's life and legacy appear to be more legible *now* than ever before? To be sure, the number of elements that could be listed as part of this event's historical infrastructure is no doubt too large to yield anything that may look like a well-defined set or, to be more precise, a saturated historical context. Besides, the very status of this *now* is itself highly suspect. For, although it could be the case that most of my Anglophone readers encountered de Burgos for the first time in the pages of the *New York Times* or the *New York Review of Books*, the fact remains that the figure of Julia de Burgos never fell out of fashion in Puerto Rican and Caribbean letters. The *New York Times* may have *overlooked* Julia de Burgos, but in the Spanish Caribbean, and especially in her natal Puerto Rico, her figure has been submitted to a curious form of *over-reading* ever since the publication of her very first poems in the mid-1930s.

To begin taking the measure of de Burgos's historical significance within the Puerto Rican cultural milieu on both sides of the Atlantic, we would do well to recall a conceptual opposition that Hayden White borrowed from Michael Oakeshott in his last book, *The Practical Past*, namely, the distinction between the *historical* and the *practical* past. For, as we will see, the privileged place that de Burgos occupies within Puerto Rican historicity encompasses both these species of history—which, if we follow White's line of thinking, appear to divide the totality of the genus "history." According to White, the historical past is the name for "a theoretically motivated construction, existing only in the books and articles published by professional historians";[67] as such, it could be said to include all historiographical endeavors whose evidentiary claims and onto-epistemic presuppositions are answerable to the professional guild of the historians, regardless of whether their authors are themselves academic historians.

When it comes to Puerto Rico's historical past, it would be possible to argue that de Burgos remains the twentieth-century literary figure about whom more ink has been spilled and more conference papers have been delivered than any other. This is even more so since the celebration of the centenary of her birth in 2014. In the last decade, a considerable number of her texts that remained unpublished or out of print have become available: *Cartas a Consuelo*, de Burgos's correspondence with her sister; a hauntingly beautiful *Diario*, which de Burgos kept while she was hospitalized at New York's Mt. Sinai Hospital in 1948;[68] and even the FBI file that was opened after her Hatch Act investigation in 1944, which shows that she remained under surveillance by US intelligence for the remainder of her life. Likewise, several new collections of her poetry have been published by presses in Madrid, Caracas, and La Habana, where Casa de las Américas, one of the most prestigious cultural institutions in the Spanish-speaking world, published her complete works. If before her centenary a complete bibliography of criticism of de Burgos could be counted in the dozens, since 2014 there has been a veritable explosion in the number of academic and para-academic publications on de Burgos. While the publication of Vanessa Pérez Rosario's *Becoming Julia de Burgos*—the first monograph devoted to her work published by a North American university press—and her forthcoming bilingual anthology of de Burgos's prose and poetry, *I Am My Own Path/Yo misma fui mi ruta*, mark watersheds both in her US academic reception and in the poet's textual archive available in English, these volumes are part of a veritable tidal wave of scholarship and criticism on de Burgos that has been published in the last decade across the Caribbean, which includes more than a dozen books and several dissertations that have clearly expanded our understanding of de Burgos's life. All of this justifies my claim that no poet to date occupies the kind of privileged place in Puerto Rico's historical past that de Burgos does.

Something similar could be said about her role in the island's practical past. According to White, the practical past designates "the past that people as individuals or members of groups draw upon in order to help them make assessments and make decisions in ordinary everyday life as well as in extreme situations (such as catastrophes, disasters, battles, judicial and other kinds of conflicts in which survival is at issue)."[69] Borrowing a distinction more Husserlian or Heideggerian in nature, we may say that whereas the historical past refers to a specific mode of constructing historical objectivities that relies on a theoretical attitude to the past, the practical past reaches to our *pre*theoretical relationship to historical phenomena; it refers to the ways in which our very existence in a lifeworld is informed by a mode of historical consciousness whose vague norms are oriented toward everyday action and not toward satisfying the protocols of the historical science. If it could be easily argued that de Burgos is the most salient poet in Puerto Rico's historical past, the fact that she is the writer most often upheld as a political example is barely disputable. Perhaps the most eloquent proof of this claim are all the statues that have been erected to her figure, all the homages that have been organized in her honor, all the cultural centers, parks, buildings, and boulevards that have been named after her. Indeed, no other Puerto Rican writer to date has become so indissociable with Puertoricanness that the mere appearance of their image suffices to *symbolize* (in the strict sense that Benjamin or Paul de Man gave to this term)[70] both the island and its peoples, scattered on both sides of the Atlantic.

Why is this so? How could we explain that, of all the distinguished, canonized writers in Puerto Rico's lettered city, it would be de Burgos who would emerge as the symbol of the many "nations" that divide from within the Puerto Rican national body politic? To approach this question, we must attend to the different ways in which her reception has constructed the "image of the life" of Julia de Burgos.[71] To do so, however, requires a different kind of exercise than a mere cataloging of empirical facts. Indeed, were we to expand that catalogue ad infinitum, we would still not gain a sound insight into the reasons *why* de Burgos's legibility has continued to grow unabated since her death. That being said, an insight into the basic configuration of de Burgos's image could be gleaned from the last lines of the *New York Times*' obituary, which gives the last word to de Burgos's niece and literary executor, María Consuelo Sáez Burgos: "Julia de Burgos not only spoke her reality. She spoke about all of us."[72] This statement illustrates the extent to which the legibility of de Burgos's image continues to be determined by a longstanding tradition that pre-positions de Burgos as a universal mirror in whose life and works generations of Puerto Ricans on both sides of the Atlantic can glean the *imago* of their own idealized relation to Puertoricanness, whether conceived along hegemonic or minoritarian lines. But to become, more than any other figure in Puerto Rican letters, the very *symbolon* that secures the possibility of collective identification, de Burgos's corpus had to be submitted to an ironic form of *over*-reading that entails neglecting those aspects of her life and her writings that may maculate her mirror and interrupt her capacity to function as a glossy reflecting surface in which her readers may come to see a reflection of their own ego-ideal, however it may be understood. The result of this protocol of identificatory *over*-reading is that de Burgos's life and corpus have fallen into a peculiar condition of *historical illegibility*, which becomes more acute as her fame spreads.

The Tradition of Catastrophe and the Danger of Rescue (Benjamin/Husserl)

My overarching goal in this section is to justify my twofold claims that de Burgos's poetry remains *dehistoricized*, if not even *historically unread*, and that to restore historicity to her poetry requires a thorough reconstruction of her image, in a Benjaminian sense of the term. But in order to embark on such a reconstruction, a critical *Wirkungsgeschichte*, or "reception history," is needed to retrace the genetic process through which de Burgos became overwhelmingly a symbol of identification rather than a historical text demanding to be read. This explains why this paragraph is titled after another Benjaminian historical insight, namely, his conception of a "catastrophic tradition," which he articulates most clearly in the following entry from *Das Passagen-Werk*:

> From what are phenomena rescued? Not only and not so much from the disrepute and the disdain into which they have fallen as from the catastrophe in which a determined type of their tradition, their "enshrinement as heritage," often presents them. (They are rescued through the indication of their leap.) There is a tradition that is catastrophe.[73]

The insight in question here takes the form of two interrelated oxymorons. The first and most obvious one is Benjamin's claim that there is a mode of traditionalization that is as catastrophic as the forgetting or neglect of the past. This argument seems paradoxical or perhaps even scandalous because it challenges a deeply sedimented axiom about the constitution of historical memory that posits erasure or the forgetting of tradition as the *worst* possible scenario that may happen to the past. If the present were to vanish without leaving a trace or if it were to be so neglected and disdained that it effectively vanishes from collective memory, then that event would have failed to constitute a tradition, thereby falling prey to a mode of negativity akin to the very death of history. Benjamin's claim appears oxymoronic, however, only in light of the implicit normative preference that undergirds this axiom, namely, that any form of memory and any ritual of remembrance ought to be preferable to not being remembered at all. Tradition and memory in general thus occupy the position of historical life, being, and existence, and their absence amounts to the death, nothingness, and inexistence of history itself. Benjamin's concept of a catastrophic tradition contravenes this sedimented axiological axiom by insisting that there are forms of traditionalization or remembrance that may be, in fact, just as damaging to, if not even *worse* for, the historical *afterlife* of the object of memory or the life remembered than its fall into oblivion or disrepute. But what is truly crucial for my purposes is the fact that Benjamin here explicitly singles out the historical schemas of inheritance that transform the past into the heritage of a people, a cultural good or, better, a "national treasure" as the privileged instance of that form of tradition that he calls catastrophe and that is just as damaging to the life of the past as its forgetting. It is from this tradition that, according to Benjamin, history must try to *rescue* or *save the phenomena*.

This first aspect of Benjamin's notion of a catastrophic tradition already goes a long way toward answering the first of the two questions that I posed earlier. When I argued that de Burgos remains *historically unread*, I was implicitly making the case that Benjamin's conception of a catastrophic tradition describes to a tee the condition of *historical illegibility* to which de Burgos's corpus has fallen. In this respect, I take de Burgos's excessive presence within Puerto Rico's practical past as both cause and symptom of her catastrophic traditionality.

The second oxymoronic aspect of Benjamin's historical insight comes to the fore as soon as we begin to pay attention to the theme of historical *Rettung*, or "rescue." This idea is paradoxical on two accounts: first, because, to the extent that *rescue* is the countermovement of catastrophe, it cannot be simply equated with preventing the past from falling into oblivion, with snatching an image of the past from the jaws of forgetting. Second, and most importantly, because, contrary to what the rhetoric of salvation or redemption may suggest, Benjamin's conception of rescue is structured by the paradoxical claim that to *save* the past, that is to say, *to do history in a way that would not be simply historicist* (or catastrophic), *requires endangering historical phenomena*. Benjamin himself hints at this point when, in the passage quoted earlier, he adds that the historian rescues historical phenomena "by indicating their leap [*Sprunges*]." To grasp the significance of this statement, we must recall the key role that the motif of the *Sprung*, or *leap*, plays in Benjamin's thinking of the dialectical image and the constellation, from its first articulation in *Das Passagen-Werk*—where Benjamin describes the relation between *das Jetzt*, "the now," and *das Gewesene*, "what has been," as *sprunghaft*, or "leap-like"[74]—to the famous motif of the "tiger's leap" in his theses on history.[75] Benjamin's identification of *rescue* with making historical phenomena *leap* clarifies the ultimate grounds upon which Benjamin's critique of catastrophic traditions rests. What is catastrophic about this mode of historical remembrance is the way it institutes a temporal schema of *succession* and a mechanical schema of *causality* to ground the very possibility of a relation or connection between different moments in historical time. Understanding historical time as a successive continuum, catastrophic traditions *dehistoricize* historical time by precisely blocking the possibility of a historical experience whose clarification requires that historians see their own present as dialectically entangled with and generated out of their readerly engagement with the past.

In this respect, the schema of continuity that determines the form of catastrophic traditionalization is catastrophic not only because it reduces the historical significance of the past to the reiteration of how it has already been traditionally read—even more harmful for Benjamin is the fact that this type of traditionalization seeks to eliminate the *danger* in which alone historicity becomes something that is at stake. Catastrophic traditions thus stand in diametric opposition to a view of history that argues that the past is never more historical than when its "facts become something that just now befall upon us."[76] In other words, catastrophic traditions are *historicist*, as this book understands this term, not only because they reduce the historical meaning of the past to its "'enshrinement as heritage'"—what I call, in the context of de Burgos, the *reactivation of the totem*—but also because they deprive the present and the past of their own historicity by positing the link between the present and the past as always already guaranteed, as always already settled. In this way, catastrophic traditions configure history in a historicist key by *distributing the form of ipseity* across the entire chain of the historical continuum, from the institution of the tradition to its reactivation. Conversely, to *rescue* the past by making it leap entails endangering it, that is, undoing and dismantling the historicist continuum that posits the schema of *transcendental appropriation* as the ultimate ground that secures the ontological availability of the past *for* the historian's present.

Besides Benjamin's concept of catastrophic tradition, my efforts at a reception history of de Burgos's symbolic image also draw inspiration from the type of "historical explanation" that Husserl outlines in the *Krisis* (*Crisis*) when he describes the gesture or the "method" of the *Rückfrage*, which he glosses as a "questioning back into the originary institution of the goals which bind together the chain of future generations, insofar as these goals live on in sedimented forms yet can be reawakened again and again and, in their new vitality, be criticized."[77] Turning to Husserl here is helpful for at least two reasons. In the first place, I find that Husserl's concepts of tradition and sedimentation can be productively mobilized to lend some structural specificity to Benjamin's talk about tradition—a motif that, despite his ubiquitous use, remains somewhat undertheorized by Benjamin. More specifically, it is Husserl's way of rendering sedimentation and tradition nearly synonymous that has been key for my own attempt to elaborate de Burgos's catastrophic tradition. For instance, in texts such as "The Origin of Geometry," Husserl writes that "the geometry which is ready-made, so to speak, from which the questioning back begins, is a tradition. Our human existence moves within innumerable traditions. The whole cultural world, in all its forms, exists through tradition," and later he adds that "cultural structures . . . appear on the scene in the form of tradition; they claim, so to speak, to be *sedimentations* of a truth-meaning that can be made originally self-evident."[78] The proximity between sedimentation and tradition is such that Husserl even uses these terms interchangeably at least once in the *Krisis*: "sedimentation or traditionalization."[79]

The passage from "The Origin of Geometry" that I just quoted sheds light both on why these terms are essentially isomorphic and why their functional coterminousness is useful for my critical reception history. Sedimentation names both the *process* and the *modality* in which the intentions and goals that animated the institution of any sense-configuration are retained in the living tissue of historical experience *after* the temporal phase of their foundational activity has lapsed. This explains why the very constitution of a tradition, which Husserl represents metaphorically by using the figure of a "chain" that binds "future generations," cannot occur without sedimentation. There is no tradition without sedimentation because sedimentation names, among other things, the specific modification through which the active institution of sense gives way to the *passive* experience of already instituted sense-formations; passivity, in turn, indicates the particular manner in which the "truth-meanings" or "goals" that instituted a sense-formation settle down into habits, receding so deep into the self's experiential background that it is no longer necessary to have an active, constitutive, originary, and adequate intuition of those "truth-meanings" in order to inhabit the sense-formations that were instituted in the wake of their consolidation. Inhabiting any sense-formation becomes a matter of tradition through the sedimentation of its foundational acts, which are thereby dissimulated through their very transmission.

Husserl's example of how geometry is taught and transmitted illustrates this point. To learn geometry obviously entails that one comes *after* its originary institution by the putative protogeometer, which means that to learn geometry is to learn a scientific tradition. But this means, in turn, that it is always possible for the student of geometry to think that doing geometry means memorizing an empty set of geometrical axioms, signs, and procedures and learning how to reproduce and manipulate them to reach the right conclusion to the problem set given by their teacher. To "learn" geometry, in other words, does not necessarily require *reactivating* the originary intuitions that were given to those who first instituted geometry's axioms, which means that the "truth-meanings" on which the validity of the axioms of the new science of geometry depended are now divorced from the evidentiary ground of intuition in which alone something like a geometrical *being* could have presented itself to the protogeometer. The result, for Husserl, is that the overly sedimented appropriation of geometry blocks the very possibility of relating to geometry as a *living* tradition. This possibility of historical automatism—which Husserl designates with the term *crisis* and which Derrida calls "somnambulism"—is precisely what ought to animate the phenomenologist in their attempt to undertake a critical *Selbstbesinnung*, or self-reflection, through the *Rückfrage*, or "questioning back," of that sedimented tradition, with the goal of reactivating the originary sense, truth, and goals that lent onto-epistemic validity to the intentional acts that constituted the sense-formations of that very tradition in their normative institutionality.

In the second place, Husserl's method of the *Rückfrage* is particularly apt for the task of providing a reception history of de Burgos because Husserl's concept of tradition in general turns out to be isomorphic to Benjamin's concept of *catastrophic* tradition. Husserl's reliance on the metaphor of the chain to speak of tradition suggests that his understanding of the temporality of tradition remains wedded to the schema of continuity that Benjamin associates with historicism and the temporality of catastrophe. And his unshakeable faith in the *necessary possibility* of reawakening the meanings that have been sedimented means that the *danger* that reactivation might be *impossible* is either excluded a priori from the space of historicity or is simply understood as its death or negation. Husserl may indeed acknowledge that the possibility of a crisis brought about by the necessity of sedimentation is part of the very movement of history, but he never ceases to regard sedimentation as harboring a dangerous possibility that threatens the very *life* of a tradition, rather than a possibility that has a claim on the chance that a tradition may survive, even as it corrodes from within the very possibility of a total reactivation and restoration of the meaning of any tradition.

In this respect, the "historical explanation" that follows is highly ironic. For my goal is not to reawaken the truth of the historicity of de Burgos by reactivating the goals that determined her traditional reception, so as to ensure that my own relation to Puerto Rican historicity is not simply of the order of a passive habituality. Instead, the aim of this desedimentation is to clarify the genesis of de Burgos's totem, in order to prepare for a reading that might enable de Burgos's image to leap out of this catastrophic tradition.

Martyr/Poète Maudite: Constructing the Legends of de Burgos

To begin desedimenting de Burgos's catastrophic tradition, we must reconstruct the narratives that determined her legendary fame and shaped the images of her life that have circulated throughout Puerto Rico's lettered city ever since the publication of her first poems in 1934. To do so, I will again take Benjamin's engagement with Baudelaire as my model, this time centering on the following entry from "Zentral Park" ("Central Park") where Benjamin identifies the two main legends of Baudelaire that secured his fame: "There are two legends of Baudelaire. One he himself spread, and he appears in it as a monster and terrorizer of the bourgeoisie. The other emerged with his death and has established his fame. In it he appears as a martyr. This false theological halo must be destroyed across the board."[80] To be sure, de Burgos's status as a "national poet" added dimensions to her fame that make it significantly more complicated than how Benjamin understands Baudelaire's. At the same time, I would argue that the logic behind de Burgos's multiple legends can also be reconstructed with the help of this seemingly Manichean schema. In other words, I will try to show that the establishment and expansion of de Burgos's fame relies on a sedimented conflict between two apparently incompatible images of her life, which correspond to the polarities of "terrorizer of the bourgeoisie" and "martyr" or "saint" of any number of political causes. That being said, these polarities should be seen as *functional*, not *substantial*, concepts for at least two reasons: first, because they are grammars or schemas that organize historical content in view of (re)producing the legends of de Burgos as either a martyr or a *poète maudite*. Second, and most importantly, because their formality is such that at any moment either of these legendary schemas allow de Burgos's inheritors to construct a narrative that appropriates historical content that at other moments in de Burgos's reception was ascribed to the opposite term of this polarity.[81]

The following biographical sketch of de Burgos constitutes an attempt to reconstruct the legends that have consolidated de Burgos's fame, taking the polarity just articulated as my touchstone. As already anticipated in the previous section (§10), such a reconstructive effort is a prerequisite for any attempt to construct the *image* of de Burgos (in a Benjaminian sense of the term) and thus to make de Burgos's life and, above all, her poetry, available for a protocol of literary-historical reading that would no longer be entirely dominated by the totemic, monumental grammar of historicization and commemoration that has determined her afterlife up to this point. Hence, my main goal in supplying this short biography is not simply to introduce de Burgos to a readership that may not be familiar with the main events that shaped her life. For this very reason, my main concern here is not to establish the factual "truth" of her life "as it really happened." On the contrary, since my task is to identify the key biographical elements that lent themselves to the construction of de Burgos's ambivalent fame during her lifetime—and which, after her premature death, were reactivated as part of the ongoing effort to institute her name and image as one of the totemic figures par excellence of Puertoricanness—I will give equal weight to aspects of her life for which her main biographers and other scholars have found solid, empirical evidence and to those elements that have contributed to the constitution of her fame while remaining of the order of rumor and gossip. Another caveat: since Part III of this book is primarily concerned with de Burgos's first published poetry volume, *Poema en 20 surcos*, published a year before the poet left the island in 1939, the biographical sketch in question will mostly center on those aspects of de Burgos's fame that were already instituted before her departure from Puerto Rico.

After this initial biographical narrative, we will be in a better position to track the sedimentation of what Benjamin calls "the false theological halo" that surrounds de Burgos to this day and to prepare the grounds for its desedimentation and destruction. Only then would it be possible to make de Burgos leap from the catastrophic continuity of her traditionalization and, by extension, make us leap from that tradition, thereby gaining the chance to read in de Burgos's image something other than what her theological-monumental totemism has already sanctioned.

Unlike Benjamin's Baudelaire, in the case of de Burgos the first events and meanings that contributed to her enduring fame crystallized in a politico-theological context marked by the values of martyrdom and sainthood. The legend that was retrospectively elaborated on the basis of these sedimented historical elements could be summarized with one of the monikers the poet has been retrospectively given, namely, "la novia del nacionalismo" ("nationalism's bride").[82] Regardless of the veracity of this nickname, the fact remains that de Burgos's beginnings as a poet are intimately bound to the tumultuous history of the Puerto Rican Nationalist Party. For this reason, a foray into this party's development circa the 1930s will help us situate a whole array of elements that have largely contributed to her totemization.

Under the undisputed leadership of Pedro Albizu Campos, elected president of the party in 1930, Puerto Rico's Nationalist movement underwent a striking political transformation. In keeping with Albizu Campos's motto *Acción inmedi-*

ata, the party quickly abandoned the largely ornamental defenses of Puerto Rican independence that characterized its previous leadership—mostly composed of upper-class *letrados* gathered around the Ateneo Puertorriqueño (Puerto Rican Atheneum)—and undertook an enormous effort of political reorganization characterized in equal measure by a massive effort of political persuasion and direct acts of resistance to US colonial rule on the island. This shift in the party's orientation was signaled, among other ways, by the formation of several paramilitary organizations within the movement, segregated by gender: the Cadetes de la República (the Republic's Cadets) for men and Las Hijas de la Libertad (the Daughters of Liberty) for women.[83] Although the party's surprisingly abysmal results in the 1932 elections certainly constituted a major setback for the *nacionalista* cause, Albizu Campos continued to enjoy enormous prestige and sympathy across the island. Perhaps the clearest (certainly the most mythologized) proof of his leadership came during the 1934 strike of the sugarcane industry, when the workers dismissed their labor union leaders and asked Albizu Campos to direct their strike. The worker's rejection of the Federación Libre de Trabajadores (Free Worker's Federation, affiliated, since its foundation in 1899, to the American Federation of Labor of Samuel Gompers) was also read as a rejection of the Puerto Rican Socialist Party, which supported Puerto Rico's incorporation as a US state and, since 1924, had entered into a political alliance with the Pure Republican Party of Puerto Rico, thereby producing a situation in which the party of labor was in a coalition with the party that counted among its leadership the majority of Puerto Rican capitalists and sugarcane barons.[84] The appointment of military figures such as Major General Blanton Winship and Colonel Elisha Francis Riggs as colonial governor and head of the Insular Police in 1934 marked a shift in colonial policy that led to the intensification of the police state and the increased persecution of the Nationalist leadership. After the Massacre of Río Piedras (October 24, 1935), where two *nacionalista* students died at the hands of the Insular Police, the Nationalist Party decided to abandon the electoral route and intensify its direct efforts to resist US colonial rule, opposing, in particular, the implementation of the New Deal on the island at the hands of both Puerto Rican and US liberal reformers. This turbulent period in Puerto Rican history, bookended by the massacres of Río Piedras and Ponce (March 23, 1937), was punctuated by the execution of Colonel Riggs at the hands of two young Cadets of the Republic, Elías Beauchamp and Hiram Rosado (February 23, 1936), who were then executed without trial by the police, and the subsequent imprisonment of the Nationalist Party leadership after being found guilty of charges of seditious conspiracy by a jury composed mostly of US-born settlers (July 31, 1936) after a previous case resulted in a hung jury.

De Burgos's biographers differ on when exactly the poet joined the Nationalist Party, but most are in agreement that she was already a militant in the movement before her marriage to Rubén Rodríguez Beauchamp on June 8, 1934, a popular radio host who was also a militant of the party.[85] Doel López Velázquez, for instance, claims that de Burgos even served as personal secretary to Pedro Albizu Campos as early as 1931, though no other scholar that I have consulted has corroborated that claim. José Manuel Dávila Marichal's recent history of the party's paramilitary cadres has nonetheless shown that de Burgos served as president of the Río Piedras chapter of the Damas Nacionalistas (Nationalist Ladies) and as the vice-president of the Consejo Nacional de las Hijas de la Libertad (National Council of the Daughters of Liberty), which would become the Nurse Corps of the party by the end of 1935.[86] His findings confirm the view of José Manuel Torres Santiago, whose biography of de Burgos places particular emphasis on her role in the Nationalist movement's female organizations from her time as a student.[87]

Other scholars have also hypothesized that other prominent figures in Puerto Rico's independence movement must have played a role in consolidating de Burgos's adherence to the cause of Puerto Rican independence. Key among these is Clemente Pereda, a rising academic star and a young member of the Generación del 30 intellectuals who joined the Normal School of the University of Puerto Rico right around the time of de Burgos's admission to the university (1931–1933). Before returning to Puerto Rico, Pereda had received a master's degree from Columbia University and had served as interim dean of Middlebury College's Spanish School (a key institution in the development of Hispanic Studies in the United States), where he was responsible, among other things, for hiring the Chilean Nobel Laureate Gabriela Mistral as a visiting professor.[88] According to Yvette Jiménez de Báez, who wrote the first book-length study on the poet, de Burgos must have come into contact with Pereda at the university, even if this claim remains circumstantial.[89] An ardent Catholic nationalist, Pereda is mostly remembered today for the hunger strike he staged during the Holy Week of 1934 to protest a resolution presented by the pro-statehood majority in the Puerto Rican House of Representatives demanding that the US Congress admit the island as a state.[90] According to de Burgos's most thorough biographer, Juan Antonio Rodríguez Pagán, this event had an enormous significance in her early development both as a poet and activist within the Nationalist movement, not least because it was at Pereda's hunger strike that de Burgos met Juan Antonio Corretjer, at that time secretary general of the Puerto Rican Nationalist Party; editor of its main publishing organ, *La Acción*; and one of the few writers besides de Burgos who, to this day, has been granted the title of "national poet." A certain complicity between Corretjer and de Burgos quickly took shape after their initial encounter, so much so that not long after Pereda's protests de Burgos asked Corretjer to be the best man at her wedding, which took place on June 8, 1934.

A couple of months after Pereda's protest and her encounter with Corretjer, de Burgos published her first poem—a sonnet titled "Gloria a ti" ("Glory to You")—in the October edition of *Alma Latina*, a popular journal whose poetry section was edited by Graciany Miranda Archilla, a prominent member of the Puerto Rican avant-garde poetic movement known as Atalayismo. De Burgos's first poem is dedicated to Manuel Rafael Suárez Díaz, a young student who died on April 16, 1932, when a Nationalist crowd stormed the Puerto Rican capitol to prevent the legislature from declaring the Puerto Rican flag the official symbol of the island's colonial government. Although it was the result of an accident, his death earned him the title of the party's first martyr—and it is as such that de Burgos addresses him in her first appearance in public as a poet:

Gloria a ti	Glory to You
A Manuel Rafael Suárez Díaz	*to Manuel Rafael Suárez Díaz*
Impávido y altivo ofrendaste tu vida,	Undaunted and upright you offered your life,
henchida con la savia de tus sueños en flor,	swelled by the sap of your dreams in bloom,
a la causa doliente de la patria oprimida	to the sorrowful cause of your oppressed country
que sufre los rigores de extranjera invasión.	that suffers the rigors of a foreign invasion
Gloriosamente bravo caíste en la brecha	Gloriously brave you fell into the breach
como símbolo egregio de la renunciación;	as illustrious symbol of renunciation;
ofrenda inmaculada es la primera mecha	immaculate offering you are the initial fuse
que encenderá la hoguera de la revolución.	that will ignite the bonfire of the revolution.
Por eso al recordarte, hermano, yo presiento	That's why, remembering you, brother, I sense
que no estará lejano el augusto momento	that the august moment shall not be faraway
que consagre en la historia nuestra inmortalidad.	that may consecrate in history our immortality.
Y pídote en la hora febril de la victoria	And I ask at the febrile hour of victory
que toques las trompetas sonoras de la gloria,	that you play the sonorous trumpets of glory,
clamando a voces llenas: 'Libertad,' 'Libertad.'[91]	clamoring full-throated: "Liberty," "Liberty."[92]

Before addressing the aspects of this poem that clarify the martyrological dimension of de Burgos's image, I want to remark on some of its formal aspects, beginning with de Burgos's eclectic approach to the sonnet form, which produces a poem whose "classicizing" allure is tempered by its deliberate formal irregularities. Although its stanza structure retains the classic shape of the Petrarchan sonnet, its rhythmic pattern evokes aspects of both the French *sonnet marotique*—where the first two verses of each tercet and the last verse of both tercets rhyme (in this case: eef, ggh)—and of the sonnets popularized by the French poets of *Le Parnasse contemporain*, such as the introduction of an extra rhyme scheme in the first two quartets (in this case: abac, dcdc). These French influences in the poem's prosody and, above all, de Burgos's use of the Spanish "Alejandrino," firmly situate the poem within a Latin American *posmodernista* literary landscape, decisively marked by Rubén Darío's transformation of Spanish prosody in the preceding *fin-de-siècle* through his inventive adaptation of the prosodic innovations achieved by the French symbolists.

But the poem's most striking formal feature is the result of de Burgos's decision to break the sonnet's rhyme scheme by purposely ending the second line with the word *flor*. This deviation marks the place in the poem where its form is shown to be indissociable from the poem's content, an indissociability that the poem performs as its very mise en scène. I would even describe the effect produced by the appearance of the word *flor* in this poem as akin to Roland Barthes's famous photographic *punctum*, "that chance [*hasard*] which, in a photo, *stings* me (but also bruises me, jabs me)."[93] Indeed, this word emerges as that "detail" which, once remarked in its *punctum*-like quality, dominates the poem's interpretation. To be sure, when read semantically, and in the context of both the line in which it appears and of the person who is being described, the speaker's recourse to the image of a blooming flower is not only understandable but almost clichéd: After all, the line that describes the sacrificed life of the poem's addressee as "henchida con la savia de tus sueños en flor" ("swelled by the sap of your dreams in bloom") is a self-evident reference to the fact that Manuel Rafael Suárez Díaz was still a high school student when he died. The organicist trope of "savia" ("sap") conveys the exuberant and overflowing vitality of a late adolescent already consecrated to the cause of Puerto Rican independence—and who, like a flower on the verge of blooming, was plucked too early from its vital soil. And yet, if we abstract from its metaphorical-semantic-referential function and regard this line from the point of view of the poem's prosody, the term *flor* acquires a different status; namely, it emerges as the sole word that does not participate in the system of associations that are established by the sonnet's rhyme scheme. It is this exclusion from the rhyme scheme that renders *flor* available as an allegorical mark that inscribes and stands in for the poem itself. The speaker's homage to the fallen Nationalist martyr is itself a *flor*, the poem itself is a *flower* placed at his tomb on the day of the anniversary of his sacrificial death.

In so doing, however, the poem could be read as merely remarking on the symbolic structure that already determines martyrdom as a theological limit experience. For those who are adept to the hermeneutics of martyrdom—and de Burgos was no strange to its rigors—the martyr's death, like the flowers of dreams prematurely plucked by an accidental death, means the opposite of death: It bespeaks life immortal. A material trace of this eminently politico-theological process of symbolization can be found if we return, once more, to the word *flor*. For it is not technically true that this word, as I suggested, is entirely removed from the poem's rhymical system. Although, indeed, *flor* is not compossible at the level of *consonance* with the other thirteen words that end the poem's lines, the word nonetheless rhymes in *assonance* with what is arguably the most crucial word in the poem, namely, G*lor*ia, which recurs at least three times in the poem: (1) in its title, (2) in the term *Gloriosamente* that opens the second strophe, and (3) in the second line of the last tercet. We might say that de Burgos launched her poetic career as *a* poet of Puerto Rico's Nationalist Movement by writing her *Flores de gloria* (*Flowers of Glory*).

It should therefore not surprise us that the first legend of de Burgos as a poet consolidated around the values of martyrdom and sainthood. Not only is it the case that her poetic persona took shape in a context deeply marked by the increasing Catholicism of Nationalist ideology, but de Burgos herself began her public career as a poet with a sonnet commemorating the first Nationalist martyr, inaugurating the theologico-political poetics that would characterize most of her published work until the end of 1937.

An account of de Burgos's early beginnings as a poet would not be complete without reckoning with a minoritarian strand in her early poetry constituted by the only two nonpolitical poems that de Burgos published between 1934 and 1937. Written in the Neo-Romanticist style common to Latin American *posmodernistas*—whose major exponents at that time were all women: Gabriela Mistral, Alfonsina Storni, and Juana de Ibarbourou—De Burgos's second published poem, "Yo quiero darme a ti" ("I Want to Give Myself to You"), which appeared in the February 1935 issue of *Alma Latina*, inaugurates this essential aspect of her poetic production:

Yo quiero darme a ti	**I Want to Give Myself to You**
Yo quiero darme a ti	I want to give myself to you
toda entera . . .	All whole . . .
Y vaciar con pasión mis suspiros en tu alma	And empty with passion my sighs in your soul
Sedienta de pena	Thirsty of pain
Y verter en tus ojos serenos las lágrimas negras	And pour in your serene eyes the black tears
Que el dolor del vivir	That the pain of living
Ha traído a mis puertas.	has brought to my doors.
Entonces . . .	Then . . .
Tú sabrás el misterio	You will know the mystery
que mis tristes pupilas encierran;	That my sad pupils contain;
y sabrás que la vida no es sueño	and will know that life is no dream
Con el cual has bañado en el mundo tu corta existencia.	with which you have covered in the world your brief existence.
Entonces . . .	Then . . .
Llenarás el vacío	You will fill the emptiness
Que anida tu alma	that nests your soul
Con el dulce vibrar de mi pena	with the sweet vibrating of my pain
Henchida de calma;	Swollen of stillness;
Y sabrás una vez en la vida	And you will know once in life
Que el dolor es sublime santuario del alma.	That pain is sublime sanctuary of the soul.
Yo quisiera vaciar en tu alma	I would like to empty in your soul
La flor de mi pena	The flower of my pain
Y entregarme a ti	And surrender myself to you
Toda entera . . .[94]	All whole . . .

If, as I suggested earlier, de Burgos launched her poetic career under the heading of *flowers of glory*, her second publication retains the tutelar image of the flower but modifies its prevailing quality, so that the flower is now quite literally marked by *pain*. And yet we might say that this change is epiphenomenal. This is not the case because the flower here would have the status of a substance or substrate that remains the same despite a change in attribute but rather because the movement from glory to pain barely entails an alteration. For, within a worldview in which life is literally conceived as a vale of tears, pain and glory maintain an intimate affinity. And, as a matter of fact, the poem appears to be conceived within such a worldview; its voicing unfolds within a theologico-metaphysical atmosphere in which love is marked by sacrifice, life is pain, and earthly existence is conceived as irremediably fallen, hence as only redeemable through the mortifications of the flesh. Indeed, the most audacious lines of this otherwise unremarkable poem transform the very erotic relation with the lover into a medium for such mortification, which would alone awaken the lover from the mundane dreams in which he has clothed his existence. By sharing in her lover's pain, the lover may experience the true sacrificial glory of human life, thereby knowing for the first time the true sublime glory of the soul in pain.

Despite the stark differences in theme, prosody, and voice, de Burgos's first two publications unfold within a parareligious or crypto-Christian, more precisely crypto-Catholic, metaphysics deeply marked by an insistence on pain, suffering, passion, and sacrifice as irreducible dimensions of human life.

This quick foray into de Burgos's first poems yields a picture of her poetic beginnings that, in many ways, ratifies Corretjer's lapidary claim that "never has there been a poorer beginning to such a great poetic career."[95] Corretjer's testimony is based on firsthand familiarity with de Burgos's earliest poetic compositions, which he read as early as April 1934. In a short column published almost thirty years after his first encounter with de Burgos's poetry, Corretjer writes that during one of their first meetings, not long after Pereda's hunger strike, de Burgos showed him several of her poems, hoping to get some feedback. Already an accomplished poet, Corretjer judged the poems to be of very poor quality, but he didn't share his opinion with de Burgos and simply encouraged her to continue writing. It was during that same conversation that de Burgos asked him to be the best man at her wedding. Corretjer doesn't go into further detail about the type of poems that de Burgos gave him to read on that day, but Rodríguez Pagán relies on his negative response to make a twofold hypothesis about the possible nature of those poems: First, he claims that it is quite likely that poems such as "Yo quiero darme a ti" were included in the folder she gave to Corretjer and, second, that these poems could have been included in *Poemas exactos a mí misma*, a poetry volume that de Burgos typewrote and circulated among her friends as late as 1937 but that has since vanished, after the poet herself presumably destroyed it because she was unsatisfied with the quality of the poems contained in it.[96]

The disappearance of her first poetry volume and the mantle of mystery that still shrouds its content provide perhaps the most eloquent proof of the pertinence of Corretjer's assessment of de Burgos's poetic beginnings. Indeed, I would go so far as to argue that most *significant* document of de Burgos's early career is not any of her poems but the speech "La mujer ante el dolor de la patria" ("Women Facing the Fatherland's Pain"), which she delivered on October 24, 1936, in the first General Assembly of the Frente Unido Femenino

Pro Convención Constituyente de la República de Puerto Rico (United Women's Front for the Constitutional Convention of the Republic of Puerto Rico). This women's organization emerged in response to the imprisonment of the leadership of the Nationalist Party in the immediate aftermath of the assassination of Colonel Elisha F. Riggs, head of the colonial Insular Police. The Frente Unido was part of a broader effort organized by prominent leaders of Puerto Rico's independence movement who were not necessarily members of the Nationalist Party to advocate for the release of Albizu Campos, Corretjer, and other political prisoners. De Burgos's speech constitutes arguably the clearest manifestation of her commitment to the martyr logic of political struggle, saturated within an onto-theological, Catholic metaphysics, which was in alignment with the ideological makeup of an increasingly conservative Nationalist Party under Albizu Campos's leadership.[97] And yet this speech also challenges the patriarchal strictures of Albizuist ideology. The following anecdote, relayed by Rodríguez Pagán, suffices to illustrate this:

> Several days before the celebration of the Frente Unido's General Assembly, Albizu Campos himself wrote a letter to de Burgos and the rest of Frente Unido's leadership urging them to cancel a public parade planned in support of their release; his reasons for making this request were telling: "Only when the enemy has managed to run over all the cadavers of men would it be permissible to offer the life of women, who are the source of nationhood. We have received information that enemies of independence harbor plans to produce a riot with unspeakable aims on the day of the parade."[98]

This letter of Albizu is crucial if we are to measure the weight, indeed the gravitas, of the following moment from de Burgos's speech:

> Y vuelvo a repetir, como he dicho en varias ocasiones, movida tal vez por un presentimiento terrible, que glorioso y bendito el día en que caiga una mujer puertorriqueña defendiendo el Santo Ideal de nuestra libertad, porque ese día habrá Revolución en cada alma, y en cada hogar puertorriqueño, y la tiranía se estremecerá ante el resurgimiento pleno de nuestra conciencia nacional.[99]

> And I repeat again, as I have said on multiple occasions, perhaps moved by a terrible presentiment, that glorious and blessed [will be] the day in which a Puerto Rican woman falls defending the Holy Ideal of our freedom, because on that day there will be a Revolution in each soul, and in each Puerto Rican home, and tyranny will tremble before the complete resurgence of our national consciousness.

In many respects, this moment of her speech constitutes a summary of both her poetics of Nationalist glory and her metaphysics of erotic pain and mortification. Indeed, note the repetition of many of the elements that appear in "Gloria a ti," such as the insistence on the foreseeable glorious advent of independence and, above all, the belief that "the blood of the martyrs is the seed of the nation," to paraphrase the classic martyrological dictum attributed to Tertullian.[100] But perhaps what is most crucial about this passage for our purposes is the way it makes explicit what remained implicit about the concept of life that underpins "Yo quiero darme a ti." To see this, note how this passage directly challenges a crucial aspect of Albizu's patriarchal view of the political role of women within the independence movement, which he reduced to their role as mothers who literally birth the nation.[101] Indeed, in prophesying that a feminine sacrifice would be needed for the liberation of the nation, de Burgos is contesting Albizu's restriction of the role of *independentista* women as mothers of the nation to the biocultural reproduction of the nation's children. Instead, their willingness to give the ultimate sacrifice for the constitution of the Republic would allow Puerto Rican women to attain an even more dignified and spiritual form of maternity, namely, becoming the mothers who birth the *soul* of the nation and not just its biocultural *bodies*. And yet through this very move, de Burgos is not only indexing an aspect of an historico-ontological process that Rocío Zambrana has aptly described in terms of the "actualization" of the modern gender system—and its compulsory heterosexual matrix—as a key technology of modernity and coloniality.[102] She is also reinstituting a metaphysical conception of life in which the earthly, mundane, or worldly life of the *flesh* is not only *sacrificable* but *must* be sacrificed (whether literally or symbolically) in order to accede to a truer, more authentic form of life—a life that is all spirit or *soul*. Indeed, only such a sacrifice could awaken Puerto Ricans from their assimilationist dreams of mundane progress to, like the lover addressed in "Yo quiero darme a ti," finally discover that life is pain and that, in the words of Albizu Campos addressed to Corretjer, *la patria es valor y sacrificio* ("the fatherland is valor and sacrifice").[103] If we keep in mind what Derrida says about "the essence of the religious" in the first year of his seminar on the death penalty—namely, that "all religions are capable of preferring something to life, at the price of life," since "what is religious about religion is always the acceptance of sacrificial death and the death penalty in the shadow of a sur-viving that would be worth more than life"—then we might say that the first sedimented layer of what would become de Burgos's totemic fame remains essentially religious.[104]

Up to this point, I have been exclusively concerned with tracking some of the events and contexts that led to the constitution of de Burgos as a saint- or martyr-like figure. As is clear, this legendary script was initially sedimented through her impassioned support of the cause of Puerto Rican independence and her militancy in the island's nationalist movement—though as I have shown, the reach of her commitment to martyrdom was deeply rooted in a metaphysical conception of the essence of life as sacrifice. But de Burgos also cultivated a different legendary image of her poetic persona, in which the speaker of her poems appears, not unlike Benjamin's Baudelaire, as a "terrorizer of the bourgeoisie."[105] It is this legend that has played the decisive role in establishing her fame, especially since the 1970s. This doesn't mean that Burgos's legend as martyr has dropped entirely from her sedimented totemic image. But, as we will see, her contemporary inheritors are more prone to rely on the sedimented legends of de Burgos as a free-love feminist icon; as an antifascist, socialist activist; or as a poor *mestiza* who heroically struggled against racism and poverty in order to erect their Burgosian totems.[106] It is to these other images of de Burgos, summarized under the heading of the "antibourgeois," that I now turn.

De Burgos's explicit poetic self-fashioning as an antibourgeois icon is perhaps best exemplified by another anecdote told by Rodríguez Pagán in his biography. In 1940, during her brief stay in New York before embarking to La Habana to join her lover, the anti-Trujillo Dominican activist Juan Isidro Jimenes Grullón, the Association of Puerto Rican Journalists and Writers organized an event in honor of both de Burgos and Antonio Coll y Vidal, an older Puerto Rican writer and journalist. Coll y Vidal had written a rather mediocre poem on de Burgos expressly for the occasion in which the speaker at one point says: "In Julia de Burgos I love the bourgeois Julia/the one who uses lipstick and curls her hair."[107] As Rodríguez Pagán tells the story, de Burgos read the poem while they were together on stage, went backstage for a moment, and improvised a brilliant poem, aptly titled "Replica" ("Response"), that begins declaring: "Sigue siendo poema Julia de Burgos/la que no tiene nada de ser burguesa" ("Julia de Burgos keeps being poem;/who has nothing of being bourgeois") and closes with the following remarkable strophes:

Será siempre poema Julia de Burgos;	Shall always be poem Julia de Burgos;
la que no tiene nada de ser burguesa;	who has nothing of being bourgeois;
la que rompe los siglos en sus vestidos,	who breaks centuries in her dresses
¡y se suelta la vida por las estrellas!	and unleashes her life through the stars!
. . .	. . .
Envío.	Sending.
Si en tu verso tendido fui creadora	If, in your extended verse, I was creator
de un enorme espejismo de flor burguesa,	of an enormous mirage of bourgeois flower,
con mi impulso salvaje de golondrina	with my savage impulse of swallow
desataré tu erguida voz de poeta.[108]	I will loosen up your erect poetic voice.

CATASTROPHIC TRADITIONS 75

These stanzas are perhaps less eloquent for what they contain than for what is missing from them, namely, the motifs of pain and suffering that constituted the religious metaphysics within which de Burgos determined the essence of both erotic and political life as sacrifice. This absence is all the more significant in light of the fact that the poem indeed mobilizes the word *life*. The contrast between these two poems could not be more striking. The movement of life has now been removed from the cycle of pain, mortification, and glory that found expression in de Burgos's earliest poems and political speeches, and a new understanding of life has taken hold. As we will see, *life* now emerges in de Burgos's poetics as the cipher of a humanity that has finally undone centuries of sedimented traditions and bourgeois conventions and has been restored to its originary creative powers, to the purity of its embodied autoaffection, to its a-historical wildness.

How did de Burgos become this emblem of an anti-, post-, or simply non-bourgeois humanity? To desediment this layer of de Burgos's legend as a "bourgeois terrorizer," we must retrace some key events in de Burgos's life before 1937 as well as reconstruct other institutional formations and sense-configurations within Puerto Rico's lettered city beyond the Nationalist Party and its sphere of influence. Crucial among these key events is the publication of de Burgos's second romantic or erotic poem, "A plena desnudez" ("In Complete Nakedness"), which appeared in *El Imparcial*—a major opposition daily—in March 27, 1936, barely a month after the assassination of Elías Beauchamp and Hiram Rosado after they executed Col. Elisha Francis Riggs:

A plena desnudez	In Complete Nakedness
Un día,	One day,
me iré a danzar contigo	I will go dance with you
a un sitio bien lejano	to a faraway place
donde la ley no existe, ni mande la razón;	where law does not exist nor reason rule;
donde el agua sea brisa, donde el ave sea flor;	where water is breeze, where the bird is flower;
donde todo lo puro y natural se confunda	where everything pure and natural blends itself
con la Gracia de Dios.	with the Grace of God.
En un paraje	In an expanse
limpio de convencionalismos;	cleansed of all conventionalisms;
estéril	sterile
al abrazo mundano que amenaza su dicha;	to the mundane embrace that threatens its joy;
fecundo a todo lo espontáneo:	fecund to everything spontaneous:
a la lluvia,	rain
al amor.	love.

Allí,	There,
a plena desnudez,	in complete nakedness,
despojados del ropaje de fino formalismo	stripped of the robes of refined formalism
con que cubren, pomposos, los humanos esbirros,	with which human minions pompously cover
cicatrices de orgías de la noche anterior,	scars of orgies from the previous night,
bailaremos la danza de la vida	we will dance the dance of life
al ritmo de un incendio de luz	to the rhythm of a conflagration of light
que brotará del sol.[109]	that will sprout from the sun.

In one of the few commentaries available on this poem, Edwin Cuperes claims that it amounts to a "prank," since just a week earlier (March 19, 1936) de Burgos had published another political poem in the same newspaper, "Despierta: A la mujer puertorriqueña en esta hora de transcendencia," ("Awake: To Puerto Rican Women on this Transcendental Hour"), in which she admonishes Puerto Rican women in the following way: "deja a un lado las orgías / deja a un lado los placeres / y defiende heroicamente de tu patria la inocencia y la virtud" ("set aside orgies / set aside pleasures / and heroically defend of your country innocence and virtue").[110] For Cuperes, de Burgos's prank consists in the fact that one week she presents herself as the chaste Athena of the nation and the next week she publishes a poem "in which a poetic voice projects itself, precisely, in orgies and sexual pleasures."[111] Moreover, for Cuperes, this oscillation is proof that, already at this point, de Burgos had begun to transition out of the narrow confines of *nacionalista* ideology and its irreducible crypto-Catholicism and toward the communist and atheist commitments that will eventually mark her mature poetry and find expression in *Poema en 20 surcos*. Although I agree with Cuperes on this second point, his claim regarding the existence of this prank is not only textually mistaken; it also prevents us from both tracking the metaphysical abyss that separates these two poetics and grasping the continuity that connects this poem with de Burgos's previous production. Indeed, only a highly superficial reading of "A plena desnudez" would equate the poetic voice's fantasy of an erotic connection with her lover with the "pleasures" and "orgies" denounced by the speaker of "Despierta." What is more, "A plena desnudez" contains an even more powerful condemnation than "Despierta" of the superficial pleasures of conventional love. Indeed, the speaker of "A plena desnudez" establishes an absolute opposition between the "night orgies" that unfold in accordance with mundane conventionalisms and the erotic pleasures that the speaker allegorizes in the figure of "dancing the dance of life." What Cuperes's shallow remark occludes is the way de Burgos's embrace of a quasi-Marxist critique of bourgeois civilization retains, while radically transforming, the theologically inspired critique of mundane life as a life not worth living and in need of sacrifice that characterized her *nacionalista* worldview and that was in full display in "Yo quiero darme a ti." Rather than relying on the cycle of pain, suffering, sublimation, and glory to disentangle life in its ensouled purity from an always-mundane fleshiness, nakedness will progressively become one of the ciphers of de Burgos's life-philosophical poetry, which will now attempt to "take possession of 'true' experience, as opposed to the experience that sediments in the normed, denatured existence of the of the civilized masses," by less politico-theological and more *transcendental-aesthetic-erotic* means.[112]

This shift in de Burgos's poetics became more pronounced in 1937—a year that saw dramatic changes in de Burgos's personal life and effectively transformed her relation to the Nationalist Party and to San Juan's broader lettered city—though it was already anticipated by other poems that de Burgos published or at least wrote during 1935 and 1936. At a political and historical level, this period was marked by the intensification of US colonial repression against the Nationalists, the end of the Puerto Rico Emergency Relief Agency and its substitution by the Puerto Rico Reconstruction Agency (the two New Deal agencies created to address the island's dire economic situation in the aftermath of the Great Depression), the onset of the Spanish Civil War, and the escalation of regional tensions in response to the increasingly brutal dictatorship of Rafael Leónidas Trujillo. As Luis A. Ferrao has shown, all of these issues polarized the Nationalist intelligentsia, creating effectively two ideological currents within the party's sphere of influence, with Julia de Burgos consistently occupying the progressive or left-wing side of the *independentista* movement.[113] Whereas the Nationalist Party officially adopted a neutral position with regard to the Spanish Civil War, and an imprisoned Albizu Campos, writing a letter to his wife on Christmas Eve 1937, expressed his hope that "Spain, the Mother Fatherland of modern civilization, will rise again in its pristine glory and power, fulfilling its mission as the depositary of Christian civilization,"[114] de Burgos and other Nationalist leaders and sympathizers embraced the cause of the Second Spanish Republic. In this respect, it is very telling that two of the three explicitly political poems in *Poema en 20 surcos* deal with the Spanish Civil War and not with Puerto Rico's own struggle for independence. Something similar can be said about the divergence between the orthodox, Albizuist position with regard to the third International and de Burgos's stance. Throughout the 1930s, several efforts by Puerto Rican communists to form an anti-imperialist front with the *nacionalistas* foundered on the ideological and antidemocratic rocks of the party's ideology—which understood itself not as a political entity within a broader ecosystem of political agents but, in keeping with its motto, as *La patria organizada para el rescate de su soberanía (The fatherland organized to rescue its sovereignty)*.[115] De Burgos published in *La Acción* (an official venue of the Nationalist Party) poems such as "Es nuestra la hora" ("The Hour Is Ours"), where the speaker addresses the peasant, sickle in hand, and urges them to join the urban worker and the poor masses in a revolutionary struggle that would be equal parts nationalist and proletarian.[116] Likewise, whereas prominent members of Puerto Rico's independence movement openly praised aspects of Trujillo's modernizing nationalist policies in the Dominican Republic, de Burgos cultivated personal and intellectual relationships with some of the most prominent figures in the anti-Trujillo movement—including Juan Bosch, who became the first (and short-lived) democratically elected president of the Dominican Republic after Trujillo's assassination in 1961 and who wrote a critical commentary on her poetry that was included in the preface to *Poema en 20 surcos*—and published in 1944 a poem "Himno de sangre a Trujillo" ("Bloody Anthem for Trujillo"),[117] which the Dominican writer Chiqui Vicioso describes as "the most scathing poem written by any woman against one of the most repressive dictatorships in America."[118] In short, already by 1936, we find multiple traces of de Burgos's unwillingness to adhere to the party line both in her poems and in some of the most fundamental aspects of her personal life, including her decisions to work at a milking station that was part of the federally run PRERA policies; at the colonial government's Department of Public Instruction on their radio education program, "La Escuela del Aire"; and to accept a position as a teacher in the rural town of Naranjito through the intervention of the town's Liberal mayor[119]—labor arrangements that would have been anathema for an orthodox party member.[120]

That being said, it is really only after 1937 that the most enduring legends of de Burgos begin to take shape. A key catalyst in this process was the decision of de Burgos and Rodríguez Beauchamp to end their marriage. As Edwin Cuperes has forcefully shown, most scholars of de Burgos's have failed to take note of the fact that it is only after her divorce that de Burgos's career as an acclaimed poet, rather than as the bard of the *nacionalista* cause, began in earnest. Corretjer's testimony bears witness to this transformation. In the same article quoted earlier, Corretjer narrates that while he was in prison in Old San Juan during 1937 he received another folder containing de Burgos's most recent poetic production, which corresponded to the poems that were eventually published in December 1938 as *Poema en 20 surcos*. His assessment this time couldn't have been more different than what he said three years before: "A first-rate poet has been born to Puerto Rico and to the Spanish-speaking world."[121] Corretjer was not the only major *letrado* to think so. On November 13, 1937, Luis Lloréns Torres, at that time the most venerated literary figure in the island, introduced Julia de Burgos to the broader reading public of the *Puerto Rico Ilustrado*—the island's equivalent of *Life* or *Time*—in an article featuring the poetry of "Cinco poetisas de América" ("Five Poetesses of América"), thus consecrating de Burgos among the likes of Gabriela Mistral, Juana de Ibarbourou, Alfonsina Storni, and Clara Lair. More significant for our purposes than the sheer fact of this inclusion are the traits that Lloréns Torres claims distinguish de Burgos from the rest of the group, of which she was the youngest by at least two decades:

> Julia de Burgos, Puerto Rican, is today the highest promise of Hispano-American poetry.... In those purely metaphysical flights, when thought surpasses the whole plane of sensibility to plumb the depths of pure abstractions, Julia de Burgos is unique, because today there is no poet in our América that can follow her to the heights of her ideological flights. Through her paternal grandmother she is a quarter German, which can be divined in some traits of her rounded face and even more so in her mental propensity for Kantian abstractions. She finds solace in her ironic verses (see the poem *Nada*), where she firmly roots in prose her pure mind (Kant would say her pure reason) disintegrated from all sensibility, from all experimental apprehension, from all intuition of what exists, from all sense data.[122]

I will return to this passage in Part III in order to remark both the racialism that determines Lloréns Torres's presentation of de Burgos (which marks a counterpoint to the most common strand in her reception, which has reclaimed de Burgos as an Afro–Puerto Rican poet) and the curious characterization of de Burgos as a Kantian poet. For the time being I simply want to note that this text constitutes a crucial item in the dossier of the constitution of another image of de Burgos that is as distant as could be from the image of de Burgos as a martyr-like figure ready to give her life to the cause of the Nation.

But de Burgos's divorce also contributed to the consolidation of her legend as a "terrorizer of the bourgeoisie" in a more harmful way, namely, by intensifying the rumors about her promiscuity, alcoholism, and bohemian lifestyle that were already circulating around the island. To be sure, much has been speculated about the reasons that led to de Burgos's separation from Rodríguez Beauchamp. According to the testimony of Raúl Grau Archilla—a friend of de Burgos that Rodríguez Pagán interviewed in 1990—their divorce was caused mostly by irreconcilable differences between de Burgos and Rodríguez Beauchamp regarding both gender roles and sexual mores: whereas Rodríguez Beauchamp wanted a traditional wife, de Burgos was apparently an avid nudist who always had a less "antiquated" outlook on gender and sexuality in her private, conjugal life than her public speeches and poems would have led us to believe. Whether this candid anecdote is true or is instead a projection retroactively imposed by Grau Archilla upon events that happened more than five decades before (perhaps on the basis of poems like "A plena desnudez") matters less for our purposes than the anecdote's capacity to substantiate the claim that the construction of de Burgos's legend as the embodiment of an antibourgeois form of life continues to mobilize to this day her reputed promiscuity and flaunting of societal norms around sex and gender. The publication in 1969 of six erotic poems written by de Burgos in 1936 that were never published and that refer to an unidentified lover from Aguadilla[123] and Roberto Ramos Perea's recent archival discovery and publication of several unpublished poems written by Luis Lloréns Torres between 1937–1938 that refer explicitly to his love affair with Julia has only amplified the rumors that have been circulating about her sexual life among Puerto Rico's lettered city from the moment of her divorce.[124]

Moreover, we may say that de Burgos herself fanned the flames of this legend by publishing in *El Imparcial* poems like "A Julia de Burgos" ("To Julia de Burgos") and "Pentacromía" ("Pentachrome"), both of which refer or at least include in the body of the poem the poet's nom de plume and both of which end in the threat of violence to the person or figure that bears that name. The latter of these two is particularly important in this context because of its scandalous conclusion, which is barely mitigated by the playful, explicitly fictional context in which it unfolds.

Hoy, día de los muertos, desfile de sombras . . .	Today, Day of the Dead, parade of shadows . . .
Hoy, sombra de sombras, deliro el afán	Today, shadow of shadows, I conjure the yearning
de ser Don Quijote o Don Juan o un bandido	of being Don Quixote or Don Juan or a bandit
o un ácrata obrero o un gran militar.	or an acratic worker or a great military man.
. . .	. . .
Hoy, quiero ser hombre. Subir por las tapias	Today, I want to be a man. Climb through the walls
Burlar los conventos, ser todo un Don Juan,	Mock the convents, be a perfect Don Juan,
Raptar a Sor Carmen y a Sor Josefina	Capture Sister Carmen and Sister Josephine
Rendirlas, y a Julia de Burgos violar.[125]	Conquer them, and rape Julia de Burgos.

Gestures like this consolidated de Burgos's image as the "terrorizer of the bourgeoisie" at yet another level: She would not only call for the necessity of destroying "bourgeois man" at the economic and metaphysical or philosophico-anthropological levels—as she poetizes forcefully in "Amaneceres"

("Dawns")— but also at the level of sexual politics. In *Becoming Julia de Burgos*, Pérez Rosario summarizes the predicament that de Burgos faced in the last three years of her stay in Puerto Rico quite succinctly:

> Burgos's assertiveness, outspokenness, divorce, affair, and bohemian lifestyle resulted in substantial gossip and prejudice on the island. One New York–based friend, Emelí Vélez de Vando, remembered that the women of San Juan's cultural circles accepted Julia de Burgos the poet but could not be associated with Julia de Burgos, the woman. Burgos's rejection of marriage and traditional roles for women, her poverty, and her race all factored into her conflicted relationship with her home country and significantly influenced her decision to depart.[126]

As I have already mentioned, de Burgos's departure from the island happened barely a year after the publication of *Poema*, in late 1939, not before she published a second poetry volume, *Canción de la verdad sencilla*. But even her departure was shrouded in a romantic controversy that pitted de Burgos against another rising star in the Puerto Rican lettered city, Nilita Vientós Gastón, who claimed to have been romantically involved with the Dominican intellectual and anti-Trujillo activist Juan Isidro Jimenes Grullón at the same time as de Burgos and Jimenes Grullón began seeing each other during his stay in Puerto Rico at the invitation of the Association of Alumnae of the University of Puerto Rico, which Vientós Gastón led at that time. Hence, although there were many factors that contributed to de Burgos's decision to leave the island, the fact that the proximate efficient cause of her departure was her budding relationship with Jimenes Grullón may have deepened a rivalry with another intellectual who would later become the president of the Ateneo Puertorriqueño (Puerto Rican Atheneum)— the island's leading elite cultural institution—and Puerto Rico's most influential literary critic for at least three decades. Whether this rivalry had anything to do with the ambivalent if not outright negative review of *Poema* that Vientós Gastón published in *Puerto Rico Ilustrado* in April 1939, which praises de Burgos as a promise of Puerto Rican poetry even as she classifies many of the poems in the volume as communist political propaganda, remains an open issue.[127]

What is less of an open issue, judging from the occasional comments in de Burgos's letters to her sister and the testimonies of many of her contemporaries, is that by the time de Burgos left the island, the elements that would eventually nourish the legendary narratives of de Burgos as a patron saint of the cause of Puerto Rican independence or as the accursed, bohemian *poète maudite* who flouted bourgeois conventions, as the socialist defender of the poor and downtrodden or as the protofeminist who challenged gender expectations under patriarchy, as the poet of a life purified through pain and sacrifice or as the poet of a life reduced to its originary nakedness had already been set.

Imitatio Iuliæ: Re/De/Constructing the Totem

After this biographical sketch, we are now in a better position to track the sedimentation of de Burgos's catastrophic tradition. To do so, I want to center on two specific interpretive or critical events that took place after de Burgos's death and that I argue economically condense the two major regimes of totemization to which de Burgos's image has been submitted.

The first of these events was a eulogy of sorts delivered by José Emilio González in an event celebrating de Burgos's life, which was held just two days after her burial in Carolina, Puerto Rico, at the Ateneo Puertorriqueño (Puerto Rican Atheneum) on September 8, 1953. Given both the funereal context in which this address was delivered and the abject conditions in which de Burgos died, it is not surprising that the institution of this totemic tradition begins with a mea culpa: "We must make a confession: We are all in part guilty of Julia's death. To the extent that we do not fulfill our charitable duties, that each of us shields themselves in their 'I,' closing the doors to human communication; to that extent, I repeat, we are guilty of Julia's death. And if we insist on our fallacious negligence, we will continue to kill and bury her."[128] Note the collective nature of this confession; although the first "We" can be explained away as the result of González's innocuous rhetorical choice of the Royal We, the second sentence clarifies that there is nothing rhetorical about González's decision and that he is not only speaking in representation of a collectivity but also atoning for a sin committed by the entire collectivity. González is here putting himself and his audience in an imaginary position analogous to the one Sigmund Freud assigns to the members of the mythical *mob of brothers* in *Totem und Taboo* (*Totem and Taboo*) and much later to the proto-Hebrew people of *Der Mann Moses und die monotheistische Religion* (*Moses and Monotheism*), but with one major difference: González's audience, gathered in the most emblematic institution of Puerto Rican cultural nationalism, must atone for killing the nation's mother through inaction and omission, rather than through direct violence.[129]

From the moment González begins his speech, we enter the terrain in which the constitution of de Burgos's catastrophic tradition will take hold; indeed, we are in the affective, psychosomatic soil upon which her religious totem will be erected. For González places himself and his audience—and by extension us readers who presumably belong to the tradition, the same Husserlian "chain of generations"—within that phase in Freud's mythical allegory in which ambivalence asserts itself among the "mob of brothers" after the repressed feelings of affection for the father return to haunt the surviving sons. Like the body of the deceased father in Freud's psychoanalytic myth of the origin of both totemism and the incest taboo, de Burgos's corpse bears witness to "our" transgressions and is therefore the very source of the guilt that emerges as the affect that maintains the communal or social bond of this fraternal band.

And yet, González institutes a totemic tradition in the more strictly anthropological (and, dare I say, idealistic) sense that Claude Levi-Strauss gives to this phenomenon, for instance in his famous essay "Le totémisme du dédans" ("Totemism from Within"). For note that the precise content of the sin that he claims we have all committed is not limited, as one might expect given the context, to the fact that those present at the poet's homage did little, if anything, to try to spare the poet from the humiliations and suffering that characterized her last years in New York City and especially since her hospitalization in 1948 at Mt. Sinai. (As a matter of fact, González should be given credit for the fact that he avoids turning de Burgos into a hapless victim that could have been rescued by her friends or family, even if, as we will see in a moment, he can't avoid turning this decision into de Burgos's ultimate sacrificial act for the nation.) Instead, González presents the *form* of the sin that we have all committed against de Burgos via a strict analogy with the status of sin in Christian theology, whose most basic definition is an offense against God's law. In the case of the sins against de Burgos, however, the law we have all transgressed is not natural or divine law but the law of "human communication." It is this definition of the Burgosian law that evokes the sole eidetic content that Levi-Strauss seems comfortable with ascribing to the "phenomenon" of totemism and that, according to him, had already found expression in Jean-Jacques Rousseau's insight into the conditions of possibility of totemism, namely, "*compassion*, or, as Rousseau also writes, *identification with the other*," which he glosses as "the natural condition of man by means of the sole psychic state whose content is indissociably psychic and intellectual."[130] Moreover, bringing Levi-Strauss to this scene has the added benefit of clarifying the metatotemic, if you will, nature of González's gesture. For not only is it the case that de Burgos herself is a totemic figure in the Freudian sense, but the content for which she was erected into a totemic figure is presumably *totemism*, that is to say, the supposedly inherent tendency for *compassion* and *identification with the other* that characterizes humanity in its "natural condition."

But, according to González, the constitution of de Burgos as a totemic figure whose sacrifice embodies the very *universal* ideal of a natural humanity defined by its capacity for compassion also has a *particular* dimension. Not surprisingly, this particularity is linked to the cause of Puerto Rican independence. De Burgos's death, like that of Christ, not only renders all her successors guilty for sinning against the very idea of humanity; it also renders the entire Puerto Rican body politic both guilty of the sin of not having shaken the shackles of colonialism and, paradoxically, rendered innocent of that very same sin by her own sacrifice. Consider the following moment:

> Let us declare this truth that has been on the tip on our tongue for quite some time: her life as much as her death constitute one single protest. Julita de Burgos chose her life and with it she also chose her death as well. Like Rilke, she didn't want to die the death of the doctors. She wanted to live her death like she lived her life, both of them forged in the vigor of her intense protest.... If she had wanted to come she would have done do. People both here and there would have made it possible. But she herself constructed her own death; she wanted it thus and she preferred to end there, in exile, anonymous, on the cold pavement of a hostile city, so that in her [person] the parable of our national tragedy would be fulfilled. Is there not here a lesson or a warning for our conscience?... The life and death of Julia constitute the epitome of the crime that is being committed against our culture.... We are still not worthy of burying Julia by the Río Grande de Loíza because we are still far from achieving her greatness.[131]

Note the tension that emerges here. At first, it seems like González, who was a close friend of de Burgos, is making a case for recognizing the poet's agency in her own death, a gesture that is more than understandable, especially given the importance that the narrative of victimization continues to place in her reception. And yet González is not that interested in asking his audience to respect the choices that de Burgos may have made and that led her to die in abject conditions in the summer of 1953 in the city of New York. Rather, de Burgos's agency in constructing her own death is, for González, the decisive proof of her Christological sacrifice. In fact, her decision not to return to the island is even more convenient for the nationalist protocol of totemization because only this way can her death be the ultimate sacrifice for the nation: In choosing to die alone, abandoned, an exile in the largest city of the empire that colonized her people, de Burgos becomes the martyr for Puerto Rican nationalism that she had wanted to be in her early adulthood, before she began to "write herself out of the nation," as Pérez Rosario has eloquently put it.[132]

Finally, note that the Christological vein of this passage becomes even more transparent in the last sentence, where González, echoing the Centurion's Prayer, casts all of de Burgos's inheritors as not worthy of receiving the gift of her sacrifice. *Imitatio Iuliæ* is the name that I suggest should be given to the tradition that crystallizes in González's speech. Not unlike the devotional practice of the Imitation of Christ, this tradition takes the form of a secularized Christology in which de Burgos emerges as a totemic figure that brings together or reconciles two different scripts of identification.

On the one hand, de Burgos's life and, especially, her death become *the* symbol of an *intensive, qualitative, humane* humanity that is perennially caught up in a Manichean struggle against the dehumanizing forces of modernity and its regime of extension—number, commodification, fungibilization. Indeed, given that Rilke did die at the hands of his doctor, González's reference to the Austrian should perhaps be taken as an attempt to position de Burgos alongside the author of *Briefe an einen jungen Dichter* (*Letters to a Young Poet*), that is, as an emblematic figure of the modern poet as an inward-looking vessel for a creative word that is meant to express the very flow of life. As a leading scholar who wrote one of the most authoritative histories of Puerto Rican poetry and especially as the author of the prologue to the first anthology of de Burgos's poems, *Critatura del agua* (1961), González was in a unique position to contribute to the consolidation of an interpretive framework in which de Burgos's image as a poet is understood in terms of an aesthetic ideology that corresponds with the project of *Lebensphilosophie* as Benjamin describes it:[133] "Julia was the perpetual outcast. And to defend herself from so many frustrations she built for herself a compartment: her poetry."[134]

On the other hand, de Burgos's Christological totemization buttresses the narratives of martyrdom and victimization that have characterized (for good reason, one should add, though perhaps to ill political effects) the different institutions that defend the cause of Puerto Rican independence. González's *Imitatio Iuliæ* becomes a crucial formation within the historicity of Puerto Rican nationalism precisely because, if we follow the logic of González, it becomes clear that our debt to de Burgos cannot be settled until Puerto Rico is no longer a colony. And so, reading de Burgos's poetry, like consuming the body and blood of Christ in the Eucharist, becomes an ambivalent (though repressed) ritual that harbors the possibility of absolution even as it remarks on the persistence of an unpayable debt. Paradoxically, it is precisely because this debt can't be settled that reading de Burgos can function as the ultimate dialectical resource, as the Puerto Rican sacrifice to end all sacrifices. Her poetry and, above all, her life become the medium that allows de Burgos's heirs to affirm their moral superiority and their authentic Puertoricanness on the basis of belonging to that select group within the country that constitute the soul of the nation precisely because they are aware of their infinite debt to de Burgos—because, like the Centurion said of Christ, they know that "they are not worthy" of her.

Rebellious Symbol: de Burgos as the Nomadic Subject of Puerto Rican Counterhegemony

De Burgos's reception took a progressive turn roughly from the 1970s onward, when a new generation of intellectuals and writers such as Anjelamaría Dávila, Rosario Ferré, Manuel Ramos Otero, María M. Solá, and Edgardo Rodríguez Masdeu began to rescue the feminist, communist, internationalist, and Afro-Caribbean aspects of de Burgos's life and poetry whose importance for de Burgos's poetics had been understated by previous generations of critics. This profound revision of the historical grammars that had ensured de Burgos's survival until that moment in Puerto Rican culture should be seen as part of a broader shift in Puerto Rican intellectual life, one characterized by the rise of the Nueva Historiografía Puertorriqueña (New Puerto Rican Historiography), the joint formation of the Center for Puerto Rican studies at Hunter College and the UPR's Centro de Estudios de la Realidad Puertorriqueña (Center for the Study of Puerto Rican Reality), and the emergence of a new generation of writers known as the Generación del 70. These new intellectual and cultural movements, coupled with the resurgence of a combative Puerto Rican Socialist Party, could be taken as key symptoms of the arrival of the New Left on the island's political and intellectual life. At the risk of caricaturing this process, we may say that whereas the *maître penseurs* of those intellectuals and writers who shaped elite discourse on the island from the 1930s to the 1950s were José Ortega y Gasset, Oswald Spengler, José Vasconcelos, or María Zambrano, the intellectuals, academics, and writers of the 1970s drew inspiration from Karl Marx, Antonio Gramsci, Franz Fanon, and Simone de Beauvoir.

It is within this broader historical context that a different totem of de Burgos will be erected, a monumental image that does not present de Burgos simply as an icon of Puerto Rican cultural nationalism or as an emblem of the predicament of the modern artist in a bourgeois society; rather, de Burgos will also become a foundational figure in the ongoing effort to construct a counterhegemonic Puerto Rican literary canon that could challenge the reduction of the politics of Puerto Rican artistic and intellectual expression to the erection of a last line of defense against the threat of Anglo-Saxon cultural assimilation. At the same time, the figure of de Burgos will also begin to play a crucial role in the formation of a pan-Caribbean, Latino diasporic identity in urban centers such as New York City.

Pérez Rosario has perhaps summarized this alternative reception best when she writes that "as time passes, her story is co-opted and serves the nation as well as the diaspora. Yet understanding Burgos's life and works requires understanding her struggle against hegemony and her enduring belief that political action will enable radical democratic principles of social justice and equality to shape a better world."[135]

With the formation and consolidation of this layer in de Burgos's reception we would seem to be as far away as possible from the totemization of de Burgos's image that González's speech crystallized, if not instituted. And yet, as a way of closing this section, I want to make the case that there is a profound continuity between these two seemingly opposed receptions.

To do so, I want to turn to another critical intervention that took place four decades after González's speech, namely, the publication of Juan Gelpí's essay "El sujeto nómada en la poesía de Julia de Burgos" ("The Nomadic Subject in the Poetry of Julia de Burgos"). As Lena Burgos-Lafuente argues, this essay has "marked a watershed [*un antes y un después*] in the criticism on de Burgos's work."[136] Claiming for de Burgos the status of a Deleuzian-Braidottian nomadic subject, Gelpí's essay constitutes the most influential and rigorous attempt to erect an alternative totem of de Burgos, according to which the poet serves as the exemplary "line of flight" that may lead different Puerto Rican subjectivities to unforeseen becomings, in the process widening the island's political imaginary beyond the constrictive insularity of the cultural nationalism that took shape around the time of de Burgos's poetic debut.

But how does Gelpí reconstruct the figure of de Burgos as a nomadic subject? In keeping with the role that the Deleuzian motifs of deterritorialization and the line of flight play within Deleuze and Guattari's thinking of nomadism, Gelpí's reading of de Burgos's nomadic poetics begins by demarcating the territory against which de Burgos's poetry will take flight. The boundaries of this territory were initially drawn by Antonio S. Pedreira, the main intellectual of the Generación del 30 and author of *Insularismo* (*Insularism*; Madrid, 1934), widely regarded as a foundational text in the study of Puerto Rican matters. Pedreira's *Insularismo* is a book dominated by a telluric, patriarchal nostalgia that couples anxieties about the empowerment of women and Black Puerto Ricans by US modernizing efforts with a geographical and biological determinism that naturalized Puerto Rico's political subservience as a result of both its racial mixing and its geographical condition as a small island. With the rise to power of the Partido Popular Democrático in the 1940s and the drafting and approval of a colonial constitution for the island in 1952, the political conditions were met for the cultural nationalism articulated by Pedreira and his fellow young intellectuals to become the state's official nationalist discourse.

It is in this context that de Burgos emerges as a nomadic figure, according to Gelpí. As Deleuze and Guattari write in their introduction to *Mille Plateaux* (*A Thousand Plateaus*), "One writes history, but one has always written it from the point of view of sedentary people, and in the name of a state apparatus, at least a possible one, even when we were talking about nomads. What is missing is a nomadology, the contrary of a History."[137] De Burgos's poetry, as read by Gelpí, constitutes in its own right such a nomadology, that is, the writing of an alternative, counterhegemonic history. For Gelpí, De Burgos mounts a challenge to Pedreira's discourse on various fronts: As opposed to the tellurism and insularism of Pedreira, her poetry "inscribes a symbolic geography marked by nomadism, expansiveness and dynamism"; her combination of irony, metaphysics, and eroticism—already signaled by Luis Lloréns Torres as the distinguishing feature of her poetry—could be read as a challenge to "the stereotype of feminine frivolity that is present in Pedreira's text"; moreover, against Pedreira's privileging of Whiteness and his claim that Puerto Rico's social, political, and cultural problems are the result of *mestizaje*, Gelpí insists that de Burgos's poems, in particular "Ay ay ay de la grifa negra" ("Ay Ay Ay of the Griffe Negresse"), mount "a defense of African heritage and a celebration of racial miscegenation in the Americas"; and, finally, de Burgos's personal nomadism, emblematized by her decision to never return to Puerto Rico, make her into a foundational figure of "that other strand of Puerto Rican literature which is the literature of migration or Diaspora."[138] In this way, the nomadic de Burgos that Gelpí constructs emerges as the major representative of the marginal, counterhegemonic tradition within Puertoricanness—which we may perhaps call, this time with Benjamin, the Puerto Rican "tradition of the oppressed."[139]

A superficial examination of the elements of de Burgos's life and works that Gelpí emphasizes in order to construct the image of de Burgos as a nomadic subject might lead us to think that his critical intervention consolidated the formation of an alternative mode of traditionalization, a different protocol for inheriting de Burgos that breaks with the ideological, metaphysical, and even ontotheological aspects that determined her construction into the totemic figure of what authentic Puerto Rican humanity should look like. If, as Burgos-Lafuente and other scholars have argued, Gelpí's reading of de Burgos marks a watershed in her critical reception, this is so because of the way his essay rearticulates de Burgos's afterlife, namely, by gathering and intensifying the different historical elements that previous scholars and writers had already begun to accentuate in their attempt to render de Burgos available as a symbolic figure for a different framework of political demands. Gelpí's reliance on a Deleuzian-Braidottian conception of nomadism allows him to iterate the universalism that has always determined de Burgos's traditionalization while also expanding considerably the grammars of political particularization that find a privileged expression in her life. In this way, de Burgos appears as the minoritarian subject par excellence within the constitution of Puerto Rican historicity precisely because she embodies all the different grammars of what Deleuze and Guattari may call *becoming-intense* within Puerto Rican history-as-nomadology: As *feminist* icon, she's the emblem of *becoming-woman*; as the supposed Blackened mestiza who writes "Ay ay ay de la grifa negra," she emerges as the icon of *becoming-Black* in a mestizo country that is slowly gaining awareness of the extent to which it was whitened; and as the defender of the poor and downtrodden, she remains the symbol of *becoming-proletarian*. That being said, although it certainly registers the displacement of the more explicit Christological resonances that determined the institution of de Burgos's totemization, Gelpí's critical intervention nonetheless attests to the fact that her more political or progressive reception has actually expanded the scope of de Burgos's catastrophic tradition *without troubling its totemic constitution*.

As a way of substantiating the claim made earlier, I want to briefly unpack the concept of totemism that Sylvia Wynter elaborates on the basis of Levi-Strauss's. As we saw in passing, Levi-Strauss holds that totemism boils down to a mode of thinking that ritually institutes a set of oppositions, such as the distinction between human/animal or culture/nature, that lend structure and order to the human world. In "The Ceremony Must Be Found," Wynter retains Levi-Strauss's emphasis on totemic schemas as operating along binaristic lines that ultimately boil down to the distinction between sameness and difference. But Wynter parts ways with Levi-Strauss's idealistic universalism and his facile critique of ethnocentrism by transforming the concept of totemism into a critical tool that allows her to track the "regularities of the 'figuring' of an Other excluded series" across different stages and at different scales in the long history of anthropogenesis.[140] Rather than indexing a presumed universal humanity, Wynter's totemism accounts for the systemic fact that entire swaths of humanity—that is, native-Blackened-impoverished-illiterate humanity—continue to serve as the "totemic operators" for the consolidation of the specific systems of totemically instituted oppositions that lend order and structure to the world since the advent of modern coloniality.[141] In other words, totemism, for Wynter, is a mode of thinking or an onto-epistemology, but one that entails the ritualized figuration *as other* of human beings from different classes, castes, genders, religions, or, especially, races, which thereby become bearers of an intrinsic difference-within-sameness that then justifies the hierarchical and unequal distribution of humanness across the *Homo sapiens* species. Moreover, for Wynter, totemism reaches its apex in modernity with what she calls the "overrepresentation of Man,"[142] or, putting a finer point on this insight, the overrepresentation of "Western bourgeoisie's liberal monohumanist Man2."[143] Man2 institutes and replicates its onto-epistemic and geopolitical hegemony precisely through totemism, that is, through "the 'figuring' of the Other excluded series." The "regularities" of this totemic procedure produce the stability of the world's hierarchies by tautologically positioning those genres of the human that are taken as "totemic operators" of *difference* or otherness—that is, as embodying a genre of humanity that is "dysselected" for replication—in a differential/debased relation to the *sameness* of the human norm, which Man2 symbolically encoded through the totemic procedures that guaranteed its self-institution and stable replication.

This latter point is crucial to understand why Wynter, in a suggestive footnote in "Beyond Miranda's Meanings," makes an intriguing claim about the link between totemism and abolitionist politics: "Since all the *isms* constitute a totemic system or set, the attempt to abolish any of these as an isolated ism is everywhere a 'strategy set' of the specific group for whom . . . the abolition of a specific ism will be empowering."[144] I take Wynter's point here to be that the isolated *isms* that regulate and order our contemporary world, such as racism, classism, sexism, elitism, etc., should be seen as discrete articulations (hence, *isms*) of the specific historico-metaphysical totemic system of differences reinstituted by coloniality/modernity, where racialization emerges as a privileged level for totemic dysselection/othering. In this respect, the abolitionist vocation of an isolated *ism*—say, femin*ism*—is precisely to undo the "totemic system"—in this case, patriarchal*ism*—that relies on "women" as a totemic operator for the differential allocation of sameness or humanity to maleness and difference or less-than-humanity to femaleness. Abolitionist projects, such as feminism, may well succeed in combating isolated totemic systems, thus empowering female-identifying people, but I take Wynter's point here to be that the task she articulates elsewhere of replacing "the ends of the *referent-we* of liberal monohumanist Man2 with the ecumenically human ends of the *referent-we in the horizon of humanity*" requires a different "strategy set," one that targets the workings of *totemism in general*, that is, the self-production of humanity through the differential distribution of humanness by recourse to totemic operators.[145] Wynter's philosophical and political project could thus be construed as that of bringing an *end to any and all totemisms*.

The abolitionist dimension and horizon of Wynter's concept of totemism is key to an understanding of the specific modes of subversion, if not perversion, that are at stake in de Burgos's reconfiguration as a progressive totem. The fact that, to borrow a description from Aurea María Sotomayor, de Burgos has become the near-universal symbol of the *outsider*[146] within Puerto Rican historicity is proof that de Burgos continues to function totemically in a Wynterian sense of the term: She emerges as the privileged emblem for all of the itineraries within Puerto Rican historicity that, throughout the island's colonial modernization, have been positioned as totemic operators against which to demarcate what counts as a proper Puerto Rican humanity. In other words, de Burgos functions as the totem (this time in a Freudian sense) of all the *isms* that vie for cultural and political hegemony within Puerto Rican historicity—feminism, socialism, independentism, Afro-Caribbeanism—because de Burgos is explicitly or implicitly positioned as a privileged figuration of the *others* within Puerto Rican historicity: the woman, the worker, the nationalist, the Afrodescendant person, etc. But it is precisely because she is constructed as the iconic figure that can gather all of these different isolated *isms* that she is able to emerge as a universal totem for a project of universal emancipation that, not unlike Wynter's own utopian task, would finally bring about the advent of a truly ecumenically human humanity— a *humanity beyond totemism*.

We are now in a better position to understand why Gelpí's text and the critical tradition that it summarizes stand in a profound continuity with the more Christological constitution of de Burgos's totemic image. For these two sedimented protocols of reading rest on a key aspect of the ritual of totemism, namely, the specularity of idealized identification; as such, they require restricting the legibility of de Burgos's image to those elements that facilitate her reduction to a flattering mirror in which her inheritors may see the imaginary projection of their own ego-ideal. In other words, the alternative, counterhegemonic tradition that Gelpí represents may expand the *content* of what can be read in and through de Burgos, but it maintains the totemic, monumental, catastrophic *form* of traditionalization, which thus informs whatever "new" content can be read off of her image. We can now see why writing or speaking about de Burgos almost inevitably entails reerecting her totem, engaging in a communal ritual that is never as effective as when it appears to be nowhere on stage. This ritual is characterized by the mutually reinforcing dialectic of guilt and absolution: To read de Burgos within the constraints of this catastrophic tradition entails that the reader must confess their guilt for not being quite as radical, quite as authentic, quite as progressive, quite as feminist, quite as nationalist, quite as communist, quite as rebellious as she was. And yet the sheer fact of engaging in the ritualized reactivation of de Burgos's totem is enough to ensure the partial absolution of this guilt through the hermeneutic performance of what I would call vicarious moral(istic) uprightness. Indeed, by choosing to recognize and champion de Burgos as the symbol, icon, or emblem of all the marginalized trajectories and forms of life within Puerto Rican historicity, her readers implicitly gain that unassailable moral high ground in which culpability and absolution cannot be distinguished, since the very admission of guilt constitutes its momentary pardon. Once this circuit has been closed, the catastrophic tradition can run on its own. This specular circle of reappropriation, in which de Burgos each time appears both as our most inalienable national treasure and as the mirror in which we will always see the best version of ourselves that we may ever be, neutralizes her historicity, blocking the very chance that de Burgos may leap from out of her catastrophic tradition. Henceforth, de Burgos's totem will always be *there*, available to her readers as the mirror that will allow them to write the *same* old history, namely, the history of how they belong, as if by destiny, to the catastrophic tradition of Puerto Rican historicity.

§12. CODA: INTERRUPTING THE CATASTROPHE; OR, THE PROMISE OF LEGIBILITY

In the previous section, I put forward the following three claims: first, that de Burgos's reception has been determined by the mode of traditionalization that Benjamin calls "catastrophe"; second, that the grammar of totemization—understood along Freudian, Levi-Straussian, and Wynterian lines—can help us analyze the different layers and phases in the constitution of this catastrophic sedimentation; and, finally, that this catastrophic totemization has produced a paradoxical form of *historical illegibility* that becomes more intense the more her fame as the polyvalent symbol of different scripts of Puertoricanness expands. To bring Part I to a close, I want to clarify what I mean by "historical illegibility" and, by extension, explain how a Benjaminian approach to (literary) history, informed by his key concept of the dialectical image, might help us interrupt the ceaseless actualization of this tradition.

This point of clarification is necessary at this precise moment in my itinerary because, as readers familiar with scholarship on de Burgos know, I am not the first to diagnose or bemoan de Burgos's descent into historical illegibility. As a matter of fact, I would even argue that similar complaints play a crucial role in the institution and consolidation of her totemic reception. This is particularly (though by no means exclusively) true of those readers of de Burgos who emphasize her engagement with the Nationalist Party or her communist sympathies. The recent study of de Burgos's FBI file by Ángel Rodríguez or Torres Santiago's aforementioned biography provide eloquent illustrations of how this complaint continues to function: For both these authors, de Burgos's image has not been *read historically* because her enshrinement within the cultural pantheon molded by the colonial and depoliticized forms of cultural ethnonationalism instituted in the wake of the Generación del 30, the advent of PPD hegemony, and the establishment of the Commonwealth required the erasure of her commitments to Puerto Rican nationalism, internationalist or pan-Hispanic antifascism, or communism.[147] Whether this claim is true today (I have my doubts) matters less than the fact that these gestures illustrate how even her totemic readers rely on claims about her historical illegibility in the service of reinstituting the identificatory-idealistic "reading" protocols that constitute her catastrophic tradition. Indeed, this is but one example of the battle of totems, the symbolic gigantomachy that largely constitutes de Burgos's scholarly and cultural reception, with different totems of de Burgos facing one another in a struggle to determine which de Burgos is the truest: the feminist or the nationalist, the communist or the tragic, the Puerto Rican or the Niuyorican, and so on.

My diagnosis of de Burgos's historical illegibility is *toto cælo* different from these gestures for at least two reasons. In the first place, because I am not interested in rescuing aspects of de Burgos that her reception has supposedly neglected in order to produce the *real, authentic,* or *true* image of de Burgos, in order to project yet another version of her life and poetry that would have remained hidden under decades of censorship. This is the case not only because, in keeping with the Benjaminian commitments that inform my concept of historical reading, the *truth* of de Burgos's image could not simply be understood as a state of affairs that corresponds to empirical elements of her life that had been ignored and are now identified. (Indeed, following Benjamin, I take the *truth* of de Burgos's image as having necessarily the character of what Derrida would have called an *event*, namely, that which cannot be foreseen, since its happening *generates* in the first place both the historicity of the historian who *reads* de Burgos's image and the historicity of that very image.) Second, because the way I understand historical legibility requires the interruption of the *idealistic* determination of the time-space of what attains legibility in and through the presentation of de Burgos's image. Without *endangering* her historically sedimented status as the *flattering* mirror of Puertoricanness, without giving her the chance to take leave of our totemic schemas, and without giving us the chance to become something other than the fraternal mob reaffirming our communitarian bond through the consumption of her spiritual flesh, de Burgos will not attain *historical* legibility (in an emphatically *nonhistoricist* sense of this term).

This claim is not without precedent in de Burgos's storied reception. José Quiroga, in a beautiful review of the Cuban edition of her complete poetry, writes that the celebration of her centenary "could be an invitation to remove her from where she is or was and put her in a different place. Or put her in the same place but after this place has been rendered other: less example, less normative, more country and less landscape."[148] Likewise, Juan Carlos Quintero Herencia, in a review of *Cartas a Consuelo*, perceptively diagnoses the tendency to treat de Burgos as a "talisman," noting how "discursive cleansings and spiritualizations, identitarian tautologies of all types, have been hoisting de Burgos's works (her picture, some poem, that letter) like an amulet that will fend off the calamity of thinking de Burgos from and with the complexity that pervades her."[149] Along similar lines, Burgos-Lafuente concludes her compelling preface to *Cartas a Consuelo* by expressing her hope that the publication of de Burgos's letters may contribute to rescuing de Burgos from the historical illegibility to which her own monumental reception has consigned her:

> Reading these letters may help to walk back a little that mythical, heroic and mercilessly monumental de Burgos that we have forged for ourselves and against which her own writing wagers on occasion. Perhaps it is a matter of catching a glimpse in the correspondence—in this fiction of the I—of the place in which the Julia of the little sandals, the little robe and the half-mourning dress and the hermetic Julia cross each other, the op-ed contributor to *Pueblos Hispánicos* and Rockefeller's clerk, the pro-Soviet and the anarchist Julia, the composer of popular verses and the avant-gardist, the sarcastic and the melancholic. This exercise may allow us to take note of the contiguity between her rapist Don Juans, the irony of her nothing, the weight of her negativity, the density of her philosophical wager, and the imprudence of her desire. In this way, we may perhaps recover the political texture of her literary word. In this way, we may perhaps read Julia again.[150]

What would it take for de Burgos to become legible again? Before examining briefly how Burgos-Lafuente answers this question, we must take notice of the *promissory* nature of her remarks here: At stake here, in other words, is not the certain actualization or the effective realization of such a reading but the precarious, contingent bestowal of its *possibility*, that is, of a legibility that has not yet become ontically bound to an actual moment of reading. As Derrida never ceased to insist, a promise is not a promise if it can't be broken.[151] A promise is therefore possibly impossible; its modality is such that its very *actuality* harbors its impossibility within itself. Burgos-Lafuente's prudent use of modal verbs like *puede* (may) and of modifiers like *quizás* (perhaps) reflects a keen awareness of what is at stake in the task of preparing the ground for the possible arrival of the chance of reading de Burgos—this may or may not happen, and it is precisely in its *ineliminable contingency* that its historicity resides.

Burgos-Lafuente's passage suggests that a twofold process would be necessary for de Burgos to become legible again. First, there is the necessity of *walking back* (in Spanish, literally *desandar*) de Burgos's mythological and heroic monumentalization. Though she doesn't mention Nietzsche by name here, this suggestion recalls Nietzsche's characterization in the second of his *Unzeitgemäße Betrachtungen* (*Untimely Meditations*) of *critical history* as the mode of engagement with the past that endangers the anxious efforts of monumental historians to secure the continuity of genealogy by narrating history as a chain of great deeds of a single nation or "race" (*Geschlecht*) across the "alternation of its generations" (*Wechsel der Geschlechter*). Against monumental history's attempt to secure the nation (and the historian themselves) a place in history, critical history

> is always a dangerous process, namely, dangerous for life itself: and men or times that serve life in this way, that judge and annihilate the past, are always dangerous and endangered men and times. For since we are indeed the result of earlier generations, we are also the results of their equivocations, passions, and mistakes, even crimes; it is not possible to free oneself completely from this chain.[152]

Critical historians endanger themselves because their historical judgments endanger the past they historicize. This opens the door to a breach in their own genealogical linkage to the past that is the target of their critical exertions, which, in turn, threatens the very life of critical historians, who cannot achieve a total separation from the past they criticize and condemn, since they are the result of that history. If, as Derrida puts it in *Spectres de Marx*, "*being* . . . means . . . *to inherit*,"[153] then the exercise of critical history always endangers the past in its very being by harboring the promise of its negation. By extension, critical historians also endanger their own ontological status as inheritors of the past they might always consign to the dustbin of history.

Nietzsche's thinking of critical history resonates and amplifies Burgos-Lafuente's call for the partial undoing of the monumental myth of de Burgos that, as she herself puts it, "*nos hemos labrado*," which "*we* ourselves have forged." It is *we* who belong to the many *Geschlechtern*, the many peoples, nations, sexes, or "races" that lay claim to her *corpus* and are, in turn, shaped by it who have produced this monument. The *we* used here by Burgos-Lafuente betrays the fact that even the most critical of histories of de Burgos would have to undergo a form of *self*-endangering given the fact that de Burgos's history and that of her readers can't be entirely extricated from her monumentalizing tradition. A *critical* history of de Burgos must therefore dare to interrupt the genealogical chain that would irremediably inscribe said critical historians—whether or not they themselves are Puerto Rican, Caribbean, Latin American, or Latinx—within the national and popular traditions that have by and large taken shape through the symbolic interpretation of de Burgos's *corpus*, which reduces her literary word to an icon and transforms her image into an *imago*—or, at worst, into a sort of Freudian totem, if not even a fetish. Such a literary history would thus be both dangerous and endangered.

Burgos-Lafuente's passage, however, suggests not only a critical operation but also an operation of *retrieval*. At stake is not only a radical critique of the monumental tradition that has captured de Burgos's writings but, above all, the possibility of having once more a *readerly encounter* with de Burgos's poetry that might recover its political force. Here Burgos-Lafuente recalls Benjamin, rather than Nietzsche. Benjamin, himself a reader of Nietzsche's second *Untimely Meditation*, offers an image of what this retrieval might look like in *Über den Begriff der Geschichte (On the Concept of History)*:

> Historical materialism is concerned with holding fast to an image of the past as it suddenly presents itself to the historical subject in a moment of danger. The danger threatens the existence of tradition just as much as those who receive it. For both it is one and the same: to give themselves away [*herzugeben*] as a tool of the ruling classes. In each epoch, the attempt must be made to reclaim tradition from the conformism that is about to overpower it.[154]

As Werner Hamacher reminds us,[155] the conformism that he identifies here as always threatening to overcome tradition is not simply to be countered through the adoption of a Marxist or proletarian position, since such a position might itself be constructed in accordance with the mythological, monumental, or epic principles of historicist historiography. Hence the need for a historical mode of reading that makes the past *leap*, removing it from its assigned place within a catastrophic tradition as the condition of its renewed historicization. In exhibiting such a leap in the very past they historicize, historians both avert the danger of conformism while at the same time exposing both the past and themselves to a more enigmatic danger—enigmatic, since here danger and rescue, peril and salvation, are no longer opposed to each other, or, better stated, are undecidable.

CATASTROPHIC TRADITIONS

If, as Benjamin writes in *Das Passagen-Werk*, "The image *that is read*, that is to say, the image in the now of knowability, bears to the highest degree the stamp of the *critical, dangerous* moment that underlies all reading,"[156] then to read the image of de Burgos in a Benjaminian sense, that is, to exhibit the leap in which that image *comes* intempestively in our *now*, would require letting de Burgos's image be marked, to the highest degree possible, by the danger that characterizes the moment of her arrival—and ours—in the constellated scene of legibility.

The chance that de Burgos might become legible requires reading her life and above all her works against the grain of her catastrophic tradition and its symbolic protocols of reappropriation and idealized specular identification, which have rendered de Burgos into a privileged vector for the institution of a specifically Puerto Rican mode of *historical ipseity*.

A foreseen event is already present, already presentable, it has already arrived and has been neutralized in its irruption. Wherever there is horizon and where one sees coming from a teleology and from the ideal, eidetic horizon, that is to say, from the seeing or the knowing of an *eidos*, wherever ideality is possible (and there would be no science, no language, no technique, as we well know, nor experience in general, without the production of some ideality), this horizontal ideality, the horizon of this ideality, will have everywhere neutralized in advance the event and thus that which, within *a historicity worthy of this name*, requires the eventuality [*événementialité*] of the event.

—Jacques Derrida

Part II
THE CLOSURE OF HISTORICISM; OR, HISTORY IN DECONSTRUCTION

§13. REPRISE: CATASTROPHIC HISTORICISM, NARCISSISTIC IMAGES, DANGEROUS READINGS

Near the end of Part I, I suggested that the ultimate goal that oriented both the specificity of de Burgos's catastrophic tradition and the sedimented institution of continuity as the grammar of historical time *in general* is the constitution of what I call a *historical ipseity*. The constant reactivation of her catastrophic tradition aims to keep a tight grip on the Burgosian mirror and, above all, to restrict what can be seen in this mirror to those elements that both ratify her sedimented totemization and secure her readers' privileged place in the liturgical procession of her reception. Her totemization may unfold through pious rituals and manifold symbolic genuflections, but the unintended aim of all this display of humility is, in fact, the attainment of mastery over the *dangerous* historicity of her image. This irrepressible desire for ipseity and self-presence has determined both the *arkhē* and the *telos* of de Burgos's tradition.

In this respect, Part I already provides an initial justification of the definition of *historicism* that I advanced in the Introduction, according to which historicism is *the sense-configuration within the history of history that instituted the possibility of historical appropriation by endowing the historian with the power to resurrect, as it were, the past through the composition of historical narratives*. Totemization and catastrophe are two conceptual headings that capture the specific dynamics that presided over the constitution of de Burgos as an object of history in accordance with this revised concept of historicism. Accordingly, de Burgos's reception is historicist not because it grants us access to her history "as it *really* happened." Rather, her reception is historicist because it positions her readers as those to whom de Burgos would have always already "*properly* happened." Historicism here functions at a level that is much more fundamental, indeed foundational, than that of a mere empiricism. Her catastrophic tradition ensures that the task of historicizing de Burgos's image remains firmly ensconced within the metaphysical boundaries of an *appropriative* mode of *correlation* that necessarily neutralizes her historicity. Detained within these idealized scripts of identification, the phenomenality of de Burgos's afterlife can only manifest itself as the intuitive material that fulfills the idealizing intentions sedimented as her catastrophic tradition, whose unstated goal is thus to further sediment its authoritative interpretations of who de Burgos ought to be within Puerto Rican historicity and who her readers ought to become in light of her example as the Puerto Rican totemic figure par excellence. Following a suggestion from Juan Carlos Quintero Herencia, I would argue that her totemic feast is precisely organized to avert the *danger* of having an *eventful* encounter with de Burgos's image, to "fend off the calamity of thinking de Burgos from and with the complexity that pervades her."[1]

But if de Burgos's historicist capture is ultimately an attempt to domesticate her event-like character, then what conditions would have to be met if an eventful encounter with de Burgos's image is to take place? How could we have an experience of de Burgos's historicity in which said historicity becomes "worthy of this name," as Jacques Derrida puts it in the epigraph to this part?[2] Before providing an outline for the work that I carry out in this part, I want to take a moment to explore some of the implications of this question by making explicit two of the assumptions that remained implicit in my attempt to clarify the historicism that has determined de Burgos's reception.

First, I want to make clear that I regard the task of dismantling de Burgos's fetishistic totemization as a *necessary* but not a *sufficient* condition for delimiting her historicist capture. To be more precise, the desedimentation of her catastrophic tradition should be seen as a preliminary task, akin to a *pars destruens*, whose goal is to clear the ground and thus facilitate the chance of an eventful encounter with her image. For this very reason, it cannot take the place of that improbable encounter itself, and pretending that the contrary is the case would amount to presenting a false exit as a felicitous shortcut—that is, it would amount to self-delusion. A different mode of engagement and a thorough reconfiguration of the scene of reading is necessary for the *pars construens* of this exercise to take place.

In Part I (see §10), I argued that Walter Benjamin's concept of the dialectical image could provide a model of sorts, if not a method, for a historical engagement of this constructive type. The reason that I adduced to justify this decision was simple: Benjamin's conception of the image constitutes, to my eyes, the most rigorous attempt within the Western European philosophical milieu to challenge historicism on its own terrain, namely, to contest historicists' monopoly over historical presentation. Before I turn to my second point, I want to synthesize some of the arguments that I made in the previous part of this book to justify the privilege I grant to this concept.

To be sure, critiques of historicism abound both within the Continental philosophical tradition and beyond the boundaries of philosophy: Marxist materialist historiographies; Nietzschean genealogies; Husserlian critical desedimentations; Heideggerian *Seynsgeschichten*, or "histories of beyng"; Foucaultian histories of the present; postcolonial and decolonial alternative histories of modernity—these are some of the (presumably) nonhistoricist attempts to contend with history that have been formulated since the institutionalization of historicism and the pervasive expansion of "historical consciousness" throughout the imperial West and its (post)colonies. That being said, I would argue that Benjamin's concept of the image stands out among these alternatives, especially in the context of providing an alternative historicism: first, because the image's transcendental dimension allows it to function—in a way somewhat analogous to a Kantian schema—as the *form* of historical synthesis that enables the constitution of historical "objects" and historical "subjects" in their post-Copernican *historicity*, that is, as historical phenomena whose reality is itself instituted within the space of a correlation through which they attain mutual differentiation.[3] Second, because this hypertranscendental dimension of the image is, paradoxically, characterized by a radical mode of empiricity, which Benjamin captures with the concept of the image's split indexicality. But since indexicality not only belongs to the image but also determines its own mode of givenness, and since the image, by virtue of its constellation, is nothing other than the singular configuration that arrests and spatializes the temporal continuum so that two times may enter into a relation of absolute proximity and radical difference, it follows that the image itself *must happen* in historical time. As such, the image is the form in which the historian experiences their own historical experience crystallized in a spatial moment of temporal suspension. In other words, since the historians' historicity—that is, their capacity to historicize—is itself a function of the image and not its transcendental condition, what happens when and if an image happens is not only the givenness of a historical object in its post-Copernican phenomenality but the givenness of this phenomenality itself in its radical *a*subjectivity. Benjamin's "theological" title for this *a*subjective phenomenality is the "*weak* messianic force" with which the historian is "endowed."[4] The lexicon of *endowment*, as translation of the German *mitgeben*, lends itself to confusion, since it suggests precisely the opposite state of affairs. Phenomenality is "*weak* messianic" because it is not an inherent principle of the historical subject or an essential power with which historians would always-already be endowed. Rather, historicity is a force that is *lent* to them by the past's historical intentionality, which, in turn, does not have this intentionality as a capacity that would necessarily belong to it in general, but which emerges out of the "the mass of [the past] that has not yet become history at all."[5]

As I have argued in more detail elsewhere, the dialectical image configures historical phenomena through the thoroughgoing entanglement of the transcendental and the empirical or the a priori and the historical,[6] producing a situation in which what is experienced each time through its formal strictures is not simply a historical object but rather the manifestation of the concrete conditions of possibility of historical experience. This goes a long way to explaining the privilege I grant to Benjamin's theory of history vis-à-vis other "theoretical" alternatives. But Benjamin's insistence on the "tradition of the oppressed" and his commitment to a view of history that locates the historicity of historical time in what Werner Hamacher aptly glosses as the "excess of the unactualized, the unfinished, failed, thwarted," also explain the explosive nature of Benjamin's theory of history from an ethico-political perspective.[7] For Benjamin's insistence on historical intentionality as something that emerges with a past that became *impossible*, hence *unactualized*, places us before an aporia that other counterhegemonic approaches to history often sidestep. Indeed, Benjamin's understanding of the "tradition of the oppressed" not only asks us to contend with the desire for mastery that manifests itself whenever historical agents claim to already know *who* the oppressed are and arrogate to themselves the right to speak for them; it also demands that the *tradition* in the "tradition of the oppressed" be rethought and relived from the ground up, as far removed as possible from the schema of continuity and the guaranteed inheritance of filial genealogy.

To be sure, the (quasi/ultra)transcendental aspects of Benjamin's theory of history would appear to be enough to vouch for the nonhistoricist credentials of Benjamin's theory of history—so long as historicism is restricted to its traditional interpretation as a *realism* of historical facts. But could we say the same about Benjamin's dialectical image if, instead of continuing to adhere to this sedimented and indeed catastrophic understanding of historicism, we paid heed to the definition that I laid out previously, according to which the essence of historicism is concerned with securing the transcendental correlation that allows historians to appropriate for themselves the very being of the past? Doesn't Benjamin's insistence on the schema of historical *specularity*, according to which the presentation of the past in its historicity necessarily entails the clarification of the historicity of the present, prove that his concept of the image remains historicist at its core? For isn't the circuit of specularity, that is, the schema and movement through which the present and the past, the self and the other, become what they are through their self-differentiation, precisely the means by which the historicist appropriation of the past obtains? If so, wouldn't this compromise the suitability of Benjamin's image for the twofold exercise to which this book is devoted, namely, to sketch, if not institute, a nonhistoricist concept of historicity that is not divorced but rather finds its bearings in the terrain of historical representation—of historical writing and reading—and to rescue de Burgos's *afterlife* from its historicist capture?

Although a full-blown answer to this question cannot be given at this moment, in the rest of this section I want to rehearse the beginnings of an oblique response to these concerns by examining their core more closely, namely, the claim that the very schema of specularity suffices to reinscribe historicism even at the heart of a theory of history like Benjamin's. This response will be oblique, however, because it will take the form of an attempt to make explicit the second assumption that remained implicit in Part I of this book, which concerns the decisive status of *idealized specularity* in de Burgos's reception.

One possible way of summarizing my argument in the first part of this book is that the historicism that has dominated de Burgos's reception necessitates the reduction of her image and her textuality to a *symbolic mirror*. Her catastrophic tradition treats de Burgos's as a glossy surface that reflects the many ego-ideals that constitute the phantasmatic, normative correlates that determine the idealizing trajectories of different identity scripts within Puerto Rican historicity. And indeed, this is a core aspect of my argument. That being said, it would be very easy to assume that, since the interruption of this historicism requires an interruption of this tradition, and since her historicist reception is bound to her reduction to a mirror, the most expedient way to undo her historicism would be to *shatter* the Burgosian *mirror*. It is this assumption that is not warranted, however seductive it may be. The reasons why this logical leap is unwarranted go to the heart of the question I just posed regarding the seemingly coterminous nature of specularity and historicism.

But why is the interruption of her catastrophic tradition not the same as the shattering of her mirror? I would begin to respond to this question by posing a counterquestion: Is shattering her mirror even possible, let alone desirable? At first sight, it would seem as if the interruption of all forms of specular identification would be the precondition for freeing the image of de Burgos from the narcissistic attachments that have congealed her afterlife into a totemic figure. On this account, the only way to respect her alterity and opacity and indeed to take de Burgos's historicity seriously would be by shattering her mirror. Contrary to this position, I want to argue that, ironically, this desire to break her mirror and free both de Burgos and ourselves from this symbolic circuit of identification might not only be a sort of transcendental illusion—that is, a ruse of an even more deeply entrenched specularity—but also a deeply narcissistic fantasy of sovereignty. Indeed, I would argue that a "speculoclastic" approach that assumes as the condition for undoing the historical illegibility of de Burgos the elimination of any narcissistic moment of self-reflexivity would ultimately amount to a misguided attempt to short-circuit the painstaking work of deconstructing historicism, both in general and in the particular case of de Burgos's reception.[8]

In making this claim, I am following Jacques Derrida, who, in an interview titled "Il n'y pas le narcissisme (Autobiophotographies)" ("There Is No *One* Narcissism (Autobiophotographies)"), writes that "without a movement of narcissistic reappropriation, the relation to the other would be absolutely destroyed, would be destroyed in advance. The relation to the other must—even if it remains asymmetrical, open, without possible reappropriation—trace a movement of reappropriation in its own *image* if love is to be possible, for instance."[9] As is well known, this argument can be traced back to his early groundbreaking engagement with Emmanuel Levinas in "Violence et métaphysique" ("Violence and Metaphysics"), where Derrida famously exposes the limits of Levinas's insistence that the *visage*, or "face," of *autrui*, or, "the other"—whose reputed excess with regards to classic phenomenology Derrida captures with the oxymoronic phrases "the phenomenon of its [the other's] non-phenomenality, the theme of its non-thematizability"—cannot be thought, let alone "experienced," within the dimension of intentional consciousness:

> That I am also essentially *the other of the other*, that I know this—here lies the evidence of a strange symmetry whose trace does not appear anywhere in Levinas's descriptions.

> Without this evidence, I would never desire or respect (or desire to respect) the other in its ethical dissymmetry. This transcendental violence, which does not proceed from an ethical resolution or freedom, from a *certain way* of approaching or overflowing the other, institutes originally the relation between two *finite ipseities*.[10]

Note that Derrida concludes this crucial moment by using the concept of *finite ipseity* to refer to the self and the other in their irreducible "dialectics" or, rather, in their *différance*. At first sight, it might seem that this use of ipseity is irreducible to or cannot be simply mapped onto his later use of this term, which is the sense of ipseity with which this book is primarily concerned. As I indicated in the Introduction (and will explain in more detail later; see §19), Derrida's later engagement with ipseity designates economically the indissociability of mastery, possibility, sameness, and self-referentiality, entangling a thinking of logical modality and ontological sameness with an attempt to disclose the sovereignty implicit in the autopoetic institutionalization of the self itself.[11] That being said, the juxtaposition of these two passages shows to what extent it is possible to read Derrida's more explicitly or overtly political mobilization of the lexicon of ipseity already in his early, apparently more affirmatively phenomenological work. And, not surprisingly, it is the language of psychoanalysis that will serve here to translate one ipseity into another. Indeed, I would argue that Derrida's turn to the language of narcissism at this precise point in his itinerary puts a spin at once *genetic* and *political* on the motif of a "transcendental violence" that constitutes the *origin* of finite ipseity itself, that is, the origin of both the self and the other. As origin, this violence must be located *prior* to the constitution of these ipseities. And yet, this violence cannot be understood in ontic or ontological terms. In other words, this violence is neither an entity nor a ground or essence that would be constituted in itself before and outside the economy that Derrida calls "the relation to the other." To be sure, it is always possible to interpret this originary violence onto-theologically, but for Derrida this would amount to reducing the very historicity of this violence by hypostatizing it as a sort of god who would stand as the alpha and omega of history understood as the economy of violence between finite ipseities. But the fact that the transcendental violence at the origin of "ipseity in general" cannot be located simply *outside* the zone of ipseity nor simply *inside* its purview (as something that an already instituted ipseity *would be able to do* in the mode of an activity or an *ergon*) necessarily raises the question of its *genesis*—and, by extension, raises the question of the genesis of ipseity itself.

This is a question that classic phenomenology—despite Edmund Husserl's genetic turn[12]—has a hard time hearing, because the way phenomenology approaches the "I am" and the living present as the evidence of all evidences and the fact of all facts renders it incapable of inquiring deeply enough into precisely the genesis of this "I am." The following passage from *Formale und Transzendentale Logik*, which Derrida quotes and comments on in "Violence et métaphysique," is, in this respect, telling:

> This "*I am*" is for me, who says this "I" and does so in sound understanding, the intentional originary ground for my world. . . . Whether convenient or inconvenient, and even though it may sound monstrous to me (no doubt out of any given prejudice) it is the originary fact [*Urtatsache*] to which I must hold fast, which I, as a philosopher, may not disregard for a single instant. For children in philosophy, this may be the dark corner haunted by the specters of solipsism and, perhaps, of psychologism, of relativism. The true philosopher, instead of running away, will prefer to fill the dark corner with light.[13]

Husserl's reference to children philosophers here is highly ironic, both on its own but, especially, within the constellation in which I have placed this passage. What characterizes these childish thinkers is the inability to admit the potentially monstrous *Urtatsache* of the "I am," or, even more foundationally, of the "I can," as the *"intentional originary ground for my world,"* which, as Husserl adds, encompasses not just "my world" but *the* world, insofar as no world could be given to me that wouldn't become by that very fact *mine*.[14] Whereas the childish philosopher would shy away from this insight, the true, mature philosopher would take up the task of thoroughly illuminating this dark corner that is the transcendental monad. But in the process of carrying out such illumination the philosopher perhaps runs the risk of being blinded by the light that his own ego has cast on this "I am." In this case, I'd argue that this blindness produces an ironic counterinsight, which could be exposed if we translate Husserlian egology into the Freudian lexicon of narcissism (a gesture that a dogmatic phenomenologist would no doubt find illegitimate). This, I'd argue, is precisely what Derrida is doing in the two passages quoted here, which yields the following insight: Husserl's unwavering commitment to the ego as the "originary fact" of all facts may well entail a commitment to something like a transcendental narcissism that would resemble in content (if not in structure and level of generality) the narcissism that, for Sigmund Freud, is not "a perversion, but the libidinal complement to the egoism of the instinct of self-preservation, a measure of which may justifiably be attributed to every living creature."[15] But this translation has other, more ironic, turns in store. For primary narcissism in psychoanalysis is not just "normal" or "healthy" (given its key biological function as the drive for self-preservation); it also designates, as Jean Laplanche and J. B. Pontalis remind us, "the first narcissism, that of the infant who take themselves as the object of love before choosing external objects. Such a state would correspond to the child's belief in the omnipotence of their thoughts."[16] As a result—and this is where the irony lies—if Husserl's commitment to the "I am" betrays something like a transcendental narcissism, then this phenomenological narcissism could also be taken as a symptom of philosophy's childish belief in the ego's omnipotence. The true, mature philosopher and the childish philosopher would thus exchange positions or become indistinguishable.

At first sight, it would appear that I have strayed from the original point that I wanted to make regarding the role of narcissism in Derrida's thinking concerning the genesis of ipseity. But this Husserlian-Freudian excursus is important to clarify why Derrida, from *Droit de regards* onward, will at times speak of the need for a "new intelligence of narcissism, a new 'patience,' a new passion of narcissism."[17] For the contamination of the Husserlian monad or the transcendental life of the living present with the psychoanalytic lexicon of narcissism introduces the question of *identification* as a crucial feature in the very *genesis* of ipseity itself. Ranjana Khanna makes this point very clearly in passing when she writes that "the very constitution of the ego as *something produced out of narcissism* caused Freud to understand *narcissistic identification* as a reversion to an earlier stage of development."[18] The fact that the ego is not the subject of narcissistic identifications but is itself produced or constituted through narcissism clarifies why the contamination of transcendental ipseity with psychoanalysis enables Derrida to produce a different *transcendental narcissism*, which renders explicit the role of identification and hence of *appropriation* for the constitution of any ipseity that remained implicit in Husserlian monadology. Whereas Derrida's discussion of the transcendental violence at the heart of the self-other dyad in "Violence et métaphysique" does not go beyond simply identifying this violence as the origin of both the self and the other, the metaphorical substitution of this transcendental violence with the lexicon of narcissism allows Derrida to implicitly produce a prehistory of ipseity that locates its genesis in the pre-egological, impulsive, and violent processes of identification through which the self consolidates its imago precisely by "tracing a movement of re-appropriation [of the other] in its own *image*." If this reading is correct, then it follows that narcissism, for Derrida, is another (highly ironic) name for *différance*: Narcissism would thus name the differing deferral in which the self and the other *become-differentiated*. But self and other here no longer designate "two finite ipseities"; rather, self and other are functional rather than substantial concepts that refer to an "originary division" "within" a "single" self. The "first" movement of narcissism—what we may call *arche-narcissism*—does not produce the self and the other except by an "originary" expropriation that deports the self from itself by exposing it to an internal radical alterity. Narcissism "begins" when the self's imago emerges as the wholly other, as the site of an uncanny sameness that resists the self's attempts to make it its own, to appropriate it. The movement of reappropriation—which corresponds to what in psychoanalysis is called "primary narcissism"—is in fact a secondary and derived form that takes place through the self's phantasmatic (re)appropriation of *its own imago*, which enables it to disavow the "wholly other" within and constitute itself as a "finite ipseity." It is only on the basis of this second narcissism that the most common form of narcissism—which Freud called "secondary" and which is the most pathologized—obtains, with ipseity redirecting its outward, objectual libidinal investments inward.

Following Derrida, I take narcissism to be irreducible, constituting an ineliminable condition of the very chance of historicity—both in its historicist-ipseitological determination and in the nonhistoricist, *dangerous* version that this book seeks to elaborate. Rather than conflating narcissism, specularity, and ipseity, this book assumes that narcissistic specularity is not *necessarily* destined to produce a self that has the form of ipseity. This insight is forcefully articulated by Pleshette DeArmitt's work on Derrida's rehabilitation of narcissism, which, according to her, sketches the possibility of what she calls "an ex-appropriating 'self,'" that is, a self whose differential constitution through hetero-auto-reflexivity is not programmed by the form of ipseity.[19]

Moreover, at the risk of proceeding by metonymical contiguity, I would like to suggest that Derrida's use of the term "image" in his discussion of narcissism can help us approach the structural affinities between Derrida's claim regarding the necessity of narcissistic reappropriation and Benjamin's conception of the dialectical or historical image. For Benjamin's concept of the image entails an ultra- or quasi-transcendental schema of dialectical reflexivity that paradoxically divests the historian and its now of historical ipseity. Rather than being the sovereign historio*grapher* who occupies the position of the master of historical narration and is thus able to resurrect at will the past, the Benjaminian historian is *generated* as a historical *reader* by the very past that, paradoxically, has no ontological solidity outside the now in which it may (or may not) be read. Such a reading would also be a self-reading, but a self-reading that "knows" (assuming that speaking in terms of knowledge here makes any sense) that its own historicity could have only been bestowed by the past's leaping movement, through which it took leave of its determined place within the historico-temporal continuum and became an event in its own right, something that befell us, as it were, for the first time.

This attempt to unpack and extend Derrida's inchoate rethinking of narcissism explains why the effort to construct the image of de Burgos does not require that we step outside the narcissistic scene that has turned her image into a privileged possession for all the different itineraries of Puerto Rican identitarian reappropriation and communitarian constitution. For such a stepping outside would relinquish the very terrain of historical reading. On the contrary, the task is *to read what was never written* and indeed what *could not have been written* in that mirror for her catastrophic reception to have consolidated itself as it did.[20] Accepting the *danger* of reflexivity is a precondition for entering into the scene of historical reading, where the chance of becoming-*other*-than-ourselves lies.

But if the essence of historicism lies in the institution of the historian as the *ipse* or the master of history, is a nonhistoricist understanding of historicity possible at all? Is it *possible* to engage in the activity of historical representation—even armed with Benjamin's dialectical image—without acceding to the mastery of the historian as the subject or, better, the self who *presents* the past? If, as Jacques Derrida suggests in the epigraph to this part, a "historicity *worthy* of this name . . . requires the eventuality [*événementialité*] of the event," and if the event-character or "the essence" of the event necessarily entails a rupture in the very structure of ideality, then how could a history be written or read without the production of some ideality and thus without participating in the neutralization of the event in its very irruption?[21] In other words, and to put it bluntly, can a history be written or read in a way that does not simply domesticate the event-like character of the events that it is historicizing, so that the historicity of its "phenomena" is shown to be "worthy of this name?"

The following sections circle around this question, in whose formulation I discern an abridged articulation of the aporia that underlies the task of a *deconstruction of history*. Answering this question, however, requires that the concept of historicism be clarified in its essence and structure. So long as this analysis has not been given, all the conceptual gestures and theoretical arguments I have made so far in this book will remain marked by an index of provisionality and dubitability, however sound or compelling they may seem. A prior desedimentation of historicism itself is required both to clarify my previous efforts at dismantling de Burgos's catastrophic tradition and to sketch the outlines of the concept of a nonhistoricist historicity, which is the theoretical task that determines this book's horizon.

§14. RECONSTRUCTING THE CONCEPT OF HISTORICISM AS A PROBLEM FOR THOUGHT

This part of the book is precisely devoted to such a desedimentation. As I anticipated in the opening section of the Introduction (see §0), the goal of this exercise is to restore the concept of historicism to the status of what Nahum Chandler calls "a problem for thought" by exposing the limits of the *realist* conception of historicism that continues to determine the meaning and scope of this term in most scholarly debates about the theory of (literary) history. In other words, what the reader will encounter in the following sections is a sustained attempt to challenge the reduction of historicism to a realism and reconstruct a concept of historicism that may be a worthy adversary for philosophical critique. To do so, the following pages will not only attempt to restore the *transcendental* and *poetic* dimensions that are constitutive of this concept but also to shed some light on some of the deep, structural reasons why these dimensions have dropped out of the sedimented concept of historicism that we have inherited. Hence, my task here is not simply to craft a new concept of historicism but, as it were, "to read what was never written" in the concept of historicism that we have inherited.[22] This exercise should produce a different concept of historicism by *transforming* what Gilles Deleuze and Félix Guattari call the "field," "plane," or "ground" in which this concept was initially constructed.[23]

Roughly speaking, the argument of this part of the book unfolds in three different phases. The first phase is the most explicitly committed to the task of carrying out this conceptual reconstruction. At the same time, my efforts at conceptual exposition take a cue from Adi Ophir's critical remarks regarding the limits of Deleuze and Guattari's view of the concept, which "always appears in relation to a problem as its *solution*."[24] Following Ophir, my efforts at conceptual reconstruction take as a point of departure a view of philosophical problems as "something that *happens* to a thinking subject . . . a kind of question that requires thinking, pausing, lingering, and *wandering*."[25]

Fittingly, in the next three paragraphs I will provide an autobiographical account of sorts outlining how the problem of historicism happened to me as a thinker. This event could be dated to the fall of 2012, while I was a DAAD research fellow at Goethe Universität-Frankfurt under the auspices of the late Werner Hamacher. A few months before, I had defended a dissertation prospectus in comparative literature at Emory University in which I assumed that historicism remained a problem for the practice of literary history but not a problem for thought. The abandonment of this belief was brought about by three chance textual encounters that took place during my time at Frankfurt. Accordingly, each of the following paragraphs restages the experience of reading these texts and realizing that the concept of historicism that I had inherited needed to be rethought from the ground up.

The first of these encounters occurred when I stumbled upon a letter that Benjamin wrote in French to Max Horkheimer on February 22, 1940, announcing the "completion" of a draft of his famous *Über den Begriff der Geschichte (On the Concept of History)*.[26] What most caught my attention about this letter is the fact that Benjamin admits that historicism continues to survive and thrive incognito even within the alternative, presumably nonhistoricist concepts of history proposed by himself and his fellow members of the Frankfurt School's first generation. If Benjamin, arguably the thinker who struggled most intensely and earnestly with historicism as a problem, thought that historicism remained alive and well in the work of even his closest colleagues, then how could I be sure that historicism's afterlife did not also cast enough of a shadow on Benjamin's own concept of history to question my own reliance on it as a foundation on which to theorize a nonhistoricist literary history?

This suspicion intensified when I encountered Frank Ankersmit's *Meaning, Truth, and Reference in Historical Representation*, which had just been published that year. Ankersmit's book puts forward what is arguably the most rigorous case for the irreducibility of historicism, which he claims is the only ontology of history that can account for what it is that historians actually do when they write historical narratives.[27] Ankersmit's redefinition of historicism, which is predicated on a deflationary, postmetaphysical (in the Rortyan sense of the term) interpretation of the Humboldtian concept of the *historical idea*, forced me not only to revise my understanding of historicism as a realism and admit its transcendental-idealist dimension but also to question whether Benjamin's concept of the historical idea—and, by extension, the dialectical image—is actually nonhistoricist.

Finally, reading Hamacher's "Über einige Unterschiede zwischen der Geschichte literarischer und der Geschichte phänomenaler Ereignisse" ("On Some Differences between the History of Literary and the History of Phenomenal Events")—a short but decisive talk delivered in 1985 but which remained untranslated into English until very recently[28]—allowed me to see how Ankersmit's transformative work on historicism, and especially his interpretation of the historicist idea, could be understood and located within a deconstructive approach to the history of Western metaphysics, which compelled me to adopt a more genealogical approach to the question of historicism's essence and concept. More specifically, Hamacher's essay helped me bring into focus the crucial role that Aristotle's institution of tragic plots as organic totalities in the *Poetics* had in the constitution of historicism as a historico-metaphysical formation.

After retracing the process through which historicism became a problem for my thinking and restoring historicism to its constitutive transcendental cosmopoetics, I will conclude Part II of this book with two sections devoted to sketching out a *nonhistoricist concept of historicity*. In §18, "The Closure of Historicism," I rely on Derrida's concept of closure, and on his general historico-structural approach to Western metaphysics, in order to undertake a preliminary attempt at a solicitation of the historicist formation, after its restoration as a transcendental-narratological form of appropriative correlationism. The task of this section is to provide an outline of the broader task of a *deconstruction of history*, whose first step requires drawing a *closure* around the historicist formation by demonstrating, as rigorously as possible, how historicism rearticulates and reinscribes the ultratranscendental strictures of Western onto-theology and of the metaphysics of presence. The goal of this section is to make the case that, *pace* Derrida, the old name of history may yet mean something other than "knowledge and mastery."[29] Finally, in §19, "Endangering Ipseity; or, Another Historicity," I take a further step toward this *deconstruction of history* by outlining some of the modal intuitions that, I claim, must be elaborated if *another* concept of *historicity*, one that would no longer be entirely dominated by historicism, is to be articulated. If historicism is now understood as the ontology of history that instituted the figure of the historian as the *ipse* or the "self itself" who, as sovereign history-teller, lords over historical being, this section argues that Benjamin's motif of danger holds one of the keys to displacing the figure of the historian from its unassailable transcendentality. In other words, my claim is that Benjamin's notion of danger *endangers ipseity*, compromising the desire for sovereignty that constitutes the dissimulated origin and end of the institution of historicism. Benjamin's notion of danger contravenes the logical space within which history was able to both constitute itself into a "science" (in the broader sense of *Wissenschaft*) and secure its institutionalization as an academic discipline. The constitution of this logical space not only required the absolute decidability of the possible against the impossible as well as the former's indubitable privilege over the latter; it also required the institution of a network of arch-transcendental associations that renders possibility indissociable from selfhood, sameness, and sovereignty. Thinking historical knowledge as intrinsically bound to an experience affectively modalized by what Benjamin calls "danger" transforms the very historicity of history, which has been determined, since the advent of modern historicism, by the metaphysics that attained closure through the institution of ipseity as the *form of being itself*.

§15. THE AFTERLIFE OF HISTORICISM

On February 22, 1940, Walter Benjamin wrote a letter (in French) to Marx Horkheimer that, among other things, includes the first mention in his correspondence of his famous theses on history:

> I have just finished a certain number of theses on the concept of history. These theses are linked, on the one hand, to the views sketched out in the first part of the Fuchs essay; on the other hand, they should serve as the theoretical armature for the second essay on Baudelaire. They constitute a first attempt to fix an aspect of history that should establish an irremediable split between our point of view and the survival of positivism which, in my opinion, so deeply delimits even those concepts of History that, in themselves, are closest and most familiar to us.[30]

Note that Benjamin assigns to his theses on history a *critical* function that is in line with the traditional understanding of the Kantian sense of *critique* as the drawing of a negative boundary or limit. Indeed, the situation that Benjamin describes here recalls the classic Kantian image of reason overstepping the boundaries of experience, except that in this case the overstepping is done by positivism's survival, which continues to delimit from within even those presumably nonhistoricist or nonpositivist historical concepts crafted by Benjamin and his collaborators in the first generation of Frankfurt School critical theory. The critical task of the text that was published posthumously under the title *Über den Begriff der Geschichte (On the Concept of History)* is thus to articulate conceptually an "aspect of history" that is so devoid of positivism that its delimitation would at the same time draw a firm boundary around those aspects of the Frankfurt School's conception of history that remain informed by unexamined historicist sedimentations. Moreover, since, as any reader of Benjamin's theses knows, this "aspect of history" that is *toto cælo* dissociated from positivism coincides with the concept of the image, it stands to reason that Benjamin seems to believe that the *critical* success of his theses should have ushered in a situation in which historicism-cum-positivism has been finally overcome. To the extent that scholars and nonscholars alike continue to believe that the historicist-positivist account of historical reality coincides with the ontology of history, historicism may remain a pragmatic problem. But in the wake of Benjamin's articulation of the concept of the image, historicism should no longer be alive as a *philosophical* problem. After articulating the (post-)Copernican turn in historical intuition and disclosing the sense of historical phenomenality as necessarily irreducible to the status of a *realistically* conceived *positive* fact, the untenability of historicism-cum-positivism should be self-evident.

Still, as the reader surely noticed, it is telling that Benjamin here does not speak of historicism per se but of positivism. What should we make of this crucial detail? Doesn't it prove that Benjamin was also sleepwalking on the compacted grounds of the sedimented *realist* conception of historicism? And if so, then shouldn't this lead us to reconsider the utility of his concept of the image? For if we have good reasons to assume that the reduction of historicism not just to positivism but to any sort of *realism* is unwarranted, and if, as a quick glance at the actual text of the theses would show, Benjamin holds historicism and positivism to be coterminous, then shouldn't we question Benjamin's belief in the capacity of his concept of the image to draw a critical cordon sanitaire around historicism? Even more pressing in the context of this quasi-autobiographical sketch is the question regarding how reading this letter forced me to realize that these two concepts need to be dissociated. Wouldn't Benjamin's letter in fact block the way to this realization?

Notwithstanding the pertinence of these questions, I must say that what really struck me about this letter and brought me closer to becoming aware of historicism as a *problem* for thought was not Benjamin's insistence on conflating positivism with historicism but Benjamin's curious use of the term *survival* (*survivances* in the French original) to describe historicism's uncritical sedimentation. For, as readers familiar with Benjamin surely know, *survival* is not just any word in Benjamin's conceptual lexicon. Indeed, Benjamin's talk of historicism or positivism's *survivance* invites reading this passage as both a translation of Benjamin's own historical reinterpretation of the concept of life—which finds expression throughout his corpus in his idiosyncratic usage of terms such as *Fortleben* ("living on"), *Nachleben* ("afterlife"), and *Überleben* ("survival")[31]— and an application of this concept to the *historical life of historicism itself*. We can clarify what would be at stake in such a reading if we bring to bear on this letter Benjamin's insistence, in his celebrated 1923 essay "Die Aufgabe des Übersetzers" ("The Task of the Translator"), that "the thought of the life and the living on [*der Gedanke vom Leben und Fortleben*] of works of arts is to be grasped in a wholly unmetaphorical objectivity [*Sachlichkeit*],"[32] alongside his lapidary claim in the 1937 Fuchs essay that "historical materialism grasps historical understanding as an afterlife [*Nachleben*] of what is to be understood [*des Verstandenen*], whose pulse can be traced in the present."[33] If, for Benjamin, historicism has an afterlife, and if tracking this afterlife can itself be interpreted as the result of the deployment of the mode of historical understanding characteristic of Benjamin's sui generis approach to historical materialism, then it follows that Benjamin remains somewhat *alive* to the question of historicism as a *historico-philosophical* problem, even as he also uncritically inherited the sedimented concept of historicism as a positivism.

If Benjamin saw his theses as an attempt *to understand the afterlife of historicism*, then my own attempt to follow Benjamin's steps should not be exempt from this historical injunction. Coming to terms with this realization explains how this rather minor document in Benjamin's corpus forced me to shift my own understanding of the task of critiquing historicism. Rather than resting on the critical laurels earned by figures like Benjamin or Derrida (or Heidegger, de Man, or Foucault, to name just a few) through their engagement with historicism, a critique of historicism needed to take the form of a *genealogy* that would track the mutations of historicism's afterlife in the present. The theoretical critique of historicism must therefore give way to a historico-philosophical attempt to intercept the signal of historicism's afterlife in our now, to trace its pulse in our own present. As Benjamin claims in a memorable passage from the sixth thesis, "in each epoch the attempt must be made to reclaim the tradition from the conformism that is about to overpower it."[34] Benjamin's injunction regarding the need to rescue tradition from conformism—which is indeed another name for what he elsewhere calls *catastrophe*—is nowhere more binding than when the tradition in question is precisely the tradition of tradition, that is, the tradition of history itself, understood prior to any separation between *res gestæ* and *rerum gestarum*, historical deeds and historical representation or narration. Benjamin's own sleepwalking iteration of the positivist definition of historicism attests to the depths of the conformism to which the philosophy or the theory of history has fallen and thus gives us a measure of the difficulty involved in this genealogical endeavor.

Thus, my own attempt to articulate a nonhistoricist literary history required first of all tracking the survival of historicism *today* by rereading its own genesis and development as a historical life form that endures in the present. This explains the semantic undecidability of the *after* in the phrase "literary history *after* historicism": On the one hand, it anticipates the chance of historicism's closure, the delimitation of its unbridled claim to saturate and determine the entire field of the historical. On the other hand, it points to the more immediate task of *going after* historicism, as if for the first time.

§16. HISTORICISM, RESTORED: ANKERSMIT'S TRANSLATION OF THE HISTORICAL IDEA

Fortunately, I was lucky enough to embark on this search mission right around the publication in 2012 of Frank Ankersmit's *Meaning, Truth, and Reference in Historical Representation*. At the risk of sounding immodest, I would say that reading this book woke me up from the proverbial "dogmatic slumber." Although I was familiar with Ankersmit's previous work on history and tropology (where his debt to Hayden White is most clearly legible) and on the historical sublime,[35] my unfamiliarity at that time with his first book, *Narrative Logic: A Semantic Analysis of the Historian's Language* (where he lays out the agenda for his neohistoricist philosophy of history) meant that I was not prepared to encounter a book of his that opens with the following statement:

> There is one basic assumption underlying this entire book: that the historicist account of historical writing, here associated primarily with the writings of Leopold von Ranke and Wilhelm von Humboldt, is basically correct. . . . Ranke and Humboldt's historicism was formulated in the idealist and romanticist idiom of the 1820s and 1830s, which can no longer satisfy us in the second decade of the twenty-first century. Their argument therefore needs to be translated into more contemporary terms. Doing this is a major part of my project in this book.[36]

A thorough, critical exposition of Ankersmit's attempt to translate nineteenth-century historicism into twenty-first-century postmetaphysical thought exceeds the purview of this section. Still, in what follows I want to touch on some of the major aspects of Ankersmit's revised account of historicism in order to draw the chiasmus into which I felt pulled after encountering this book.

I speak here of "chiasmus," that is, of the figure of a crossing, as a way of conveying the ambivalence that marked my encounter with this text. On the one hand, in decisively cutting the ground from under the ongoing conflation of historicism with positivism while insisting on historicism's vitality and indeed necessity for the theory and practice of historiography, Ankersmit offered me what I was looking for, namely, a different way of approaching historicism's life—and, especially, its contemporary afterlife. Moreover, in restoring the centrality of the concept of the *historical idea* for historicism all the while providing a deflationary translation of this concept with the goal of purging its metaphysical residues, Ankersmit retroactively allowed me to gain a deeper understanding of the strange proximity that Benjamin hints at in the letter to Horkheimer between their own theory of history and historicism. On the other hand, as the passage just quoted makes patently obvious, Ankersmit's trajectory is clearly at odds with mine: Whereas his avowed goal is to show that "no historian can avoid subscribing to historicism,"[37] my goal is precisely the opposite, namely, to trouble the necessary conflation of historicism and the theory and practice of history. Ankersmit's revamped concept of historicism therefore presented a double challenge: It confirmed my suspicion that conventional realist definitions of historicism are largely misguided, and it raised the bar on what would be required to carry out a critique of historicism.

As I mentioned before, the pièce de résistance of Ankersmit's work is his translation of the concept of the historical idea, which is operative in Ranke's theoretical and historiographical work and is explicitly thematized by Humboldt in his crucial essay "Über die Aufgabe der Geschichtschreibers" ("On the Task of the Historiographer"). The deflationary retrieval of this concept is the final nail in the coffin of historical positivism, signaling at once the recuperation of essentialism in the theory of history. For only the historical idea, as Ankersmit argues in the wake of Humboldt, designates "what is unique to or characteristic of" epochs, nations, historical processes, etc.[38] In other words, the site of historical individuation in the scene of historical writing is paradoxically not located on the site of historical *facts* but in their configuration, whose ground and totality is indeed guaranteed by the construction of the historical idea.

But for Ankersmit, the essentialism or idealism that is irreducibly at work in historiography should be understood in postmetaphysical terms, which means that the historical idea needs to be extricated from the historical context of its emergence under the dominance of German idealism and located squarely within the language or the discourse of the historian. Rather than developing a postphenomenological *eidetics of history* that would have required privileging the historian's *consciousness* as the site in which the essence of any historical entity is constituted, Ankersmit's translation of the historical idea positions the idea's presentational power solely within the realm of historical *representation*. In other words, the historical idea is not a transcendental noema constituted by the historian but an immanent feature of the historian's discourse, and, more specifically, it is an immanent function of what makes historical narratives *historical* in the first place. Moreover, the postmetaphysical status of Ankersmit's historical idea is further buttressed by the fact that his account of historical representation is explicitly framed as a continuation of both the linguistic turn in (analytic) philosophy in the wake of the work of W. V. O. Quine and Donald Davidson and the shift in Continental philosophy from epistemology to ontology brought about in the aftermath of Heidegger's awakening of the question of the meaning of being. Of crucial importance for Ankersmit's project is the way these two philosophical strands converged in Richard Rorty's debunking of representationalism, or "the notion of knowledge as accurate representation, made possible by special mental processes, and intelligible through a general theory of representation."[39] For Ankersmit, these philosophers "cleared away all frameworks that had been thought to provide some background allegedly shared by language and reality, in terms of which their epistemological relationship could be defined."[40] In so doing, they also cleared the historico-philosophical ground for a postmetaphysical retrieval of historicism and, especially, of the historical idea as the key concept of a revamped notion of representation that is no longer constrained to "mirroring nature" or reality.

Writing in the aftermath of these tectonic shifts in philosophy, Ankersmit takes up the task of reconstructing how reference, truth, and meaning (in that order)[41] should be understood within the context of a concept of historical representation that is no longer tethered to representationalism. According to Ankersmit, if the benchmark of reference is to be located in the "rigid designation" canonically achieved by proper names,[42] then reference astonishingly plays little to no role in historical representation. For historical representation does not aim to provide an accurate or *true description* of what is represented in it; its concern is rather with "what is presented by a representation," and what representation *presents* cannot be thought on the model of resemblance or correspondence between the representation and what it represents but in terms of the offering to legibility of "an aspect" of that presented thing, for which Ankersmit retrieves the (perhaps Nietzschean?) motif of "style."[43] Given this decoupling of the semantics of historical representation from the paradigm of strict or rigid reference, it is not surprising that Ankersmit also distinguishes the concept of truth at work in historicism from any correspondence, coherentist, or pragmatist theory of truth. What might be more surprising to some readers is the fact that Ankersmit turns to Heidegger's etymological rethinking of truth as *a-lētheia*— that is, as the movement that brings a presence into unconcealment from out of concealment—in order to articulate a concept of truth in accordance with the aspect-disclosive function of historical representation: "Representational truth is a *revelation of reality*. Not language but reality itself ignites here the light of truth, although this self-revelation of reality can be achieved only through representation."[44] Only in the wake of Ankersmit's redefinition of historical reference and truth can we begin to grasp the implications of a point made in passing by Richard Evans in his influential book *In Defense of History* regarding the symptomatic and enduring misinterpretation of Ranke's *wie es eigentlich gewesen*: "This last phrase is perhaps Ranke's most famous, and it has been widely misunderstood. The German phrase which Ranke used—'*wie es eigentlich gewesen*'—is better translated as 'how it essentially was.' By it, Ranke meant that he wanted to penetrate by a kind of *intuitive* understanding to the inner being of the past."[45]

Extricated from the context of German idealism and reinterpreted as a category that gathers together the accounts of reference and truth that constitute the structural components of historical representation, Ankersmit's historical idea creates the conditions for a different understanding of Ranke's *wie es eigentlich gewesen* that no longer reads this phrase as a positivistic rallying cry. As the ontology that alone accounts for the *re-presentation* of the past, historicism does not entail *intuiting* the past "as it really" or "as it actually was" but rather *narrating* it in such a way that an *aspect* of the past is brought into unconcealment by the historian. We are as far away as possible from the proverbial accusations of historicism as a positivism or an empiricism of historical facts.

Ankersmit's transformative restoration of historicism raises difficult questions that cut to the heart of many unexamined assumptions shared by many in the theoretical humanities, in particular about the nonhistoricist bona fides of thinkers of history such as Benjamin himself. For instance, if we assume that this definition of historicism is correct, wouldn't it be the case that Benjamin's concept of *Ursprung*, or *origin*, which he identifies in the *Trauerspiel* as the *idea* of history, is of a piece with historicism?[46] And if Benjamin's dialectical image constitutes something like the afterlife of his theory of historical origin—as major readers of Benjamin such as Hans Heinz Holz and Samuel Weber have suggested[47]—then wouldn't that make the concept of the image also historicist? Might this perhaps have something to do with the reasons why Benjamin suspected that historicism survives incognito in the midst of his own theoretical efforts?

Given the centrality of Benjamin's theory of history for my own efforts to critique historicism, it should be clear by now to the reader just how destabilizing this encounter with Ankersmit's book ultimately was for me. Indeed, his work forced me to either find a way of theorizing the practice of historical representation without relying on historical conceptuality that, like Benjamin's category of the origin, may claim to be nonhistoricist on the basis of an insufficient concept of historicism but are actually historicist through and through or concede to Ankersmit that, indeed, "no historian can avoid subscribing to historicism."[48]

Although I have barely scratched the surface of Ankersmit's challenge to the status quo definition of historicism, I trust that the preceding pages have given the reader enough reasons to grasp why I described this encounter as having the shape of a chiasmus. That being said, as the spatiality of this figure necessarily suggests, this chiasmus is a two-way street, and upon further study, several aspects of Ankersmit's concept of historicism revealed themselves to be ripe for a deconstructive reading—beginning precisely with the ideality that is implicit in his own postmetaphysical retrieval of the historicist motif of the historical idea. For my interest in exploring Derrida's contributions to a rethinking of historicity had already alerted me to a certain deep, intractable antagonism between what Derrida in *Voyous* (*Rogues*) calls a "historicity worthy of this name," which engages necessarily a concept of the event and hence of the im-possible, and the type of teleological fore-seeing that an *idea* or an *eidos* afford.[49] Putting pressure on Ankersmit's idealism seemed therefore a promising way of taking up again the task of a critique of historicism after Ankersmit's own work had forced me to revise or even abandon many of the theoretical premises on which my work was built up to that point.

As I already mentioned, the gist of Ankersmit's whole intervention is to give an update to historicism by translating it philosophically, linguistically, and temporally from the context of its emergence, marked by the dominance of German idealism in its Hegelian variant, into our contemporary philosophical context, which he describes as postmetaphysical, given the privilege he grants to figures like Wittgenstein, Rorty, or even Heidegger. And yet, although the historical idea is for Ankersmit the fundamental conceptual figure or structure of both traditional historicism and of his own neohistoricist variant, the reader of Ankersmit's *Meaning* will struggle to find a discussion in which this concept is explicitly articulated and the precise nature of its postmetaphysical ideality is accounted for in detail. This lacuna, however, seems to be entirely justifiable. For if what Ankersmit calls the historical idea in the wake of its postmetaphysical translation must be situated "in the historian's language about the past. It is not an entelechy determining the temporal development of historical objects but rather the principle structuring the historian's stories of the past. Moreover, we must avoid the assumption that the past itself contains some real counterpart to this structuring principle," then it is perfectly clear why the historical idea does not receive more thorough theoretical treatment.[50] In fact, any such account would be counterproductive, since it would suggest that the idea has some features beside its function as a name for the essence of historical narratives. Another way of putting this is that the account that Ankersmit offers of how historicism understands the referential or representational, meaning, and truth conditions of historical narratives *already constitutes an account of the postmetaphysical historical idea*, since the historical idea is nothing other than a pure categorial title for what structures historical language.

Although in the brief engagement with Ankersmit's thinking of historical truth and reference we examined some of the elements of that structure at a more categorial or formal level, the best place to see the historical idea in action is by turning to the examples that Ankersmit gives of how the historian's stories of the past are structured. Perhaps the best example in all of *Meaning* occurs toward the end of the crucial fifth chapter, devoted to the status of reference in historical representation, where we find the following passage:

> Apparently our universe is not at all like the one the philosophers of the "great chain of being" liked to speculate about or that Leibniz had in mind when he said that the realization of a "full universe" is the token of its perfection. . . . But this *could* have been different. Consider the following thought experiment. Suppose interstellar travel becomes possible in the near future and we then decide to take a trip to some planet circling Sirius. . . . Observe, furthermore, that this universe of Sirians has come into being through the actual realization of all possible Sirians; only this endows their universe with the property of being without gaps. . . . Since this kind of universe, then, closely resembles the universe of *historical writing* (not that of *history itself*, of course!) in that both are full universes (in Leibniz's sense) without gaps between the individuals inhabiting it, it follows that we can expect from Leibniz's variant of modal logic useful insights into the logic of *historical writing*.[51]

In his earlier *Narrative Logic*, Ankersmit provides a longer and more exhaustive elaboration of the idea illustrated is this passage, which he labels "the thesis of the harmonious constitution of the narrativist universe."[52] Ankersmit's use of the language of a *harmonious universe* and, more specifically, his endorsement of Leibniz's version of the rationalist conception of the universe as a *plenum* as opposed to a *vacuum* populated by atoms are indicative of the metaphysical strictures that tacitly inform his version of historicism, if not historicism tout court. Indeed, for Ankersmit the relative autonomy of historical representation vis-à-vis historical reality is ultimately grounded on the ontological discontinuity between the historiographical universe, the world of the *rerum gestarum*, and the universe of historical realities, of the *res gestæ*: Whereas the latter is not a *plenum*, the former is indeed structured as the best of all possible worlds, that is to say, as a world in which harmony has reached such a degree of perfection that even the existence of sin and nonbeing are nonetheless admitted for the sake of "bringing forth a universal harmony of things, thus distinguishing between the light by means of shadows."[53] Within such a universe, all the infinite *possibilities* that determine its totality are always-already *actualized*, a possibility that itself presupposes as a prior ontological *factum* of that universe the *a priori com-possibility* of all of the possible possibilities that make up this cosmos.

But there's more to this passage than initially meets the eye: I'm referring to Ankersmit's *presupposition* that the discourse of the historian, and indeed that of historical textuality itself, is endowed precisely with a power that is analogous to the power of the Leibnizian god, namely, the power of calculating the best possible narratological world. In a passage that occurs much earlier in his book, Ankersmit makes explicit the extent to which historicism necessarily entails a "secularization," in the strict Schmittian sense, of theological frameworks, be they Spinozist or Leibnizian: "Once we locate the historical idea in the historian's discourse, what historicists like Ranke and Humboldt say about the historical idea suddenly falls into place. Yes, in history the focus is on the individual. . . . And, finally, yes, the historian's breath permeates the past as presented by him, in much the same way that the pantheist God is present in His creation."[54] What Carl Schmitt says about "all incisive concepts of the modern theory of the state" also holds for Ankersmit's conception of historicism: They "are secularized theological concepts. Not only according to their historical development, because they were transposed from theology into the theory of [history]—as, for example, the all-powerful god became the omnipotent [historian]—but also in their systematic structure."[55]

The reader can hopefully grasp by now the extent to which Ankersmit's brand of historicism played a key role in the genesis of this project. Only after engaging Ankersmit's work, I came to the full realization that historicism, far from being an empiricist or a positivist theory of history, presupposes a *modal* logic whose function depends upon a *poetics* animated by the metaphysical belief in the power of narrative to constitute a world or a universe of fully com-possible *actual* possibilities. As a matter of fact, it was Ankersmit's passing remark about the importance of Leibniz's "variant of modal logic" for understanding historical narratives that gave me an opening to begin articulating a deconstructive engagement with historicism. If, from the outset, I imagined that a deconstruction of historicism *after* Ankersmit would have to target its particular form of idealism, a careful engagement with *Meaning* made clear that questioning historicism's idealist foreclosure of historicity and the event would require addressing the *cosmo-ontological* poetics of possibility that, according to Ankersmit, constitute the very principle and structure of how the historian *writes*.

It is at this point that Benjamin, again, became urgently needed as a theoretical resource. Despite the idealist sediments that inform his concept of history,

Benjamin's insistence on both *reading* as the activity in which historical knowledge is eminently at stake and *danger* as the precarious *modality*, marked by radical contingency and im-possibility, in which alone historical reading attains its most intense historicity, provides a strikingly lucid anticipated response to Ankersmit. For if historicism boils down to the belief that the poetics of historical *writing* requires that the space of historical narrative be purged of the very dangerous chance of im-possibility in order to become a *plenum* of com-possible actual possibilities and thus serve as a reliable medium for the constitution and transmission of historical knowledge, then Benjamin's insistence on *reading danger* shakes this dogmatic, metaphysical belief to its core. Not only would Benjamin remind the historicist that reading is not a mere accessory to writing, but also, and more importantly, his view that historical reading is only historical when exposed to *danger* allows us to both measure the hold that the metaphysics of ipseity has on historicism and begin to displace its authority. For, on this account, historical narratives themselves would attain their most intense historicity only when they're read against the grain of their supposed cosmo-poetic constitution, that is to say, when they're read dangerously, shown to be incapable of constituting the very totalized *plenum* that Ankersmit needs historical writing *to be*. Perhaps we may now grasp the reason why Benjamin repurposed the last lines from Hugo von Hoffmannstahl's *Der Tor und der Tod* into a motto for his theory of history: "'To read what was never written': the reader who is to be thought of here is the true historian."[56]

§17. HISTORICISM AND ERGONTOLOGY:
HAMACHER'S LITERARY EVENTS

As I mentioned before, the third textual encounter that contributed the most to the reformulation of my initial project was Hamacher's "Über einige Unterschiede zwischen der Geschichte literarischer und der Geschichte phänomenaler Ereignisse" ("On Some Differences between the History of Literary and the History of Phenomenal Events"). It was only after reading this text that a way forward presented itself in the form of the necessity of a deconstructive *genealogy* of historicism. The fact that Hamacher's short conference paper led me to undertake a whole genealogical inquiry into the philosophical prehistory of historicism speaks both to its capaciousness and its rigor.

As its title suggests, Hamacher's essay is largely concerned with distinguishing between *literary* events and *phenomenal* events. In a not at all surprising move, Hamacher begins his exposition by turning to Hegel's conception of history, where he finds the paradigmatic articulation of the type of historicity that characterizes what he calls "phenomenal" events. As a way of getting at the essence of the type of phenomenality that animates Hegel's philosophy of history, Hamacher coins the portmanteau word *ergontology*, which foregrounds the privilege of the *ergon*—the actuality, activity, action, deed, or work—that Hegel identifies as the very existence of *Geist* or spirit in its historical concretization. As Hamacher points out, Hegel's oft-quoted remark about the speculative unity of the *res gestæ* (history as *deeds*) and *rerum gestarum* (history as *narration*) in the German noun *Geschichte* points to the ergontology that determines the very essence of history for Hegel:[57] "The being of spirit is its deed, history is thus nothing other than this active being, and conceptualized history [*begriffene Geschichte*] in turn comprehends being in its activity as exposition [*Auslegung*]."[58] The phenomenal event is the medium in which the unity of historical deed and historical narration is enacted, allowing the subject of history to comprehend itself by comprehending its own past historical appearances, appropriating its own historicity to itself in a recognitive movement.

In a move that could be read as symptomatic of "the linguistic turn," Hamacher's characterization of Hegel's concept of history as ergontological pushes past Hegel's thinking of the phenomenal event in order to identify the ground and possibility of its phenomenality in a particular philosophy of language, which is characterized by "the linguistico-ontological assumption of an undisturbed symmetry between the cognitive and the performative character of linguistic expressions."[59] Although his ultimate claim (in a gesture that recalls Paul de Man's late work on phenomenality and the materiality of history)[60] is that the ontologico-linguistic presupposition that underlies Hegel's thinking is at bottom illegitimate, Hamacher nonetheless shows that this presupposition is entirely justified by the metaphysical strictures of Hegel's thinking, for which the essence of language must be ultimately understood as phenomenality, that is, as the medium for both the *appearance* or the *externalization* of Spirit and for its *recollection* or *interiorization* in historical *Erinnerung*: "If one comprehends the concept of history as radically ergontologically as Hegel does, then there is history only under the presupposition that action and cognition interpenetrate themselves in appearances as the medium of their correspondence and that, through this medium, they can transform themselves into each other and into themselves."[61] The phenomenal event is that *Geschehen* or occurrence whose historicity is determined on the basis of the assumptive logic of ergontology and its postulation of the symmetry and convertibility of cognition and action, of constative and performative language, of nonreferential positings and referential descriptions. The language of phenomenality—for instance, the language of historicist historiography—emerges in Hamacher's essay as the medium in which this convertibility takes place. The realm of manifestation is the exteriority that enables *Spirit* or the subject of history, who must have necessarily become *other* to itself when it acquired substantive determinacy and became concretized in different historical shapes, formations, and institutions, to reconcile itself with its historical alterity by re-cognizing and hence by knowing itself again as the *same* historical ipseity, as the *self-same agent* of *its own* objectification. Although Hamacher doesn't rely on this terminology, it is clear from his description that what he calls *ergontology* implies a conception of possibility understood as *ipseity*, that is, as implying both selfhood and mastery.

As I mentioned earlier, Hamacher's theoretical proposal is informed by the belief in the illegitimacy of the basic onto-logical or onto-linguistic presuppositions that inform Hegel's reduction of language to phenomenality and of phenomenality to the medium of absolute knowledge as the reconciliation of action and cognition. From this perspective, it is not at all difficult to ascertain what is the role that Hamacher ascribes to the concept of the *literary event* and to the notion of "literariness" that such an event presupposes: Both are called upon to interrupt and displace the conception of historical being as consisting of *phenomenal events* that are already preformed in advance in order to either secure the unity of action or cognition or at least prevent any possible discontinuity between performative and constative language from casting an irreversible doubt on the possibility of historical reappropriation, that is, on the constitution of historical ipseity.

What is perhaps less predictable and more compelling is the text that Hamacher chooses as an example of a literary event, namely, the famous scene in Book VIII of the *Odyssey* in which Odysseus breaks into tears twice at the court of King Alkinoös while he listens to the bard Demodokos sing a song of his deeds during the Battle of Troy. Readers familiar with this passage and its reception (especially in philosophy) might already have a sense of the boldness of Hamacher's gesture. For a passage that stages a classic scene of identification and recognition becomes after Hamacher's reading the site of a radical disidentification. According to Hamacher, Homer does not figure an Odysseus who experiences the encounter with his own story as an occasion for

> the reappropriation and internalizing recollection of his life, externalized into an epic—as Hegel would interpret the act of historical self-exposition. Rather, he experi-

ences the narration of his deeds as an enemy attack on his proper person, which was determined to secure the economy of his life and gender. The narration of history is a robbery on the life of those to whom it occurs.[62]

Although Hamacher's notion of a literary event was of crucial importance for the elaboration of the notion of dangerous historicity, the aspect of Hamacher's essay that most shaped the conception of my project appears in the second half, which centers on Aristotle's *Poetics*. Hamacher's goal in these pages is to show that Hegel's phenomenal ergontology and its onto-logical assumption regarding the symmetrical convertibility between the language of action and cognition relies on a powerful, authoritative, and deeply sedimented tradition of philosophical aesthetics that reaches back to the locus classicus of ancient philosophical reflections on historiography, namely, *Poetics* 9, 1451a36–b11:

> According to Aristotle's presentation of his poetics, historiography is not capable of entering into the domain of a theory of actuality. "For the historian and the poet differ," I cite from chapter 9, "in this, that the one speaks of things that have happened [*ta genomena*], but the other of the sort of things that might happen [*ta dunata*]. . . . Poetry speaks more of things that are universal, and history of things that are particular. It is what is universal, the sort of things that a certain sort of person turns out to say or do as a result of what is likely or necessary, that poetry aims for. . . ." And one is free to think of the particular, which holds for historiography, as characterized by the fact that a certain sort of person turns out to say or do certain things neither out of what is likely nor what is necessary: their comportment, as "actual" as it may be, is neither bound to universal laws of nature nor to the average conventions that regulate action. In view of the phenomenal actuality of being, which comes to intuition in poetry, the proposition that "an impossible thing that is believable is preferable to an unbelievable thing that is possible" holds; in contrast, history is the ample field of the actual that cannot find any organic, self-enclosed shape, since the possibilities that are actualized in it have at their disposal no common telos and, for this reason, no theoriz-able [*theoriefähige*] form: hence, the impossible of poetry is ranked higher in the ontological hierarchy than the actual of history, since the former grasps the paradigmatic as it exceeds actuality, whereas the latter, the historical, offers no guarantee that it may be grasped in general, much less be conceptualized.[63]

What is perhaps most striking about Hamacher's characterization of Aristotle's conception of historical *mimesis* is how far we seem to have come from Hegel's phenomenal events and their mediation of historical ergontology. It is well known that Hegel begins his lectures on world history from 1830 by grounding the possibility of a philosophy of world history on the presupposition that "reason governs the world, and that therefore world history is a rational process."[64] Conversely, for Aristotle, the writing of history amounts to a rhapsodic, infinite mimesis of the open and indeterminate field of *ta genomena*, of realities, actualities, or deeds that appear intrinsically incapable of constituting anything like a *world*, since they are essentially deprived of even the *possibility* of ergontology, that is, of being gathered by a logos that might compose a world out of their reality. Perhaps more striking than this contrast is the abyss that opens up between poetry and history, and thus between ergontology and its radical impossibility, as soon as Hamacher brings the famous passage from *Poetics* 1461b10—where Aristotle enjoins the tragedian or poet to choose plausible impossibles over implausible possibles—to bear on Aristotle's crucial distinction between poetry as the mimesis of the possible and history as the representation of the actual or the real. For the fact that something impossible though believable is ontologically privileged over something that actually did happen simply by virtue of being contextualized within the bounds of poetic mimesis points to the absolute power of poetics-cum-ergontology, which is able to integrate even the impossible into the constitution of its organic, self-enclosed shape. The ergontology of poetics is thus not only a *dunatology* but even an *adunatology*. The specific modalization of experience that is at stake in belief can turn even the *adunaton* or the *impossible* into a modality higher in being and closer to the universality of philosophy's eidetic actuality than the *actual realities* of history.

One of the far-reaching consequences of Hamacher's engagement with Aristotle's opposition between history and poetry is that the concepts of the impossible and the possible in Aristotle appear now to be *functional* rather than *substantial* concepts.[65] Although their meaning is generally determined by reference to the metaphorical or semantic core that Aristotle isolates in *Metaphysics* 1020a, where the "primary sense" of the word *dunamis* is defined as "a source of change in something else or as something else,"[66] the source of this becoming-functional of Aristotle's modal concepts lies in the overarching metaphysical commitments that inform his conception of the ontological capacities of the activities within which these modal categories operate. To put it bluntly, the reason why the impossible can be implicitly held by Aristotle to be higher or more in being than the actual is grounded in the specific capabilities that inform poetry as the mimesis of *ta dunata*, "possibilities" or "things that might happen," and that are actualized through the construction of a totalizable series of possibilities in accordance to the law of necessity (*to anangkaion*) or the regularity of likelihood (*to eikos*). At the heart of Aristotle's declaration that "poetry is a more philosophical and more serious thing than history"[67] is not simply the modal distinction between *ta genomena*, "what has happened" or "actualities," and *ta dunata*, or "possibilities." Rather, what grounds and justifies this judgment is the second-order modalization that only obtains in *poetic* (im)possibilities, since only they admit being organized in such a way that their sheer juxtaposition may give rise to a series capable of yielding an organicist totality or a beautiful whole—a totality that is only total and beautifully organized because of the *necessity* or *likelihood* that determines how the different possibilities within the poetic series relate to one another.

The basis for this key argument of Aristotle comes to the fore more explicitly in *Poetics* 8, 1451a20–30, in a passage that Hamacher does not engage explicitly in his text:

> A story is one, not, as some people suppose, if it is about one person, for many—countless many—things are incidental attributes of one person, with no unity taking in some of them. . . . Homer . . . seems to have recognized this beautifully. . . . For in making an *Odyssey*, he did not make it out of all the things that happened to the man, such as being wounded on Parnassus, or pretending to be insane at the calling up of soldiers, things of which none was *necessary* or *likely* to happen because of another thing that happened, but the *Odyssey* is organized around one action of the sort we are speaking of, and similarly also with the *Iliad*.[68]

Notice the reappearance of the modifiers *necessary* or *likely* at the precise moment in which Aristotle is accounting for why Homer is the paradigmatic poet—and by extension the antihistorian. The historian, at this moment in the history of Western metaphysics, remains imagined within philosophy as constitutively deprived of the very poetic power that, ironically, historicism will grant to their narrative representations, that is, the power of constituting the kind of "organic, self-enclosed shape" that a historical narrative must have if it is to present "the phenomenal actuality of being," that is to say, if it is to yield to the demands of ergontology.

I took this somewhat detailed excursus through Hamacher's reading of Aristotle because his engagement with the ontological and modal aspects of the Aristotelian hierarchy between philosophy, poetry, and history not only led me to ask the questions that put me on the path toward formulating the task of a deconstructive genealogy of historicism but also allowed me to situate Ankersmit's historicist modal metaphysics within the broader history of metaphysics. Indeed, Hamacher's essay made clear for me the extent to which Ankersmit's Leibnizian poetics and its commitment to a view of historical narratives as constituting totalized worlds or *plena* is firmly rooted in the soil of Aristotle's *Poetics* and its debasement of history vis-à-vis poetry.

The last pages of Hamacher's essay confirmed even more this intuition by making a link between Aristotle's *Poetics* and a text that Ankersmit himself singles out as one of the major philosophical contributions to the theorization of the historical ideal in nineteenth-century historicism, namely, von Humboldt's "Über die Aufgabe des Geschichtsschreibers" ("On the Task of the Historian"), from which Hamacher quotes the following moment: "Historical presentation, like artistic presentation, is an imitation of nature. The basis of both is the cognition of the true shape, the discovery of the necessary, the separation of the accidental."[69] Hamacher's gloss on this passage centers precisely on the Aristotelian legacy that informs Humboldt's characterization of the task of historical presentation:

> If historiography carries out the "separation of the accidental," then it places itself in the service of the necessary universality of an *eidos* and of an idea, whose "true shape" and whose cognition can only establish themselves at the cost of the denial and the silencing of the contingent and therefore of a non-ontologizable, actual-possibility of human action. The writing of history must become the writing of poetry, history must become nature, so that the intention for cognition and the belief in the autarchy of intentional action can attain a secure ground and consistency, respectively.[70]

To be sure, Hamacher only addresses von Humboldt's historicist concept of the historical idea obliquely. That being said, Hamacher does tease out what is required for the sake of the constitution of any such ideal history, namely, the "separation of the accidental," that is to say, the removal of contingency and impossibility from the field of historical mimesis. For Humboldt, history cannot purge all that may bear the imprint of danger without becoming a mimesis or representation of nature, which means that historical poetics must become like the poetics of poetry. And this can only happen if historical narratives adopt the principles of com-position that a thinker like Aristotle assigns to the writing of poetry at the expense, precisely, of historical writing. What this brief quotation from Humboldt exposes is that the *accidental*, that which bears the eventful aleatoriness and dangerous unforeseeability of chance, remains at the core of historicism as what the latter must exclude from its narrative metaphysics in order to attain its closure. Returning to Hamacher's felicitous portmanteau, we might say that historicism necessitates an *ergontological* account of historical representation. As the term's composition (*ergon* + ontology) suggests, historicist ontology presupposes a view of modality that privileges both the *ergon* and *energeia*, an *effective* entity that is *at work* and its ontological condition of *actuality*, to the point of insisting that, within the boundaries of the historian's narrative universe, not only all possibilities but even impossibilities are compossible, hence, *actualized*. Even more important for the sake of drawing historicism's *closure* is the well-known fact that the constitution of any such harmonious modal universe requires the exclusion of *incompossibilia*, that is, of those possibilities which, though possible per se, are incompatible with one another.[71] This philosophical principle, in turn, presupposes an even more basic exclusion, namely, the necessary subtraction of the *impossible per se*, or what is also known as the *nihil negativum*,[72] from the structure of the narrative cosmos.

In this way, Hamacher's essay allowed me to formulate the basic *historico-metaphysical* hypothesis that informs my redefinition of the concept of historicism: If the historical idea constitutes the essence of historicism, and if that idea necessitates the adoption or even usurpation of the principles of emplotment that Aristotle ascribed to poetics over and against the writing of history—which, for Aristotle, was characterized precisely by its structural inability to yield the mode of necessary-possibility that alone can ensure that a plot constitutes a totalized whole—then the onto-genesis of historicism, its emergence as a sense-formation within the history of Western historiography and metaphysics, could be characterized as the result of a powerful and decisive reversal of the hierarchy that Aristotle established between philosophy, poetry, and history. In other words, historicism came to its own through an inversion of Aristotelianism that paradoxically ratifies the strictures of Aristotelian metaphysics (which is to say, of metaphysics tout court) by *expanding* the very Aristotelian principles of poetic production—in particular, the *telos* of unity and totality as achievable through the selection of serializable "necessary (or likely) possibilities"—into the realm of historical events. History is now higher than poetry and closer to philosophy, since historical representation not only is now informed by the same cosmo-poetics that characterizes poetry for Aristotle, but its necessary-possibilities nonetheless remained marked by an index of actuality, which makes it so that history is like poetry, in that it can constitute a total narrative whose moments are linked necessarily, leaving no gaps between them, but, unlike poetry, its moments or possibilities are intentionally related as being real, *not fictional*, representations.

Although the question of historicism had already become for me a *historical* matter in the wake of my encounter with the letter from Benjamin to Horkheimer discussed earlier, it is only after reading Ankersmit's *Meaning* and Hamacher's short essay that the problem of historicism became a historico-*metaphysical* question. A deconstructive genealogy of historicism requires an inquiry into the history of history for the sake of carrying out a desedimentation of historicism. That historicism remains to this day still mostly known by humanists as a form of positivism or empiricism provides only a preliminary measure of the cognitive and scholarly difficulties that this task faces. This desedimentation entails prying open the history of history in order to *situate* historicism within this historical "field," locating its genesis, identifying its prehistory by delimiting its historical and transcendental conditions of possibility, and marking as rigorously as possible its effects and its afterlife in the wake of its *closure*.

§18. THE CLOSURE OF HISTORICISM

In speaking of "closure," I am taking a cue from Derrida, who distinguishes the terms *clôture* ("closure") and *fin* ("end") in *De la grammatologie* and elsewhere in his corpus in the following way:

> The epoch of the sign is essentially theological. Perhaps it will never *end*. Yet, its historical *closure* is delineated. We must not in the least renounce those concepts which are indispensable to us for making the tradition to which they belong tremble. Inside the closure, through an oblique and always dangerous [*périlleux*] movement that ceaselessly risks falling back again on this side [*en déçà de*] of what it is deconstructing, one must surround the critical concepts with a discourse both prudent and meticulous, mark the conditions, the milieu, and the limits of their efficacy, indicate rigorously their belonging to the machine whose deconstitution they allow and, at the same time, the fault through which one can glimpse, still unnamable, the glimmer of what is beyond-the-closure [*l'outre-clôture*].[73]

The drawing of closures remains agnostic to the adjudication of the ends of an epoch (understood in realist terms as the demarcation of its spatio-temporal limits within historical time); its purpose is instead to provide an account of the historico-ontological process through which any sense-configuration— e.g., a discourse, an epoch, an institution, an idea, etc.—acquired a relatively stable semantic identity or essence and, most importantly, to indicate the cracks in the conceptual walls that enclose and secure that essence. To invoke a formula from Jean Hyppolite that Derrida himself often mobilized in his writings, we might say that the drawing of closures entails a mode of reading that is at once *genetic* and *structural*, attuned to the "internal" historicity of sense-configurations.

But the motif of closure also has a more explicitly "historico-philosophical" dimension, which is even more crucial for my effort to redefine historicism. I'm referring to the fact that the drawing of the closures is also meant to reveal the intimate relation between what enables *sense-configuration*s to have stable meanings and fixed essences and the closure of the history of metaphysics through the determination of *"being as pre-sence."*[74] We might even say that deconstruction entails the belief in the isomorphicity of these two closures, so that wherever the determination of the bounds of the *sense* of any "ontic" configuration are at play at stake is also the redrawing of ontology's closure. Something along those lines is suggested by Derrida toward the end of *La voix et le phénomène* when, addressing some of the structural affinities between Hegel's culmination of the history of Western metaphysics and Husserl's own restoration of metaphysics to its origin as a *prima philosophia*, he writes the following:

> We simply believe in absolute knowledge as the *closure*, if not as the end of history. We believe in it literally. *And that such a closure has taken place.* The history of being as presence, as presence to itself in absolute knowledge, as consciousness (of) itself in the infinity of parousia, this history is closed. The history of presence is closed, for "history" has never meant anything but this: the presentation (*Gegenwärtigung*) of being, the production and gathering of beings within presence, as knowledge and mastery.[75]

Although Derrida explicitly refers to the Hegelian motif of absolute knowledge as the "event" that has brought the history of being to a close, I would argue that he could just as well be speaking of historicism in this passage. Indeed, Ankersmit would hardly disagree with this substitution, since he himself argues that "the historicist notion of the historical idea can be seen as a fusion" of Hegel's notions of *Begriff* ("concept") and *Idee* ("idea"), which suggests that historicism is at bottom nothing but a slightly different form of the Hegelian absolute.[76] But the relation between historicism and the closing of the history of being is even more intimate, their respective closures all the more isomorphic than such a substitution might indicate. For if, according to Derrida, the *history* of being as presence is closed, this situation presupposes that *the essence of history admits something like closure*, or, to put it in a less seemingly tautological way, the closure of the history of metaphysics assumes that the field of history can be idealized or essentialized, that it can yield something like the *eidos* that is proper to it. And such a historical eidos is precisely what historicism achieved through the institution of historical representation as a poietic technology structured by the totalizing semantic power of the historical idea. Reading Ankersmit with an eye to Derrida's own rewriting of Heidegger's *Seinsgeschichte* as the closure of being as presence and Hamacher's concept of ergontology, historicism appears not only as an ontology of history but as the name for a key mutation in the history of metaphysics, namely, the transformation of historical representation into *the* medium of ontology, thanks to which history became *the* spiritual milieu in which being re-presents itself to itself and appropriates to itself its own essence. As a result, to retrace the closure of the history of being requires also retracing *the closure of the history of history*, that is, it entails a genetic or genealogical account of how historical representation became invested with the metaphysical power of mastering the past by reducing its infinity, transforming its enduring absence into the very fertile soil in which a discourse of knowledge, indeed a *Wissenschaft* or a rigorous discipline, would finally be erected.

There is, however, one more aspect of Derrida's thinking of closure that I haven't yet addressed but that is crucial to the overall aims of this task. As a historico-theoretical exercise, the aim of drawing a closure is not only to retrace the internal historicity and the archeo-teleological structuration of any sense-configuration and to correlate this specific closure to the presumably more general closure of metaphysics. As Derrida states in the conclusion to his 1966 essay on Husserl and as he also suggests in the passage from *De la grammatologie* quoted earlier, closures are drawn in order to *reopen* those very sense-configurations and expose them to an *avenir* (a *future* or, better, a "to come") that cannot be anticipated from within their essence, since it entails the advent of possibilities that are not contained within their boundaries.[77] It is for the sake of reopening what is closed that Derrida emphasizes the need to interrogate the "critical concepts" that, as the adjective *critical* suggests, demarcate the boundaries of any sense-configuration by expressing discursively the system of essential predicates that constitutes that formation's ideal identity. For if the success of those "critical concepts" is shown to depend on their capacity to *exclude* those possibilities that do not answer to the *formal* demands of the metaphysics of presence and its privileging of certain values—presence to itself, proximity, constancy—and if, furthermore, these excluded possibilities can be shown to be as important, if not more, for the constitution of a closed sense-configuration than its essential predicates,[78] then it follows that the accidental elements that are outside the boundaries of an essence are, paradoxically, "within" the limits of the sense-configuration in question. This explains why deconstruction cannot give up those "critical concepts" that it appears to denounce as metaphysical. For its operation consists in using the very rigor of these concepts against the limits that they're meant to demarcate for the sake of bringing about an unforeseen *event* at the very heart of an essence. If historicism names a mutation in the history of the metaphysics of presence that signaled the incorporation of the past as the milieu in which being's "sublating [*relévant*] movement of reappropriation" unfolds,[79] then the task of a *deconstruction of history* is not simply to show how and why this is the case but to reopen the field of historical representation, that is, to expose historicism to what is "to come," which may take the form of something other than historicism or of *another* historicism that would no longer be simply and neatly contained within the closure of the metaphysics of presence.

Another way of saying this is that the deconstruction of history must *turn against the historicist machine* the "critical concepts" of *necessary possibility* and *writing* that played such a critical role in the closure of historicism and its overdetermination of the field of the historical in general. This explains why Ankersmit's work is such a crucial reference for such a deconstruction. Indeed, Ankersmit's restorative transformation of historicism lays bare what we might call, in a more Heideggerian idiom, the "onto-theo-logical constitution of historicism" as a key moment within the history of metaphysics.[80] Historicism is an onto-theo-logy because it thinks the ground of historical *beings* in terms of their compossibility, that is, as "*necessary* (hence *actualized*) *possibilities*." And it is a "theo-(cosmo)-logy" because it thinks this *ground*, that is, the ontological determination of historical beings as "necessary possibilities," in view of both historical writing as the totalizing, harmonious *world* within which alone historical beings can be as such and the historiographer, who emerges as the highest historical being, that is, as the secular *god* whose presentative power breathes *life*, that is, being as compossibility, into the past.

Although Heidegger's protocol of interpreting the history of metaphysics or the history of being remains a crucial presupposition for any *deconstruction of history*, the way I go about retracing the closure of historicism does not assume the entirety of Heidegger's trajectory. For instance, rather than insisting at this point on historicism's belonging to metaphysics insofar as it "remains admitted into a difference [*Differenz*] that is as such unthought," I would suggest that drawing the closure of historicism entails inhabiting more intimately, that is, *from the inside*, the sense-configuration delimited by this closure. A way of inhabiting this closure from within is by insisting that historicism cannot attain closure except by excluding from its determination of the very structure of historical writing an entire system of predicates that are part and parcel of what Derrida calls "arche-writing" or "the graphematic in general,"[81] and this will be shown to have radical implications for how we understand both history (*res gestæ/Geschichte*) and, especially, historical *writing* (*rerum gestarum/Historie*).

As a matter of fact, the ambivalence that characterizes Ankersmit's relation to the proper name "Derrida" suggests that he probably had some sense of being on a collision course with deconstruction. On the one hand, Ankersmit predictably joins the chorus of historians dismissing deconstruction, though for reasons that are somewhat sui generis: According to Ankersmit, Derrida's thinking is at bottom a perversion of Quine's linguistic turn, since it leads to "a celebration of the autonomy of language with regard to the world and a welcome exhortation to care no longer about evidence and truth at all. This attitude culminated in Derrida's notorious '*Il n'y pas dehors-texte.*'"[82] On the other hand, Ankersmit manages to extract a "good" (read: domesticated) interpretation of what he claims to be the thought that animates this Derridean formula, which just so happens to be compatible with the onto-cosmo-theological conception of historical textuality that characterizes his own rehabilitated historicism: "Derrida's statement quoted above is, after all, less outrageous than it may seem at first. For he was right in suggesting that textual meaning *defines a world* in a way that the prototypical true statement never could."[83] Despite this ambivalence, or rather because of it, Derrida remains throughout this book Ankersmit's main adversary, as the following passage from the last chapter makes clear:

> We would be well advised to have some notion of where this extratextual reality that we call the past (preceding what we say about it) is primarily to be found, of where it possesses its most obvious and securest anchors—anchors that no present or future Derrida will be able to pull free from the bottom of the sea again, however strong the winds of interpretation may blow.[84]

Sidestepping the issue of where exactly Ankersmit "anchors" the "extratextual past" so that no pesky "present or future Derrida" might ever dislodge it from its solid foundations, I want to bring the reader's attention to the grounds of Ankersmit's antagonism vis-à-vis deconstruction. We are now in a position to see that things couldn't have been otherwise. For historicism cannot attain closure and bring itself forth as a domesticated version of "arche-writing" without repeating what Derrida calls "the properly philosophical interpretation of writing." Historicism entails *reading writing metaphysically*; it constitutes itself by submitting to the telos that informs the system of predicates that philosophy assigns to written traces as their very "essence," namely, the end of *mastering absence* through its ontological incorporation as a "continuous modification of presence."[85] In order for writing to achieve this reduction of absence to a present-absence, written texts must be placed under the strict surveillance of a philosophical reading protocol that prescribes that they should be taken as *lieutenants* of their authors *in absentia*. If philosophy relies on writing as a medium that renders absence into a present-absence by turning the text into the re-presentation of the author's presence, historicism achieves an even more powerful effect of presence by turning the absence of a past that in most cases the historian *never lived through* or *experienced in the flesh* into a presence through its incorporation into that Leibnizian narrative world which is the historian's "creation." Ankersmit's question about where the past is anchored is ultimately rhetorical, for he already knows that it is anchored in the very language of the historians who breathe life into the past whenever they write it down in the form of a cosmo-poetic narrative.

In this context, the phrase "reading danger" can also be read as an economic title for the protocol of *reading writing* that a deconstruction of history requires if it is to draw the closure of the historicism. Such a protocol reckons, to the extent that it is possible, with the consequences of what Derrida calls *iterability*, "this logic that links repetition to alterity."[86] Though Derrida shows convincingly that iterability is a conditio sine qua non of writing, "philosophy" cannot but exclude it from its account of writing's essence because iterability commits us to view writing as structured by an absence "that is not a continuous modification of presence, it's a rupture of presence, the 'death' or the possibility of the 'death' of the addressee inscribed in the structure of the mark."[87] It is at this point—that is, at the site in which, to quote again Derrida, "the value or the 'effect' of *transcendentality* is linked *necessarily* to the possibility of writing and of 'death' thus analyzed"—that it becomes necessary to reckon with a possibility that is on *both* sides of the historicist closure, namely, that "necessary possibility" which marks the place of "my non-presence in general."[88] Unlike the field of the compossible, necessary possibilities that constitute the only historical beings admitted by the historicist historians precisely because they can recognize in these possibilities their own power of presentation and indeed their own presence, the necessary possibility of death, as Heidegger puts it, inhabits the scene of historical writing as "the possibility of the impossible," that is, as a possibility that, "according to its essence, offers no support for being intent upon something [*auf etwas gespannt zu sein*, which could also be rendered as 'for looking forward to something'], for 'picturing' the possible [as] actual and therefore forgetting possibility."[89] This "necessary possibility" is a possibility that interrupts the *ergontological necessitarianism* that we examined earlier by indicating a possibility that is never actual, not even virtual, but that *happens* in the mode of a nonhappening, as the erasure of an erasure, as the radical subtraction that first opens the field of all the possibilities that might be actualized. This possibility is judged as *dangerous* within the historicist closure because it *threatens* the *desire for presence* that animates the historicists' engagement with the past, undoing their own belief in their *power* to relate to the past in an analogous way to how

Jesus related to Lazarus, namely, by ordering it to "come out" from its concealing tomb and step into the unconcealing light of their totalizing narratives. That historicism entails a disavowal of this danger can now be seen as a sign of the lack of "critical" edge of its fundamental concepts, the fact that its otherwise powerful rethinking of reference, truth, representation, and writing is ultimately "destined to ensure the authority and the force of a certain historical discourse"[90] about history, whose closure is just now attaining legibility. For what danger *endangers* is nothing other than the historian's ontological self-understanding as what Derrida calls *ipseity*, a structure of autoconstitution through self-referral that is not reducible to the ego, to consciousness, or subjectivity and that entails as its basic formal structure the indissociability of *power* and *possibility*, of *mastery* and *potentiality*. The necessary possibility that emerges in the impossible experience of death, that is, the possibility of the impossible, ultimately endangers the sovereignty of the historian and of history.

If the "exclusion" of the necessary possibility of the historian's death is what enables the historicist to *appropriate* for themselves the role of the divinity as the "cosmic calculator" of historical narratives, the explicit or thematic inclusion of this necessary possibility within the scene of historiography would force historians to answer to demands that do not stem from the conatological necessity of preserving their own ipseity. These demands rather come from what Geoffrey Bennington calls "justice in general . . . openness to the other as other,"[91] whose exigency, as Derrida puts it in *Force de loi* ("Force of Law"), "demands that one calculate with the incalculable."[92] By reading historical texts as necessarily solicited by an experience of what cannot present itself, the door is open to the chance that *history* may mean something *other* than "the presentation of being, the production and gathering of beings within presence, as *knowledge* and *mastery*.[93]

§19. CODA: ENDANGERING IPSEITY; OR, ANOTHER HISTORICITY

But how could history ever mean something other than the ontology that secures our epistemic hold on the past through its re-presentation? To provide a preliminary answer to this question, I want to make more explicit some of the implicit gestures I have made throughout this book about Benjamin's motif of historical *Gefahr*—"danger" or "peril." My goal in this section is to show that Benjamin's thinking of danger is informed by modal intuitions that can be mobilized in order to articulate a *nonhistoricist* concept of historicity

"Ipseity in General"; or, "The Im-possible"

But before I can turn to Benjamin's mobilization of danger as the modality of nonhistoricist history, some clarification regarding the modal space in which this argument unfolds is required. My interpretation of Benjamin's motif of *danger* as providing a modal concept of historical experience is informed by Derrida's repeated call to rethink "the im-possible" as a limit *modal* concept whose theoretical elaboration would entail "another thinking of the possible (of power, of a masterly and sovereign 'I can,' of *ipseity itself*) and of an im-possible that would not be simply negative."[94] Derrida's emphatic, if not even pleonastic, use of the phrase "ipseity itself" (*l'ipséité même*) is crucial in this passage, for it suggests that this notion gathers the metaphysical values that determine the concept of possibility whose *closure* Derrida seeks to draw by articulating a "thinking of the possible impossible, of the possible *as* impossible, a possible-impossible that is no longer determined by the metaphysical interpretation of possibility or virtuality."[95] As will become clear in what follows, the radicality and uniqueness of Derrida's conception of ipseity is linked to the way it contaminates the *formal* and the *genetic* or the *transcendental* and the *empirical* in such a way that the onto-logical concept of possibility in general cannot be dissociated from the seemingly more narrow notions of power, mastery, and sovereignty.

Ipseity, to be sure, is said in many ways, and though this is certainly not the place for an exhaustive semantic mapping of this term, a foray into this field is nonetheless required to tease out why Derrida's thinking of ipseity is so crucial for the theoretical work that *Catastrophic Historicism* carries out. A somewhat arcane technical term composed of the Latin pronoun *ipse* (meaning *himself, herself*, or *itself*) and the suffix *-ity* (designating a quality or state), the word *ipseity* is perhaps more commonly used today in the field of psychology, where it designates that core element of the psyche that psychopathologists also call "the minimal self," which is often described as the "*pre-reflective, tacit* level of selfhood" and whose "normalcy" is disturbed in the case of schizophrenic disorders.[96] This psychological sense of ipseity, however, is indebted to phenomenology and, more specifically, to French phenomenology, where the theoretical resources of this lexeme have been most intensely developed ever since Jean-Paul Sartre used the word *ipséité* in *L'être et le néant* (*Being and Nothingness*) to refer to the essential, prereflexive *mineness* that characterizes human consciousness prior to the constitution of the ego.[97] To the extent that Sartre's conception of ipseity inherits aspects from the two major strands or styles of phenomenological philosophy—namely, Husserlian and Heideggerian—its importance for understanding Derrida's use of this term cannot be overstated.

As already noted, Sartre relies on the term *ipseity* to designate the nonegological basis of transcendental subjectivity, and this is the more Husserlian, that is, Cartesian, side of his philosophy of selfhood. That said, his thinking of ipseity also tracks closely one of Martin Heidegger's fundamental insights in *Sein und Zeit* (*Being and Time*), namely, the ontological primacy of *possibility* over *actuality*, which holds not only for the being of *Dasein*, understood precisely as *Sein-können* or *being-possible*, but also for the being of the *world*, understood as an ontic-ontological totality or as beings-as-a-whole.[98] For Sartre, the only dimension that can bestow ontological determinacy to both human existence and to the world is the "nothing," which, in turn, is to be understood as a limit "*possibility*," since by definition it cannot be found as a *real* or *actual* item or being *in* the world: "This nothing as possibility that there may be a beyond of the world . . . constitutes, along with the original presence to being, *the circuit of ipseity*."[99] From Sartre on, and to limit ourselves to the Continental milieu, philosophies of ipseity diverge significantly, although they tend to adhere to the styles sedimented in these Husserlian or Heideggerian alternatives. Whereas Emmanuel Levinas,[100] Paul Ricœur,[101] Michel Foucault,[102] Claude Romano,[103] or Dan Zahavi[104] understand ipseity in terms of a notion of selfhood that, because of their insistence on subjectivity or the first-person point of view, appears to be closer to the spirit of Husserlian phenomenology, thinkers like Michel Henry, Jean-Luc Nancy, Giorgio Agamben, or Cathérine Malabou have developed different approaches to ipseity that seem to be closer to the spirit of late Heidegger's thinking of *das Selbe* or "the selfsame,"[105] at least to the extent that being-a-self for these thinkers no longer refers exclusively or even primarily to the human person. Instead, they rely on this category to express the very essence of life as pure autoaffection (Henry),[106] the unique cobelonging that characterizes the singularity of *being itself* and the togetherness of *being-with* (Nancy),[107] the indivisibility of a *forma-di-vita* or "form-of-life" that has not yet been separated into a "natural life/qualified or political life" (Agamben),[108] or the capacity for self-organization and transformation that constitutes the plasticity of organisms (Malabou).[109]

Derrida's thinking of ipseity parts ways with this philosophical configuration on at least two major accounts, which could be characterized, *grosso modo* (and only up to a point), by analogy with the theoretical operations of *formalization* and *deformalization* that Edmund Husserl outlines in the first part of his *Ideen zu einer reinen Phänomenologie und phänomenologischen Philosophie* (*Ideas for a Pure Phenomenology and a Phenomenological Philosophy*).[110] On the one hand, Derrida's work on ipseity brings about a *universalization* of this concept that exceeds the scope of Heidegger's thinking of *das Selbe*, producing a situation in which ipseity becomes an empty onto-logical *form* or a *categorial* title. Indeed, in *Voyous* (*Rogues*), Derrida even speaks of "*ipseity* in general," a phrase that indicates that ipseity has the status of a universal form whose sole content, at this point in his itinerary, is that of "the relation to the self as being in view of itself."[111] Derrida's formalizing gesture in *Voyous* and elsewhere explains why his conception of ipseity initially appears to be so abstract, indeed *formal*, especially when compared to the robustly autoaffective, vitalistic, concrete, or materialist notions of ipseity advanced explicitly or implicitly by many of the thinkers I mentioned earlier. Indeed, the sole content that appears to fill out this form is the *soi-même*, or the "*oneself*," regarded as a pure essence insofar as it is not yet determined by reference to any type of self, be it the ego, the subject, consciousness, or the human person:

> Each time that I say *ipse, metipse* or "*ipseity*," . . . I will also mean the self, the oneself, being properly oneself, indeed being in person (even though the notion of "in person" risks introducing an ambiguity with regard to the semblable, the "oneself" not necessarily or originally having the status of a person, no more than that of an I, of an intentional consciousness, or a supposedly free subject).[112]

On the other hand, what is truly significant about Derrida's engagement with ipseity is the way he *deformalizes* this form by subsuming under this category concrete eidetic singularities that ipso facto *politicize* and *historicize* the total scope of this category in its very universality. Indeed, despite its formality (if not precisely because of it), for Derrida ipseity *in general* cannot be thought without positing the necessary entanglement of *sovereignty* and *potentiality*:

> Each time that I say *ipse, metipse* or "*ipseity*," . . . I will also mean . . . power, potency, sovereignty, or the possibility implied in every "I can," the *pse* of *ipse* (*ipsissimus*) referring always, through a complicated set of relations, as Benveniste shows quite well, to possession, property, and power, to the authority of the lord, of the sovereign, and most often the host (*hospites*), the master of the house or the husband.[113]

In the wake of Derrida's rethinking of ipseity as the entanglement of possibility and sovereign power, talk of political ontology becomes pleonastic or redundant. If the modal category of *possibility* conventionally means that something is thinkable, experienceable, or that it constitutes a possible existence in a possible world, after Derrida's retrieval of ipseity as the form that possibility acquired within the metaphysics of presence, this modal category acquires another essential valence: It now means that any and *all beings* that can be said *to be* must have some modicum of *power*, that is to say, *mastery* or *sovereignty over their innermost possibility*. Ipseity is the form of *self-relation* that constitutes being itself; it is the arch- or ultraontological category that grounds the sameness of *being* and of *being-possible*. But ipseity does so in such a way that the statement that for a being *to be* it must be *possible* necessarily implies at once that for a being to be *possible* it must be *able* to be its *own master*, which yields onto-logy's dissimulated truism in the form of an enthymeme whose unstated premise is that *being is mastery*. Moreover, Derrida's reference to the figure of the lord of the house and the husband suggests that the ontological mastery at stake here encompasses modes of ipseity that range from innocuous, formal-ontological categories such as Husserl's "being-in-itself" (to which necessarily correspond Bernard Bolzano's "truths-in-themselves")[114] to the sociopolitical modes of selfhood that find paradigmatic expression in the phallogocentric figure of the husband as the lord of his wife and children within patriarchy or the master over the slave in the context of chattel subjection. In this way, ipseity entangles, without necessarily collapsing, two systems of metaphysical hierarchies whose institution and consolidation has guaranteed the closure of Western onto-logy from the composition of Parmenides's poem and its privilege of the *to auto* ("the same" or "the self-same") onward: The logical privilege of the possible over the impossible becomes indissociable from the ontological privilege of a masculinized potency and a historically whitened autonomy over a gendered impotency and blackened/bestialized heteronomy at the highest and most formal levels of ontological generality.

A Dangerous Historicity

One of the working hypotheses that structure this book is that the motif of *danger* that Walter Benjamin mobilizes at several key moments in his writings on the theory of history articulates an experience whose modality tracks closely with Derrida's call for a different thinking of the possible *as* im-possible. My claim is that Benjamin's notion of danger endangers ipseity, compromising the desire for sovereignty that constitutes the dissimulated origin and end of the institution of historicism. To put it differently, I argue that Benjamin's notion of danger contravenes the logical space within which history was able to both constitute itself into a "science" (in the broader sense of *Wissenschaft*) and secure its institutionalization as an academic discipline. Thinking historical knowledge as intrinsically bound to an experience affectively modalized by danger transforms the very historicity of history, which has been determined, since the advent of modern historicism, by the metaphysics that attained closure through the institution of ipseity as the *form of being itself*.

Although Benjamin relies on the phrase "a moment of danger" on several occasions in *Über den Begriff der Geschichte* (*On the Concept of History*) to characterize the occurrence of the image,[115] it is perhaps in entry "N3,1" from *Das Passagen-Werk* (*The Arcades Project*)—which contains the meatiest exposition of the concept of the dialectical image, the cornerstone of his theory of history—that Benjamin weaves these aspects together in way that affords a solid entry point to this book's conceptual infrastructures: "The image *that is read*, that is to say, the image in the now of knowability, bears to the highest degree the stamp of the *critical, dangerous* moment that underlies all reading."[116] If we bear in mind that in *Das Passagen-Werk*, Benjamin also identifies the dialectical image with the "historical object" as "constructed in the materialist presentation of history," the *transcendental* stakes of Benjamin's thinking of danger become even clearer.[117] In the wake of Benjamin's sui generis brand of Messianic dialectical materialism, danger emerges as a name for the particular modality of experience in which historical objectivity becomes constituted or constructed in its historicity. In other words, according to Benjamin, danger belongs squarely within the structure of the conditions of possibility of a concept of history that would come *after* historicism.

But what is meant by *danger* here? How should we take Benjamin's claim that historical legibility and reading obtain only on the basis of their dangerousness or endangerment? One of the factors that initially moved me to write this book was the feeling that these questions have not yet been posed adequately, let alone received sufficiently good answers in Benjamin scholarship. Indeed, the more I tarried with Benjamin's provocative but elliptical theoretical fragments on history, the more I came to the realization that what Benjamin designates with the term *danger* remains either misunderstood or, at least, underexamined. For most Benjamin commentators—with the notable exception of the work of readers such as Werner Hamacher or Rebecca Comay[118]—appear to take danger as some sort of negativity that, in a quasi-Hegelian fashion, must be overcome or negated if history is actually to take place, that is to say, if a historical image is to be read effectively.[119] Such interpretations place undue emphasis on moments in which Benjamin appears to suggest that historical knowledge entails the *actual* or *successful* prevention of the dangers that threaten the image of the past. This seems to be what Benjamin is arguing in the following passage, also taken from *Das Passagen-Werk*: "The dialectician cannot look on history as anything other than a constellation of dangers which he is always, as he follows its development in his thought, on the point of averting [*abzuwenden jederzeit auf dem Sprunge ist*]."[120] How does this passage square with Benjamin's claim that the "critical, dangerous moment ... underlies all reading"?[121] These two passages seem to be at odds with each other, if not even contradictory. On the one hand, Benjamin asserts that danger underlies all historical reading; on the other hand, he seems to suggest that the type of thinking or intentionality that constitutes the historian's mode of comportment to the past must be attuned to an affective hypervigilance that is something akin to the subjective correlate to the objective danger that saturates the historical constellation.

The standard readings of Benjamin's theory of history remove this tension or self-contradiction by precisely admitting that, although danger may condition historical legibility, the success of historical reading lies precisely in averting those dangers, so that historical legibility only obtains when the danger has been finally overcome. Conversely, I draw the opposite conclusion from the one I just sketched; namely, I take Benjamin to be committed to the view that danger *can't be avoided* or *averted*, that danger must *survive* as the condition of gaining access to the scene of historical reading. In fact, the passage just quoted already supports this reading. For note that Benjamin does not say that the historian actually succeeds in averting those dangers; much less does he claim that only the effective warding off of those dangers marks the point in which the image would be, as it were, felicitously read. Instead, what Benjamin actually states in this passage is that historians must be at all moments *on the verge* of averting the very dangers that granted them access to the space of history—that is, to the constellation—in the first place. In other words, the type of materialist historiography Benjamin is calling for requires that historians relate to the dangers that lie at the basis of their reading *as if* they were about to deflect or repel them. On this account, what appeared as a contradiction that could be dialectized away through a sequential allegory of sublation becomes the *double bind* that animates Benjamin's theory of history. Historians must be vigilant about and relate antagonistically to historical dangers, but the moment they claim to have vanquished the dangers that underlie their own historical engagement with the past is the moment in which they will have ceased to *read* the past *historically*. Benjamin's thinking of danger signals the transformation of the modal space of historiography, which is now structured by a conception of *history's possibility that coincides with its impossibility*. In Benjamin's wake, historicity, that is, the "weak, Messianic force" of historicization,[122] becomes "transcendentally" *contingent in itself*.

To unpack further this interpretation of danger as the modal category of a nonhistoricist concept of historicity, I want to take as my guide Hamacher's tour de force essay "Jetzt: Benjamin zur historischen Zeit" ("Now: Walter Benjamin on Historical Time"), since Hamacher is one of the few readers of Benjamin who has come closest to capturing what I take to be at stake in Benjamin's thinking of historical legibility as endangered. In "Jetzt," Hamacher pithily conveys the upshot of this motif when he writes that, for Benjamin, "history is possible only in the danger of *not being at all*."[123] Hamacher puts a finer point on this idea when later in that same essay he writes the following:

> But the fact that danger is the index of the singularity, non-arbitrariness, and genuineness of recollection and thus is at the same time the index of the *possible failure* of recollection and history renders impossible understanding danger as a *mere external threat*. On the contrary, danger belongs so much to the *internal* structure of historical knowledge that, in each individual case, it is not only knowledge *in* danger, it must be also knowledge *out of* danger.[124]

Note the subtle irony of Hamacher's gesture in the last sentence of this passage: In deploying the German preposition *aus* or "out of" to intensify the intimacy that historical knowledge entertains with danger, Hamacher seems to suggest that the preposition *in* cannot somehow do justice to this intimacy. Moreover, this passage could be read as making an implicit claim for the necessity of thinking the grounds of the endangered facticity of historical knowledge (its "being-*in*-danger") in its genetic conditions (that is, its "originating-*out-of*-danger"). In other words, historical knowledge is each time *en*dangered because the possibility of its "not being at all" constitutes its origin or source, for lack of better words. In this way, danger becomes not only the name for the nonoriginary "origin" of historical knowledge but also the mode in which alone history and memory can be concretely experienced *in* their "singularity, non-arbitrariness, and genuineness." But if danger designates the chance that history and memory might become impossible, and if danger not only conditions the possibility of historical knowledge but also the actuality of any act of historical cognition, then it follows that *the possibility of experiencing any historical object as such requires that its impossibility also be experienced*. As Hamacher suggests near the end of this essay, the key role that the motif of danger plays in Benjamin's messianic historical materialism entails nothing less than the linking or binding of the possibility of history "to the possibility of its impossibility," which implies a total rewriting of the conditions of possibility of historical objectivity, if not of objectivity in general.[125] In the wake of Benjamin's concept of the image, *danger* emerges as both the *Ur-* and *transmodality* of history, naming both the *ground* of historicity and the very *way* that concrete historical experiences can be had.

But how is it possible for the impossible to be experienced? What would such a dangerous experience require as the conditions of its experience-ability? And, perhaps more basically, what exactly does historical danger *endanger*? Given the overarching role that the notion of a dangerous historicity plays within this book, I want to take a moment to lay the groundwork for a provisional answer to these questions. To do so, a detour through some key places in Immanuel Kant's *Kritik der reinen Vernunft* (*Critique of Pure Reason*) are in order. This step back will allow us to begin to take measure of the transformative distance that separates the "*ultra-*"or "*quasi-*transcendental" weight that *danger* acquires in the wake of Benjamin's theory of the image from the traditional, metaphysical notion of transcendentality that nonetheless constitutes a necessary point of departure not only for grasping the full implications of Benjamin's theory of history but also for the theory and practice of a literary history *after* historicism that *Catastrophic Historicism* seeks to set in motion.[126]

When I stated that Benjamin's work with danger transforms this seemingly quotidian concept into both the *Ur-* and *transmodality* of historical experience, I was implicitly suggesting that the "categories of modality," as Kant elaborates them in the First *Critique*, remain the necessary point of departure for understanding the fundamental role that danger plays within Benjamin's theory of history (especially after Hamacher's reading) and, by extension, in this book. Recall that in the "Postulates of Empirical Thinking in General," Kant lays out the triad of *possibility* (*Möglichkeit*), *actuality* (*Wirklichkeit*), and *necessity* (*Notwendigkeit*) as constituting the system of positive, *logical* (as opposed to *real*) predicates that can be affirmed of an entity in a judgment we could describe as purely formal-ontological. Indeed, one of Kant's main tasks in this section is to show that when we posit that an object could be, that it actually is, or that it must be, we are not making any determinations concerning its ontic constitution—that is to say, we are not adding any *real* content to the concept of the object in question, whose full ontic structure concerns only its *quantity*, *quality*, and its *relations*—but are simply expressing *whether* an object *is* by determining its "relation to the faculty of cognition" and specifying the *how* or the *mode* in which this relation obtains.[127] The latter point is key to understanding how Kant's discovery of synthetic a priori judgments, and the type of transcendental philosophy that emerged through this innovation, transformed the logical space of modal determinations, in the process transforming the "space" of onto-logy itself. For the reference to the faculty of cognition (and therefore to transcendental subjectivity) in the definition of the possible expands the semantic purview of judgments of possibility in such a way that to say that objects are possible no longer simply means to declare them to be *thinkable* without contradiction; it means above all that they're *experienceable*, namely, that "their concepts agree with the formal conditions of experience in general."[128]

This expansion (or restriction, depending on the point of view) of the meaning of possibility implies a concomitant change in what it means for something to be *impossible*, which is now equally submitted to the transcendental operation that transforms any ontological determinations by referring them to the "logical space" of phenomenality and thus to the "I think" whose synthetic power determines the form of experience itself. Accordingly, the impossible after Kant's Copernican turn cannot be simply defined either as what *cannot be* the case in *absolute* terms (which would imply an undue extension of our faculties of cognition beyond the bounds of possible experience) or merely as what cannot be *thought*, especially if by "thought" here we have in mind only the logical principle which states that a concept that contains contradictory properties must be self-canceling *without* referring the concept's self-cancelation to the subject's synthetic and constructive faculties. This is why Kant's definition of the impossible in the "Table of the Nothing" might be misleading. When Kant defines the impossible as an "empty object without concept"[129] and designates it by recourse to the scholastic concept of the *nihil negativum*, one might take him to be implicitly committing himself to the view that what differentiates the impossible from, say, privation (*nihil privativum*) as species of the Nothing is the fact that the former, unlike the latter, lacks conceptual or logical form. This would appear to endorse a strictly epistemological understanding of the impossible akin to a traditional idealist understanding of the impossible as what not even God himself can think. But Kant provides a corrective to this reading in the "Postulates" when he argues that "impossibility rests not on the concept in itself, but on its construction in space, i.e., on the conditions of space and its determinations; but these in turn have their objective reality, i.e., they pertain to possible things, because they contain in themselves *a priori* the form of experience in general."[130] The impossible is, accordingly, not simply the *unthinkable*; it is the *unexperienceable*—what the subject cannot synthesize because it does not agree with "the form of experience in general."

This brief excursus through Kant's thinking of modality might have heightened, rather than lessened, the abstract nature of these remarks thus far. That said, this detour was necessary to lay the groundwork for understanding the pressure that the motif or the theme of a *dangerous historicity*—whose basic feature is a conception of the possibility of historical experience as necessarily entailing its impossibility—puts on the basic presuppositions of transcendental philosophy. More specifically, I trust that the reasons why I wrote that danger is history's *Ur-* and *transmodality* are now clearer. For the prefix *trans-* here serves to mark the way danger pervades and overrides any modal distinctions within the realm of historical phenomena, so that any entity that could be said to be either *actually* or *possibly* historical becomes so *necessarily* only in their *endangered* appearance, that is to say, only if they manifest as an "image in the now of knowability, bearing to the highest degree the imprint of the critical, dangerous moment that underlies all reading."[131] A similar thing could be said for the prefix *Ur-*, which was meant to remark the fact that danger, that is, the *possibility of history's impossibility*, the *chance of its nonbeing*, constitutes both the phenomenality of historicity (i.e., how history *can* appear) and, even more audaciously, the historicity of phenomenality (i.e., how historical danger transforms what it means for phenomena to be *as such* in general).

That being said, such a dangerous, historical experience could only be regarded as nonsensical within the strictures of Kant's transcendental philosophy, if not of philosophy in general. For philosophy remains committed to the necessary separation of the possible from the impossible, a foundational "decision" for the tradition of Western metaphysics ever since the goddess of truth and justice in Parmenides's poem separated the path of being from that of nonbeing,[132] establishing in the process the linguistic conditions for the nominalization of the verbal form of being (*to eon*), without which the philosophical project of ontology could have hardly gotten off the ground.[133] From the perspective of the metaphysical tradition, to say that a historical object or event is only historical if it is historicized *in* and *out of* the impossibility of its historicization can only appear as a sophistic attempt to mix the possible with the impossible in such a way that, if taken seriously, even the principle of noncontradiction would lose its standing. For this principle, as it is clear from its first full textual articulation in Aristotle's *Metaphysics*,[134] presupposes the availability of "the impossible" as a categorematic form. This, in turn, presupposes something like the so-called Parmenidean parricide enacted by the stranger in Plato's *Sophist*, a dialogue within which the possibility of philosophical logic hinges upon admitting the impossible, namely, that nonbeing is, but only in such a way that the very distinction between truth and falsehood—and that also means between being and nonbeing or between the impossible and the possible—is ultimately preserved.[135] Philosophers such as Ludwig Wittgenstein, Jean-François Lyotard, and, more recently, Irad Kimhi have insisted that philosophy cannot avoid taking on the challenge of what Wittgenstein calls "the mystery of negation: Things are not thus, and yet we can say *how* they are *not*,"[136] which Lyotard in turn characterizes as "the faculty of presenting, for the same referent, its sense and the contrary (a negation) of its sense (for the unknown, the sense of the unknown and the known; for being, the sense of being and non-being)."[137] That being said, their solutions to the challenge that nonbeing represents (with the notable exception of some necessarily obscure moments in Lyotard's *Le différend*)[138] double down on philosophy's commitments to ontological *purity* and, indeed, *ipseity* by claiming both that the possible and the impossible (or being and nonbeing) are *not* contaminated at their origin and that a natural hierarchy determines their relationship within the space of philosophical logic, with the result that the impossible or nonbeing *can* and indeed *must* be said, but only as the proverbial shadow of the saying of what truly is, of what is-possible.[139]

We are now able to sketch an answer to the first two of the three questions that I posed earlier, which are deeply interrelated. Because danger names a specific determination or modality of experience whose conditions of possibility enjoin us to posit a contamination of possibility and impossibility at their very "origin" (a possibility that philosophy cannot countenance except under the form of sophistry), its theoretical elaboration requires that we set aside the philosophical, metaphysical, or ontological concept of experience. For this concept constitutes itself precisely through the exclusion of the *chance* experience of the possibility of the impossible, thereby restricting the general field of experience to those experiences that lend themselves more easily to what Friedrich Nietzsche, in the first part of *Jenseits vom Gut und Böse* (*Beyond Good and Evil*)—aptly titled "The Prejudices of Philosophers"—describes as "the fundamental belief of the metaphysician," namely, "the *belief in oppositions of values*."[140] Not surprisingly, in that same passage Nietzsche also mobilizes the motif of *danger* when he speaks of those "philosophers of the future," who will be "philosophers of the dangerous perhaps [*gefährliche Vielleicht*] in every sense."[141] Setting Nietzsche's bombastic tone aside, I want to suggest that his insistence on the necessity of deposing the fundamental belief in the opposition of values could help us begin thinking about the kind of mutation in the history of thinking and in the thinking of history that would be able to receive the radicality of Benjamin's motif of danger without blunting it. Such a thinking would have to be philosophy *otherwise*, if not altogether *otherwise* than philosophical (that is to say, no longer explicitly and consciously committed to the metaphysical project of ontology), if it is to experience the historicization of phenomenality that Benjamin thinks under the banner of danger. For danger can no longer be understood as simply a possibility or an impossibility; it in fact requires the suspension of this very opposition. And this requirement is not the result of misguided postmodern sophistry; on the contrary, it is the very concept of history's possibility that necessarily demands that we abandon the metaphysical belief in the mutual repugnance of the possible and the impossible if we are to place ourselves in a position that might enable us to experience how danger transforms the very form and content of experience.

I take the name *deconstruction* to be one of the possible names (by no means the only one) for this effort to think otherwise than philosophically. Another possible name might be that of "a finite thinking" (*une pensée finie*), to borrow Jean-Luc Nancy's formula, who comes quite near to the motif of *danger* when he writes the following: "From now on, one must keep to this implacable, revolting thought: that finitude is so radical that it is also the opening of this possibility through which sense is self-destroyed. Finitude is sense in its absence, and it is that up to there, up to that point in which, in a decisive instant, the *senseless* makes itself indiscernible from the sense that is missing."[142] Moreover, my references to deconstruction, to finitude, and to the "modality" of the "possibility of the impossible" already point to my debt to Heidegger's radical reorientation of thinking away from the task of traditional ontology in favor of a deeper comprehension of the intrinsic bond between finitude and historicity. To be more specific, Heidegger's remarks near the conclusion to the introduction of *Sein und Zeit* (*Being and Time*) regarding the primacy of possibility over actuality remain a crucial presupposition for this attempt to intensify Benjamin's thinking of danger[143]—especially since the grounds for that primacy of the possible over the actual lie precisely in Heidegger's thinking of finitude, whose authentic or proper "manifestation" entails, as is well known, understanding the possibility of my death as the possibility of an impossibility, that is, as a possibility that is radically outside the reach of any actualization.[144] That being said, it is above all Derrida's own transformative rethinking of possibility and impossibility that has helped me the most to articulate to the fullest extent possible the ways in which Benjamin's thinking of danger not only changes our understanding of historical being but also opens the door to a different rethinking of being as historical. Geoff Bennington has perhaps said it best when he writes that "deconstruction is an affirmative thinking of the 'necessarily-possibly-not' in general as a positive condition of any event whatsoever," wherein what he calls the "necessarily-possibly-not" produces an operation at the heart of the logical space of modality so that "in each case 'possible' is marked by an internal impossibility of achievement."[145] Not unlike Benjamin's danger, the "necessarily-possibly-not" captures deconstruction's commitment to the view that anything that is possible and indeed *actual* is not only necessarily haunted by the fact that its impossibility also somewhat *is* but *also would cease to be possible* if its impossibility didn't remain at play at the very core of its life or existence. The "result" of this could be formulated, as Derrida himself at times does, in terms of a "thinking of the possible impossible, of the possible *as* impossible, a possible-impossible that is no longer determined by the metaphysical interpretation of possibility or virtuality," to which Derrida then adds that this thinking of the possible *as* impossible also engages Nietzsche's thinking of the *dangerous* experience of the *perhaps*, thereby reconfiguring the conditions of eventhood: "The event comes under a *perhaps* that is attuned not to the possible but to the impossible."[146] Not surprisingly, it is perhaps only after Derrida that the metaphysical privileging of the possible over the impossible might be said to be undergoing and explicit and even thematic subversion. The integration of this relative privilege of the impossible over the possible within the structure of what I call *dangerous historicity* intensifies even more its danger, inscribing history's necessarily-possibly-not at the heart of any event worthy of the name.

At this point, I suspect that some readers might be wondering (and rightfully so) what all this discussion about the transcendental or metaphysical conditions of historical experience has to do with any concrete historical experience. Isn't danger always lived as a concrete, embodied experience, not just in quotidian terms but also for Benjamin himself, whose own account of the task of the messianic, historical materialist historian foregrounds at all moments the affective dimension that is required for historical knowledge to occur? Moreover, the question remains as to what or whom does historical danger endanger, as to what should be done with danger. Is danger to be averted or intensified? Or both? And what do *we* gain by thinking history as endangered? To bring this section to a close, I want to address these questions by way of a very targeted close reading of theses 5 and 6 from Benjamin's *Über den Begriff der Geschichte (On the Concept of History)*:

> The true image of the past *flits by*. The past is to be held fast only as an image that just now flashes farewell [*auf Nimmerwiedersehen*] in the moment of its knowability. "Truth will not outrun us"—this phrase from Gottfried Keller points to the exact place in historicism's image of history where historical materialism cuts through it. For it is an irretrievable image of the past that threatens to disappear with every present that did not know itself as intended in it. (The good news that the historian's fleeting pulse brings to the past comes from a mouth that *perhaps* already speaks in a void the moment that it opens itself up.)

> To articulate the past historically does not mean to know it "as it actually has been." It means to appropriate a memory as it flashes in the moment of a danger. Historical materialism is concerned with holding fast to an image of the past as it suddenly presents itself to the historical subject in a moment of danger. The danger threatens so much the existence of tradition as those who receive it. For both it is one and the same: to give themselves away [*herzugeben*] as a tool of the ruling classes. In each epoch, the attempt must be made to reclaim tradition from the conformism that is about to overpower it. Indeed, the Messiah comes not only as redeemer; he comes as the conqueror of the Antichrist. The gift of kindling the sparks of hope in the past is presented only to *the* historian that is steeped in this: that even the dead will not be safe from the enemy if he is victorious. And this enemy has not ceased to be victorious.[147]

These theses should be read in closer proximity to each other than perhaps any other of the theses—and this for two reasons. First, they mark both an inflection point within the linear unfolding of Benjamin's last work by introducing *historicism* as the antagonist of historical materialism, messianically understood. Second, they also introduce (the first tacitly and the second explicitly) the crucial role that motif of "the moment of danger" plays in Benjamin's attempt to draw a critical limit around historicism's hegemony over the very Western idea of history and the task of modern historiography. That being said, it is at this point where I imagine that a more Marxist reader of Benjamin might justifiably argue that my transcendentalizing (some might even say ontologizing) interpretation of Benjamin's motif of danger runs the risk of suppressing the concrete, *materialist* import that Benjamin gives to this motif, which he unequivocally identifies with the threat that both tradition and its inheritors might "give themselves away as a tool of the ruling classes." Isn't all my talk of danger as the possibility of history's impossibility yet another attempt to illegitimately claim Benjamin's "style of thinking" for a "deconstructive hypostasis of ruination," unjustifiably turning Benjamin into yet another so-called postmodern thinker more concerned with contingency than with redemption, with deconstruction rather than "reconstruction," as Hans Heinz Holz suggests?[148] For how could an attention to danger understood as the name for the "originary" contamination of history's possibility and impossibility help us *avert* the danger that history will continue to be appropriated by the ruling class, cast here in politico-theological terms as the very historical embodiment of the Antichrist?

My response to this critical question is not only very simple, but it also has the benefit of showing the insufficiency of its premises—which, moreover, are commonly held even among readers of Benjamin of a more philosophical or even deconstructive stripe. The problem with this line of thinking is that it assumes that Benjamin's theory of history is a methodological manual of sorts whose correct understanding should grant the historian the power to *avert* the danger that tradition might be misappropriated by the ruling classes. To be sure, Benjamin never abandons the (theological or messianic) idea of a Universal History written by a humanity redeemed, and, as the third thesis makes clear, for such a humanity any talk of danger would make no sense. And in thesis 17 A, Benjamin does describe the materialist historian as the one who "grasps a constellation in which his own epoch has entered along with a wholly determined earlier one. Thus, he establishes a concept of the present as 'now-time' in which splinters of the Messianic are scattered."[149] But as Benjamin's use of the language of the scattering of Messianic splinters suggests, the fact remains that *we do not yet live in that redeemed humanity*. Not only has the Messiah not yet arrived, but also, and above all, no amount of political commitment or conscious identification with the "tradition of the oppressed" from our part might allow us to will ourselves into becoming the Messiah. (This is why I take the allegory of the Angel of History to be an illustration of the Angel's constitutive *inability* to act on its "impulse to redeem," to borrow a phrase from Jürgen Habermas's milquetoast, reductionist reading of Benjamin's concept of history.)[150] As a result, no degree of commitment to the class struggle, let alone any amount of moralist self-confidence in our own progressive values, could ever remove us from the *danger* that our attempts to historicize the past *might* ultimately become tools of the Antichristic ruling classes, regardless of how counterhegemonic these histories might claim to be. For, as Benjamin puts it in the brief and crucial "Theologische-politische Fragment" ("Theologico-Politico Fragment"), "Only the Messiah himself completes all historical occurrence, and indeed in the sense that he himself alone redeems, completes, creates the relation of historical occurrence to the Messianic. That is why nothing historical can desire to relate to the Messianic from out of itself."[151]

But there is more at stake here. Not only is it the case that I take Benjamin to be saying that historical danger remains unavoidable (for us) for reasons that follow from the "(a)theological" and "(infra)political" commitments that shape his concept of history, so that ironically the desire to no longer be endangered—that is, the desire not to be reappropriable, not to possibly serve the ruling classes—turns out to contravene the strictures of his theory, rather than be its logical outcome or *telos*. For this desire reveals itself to be complicit with *historicism*, if not to constitute its very essence.

To see this, we should pay closer attention to Benjamin's first mention of the term *Historismus* or *historicism* in the theses, which occurs in thesis 5. Benjamin introduces historicism as a misguided theory of the truth of the historical image, whose error consists in the belief, captured by the phrase of Gottfried Keller, that historical truth "will not outrun us." Although Benjamin doesn't phrase his critique in explicitly modal terms, it is possible to read Benjamin here as arguing that historicism is constituted through the exclusion of the possibility that history might be impossible. For the gist of thesis five makes clear that Benjamin takes the statement that "the truth will not outrun us" as presupposing a view of historical truth as what *can't* outrun us, which in turn assumes that it is *impossible* for historical truth to be precisely impossible. Historicism thus shows itself as a metaphysics (in a Heideggerian or Derridean sense that, admittedly, would be foreign to Benjamin's lexicon) that requires the elimination of the possibility of the historical image's impossibility for the constitution of the structure of historical truth. Benjamin's response to Keller (who, admittedly, is an unlikely choice for historicism's emblematic figure) is precisely that historical truth is only *truly historical* if it *may always outrun us*, and nowhere more so than when we have "grasped" it. Whereas historicism constitutes itself through the exclusion of the *dangerous* chance that "disappearance" belongs to the phenomenality of historical objectivity, for Benjamin the historical image must be thought as appearing into "disappearance," as flashing by in our *now* all the while saying "Farewell!," never to be seen again. And it is only if the possibility of the image's impossibility is kept *open*, it is only if we relate to historical time in such a way that our "now of knowability" is also "a moment of danger," that we could then say that we have taken a step toward the conceptual elaboration of a nonhistoricist idea of history whose practical enactment would constitute a *history after historicism*.

This is why Benjamin's addition to thesis 5 of a parenthetical remark in which the historian appears as a prophet whose "Good News" *may* (the German is, tellingly, *vielleicht*, or *perhaps*) *always* fall into the void, may not have a past that might serve as its objective or intentional correlate, is so crucial. Indeed, this image discloses to what extent the essential structures of historicism remain unexplored, including by Benjamin himself (at least overtly). For if we make explicit what is implicitly said in these two theses, then it becomes clear that the essence of historicism does not lie in its *positivism* or its *empiricism* and that it cannot be captured by repeating ad nauseam Ludwig von Ranke's historicist motto that history should represent the past *wie es eigentlich gewesen*, or "as it actually happened," as Benjamin himself does in the sixth thesis. Rather, what characterizes historicism is the indubitable belief in what I call, following Derrida, a *historical ipseity*. In thesis 5, Benjamin provides an implicit characterization of this ipseity through the figure of Gottfried Keller and his commitment to the view that seizing the past in its truth entails vanquishing or eliminating its fleetingness, transience, contingency—in short, its im-possibility.

Earlier I used the term *ipseity* to characterize philosophy or ontology as necessarily committed to both the presupposition of the pure separability of the possible and the impossible and to their hierarchization, with the impossible being either derived from or, if coeval, then at least parasitic on the possible. Derrida's work on this motif is crucial at this precise point because he remains perhaps the only thinker in the Western tradition to have thematized *ipseity* as a formal structure of modal-ontological self-relation that has profound *political* implications. As Derrida puts it from *Monolinguisme de l'autre* onward, ipseity does not simply mean another name for the self-relation that characterizes the ego or the "I" and is therefore not simply restrictive to conscious or even rational beings or coextensive with subjectivity. Derrida instead approaches ipseity as an ontological form that clarifies the extent to which Western ontology not only posits an equivalence between *to be* and *to be possible* but also understands *possibility* as implicating above all the necessary entanglement of *sovereignty* to *potentiality*. In this respect, for any self *to be possible* means for it *to have the power over its innermost possibilities*.[152] The historicist historian who *relates* to the true image of history as something that, precisely because it is true, cannot escape its grasp may well consciously explain this belief in terms that might resemble an empiricist or positivist account of historical knowledge. But the ground of that *a priori correlation* between the historicist historian and the historicist image is *not* in itself a historical fact but rather a possibility (ipseitologically conceived). What historicism cannot but presuppose as its very core is the faith that the historian already has the *ability to historicize*, already therefore is in possession of their *historicity*, regardless of whatever may happen in the actual scene of historical representation. This is why they believe that historical truth will never outrun them. But by the same token, this is why only if we understand *danger* as involving a crisis of nothing less than historical ipseity, only if we understand historicity as endangered, might we be able to "break through" historicism. Only then could we understand the risks that we would have incurred if we were to have been given "the gift of kindling the sparks of hope in the past."

Part III
READING NOW: THE CATASTROPHIC MODERNITY OF JULIA DE BURGOS

"As for the present," writes Walter Muschg, "it may be said that, in its essential works [*Arbeiten*], literary history is almost exclusively focused on monographs. The present generation has almost entirely lost faith in the sense of a comprehensive presentation. Instead, it struggles with figures and problems which it sees mostly as gaps in that epoch of universal histories." It struggles with individuals and problems—this may well be accurate. What is true is that it should struggle above all with works [*Werke*]. Their entire life- and action-sphere—thus their fate, their reception by contemporaries, their translations, their fame—has the same, if not a predominant right to stand alongside the history of their emergence. With this, the work shapes itself in its interiority into a microcosm, or rather, a microeon. For, it is not a matter of presenting written works in the context of their time, rather of bringing to presentation the time that knows them—that is, ours—in the time in which they emerged. With this, literature becomes an organ of history [*ein Organon der Geschichte*] and this—not to make the written [*das Schrifttum*] into the subject matter of history [*Stoffgebiet der Historie*]—is the task of literary history.

—Walter Benjamin

§20. *TIEMPO MUERTO*; OR, A COLONY IN CRISIS: 1930S PUERTO RICO

¿Y Puerto Rico? Mi isla ardiente,
para ti todo ha terminado.
En el yermo de un continente,
Puerto Rico, lúgubremente,
bala como cabro estofado.

And Puerto Rico? My ardent island,
everything's over for you.
In a continent's wasteland,
Puerto Rico, lugubriously,
bleats like a stuffed goat.
  Luis Palés Matos

Thirty years after the United States invaded Puerto Rico and established colonial rule, the archipelago was in disarray. On September 13, 1928, Hurricane San Felipe (also known as Hurricane Okeechobee), one of the strongest tropical storms ever recorded in the North Atlantic, made landfall in Puerto Rico, killing at least three hundred people and destroying the homes of more than a third of the country's population.[1] A year later, stock markets around the globe began experiencing dramatic losses in a series of crashes that reached a peak on October 29 with the collapse of the New York Stock Exchange, which became the emblematic event that marked the onset of the Great Depression. The people of Puerto Rico were thus forced to face the worst crisis of the modern capitalist system while they struggled to recover from the worst "natural" disaster the country had faced since Hurricane San Ciriaco decimated the country in 1899 (only a year after the United States invaded the island), killing more than three thousand people and destroying at least 55 percent of all the coffee trees—the island's major commercial crop at the time of the US invasion.[2] To make matters worse, in 1932, another major cyclone, Hurricane San Ciprián, struck the archipelago, causing hundreds of deaths and wiping out 20 percent of the country's gross national income, which was already significantly reduced after San Felipe and the Great Depression.

Perhaps no one captured better the desperation that gripped many in the country than Rafael Hernández's "Lamento Borincano" ("Boricua Lament"), a bolero composed in New York two months after Black Tuesday. Allegorically depicting the trials of the country through the emblematic figure of a *jíbarito*, or countryside peasant, Hernández's bolero paints a depressing scenario in which small farmers and rural workers are unable to sell any of their agricultural products in the town's market square because there is simply no one to buy them. In a telling moment of self-reflexivity and historical sedimentation, the song concludes with a strophe in which the singer, after nodding to the patriotic poetry of the nineteenth-century romantic Puerto Rican author José Gautier Benítez, addresses the island by its Hispanicized Taíno name, *Borinquen*, and asks permission to sing it a song as it lies on its deathbed:

> Borinquen, la tierra del Edén
> la que al cantar el gran Gautier
> llamó la Perla de los Mares.
> Ahora que tú te mueres con tus pesares,
> déjame que te cante yo también.[3]

> Borinquen, the land of Eden,
> which the great Gautier singing
> called the Pearl of the Seas.
> Now that you're dying of sorrow
> let me sing to you as well.

The astounding dissemination of Hernández's bolero across the Américas—which remains to this day a staple of the great Latin American songbook—is not only a testament to the genius of a songwriter who composed more than two thousand songs, dozens of which were runaway commercial successes. If "Lamento Borincano" struck a chord with audiences all over the hemisphere and, especially, in Puerto Rico, this was partly because of the powerful way in which the song captured the grim economic and political situation of a country aptly described by Rexford Tugwell, the last non–Puerto Rican colonial governor appointed by a US president, as "the stricken land."[4] At the same time, another less conspicuous aspect that has contributed to this bolero's afterlife in Puerto Rican culture is hinted at by the singer's deployment of a historical analogy to Gautier, which underscores the sorrowful, mortuary nature of the historical moment that Hernández was forced to witness. If Gautier, writing in the 1870s, during the peak of the emergence of *criollo* national consciousness in the wake of the abolition of slavery, figures the nation as an idealized lover, Hernández, writing in the wake of the Great Depression, is forced to compose a mournful requiem for the nation. "Lamento Borincano" thus constitutes a canonical instance of a peculiar form of *melancholia* that, I would argue, structures the *Boricua* sensorium, even if this sorrowful sense of loss is often buried underneath the boisterousness that characterizes the affective tonality of Puerto Rico's most emblematic cultural formations.

That the situation throughout Puerto Rico circa 1930 was so desperate might come as a surprise to some, especially given that the first three decades of US colonial rule saw a remarkable increase in the archipelago's economic output.[5] Indeed, in the three decades bookended by the two "perfect storms" just described, the island's economy underwent a rapid transformation, yet it is precisely the reach and intensity of this transformation that quite likely made the country more vulnerable to the crisis of global capitalism that was just unfolding. Enabled by the colonial policies of the federal government, American capitalism quickly took the reins of the island's economy, turbocharging the previous efforts of both *criollo*[6] and foreign elites to "modernize" the island throughout the nineteenth century, which led to the establishment of an agrarian capitalist system that successfully placed several Puerto Rican agricultural products—key among which was coffee—in an increasingly global market.[7] The acceleration of the island's conscription into capitalist modernity transformed the island's economic ecosystem: If, in the nineteenth century, the island's economy was largely structured around the *hacienda*—a mode of production characterized by extensive forms of rural proletarianization that progressively forced subsistence farmers or small owners to become *agregados* or "squatters" within the expanding holdings of the *hacendado*, who would grant them access to some land in exchange for their labor during the harvest season[8]—the advent of US colonial rule consolidated the ongoing process of proletarianization of landless Puerto Ricans by both expanding the land footprint of the country's commercial crops (in particular, sugarcane) and intensifying the productivity of both the land and its workers through the transformation of many *haciendas* into heavily industrialized and highly interconnected *plantations*.[9]

At the risk of importing a model that may well need to be revised in light of the historical processes that unfolded in the colonization of the Americas, we might describe the consequences of US colonial economic policy during the first three decades of its occupation of Puerto Rico in terms somewhat analogous to the difference that Karl Marx identifies between the *formal subsumption of labor* and its *real subsumption* under a strictly speaking capitalist mode of production. Whereas the former simply marks the moment in which the capital-form captures previously extant modes of labor, the latter entails "a complete [and a constant, continuous, and repeated] revolution in the mode of production itself, in the productivity of labor and in the relation between capitalist and worker," which is achieved through what Marx calls "the development of the social productive powers of labor" that enables, among other advances, "the *application of science* . . . to the *direct production process*."[10] The enormous expansion of the dynamics of real subsumption in Puerto Rico by the 1930s both intensified the ongoing capture of the landless population through their conscription as wage earners and highly rationalized the process of agricultural production, deepening the crisis that the archipelago faced in the wake of the Great Depression. Perhaps more crucially, the rise of sugarcane "monoculture," combined with the more complex subsumption of labor under the capital-form, also increased the damaging effects that the *temporality* of the agricultural *lifeworld*,[11] dominated by seasonality, had on the lives of workers. The Puerto Rican historians César Ayala and Rafael Bernabe describe this phenomenon succinctly:

> If most rural dwellers had been propertyless before 1898, arrangements that in the past had allowed them some access to land for subsistence purposes now gave way to a starker condition of wage dependence. The situation of wage earners was particularly precarious, since the sugar industry could offer employment only during five or six months of the year.[12]

The phenomenon to which they are alluding here, namely, the time period in which agricultural workers were forced to be idle (usually after the sugarcane or coffee harvest was over), was commonly called *tiempo muerto* ("dead time"). To grasp the significance of this temporal phenomenon beyond its commonsense determination, the Marxian distinction between formal and real subsumption can be of some help. Recall that one of the key features that distinguishes these two modes of the capital-relation for Marx is the fact that, whereas in the capitalist phase of *formal* subsumption, the primary, if not the only, way of increasing surplus value is by *lengthening* the *labor time*, the constant revolution in the mode of production that occurs when labor is *really* subsumed opens up other means for valorization that do not rely on prolonging the time period of work.[13] If, to the "natural" fact that workers in the sugarcane industry could only work for less than six months every year, we add the "economic" fact that the intensive development of the capital-form opens the possibility of decoupling the extraction of surplus value from the lengthening of labor time, and if we then take stock of the fact that the intensification of agrocapitalism's grip on the archipelago's economy made practices of subsistence farming less viable than before, we may begin to understand why the *tiempo muerto* after the *zafra*, or "sugarcane harvest," acquired its grim allegorical valence in 1930s Puerto Rican discourse. *Tiempo muerto* ceased to refer simply to the period of idleness for agricultural workers—which, in other times, would have perhaps been mitigated by subsistence farming—and came to signify an experience in which mortality, taking a shape akin to what Lauren Berlant calls "slow death,"[14] saturated the very time of the lived experience of the working masses.

One of the most powerful documents that attests to the becoming-allegory of "dead time" is an eponymous play written by Manuel Méndez Ballester, one of Puerto Rico's canonical playwrights. Staged for the first time in 1940, Ballester's "tragedy" (though I would argue, following Walter Benjamin, that there are good reasons to designate the play instead as a *Trauerspiel*, or "mourning play")[15] enacts the becoming-allegory of "dead time" as the definitive marker of the temporality that structured the modern capitalist *lifeworld* of the sugarcane plantation in Puerto Rico at the turn of the 1930s. The play's first act begins right around the time in which the *zafra* is about to end. The lives of the main protagonists—a family of five, plus a homeless neighbor who relies on the family's charity and companionship—have been severely affected by the fact that Ignacio, the father and main breadwinner, was not allowed to work during the last weeks of the harvest because he is ill with tuberculosis. With the threat of *tiempo muerto* looming large, their older children, Samuel and Rosa, are forced to postpone their plans and desires in order to earn some money. Nonetheless, at the end of the first act, Ignacio's loss of income directly results in the death of a younger son, who contracts a curable, though deadly, illness. Although, within the economy of the play, this death (which is the third death of a child experienced by this family) is somehow mitigated by the fact that Samuel decides to leave the island to work as a merchant marine and Rosa secures her mother Juana's blessing to marry a close friend of Samuel named Juanito (who is also a merchant sailor), the prospects of a future not ruled by the "dead time" of the sugarcane plantation are quickly shattered. The incident that precipitates the play's tragic climax occurs when Rosa, who becomes a domestic worker for a plantation overseer to support her parents while her brother and her lover are at sea, is raped by her boss, who then takes advantage of her father's vulnerable situation by offering to give him back his job at the sugarcane plantation in exchange for his permission to take Rosa as a concubine. Tragedy ensues after Ignacio, bending the prevailing honor code, accepts the offer, which elicits the ire of his son upon returning from his first voyage at sea. Although he had made enough money to fulfill his promise of buying the family a home near the beach and removing them from the spatiality of the sugarcane plantation, Samuel is so enraged by his father's betrayal that he decides to take justice into his own hands, which results in his death at the hands of his sister's rapist, who is, in turn, killed by her father. In the first version of the play, which was staged in 1940, this cycle of death and violation drives Juana, the mother, to suicide.[16]

Although the play's allegorical structure is clearly determined by the tragic unleashing of this series of deaths, perhaps the most significant moment of the entire work occurs when Samuel, upon being asked by his family to share his experiences at sea, retells a daydream he had one night while on watch duty:

> I remember that one night, I was on guard duty, we crossed a desert islet. Everything there was so quiet . . . so still. . . . And I remembered you and I started to think: How nice if all of us, father, mother, Rosa and Simón, could one day go to the islet and construct a little house, and work the land together, and live in peace, without anybody mistreating us, without anybody oppressing us.[17]

It is not surprising that the utopian *topos* of the desert island imposes itself upon Samuel as the spatial image of refuge and rebirth. After all, as Gilles Deleuze aptly puts it,

> islands are either from before or after humankind. . . . Dreaming of islands—whether with joy or in fear, it doesn't matter—is dreaming of pulling away, of being already separate, far from any continent, of being lost and alone—or it is dreaming of starting from scratch, recreating, beginning anew. . . . It is true that from the deserted island it is not creation but re-creation, not the beginning but a re-beginning that takes place. The deserted island is the origin, but a second origin. From it everything begins anew. . . . The idea of a second origin gives the deserted island its whole meaning, the survival of a sacred place in a world that is slow to re-begin.[18]

The counterforce that animates this utopian dream of rebirth, however, is the historical nightmare that, like destiny, saturates Samuel's present and that of his family: the nightmare produced by their thoroughgoing proletarianization. Precisely because of its utopian charge, this dream is irrigated by an impossible memory, a memory that Samuel couldn't have lived but that would have likely been transmitted to him by his parents, who, throughout the play, briefly entertain feelings of nostalgia for a moment in which their access to land and hence the reproduction of their life was less onerous.[19] If the desert island is the mythopoetic image par excellence of the materiality of rebirth, the house built upon the desert island bears witness to the seductive powers of the *Robinsonade*[20] as an aesthetic ideology that posits that the restoration of *life* to its autopoietic autonomy can only be secured through the attainment and consolidation of what we might call, after Jacques Derrida, *sovereignty-cum-ipseity*.[21]

That the *desire for sovereignty* as a *desire for ipseity* would emerge near the end of Méndez Ballester's play as the sole possible way of overcoming the dead life of *tiempo muerto* should not come as a surprise. After all, Méndez Ballester is here echoing the political discourse of the island's lettered elites, many of whom saw the ascendancy of the sugarcane plantation—and especially the specter of absentee ownership—as just as much a threat to the integrity of the nation as the sheer fact of its colonial status under the United States.

A different permutation of this discourse was also articulated from the emergent sector of Puerto Rican academy, where a new generation of intellectuals, commonly known as the Generación del 30, began to craft a discourse calling for the spiritual renewal of the island's culture. Analogous metaphorics to that of *tiempo muerto* also abound in the magnum opus of this generation, Antonio S. Pedreira's *Insularismo: Ensayos de interpretación puertorriqueña* (*Insularism: Essays on the Interpretation of Puertoricannes*; Madrid, 1934). To bring this brief introductory section to a close, I want to center on one particularly telling inscription of this metaphor, which occurs in the second part of his book, titled "Biología, geografía, alma" ("Biology, Geography, Soul"), more specifically in the third chapter of this second part, "Alarde y expresión" ("Display and Expression"). This chapter corresponds to the third noun in the title of this book's second part, namely, the soul, and accordingly deals not with the "racial" or "geographical" factors that have shaped Puertoricanness but with its spiritual expression, which is mostly examined through the lens of Puerto Rican literature. According to Pedreira, the artistic and literary landscape is bleak, so bleak that even the few extant signs of hope only emphasize the generalized feeling of cultural decadence after three decades of US colonization. Indeed, toward the end of this chapter, Pedreira singles out three poets—all men—who, in other circumstances, would have lead him to harbor some optimism about the possible consolidation of a Puerto Rican soul in an adequate aesthetic form of expression:

> I admire Evaristo Ribera for his stubborn poetic vocation and because he is an admirable example of what artistic conscience can achieve. In a long, recent essay I have tried to clarify the significance of a great Puerto Rican innovator: Luis Lloréns Torres. I have not spared my applause and admiration for another captain of new attitudes, Luis Palés Matos, lonely figure in the path of Puerto Rican Black poetry. With their efforts, these three expressions of our collective personality clear the future of literary art. If instead of a funereal epoch ours was Christmas, we would have the myrrh, the incense, and the gold to offer to the boy.[22]

Note the telling end of this passage—telling not so much for its Christological resonances but for the metaphorical work that those resonances are enlisted to accomplish. For the child here is not Jesus Christ, and Pedreira is not explicitly advocating for an anchoring of literature in Christian devotional practices—indeed, although Pedreira harbors antimodern, anti-American tendencies, his Hispanism doesn't go so far as to advocate for a full-blown return to Catholicism. In other words, the nativity scene that he here alludes to is not that of baby Jesus but of the birth of Puerto Rican literature, emblematized in the figure of a young poet that might be able to till the ground that these three precursors have cleared and reap the spiritual benefits of their labor. But since the times for Pedreira are not of rebirth but of decay, these offerings to the child-poet to come will most likely go to waste, and all sorts of weeds and shrubs will grow back on the ground that these poets have cleared for the definitive growth of a literature that might finally express the collective soul of Puerto Ricans.

Pedreira's lugubrious scene, which would find an echo in Luis Palés Matos's "Preludio en Boricua" ("Boricua Prelude"), would be prophetic, even if things did not turn out quite like he predicted. For, as Juan Manuel Corretjer himself said, by 1937 a poet was finally born to the island (and, indeed, with Llorens Torres, among others, as her patron and supposed lover). Only, it was not a boy; it was a girl, née Constanza Julia Burgos Garcías, better known as Julia de Burgos. And her first poetry volume, *Poema en 20 surcos* (*Poem in 20 Furrows*), would constitute her as the most ambivalent, unexpected, and yet faithful inheritor of the project of cultural and spiritual renewal that Pedreira and his colleagues in the Generación del 30 had called for.

§21. CATASTROPHE AND MODERNITY: JULIA DE BURGOS, THE POET OF (PUERTO RICAN) MODERN LIFE

The totemic traditionalization that has determined the afterlife of de Burgos's image has also had deleterious effects on the critical and historical study of de Burgos's poetry. Perhaps the main literary-historical symptom of this catastrophic tradition is the lack of any sustained *historical reading* of *Poema en 20 surcos*, the first poetry volume that de Burgos published. Although *Poema* contains many of the poems for which de Burgos is most remembered today, and although these poems have been the subject of countless scholarly commentaries, readers of *Poema* have yet to pose, let alone offer answers to, basic questions such as the status of the structure of the volume—which is ironic given that de Burgos herself chose the singular noun *Poema* for the title, thereby suggesting that the twenty "furrows" that compose it make up a unity, a single-plural poem. But perhaps the most striking gap in the critical reception of *Poema* lies in the laxity with which this collection has been historicized. My goal in this final part of *Catastrophic Historicism* is to take a step forward in the direction of a historical, i.e., *dangerous*, reading of de Burgos's image by addressing this lacuna in her reception.

To lend some specificity to this claim, I would like to return briefly to Gelpí's thesis regarding de Burgos's nomadic subjectivity, which I examined in Part I. This choice is pertinent for at least three main reasons: first, because Gelpí anchors his reconstruction of de Burgos's nomadism in some of the poems of *Poema* that will be discussed in what follows; second, because his essay remains the most influential intervention in the scholarly study of de Burgos; and third, because the historical argument that underlies his interpretation is exemplary of the laxity that I am trying to diagnose and displace.

Still, in light of the historical basis of Gelpí's interpretation of de Burgos as a nomadic subject, my claim about this essay may appear prima facie baseless. Gelpí's construction of de Burgos as a "nomadic subject" necessarily requires the concomitant construction of the territory that her "lines of flight" deterritorialize, namely, the classist, patriarchal, and racist ethnonationalist scripts of cultural identity that had already consolidated their hold on the dominant interpretation of Puerto Rican historicity by the time of *Poema*'s publication in the late 1930s—and of which Pedreira remains one of its major proponents, if not architects.[23] Still, the historical significance of de Burgos's nomadism does not simply lie in the fact that her nomadic subjectivity mounted one of the first open challenges to what we may call, with Sylvia Wynter, the Puerto Rican "canonism" that took shape in the 1930s.[24] Rather, her historical significance is rooted in the recognition that de Burgos is a nomadic figure *now*. Gelpí's intervention renders legible the extent to which de Burgos constitutes a line of flight from sense-formations within Puerto Rican historicity that remain *today* deeply marked by the sedimentation of the "norms" and "truths" established by intellectuals like Pedreira. One is even tempted to translate Gelpí's reading of de Burgos in terms of the formal strictures of Benjamin's concept of the dialectical image, with de Burgos's nomadic "what has been" emerging in our awakened now as the messianic bearer of that promised utopia which the "tradition of the oppressed" bestows to the materialist historian. Given the possibility of this translation, shouldn't we affirm the opposite to what I claimed earlier regarding the construction of de Burgos's image as a perennial line of flight? Doesn't this reading amount to a crucial step in the direction of a historical reading of de Burgos's in general and of *Poema* in particular?

As I already suggested in the previous section, my efforts to historicize *Poema* have led me to the opposite conclusion as Gelpí: I contend that the historical force of *Poema* as a key event in Puerto Rican historicity does not lie in its figuration of a nomadic, minoritarian line of flight from the canonical interpretation of Puerto Rican historicity as sedimented in Pedreira's *Insularismo*. On my reading, *Poema* instead reinstitutes or reinscribes at a deeper level of historicity the same metaphysical or historico-ontological decisions that lend consistency and rationality to the majoritarian interpretation of Puertoricanness that crystallizes in the discourse of Pedreira and company. This interpretive difference is not simply the result of discrepancies that could be ultimately adjudicated on the terrain of historico-empirical correctness or formalistic textual hermeneutics. Instead, this divergence is rooted in a more fundamental disagreement regarding the conditions that would have to be met for us to say that a reading of *Poema* worthy of the adjective *historical* has taken place. As I already suggested in Part I, Gelpí's interpretation constitutes a major link in the long chain of catastrophic traditionalization that has determined de Burgos's reception. As a result, the historical *content* that Gelpí highlights acquires cognitive and political salience thanks to the formative role of the *grammar* of catastrophic traditionality. Since, to put it bluntly, de Burgos's historical appearance is ultimately determined by the formal conditions in which she is compelled to appear, the fact that the poet appears as the emblem of the nomadic, minoritarian tendencies within Puerto Rican historicity matters less than the totemic grammar in which she is presented. My claim is that all these supposedly dangerous (because *counter hegemonic*) aspects of de Burgos's poetic itinerary are neutralized in their event-like or perilous character the moment they are rendered into source material for another aestheticized protocol of symbolic reading that positions the poet as the mirror in which her readers will never fail to catch a glimpse of the ego-ideal of their own version of Puertoricanness. With this, her image resediments into a sense-configuration that has lost any chance of leaping beyond the horizon of *transcendental* (not merely realist) *historicism* and its sedimented "norms" and "truths" about Puerto Rican historicity. All possible analogies with Benjamin's tradition of the oppressed or Foucault's histories of the present notwithstanding, the irrevocable, if largely unconscious, commitment to reactivating the totem of de Burgos's catastrophic tradition blocks any attempt to construct an image of the poet that may actually pay heed to the danger that she may bear—the danger in which her historicity, *and ours*, lies.

This explains why the task at hand is not simply to historicize *Poema* but to do so in such a way that, through this literary-historical exercise, a preliminary sketch of the dialectical image of de Burgos may attain legibility. This requires the drawing of a constellation in which our *now* may become the *now of (self)knowability* through its emergence as the correlated pole for the manifestation of "what has been" under the guise of danger, *sub specie contingentitatis*.

But how should this image be constructed? In what follows, I want to outline two major aspects of this image, in the process furnishing the skeleton of my reading of *Poema*.

The Historicity of Modernity, the Modernity of Historicity

The most basic aspect of de Burgos's image as it perhaps may emerge in this reading of *Poema* is also the most speculative dimension of this historical "object." This dimension could be summarized with the following hypothesis, namely, that *Poema* is the *as-yet-unrecognized poem of Puerto Rican modern life*. The task of the following three sections could be thus characterized in Benjaminian terms as an attempt to "read what was never written": The goal is to encounter the textuality of *Poema*, and the *self* that voices this volume, within the space-time of a Benjaminian *constellation* bearing the title *modernity*. Whereas the totemic domestication of de Burgos's afterlife blocks any reckoning with this crucial layer of *Poema*'s historicity, the readings that follow interrupt this tradition by attempting to *decipher* the signal of Puerto Rican modernity encrypted in the textuality of de Burgos's first major publication.[25] In keeping with the formal strictures of Benjamin's concept of the dialectical image, my reading of *Poema* is also an attempt at self-clarification of both the modernity of Puerto Rican historicity and the historicity of "our" modernity. In doing so, the reading that follows also takes a cue from Benjamin's methodological intuition about the task of literary history, which finds clear expression in the concluding lines of his 1931 essay "Literaturgeschichte und Literaturwissenschaft" ("Literary History and Literary Studies"):

> It is not a matter of presenting written works in the context of their time, rather of bringing to presentation the time that knows them—that is, ours—in the time in which they emerged. With this, literature becomes an organ of history [*ein Organon der Geschichte*] and this—not to make the written [*das Schrifttum*] into the subject matter of history [*Stoffgebiet der Historie*]—is the task of literary history.[26]

Modernity, however, is defined in many ways, so I would like to clarify *how* I understand this concept both in general and in its Puerto Rican specificity. To a certain extent, my relation to this category could be summarized by Frederic Jameson's closing remarks in his introduction to *A Singular Modernity*: "Perhaps it might be better to admit that the notions that cluster around the word 'modern' are as unavoidable as they are unacceptable."[27] My way of approaching this situation differs from Jameson, however. Taking a cue from Christina León, whose recent work on catachresis as a performative trope of onto-logical imposition reminds us that catachresis is "born out of the tense relationship between a lack of a proper word and a need to make a claim,"[28] I take modernity's conceptual insufficiency and unavoidability as symptomatic of the catachrestic, hence *figural*, nature of this historical "category" or, rather, trope. Doing so allows me to develop an approach to several discourses that mobilize the term *modernity* in a way that foregrounds the allegorical performativity undergirding the referential claims that are unavoidably made whenever this term is used. In this way, we gain some distance from both the realist-historicist referential fictions that preside over the deployment of this concept—themselves modeled on a view of language according to which meaning is teleologically determined by the referential paradigm presumably at work in proper names and their "rigid designation"[29]—and from the "narrative idealism" that would treat this term as a historical idea that grounds the possibility of a totalizing cosmic narrative. In other words, rather than being treated as a *name* that either picks out a series of *really existent* historical facts or as an *idea* that gathers all *modern* phenomena into a unitary contextual-narrative structure, *modernity* will be approached as an *allegory of history* that produces often aberrant effects of referentiality.

This methodological remark has major consequences for the specific historical *content* that my reading of *Poema* privileges in order to make the case for de Burgos as a poet of modern life. To anticipate the form of this content, I want to turn to the definition of modernity offered by Bolívar Echevarría in his posthumous book *Modernidad y blanquitud* (*Modernity and "Whiteness"*):

> We should perhaps begin by stating the obvious: modernity is the determining characteristic of a set of behaviors that have been appearing in social life everywhere for many centuries and that common sense recognizes as discontinuous with and even opposed to the traditional constitution of life. Modernity further refers to a set of behaviors potentially in the process of replacing that traditional constitution of life, after having shown it as obsolete, or as inconsistent and ineffective. From another perspective, modernity can also be seen as a set of objective facts that are sharply incompatible with the established configuration of the lifeworld and that appear as substantial innovations, as facts meant to satisfy a need for transformation arising from the very bosom of this world.[30]

Much could be said about this definition, but I will only remark on Echevarría's use of the Husserlian concept of the *Lebenswelt*, or *lifeworld*, because this concept opens onto a dimension of his definition of modernity that is decisive for my reading of de Burgos—even if it is only implicitly at work in Echevarría's own definition.[31] By describing the lifeworld as having "an established configuration," I take Echevarría to be radicalizing Husserl's insight into the "originary historicity" (*Urhistorizität*) of the lifeworld by positing modernity as an event that is both *historical* and *transcendental*, since it produces something akin to a change in the "structure of experience" that Benjamin himself associated with modernity.[32] In other words, modernity for Echevarría is not simply a general name for the set of objective facts and behaviors that stand at any given moment in opposition to those facts and behaviors that are regarded as traditional, that is, as already sedimented into the particular historical shape of the lifeworld. For, to the extent that the "behaviors" that are informed by the form of modernity have the capacity to alter the very shape of the lifeworld, these behaviors cannot be understood *stricto sensu* as *objective facts*, that is, as really existing entities of the same order as those objects that are explicitly marked as modern. Implicit in Echevarría's definition of modernity is thus an account of the speculative *historicity* of egological and intersubjective lifeworld-constitution. In other words, modernity is above all a formal title for the *historical contingency* of transcendental experience. In keeping with this insight derived from Bolívar Echevarría's definition, I do not read *Poema* as *representing* Puerto Rican modernity, if by that we mean that the volume figures mimetically objects and behaviors selected and imposed as modern either by the colonial drivers of the process of modernization that took place during the first three decades of US occupation or by earlier and more deeply sedimented modernizing efforts undertaken by European and *Criollo* elites under Spanish rule. Instead, my claim is that *Poema registers*, *enacts*, and *responds* to the perceived intensification of a radical change in the sedimented style of the Puerto Rican lifeworld after US colonization. To put this in more precise terms, the volume is not only a record but a vector of the *transformation* of the Puerto Rican lifeworld and of the ongoing transformation of the "structure of experience" of de Burgos's readers.

Intimacy and Modernity: De Burgos's Poetics of Embodied/Gendered Ipseity

How does *Poema* register, enact, and respond to the increasing reach of "modern life" within Puerto Rican historicity? And what are the specific historical and ontological features that determine the physiognomy of Puerto Rican modernity as it emerges in this image?

My answer to the first of these questions is that the textuality of *Poema* registers the imperceptible yet overwhelming inscription of modernity in ways that are best described as ambivalent. One of the sides of this ambivalence explains why I disagree with the readings that, inspired by Gelpí, draw a stark opposition between de Burgos and what Bernabe has aptly described as Pedreira's "cultural-romantic critique of modernity."[33] Drawing from the works of Oswald Spengler and José Ortega y Gasset, Pedreira's critique of modernity is predicated on a series of metaphysical hierarchies that are anchored on the opposition between *life* and *death*, with the categorial distinction between *quantity* and *quality* or *extension* and *intension* and the philosophico-anthropological distinction between *civilization* and *culture* deriving from this idea of a life that is, in principle, absolutely distinguishable from death: "Culture—which, more than getting ahead, is vital intensity—should not be confused with civilization; it is something more qualitative than quantitative. Number, the symbol of our epoch, cannot capture it entirely."[34] From this foundational set of binaries Pedreira constructs a whole series of oppositions that include the ethnic or racialist conflict between a Latin-Iberian race that supposedly experiences progress as the *qualitative intensification* or the deepening of its *cultural formation* and an Anglo-Saxon race that appears as the main instigator of a *civilizational* progress that is measurable primarily in *quantitative terms*.[35] It is ultimately this conflict that, for Pedreira, characterizes the political and indeed ontological crisis that the Puerto Rican nation has faced since 1898, spurred by colonial policies that imposed the primacy of modernity-cum-civilization at the expense of fostering the organic development of the island's "culture": "If I were to join the group of those who define everything in terms of more or less, I would say that today we were are more civilized, but yesterday we were more cultivated."[36] *Insularismo* should be seen not only as the book that instituted on the island the Latin American genre of the "interpretation essay," thereby setting the discursive terms for the academic or elite discussion of matters pertaining to Puertoricanness. For this book also instituted a *criollo* version of what Benjamin calls *Lebensphilosophie*: Pedreira's emphases on intensity, vitality, soul, and, above all, culture are all part of his attempt "to take possession of 'true' experience, as opposed to the experience that sediments itself in the normed, denatured existence of the civilized masses,"[37] a true experience that would then furnish the ontological ground for his normative critique of the island's increasing cultural degradation under US colonization.

Poems such as such as "4. Dáme tu hora perdida" ("4. Give Me Your Lost Hour"), "5. Momentos" ("5. Moments"), "6. Se me ha perdido un verso" ("6. I Have Lost a Verse"), or "8. Amaneceres" ("8. Dawns") attest to the fact that, barring some no doubt significant differences, de Burgos's poetization of modernity resonates with Pedreira's critique of modern life as alienated, commodified, and fungible to the point of being largely submitted to the rule of quantity, extension, matter, and mediocrity. Consider the following lines from the poem "8. Amaneceres":

Allí adentro,	Inside there,
bien adentro,	deep inside,
asomarse a la vida.	to appear to life.
Ver...	To see...
Oír...	To hear...
Oler...	To smell...
Gustar...	To taste...
Y tocar...	And to touch...
tierra.	earth.
Y en la tierra...	And in the earth...
el hombre	man
perpendicular sobre su propia vida.	perpendicular on his own life.
El hombre tierra	Man earth
Hecho a dos dimensiones violentas.	Made of two violent dimensions.
La dimensión común:	The common dimension:
cinco sentidos,	five senses,
un cuerpo y una mente.	a body and a mind.
El hombre todo. Él.	The whole of man. He.
La otra,	The other,
la dimensión social:	the social dimension:
la tradición,	tradition,
la raza,	race,
el capital.	capital.
El hombre aburguesado	Bourgeois man
de cuerpo,	of body,
de mente	mind,
y de energía.	and energy.
El hombre desviado	Deviant man
huyendo ferozmente de sí mismo.	furiously escaping from himself.
A ese hombre burgués	That bourgeois man
hay que destruirlo,	must be destroyed,
ahora,	now,
en la hora presente,	in the present hour,
en la hora robusta,	in the robust hour,
en la hora universal.	in the universal hour.
¡Amanece en el mundo!	There is dawn in the world!
Cuando se abre la puerta íntima	When the intimate door opens
para entrar a una misma,	to enter into oneself,
¡qué de amaneceres![38]	such dawns!

I quote extensively from this poem because it brings together many of the most crucial aspects of *Poema*'s figuration of modernity while simultaneously clarifying the divergences as well as the deep affinities between the *Lebensphilosophien* of Pedreira and de Burgos. Arguably the most striking divergence lies in de Burgos's reliance on a more Rousseauian philosophical anthropology, which crystallizes through the poem's positing of an antagonism between "natural man"—signaled in the poem by the figure of *el hombre todo*, "the whole or all of Man"—and bourgeois or civilized humanity. Unlike the case of Pedreira's *Insularismo*, the antagonism that is established in this poem is not between culture or civilization but between acculturated/civilized humanity and natural humanity, if you will. Another key difference between de Burgos and Pedreira appears near the end of the poem, when the speaker declares that the only way to restore humanity to its true experience of its own being requires the destruction of bourgeois man. This affirmation considerably heightens the antagonistic political grammar that Pedreira had already posited through the dualistic binaries of quality/quality, Hispanicity/Anglo-Saxonness, and culture/civilization by effectively declaring the conflict between these alternatives to be so intractable as to be incapable of any form of dialectical resolution, whether via reconciliatory synthesis or via nonsynthetic apposition. What is more, de Burgos's life-philosophical or vitalistic anthropology may posit a dualism of sorts, but it does so in a way that yields a topology considerably more complicated than Pedreira's binaristic logic. This becomes clear as soon as we notice that the opposition between true and false or authentic and fallen humanity cannot be simply mapped onto the antagonism between the allegories of *el hombre tierra* ("Man earth") and *el hombre aburguesado* ("bourgeois Man"). For note that the relationship between these two allegories does not yield to the schema of a simple binary opposition; on the contrary, "bourgeois Man" is himself the result of anthropogenetic processes grounded in what the speaker refers to as *la dimensión social* ("the social dimension") of humanity, which is itself firmly rooted in the very life of "Man earth." The fact that the speaker explicates this social dimension through the apposition of "tradition," "race," and "capital" not only invites us to take these three terms as designating essential components of sociality as defined by the poem but also suggests that the sociality, and thus the historicity, of human life on earth is rooted in that very life and is thus *not extraneous* to it. Becoming-racialized, becoming-proletarian, or becoming-bourgeois would in themselves constitute historical events, indeed traditions that belong to a tradition that is ultimately nothing other than the temporal unfolding of the social life of earthly man, who is therefore endowed with historicity, as it were, naturally.

But the natural endowment of earthly human life with historicity is complicated enough that to approach it we must turn to Derrida's strange logic of supplementarity. Indeed, *la dimensión social* is figured in "8. Amaneceres" precisely as "a surplus, a plenitude enriching another plenitude, the height of presence," because it "adds itself" to that dimension of "Man earth" which the speaker calls *la dimensión común* ("the common dimension") and which is so plenitudinous that the speaker describes it as *el hombre todo*, "the *whole* of Man."[39] This dimension also has "three" essential components, which, in a logic that evokes the Christian dogma of the trinity, constitute a triune economy composed of the five traditional senses, the body, and the mind. But sociality and historicity are supplementary here in the second sense that Derrida also highlights in his work on Rousseau and the logic of supplementarity: "But the supplement supplements. It adds itself only to replace. It intervenes or insinuates itself *in the place of*; if it fulfills, it does so as one fills a void."[40] Social or historical man may supplement natural man by complementing its aesthetic totality and enriching the self-sufficient wholeness of its embodied life, but it also may dangerously usurp the place of this originary plenitude. The poem itself thematizes this second, more acutely dangerous valence of the supplement when it introduces the allegorical figure of "bourgeois Man" and then recasts this figure with the even more damning allegory of *el hombre desviado* ("deviant Man"). To see this, we should take the terms *desviado* or "deviant" both in their common senses and *à la lettre*, that is, by reading them also in relation to their shared etymology (from the Late Latin *de* + *viare*, meaning "to stray from the path," hence also "to derail or to turn off the *right* path"). The explication and resignification of "bourgeois Man" as "deviant Man" conveys the dangers to the natural economy of human life on earth that the natural historicity of social humanity poses. "Bourgeois Man" is nothing other than the allegory of modern historical humanity, which has so deviated from the path dictated by the transcendental aesthetics of its earthly existence that it has bourgeoisified the human mind, the body, and even its vital energies themselves, indeed the entire economy of the human sensorium. The transcendental sensibility that precedes and grounds human history in the soil of life has been historically displaced and substituted by the sham, artificial aesthetics of a historical, all too historical, bourgeois humanity. But since historical humanity is coeval with and belongs squarely to human life on earth, the destruction of bourgeois humanity—which alone would restore Man to its true humanity by reinstituting the proper hierarchy within the economy of natural and historical life, thereby undoing the damaging ontological effects of capitalist modernity—can only happen through historical and social means. Only history can heal the wounds that history has inflicted upon the ahistorical material substrate of human life; hence, only a "good" supplement—that is, a supplement that effaces its own historicity—can undo the effects of a "bad" supplement and restore the "natural" order. A possible name for this "good" supplement may be the proletarian revolution or communism, whose specter comes to the fore near the end of the poem, when the speaker declares that the time has come to destroy the bourgeoisie. This poem thus clarifies the extent to which de Burgos's political challenge to modernity is informed by a utopian commitment that resonates with the following aphorism of Benjamin: "The political function of utopia: to illuminate the sector of those worthy of destruction."[41]

At the same time, and without trying at all to pacify this combative text, I would like to suggest that both the *ontological* as well as the *political* stakes of the speaker's call to *destroy* bourgeois man could be better understood and, in fact, intensified, if we hear this call with an ear attuned to the Heideggerian or Husserlian motifs of *Abbau* or *Destruktion*, "deconstruction" or "destruction." Indeed, the ultimate aims of de Burgos's poetics of bourgeois destruction appear to cohere with Heidegger's earliest attempts in the 1910s and early 1920s to reconstruct a critical, destructive, or deconstructive phenomenology that would serve as "the method in which life livingly grasps itself as life [*Methode, in dem das Leben sich als Leben lebendig erfaßt*]." Such grasping, for Heidegger, entails as a concrete or phenomenological condition of possibility the experience of life as *my* life, which he grasps terminologically with the category of *Selbstwelt*, or "selfworld": "our selfworld—insofar as it encounters me directly in this or that way, and directly lends my life this personal rhythm of mine. . . . Our life is only *as life* insofar as it lives in a world."[42]

That being said, the speaker's insistence on the need to reestablish phenomenal contact with life and, especially, her listing of the five senses whose natural experience we would presumably regain after the destruction of bourgeois humanity resonates even more powerfully with Husserl's phenomenology of the lifeworld, that is, "the pregiven world, the ontic universe . . . 'ground' [*Boden*] for all praxis, whether theoretical or extratheoretical."[43] More specifically, the poem's antagonism between the *social* and the *common* dimension of the figure of Man could be read as restaging the problem of the "phenomenon" that Husserl calls *Krisis* or "crisis," which, as Derrida reminds us, is "not a simple accident. It is produced by the very progress of science and by the production of ideal objects which, as if by themselves, by their iterability and their necessarily technical structure, veil or consign to forgetting their historical and subjective origin."[44] Derrida's use of the verb *voiler*, "to veil," here is not simply metaphorical. Rather, it receives and transforms the sense of Husserl's own philosophical metaphor of an "*Ideenkleid*" or "garb of ideas," which he identifies as one of the main "culprits" of this forgetting of subjective origins.[45] This ideal garb is a historical tissue; indeed, it is made of sedimentations that produce the critical phenomenon that Husserl calls "substruction," which blocks the possibility of experiencing the lifeworld in its pretheoretical, not-yet-sedimented essence by preventing us from thematizing not only our originary historicity but also and above all the "basic subjective phenomena of kinaesthesis."[46] (In other words, substruction, for Husserl, is akin to the "dangerous" aspect of the supplement because it results in a situation in which the ideal garb takes the place of the actual body that not only wears it but that also produced it.)[47] Kinaesthesia is not to be confused with proprioception insofar as it designates, for Husserl, the qualitative, dynamic, and immediate process through which I "hold sway" (the German is, tellingly, *walten*, also translatable as "to prevail," "to rule," "to dominate") over each and all my experiences of perceiving the bodies that I may encounter in the lifeworld; experiences that encompass (though are not reducible to) the "five senses" that de Burgos locates as the very sensible essence of our common humanity.

To return to de Burgos's poem, the figure of deviant, bourgeois man could be read as an emblem of such substruction, for he threatens to veil the "common dimension" of humanity—which, tellingly for our Husserlian analogy, de Burgos locates in sensibility—with a sensorium exclusively attuned to the social demands of a historical tradition overdetermined by "race" and "capital." What Husserl called in a 1924 lecture course "*Abbau*" or "deconstruction" and that, a decade later, gave way to his mature motif of the transcendental *epokhē*, constitutes for him the sole method through which we may not only (re)gain access to "a *world of pure experience* [*eine* Welt purer Erfahrung]"—which, qua lifeworld, is the world in which we always-already live—but also *thematize* that experience and develop the scientificity that is *proper* to it (which must be *toto cælo* different from the scientificity of "historical" sciences, since these are cut from the same cloth as the *Ideenkleid* that dissimulates the lifeworld).[48] I read de Burgos's *Poema* as committed to such a destructive, deconstructive, desedimenting *epokhē*. In other words, the goal of destroying the bourgeoisie is not only political but also ontological. For at stake ultimately is the possibility of uncovering an originary mode of being-human that remains buried under the sedimentations that constitute the cultural, traditional fabric of a sociality dominated by the bourgeois style of humanity.

Although the initial aim of this brief discussion of "8. Amaneceres" was to give an example of how *Poema*'s response to modernity resonates with Pedreira's own culturalist *Lebensphilosophie* of Puertoricanness, the result exceeds by far this modest claim. For what becomes clear in this poem is that de Burgos responds to the alienation that characterizes modern human life by articulating a poetics of intimacy that opens onto a *phenomenology of life* far more radical and audacious than the *Lebensphilosophien* of Pedreira or, for that matter, Bergson. Bypassing the derivative conflict between culture and civilization or between quantity and quality that Pedreira inherited from, among others, Ortega y Gasset and Spengler, de Burgos anchors her critique of Puerto Rican modern life in the urgent need to "enter into ourselves," to regain an *intimate* experience of our *embodied, kinaesthetic ipseities* as the living, fertile soil upon which the humanity of the human must be again reerected. And whereas Bergson's ideas of *durée* or *duration* and the mature concept of the *élan vital* present us with an ontology of life in general as a *panpsychic* process of *becoming*,[49] de Burgos's attempt to retrieve a *sense* for the *experience* of *life* in its inalienable ontological dignity entails a *reinvention* of the modern, that is, Cartesian, script of subjectivity as the essence of being.

As I will show in more detail in my reading of "2. Íntima," de Burgos's phenomenology of life opens a philosophical path that, though resonant with the thought of Husserl and Heidegger, would find its closest philosophical companion much later in the twentieth century with the enstatic phenomenology of Michel Henry. For the speaker of *Poema* reestablishes the primacy of the ego along two different, if interrelated, lines: first, by situating its essence not in its *cogitare* but in its *sentire*; second, by grasping the unfolding of this essence in the experience of *intimacy*, which emerges in *Poema* as the general title for a movement of *autoaffection* that is conceived as radically "unworldly," purely immanent, endogenous, and enstatic.[50] Intimacy thus marks the sole dimension in which the ego, in the wake of *Poema*, can actually attain and secure its hold on its ipseity. The modernity of *Poema*'s historicity is thus intimately bound up with the speaker's efforts to constitute herself into what we may call with Giorgio Agamben a "form-of-life," namely, a mode of ipseity so secure in its intimate, embodied autoaffection that it *could never succumb to the ontological alienation characteristic of modern life and its biopolitical determination*.[51] We can already begin to see one of the main sources of the ambivalence with which *Poema* responds to modernity: Fighting fire with fire, de Burgos's attempt to overcome modernity's expropriating force requires her to reactivate one of the most sedimented institutions of European modernity, namely, the belief in the ontological primacy of the "self itself." This commitment to the archeological originarity of the form of ipseity—which should not *necessarily* be confused with a belief in a prelapsarian view of humanity—illustrates why I ultimately argue, contra Gelpí and company, that de Burgos's critique of modernity amounts to a radicalization of Pedreira's and not a line of flight from this foundational institution within Puerto Rican historicity.

The emergence of this embodied, autoaffective ipseity can be attested all throughout the textuality of *Poema*, including in its "erotic" poems, which are characterized by that detached, sovereign form of irony that already in 1937 Luis Lloréns Torres had recognized as a key cipher of de Burgos's poetic wager.[52] Consider the following duplets from "4. Dame tu hora perdida":

De tu existencia múltiple dame la hora perdida.	From your multiple existence, give me the lost hour
cuando vacío de todo, no sientas ni la vida.	when, empty of all, not even life you may feel.
Cuando te encuentres solo, tan lejos de ti mismo	When you find yourself alone, so far from yourself
que te pese la mera conciencia del mutismo.	that the mere awareness of stillness may burden you.
Cuando sientas tan fuerte desprecio por lo humano	When you may feel such strong disdain for the human,
que hasta de ti te rías, cual de cualquier gusano.	That you'd laugh at even yourself just as at a worm.
. . .	. . .
Entonces, ya vacío de todo, con tu nada	Then, empty already of all, with your nothing
acércate a mi senda y espera mi llegada.	approach my path and await my arrival.
Yo te daré la nota más cierta de mi vida.	I will give you the most certain note of my life.
Tú me darás la nada de tu hora perdida.	You will give me the nothing of your lost hour.
. . .	. . .
Yo te daré verdades de todo lo tangible	I will give you truths of all that is tangible
para pesar la nada de tu vida insensible.	to weigh the nothing of your insensible life.
Y así, tú te darás en mí como si fuera	And thus, you will give yourself in me as if
mi vida un aletazo de la ida primavera	my life were a wingbeat of bygone spring.
. . .	. . .
Y alzaremos en ritmo vibrante y alocado	And we will raise in vibrant and frenzied rhythm
la sublime mentira de habernos encontrado.	the sublime lie of having found each other.
Yo, en la nada de tu hora perdida,	I, in the nothing of your lost hour,
y tú, en la también nada de mi frívola vida.[53]	And you, in the also nothing of my frivolous life.

Erotic life as it appears in *Poema* is a vector of mutual expropriation and is for this very reason no fertile ground for any *proper*, that is, *ipseitological*, life.[54] The romantic or sexual encounters that the speaker figures in this and other poems (the clearest and most brilliant articulation of this layer of *Poema*'s historicity is certainly found in "10. Nada") may produce the semblance of a somatic exchange in which the lover (always figured as male) is momentarily relieved of his me-ontological condition—marked by an enduring and negatively valorized form of nothingness akin to a void or an absolute emptiness—by his exchanges with the speaker, whose lively sensibility and tangible concreteness appear to restore the male partner to being as such, that is, to life itself. But these encounters—as the speaker never ceases to insist—are a sham, the product of the speaker's calculations, who has produced exactly the version of a feminized self that her lovers expect, thus ensuring that their nonencounters, and the surplus of carnal enjoyment they figure, will indeed materialize. But the speaker enters into these exchanges from a position of indubitable self-knowledge regarding the frivolousness of this "form" of life that she nonetheless performs—a form that lacks any form, since it entails the presentation of femininity as the reified image of tangible, irrational empiricity, of sheer sensuous matter. This critical self-knowledge is, in turn, grounded in the certainty that her constitution as an autoaffective, embodied ipseity remains untouched, uncontaminated, uncorrupted by these performative descents into a sexist, materialistic sensualism. The speaker can thus have her proverbial cake and eat it too: Her intimacy allows her to exist *in this world* and extract a surplus of carnal enjoyment while living in the autoaffected certainty that both her body and soul are not *of this world*, since they are as far removed as possible from the ontological zone in which life is necessarily *enfleshed*.

Earlier I mentioned the structural ambivalence that characterizes de Burgos's response to modern life, with the retrieval of life understood as egological, embodied ipseity. This ambivalence becomes more exacerbated as soon as we take into account another crucial feature of the self that speaks its own ipseity across the textual surface of *Poema*, namely, this self's reclamation of gender differentiation and identification with a universal category of woman that is marked only in terms of sexual difference. With this aspect, we touch on the crucial matter of the nature and limits of de Burgos's feminism. My reading of *Poema* suggests that the ontological and political core of de Burgos's feminist poetics should be located in the speaker's affirmation of a gendered ipseity, rather than be superficially reduced to the speaker's repeated challenge to "societal norms" or "traditional gender roles." I offer this suggestion not because I believe that these challenges do not actually take place in her poetry but because I take them to be grounded in the speaker's effective reclamation of what we could describe, slightly modifying a phrase by Hortense Spillers, as "the monstrosity (of being a female with the potential to say *ego ipsa*)."[55] On this account, *Poema*'s feminism is largely concerned with the task of crafting a script for the assumption of *gendered* ipseity, thereby instituting a possibility presumably rendered impossible *ab ovo* by patriarchy, namely, the possibility that a body marked along sex/gender lines as feminine may accede to the position of sovereignty.

This investment in ipseity, and thus in sovereignty, already exposes the grounds for the multilayered ambivalence I am interested in tracking and rendering legible. The first and most basic layer of this ambivalent structure has to do with the modernity of feminism as an emancipatory project. Since patriarchy and, more fundamentally, phallogocentrism are not simply events or ideological discourses but sedimented formations within the established or *traditional* configuration of the lifeworld, feminism cannot but emerge as a *modern* formation that, in seeking to abolish all forms of oppression on the basis of gender differentiation, is precisely aiming to transform the very constitution of the lifeworld itself and its affective/cognitive structures of experience.

But the investment in a gendered ipseity reveals another aspect of the modernity of de Burgos's feminism that has been largely missed by her readers, namely, the way her feminist poetics not only criticizes but also participates in what Rocío Zambrana describes as the "actualization" of a modern, colonial gender hierarchy in the wake of the US colonization of the archipelago.[56] As Rita Segato has suggested, the modern system of gender imposed during the colonization of the Americas captured and intensified precolonial forms of oppressive patriarchal organization, transforming an already established gender dualism into a female/masculine gender binary grounded in a construction of sexuality rooted in biological dimorphism.[57] The modern, colonial gender system imposes compulsory heterosexuality as the anthropological norm for the intelligible presentation of *properly human* bodies, establishing a gender hierarchy that is disseminated across all the sedimented institutions that constitute the colonial lifeworld. But, as Spillers (among other Black feminist thinkers) has forcefully shown, the fact that the modern system of gender was established within ontological parameters massively determined by the African slave trade and the "peculiar institution" of chattel slavery requires that we contend with the "ungendering" that presided over the genesis of the Black(ened), enslaved "woman" as the "vestibular" figure of femaleness-*sans*-gender, or, in keeping with Zakiyyah Iman Jackson's provisional revision of this motif, as the figure of "superposition or the state of occupying two distinct and seemingly contradictory genders simultaneously."[58] From a different perspective that nonetheless builds upon the work of Spillers and Wynter, among others, Celenis Rodríguez Montero has recently retraced the ways in which modalities of *gender differentiation* began to be instituted *across* the racial, free/enslaved divide in societies throughout the Caribbean basin, driven largely by transformations in the labor structures of the plantation.[59] Echoing Saidiya Hartman's now-classic argument about the ruses of juridical emancipation within slavery's long afterlife, Rodríguez Montero shows that the partial and selective imposition of gender-like arrangements among the enslaved and the formerly enslaved should not be read as the long-awaited bestowal of full gendered humanity to Black(ened) life but as another instantiation of its enduring subjection.[60]

I contend that the work of these and other Black feminist and decolonial scholars is of crucial importance if we are to actually *read* de Burgos's feminist poetics rather than simply celebrate them. The ambivalence of this all-too-modern feminism is perhaps best illustrated by the striking contrast between "1. A Julia de Burgos" and "12. Ay ay ay de la grifa Negra" ("12. Ay Ay Ay of the Griffe Negress"). Whereas the poem that opens the collection represents and reenacts the speaker's own emergence as a gendered ipseity who has managed to extricate herself from the modern/colonial system of patriarchal domination and its positioning of woman as a subjugated gender relegated to the domestic sphere, the collection's twelfth poem features the voice of a Black woman who laments the fate of her enslaved ancestors, only to pivot into a celebration of *mestizaje-cum-whitening* in which the speaker embraces the world-historical task she's been assigned by Puerto Rico's dominant Hispanophilic culture, namely, to serve as what Jackson calls the "Black *mater*" of the Latin American future *mestizo* race by mothering the children of White men.[61] I would argue that no starker contrast between lyric voices could be found in the entire volume: Whereas the self that speaks in "1. A Julia de Burgos" and throughout most of *Poema* is already in possession of her ipseity—in spite of, if not thanks to her autonomous assumption of gender difference or of womanhood—the self that voices her "ay ay ay" can only attain a semblance of ipseity by transcending her raciality through the birthing of children whose skin is lighter than hers. In other words, it is her daughters (and perhaps only after several generations of whitening) who may eventually reach the sovereign/gendered position that the speaker of the poem has already assigned to herself. No wonder most totemic readers of de Burgos have seldom scratched beneath this poem's surface. For what the poem ultimately reveals is the persistent workings of raciality even within those sense-formations, like feminism, whose "modernity" is bound to a radical critique of "modern life" as grounded in phallogocentric and patriarchal sedimentations. A nontotemic, nonidealistic, yet specular reading of "12. Ay ay ay de la grifa" is thereby in position not only to read the structural solidarity between de Burgos's feminism, the Hispanophilic White supremacy characteristic of Puertoricanist discourse in the 1930s, and its concomitant anti-Blackness but also to read the persistence of that unholy alliance *now*.

Antagonism, Utopia: The Reinvention of the Flesh

Having just laid out the key historical elements that lend its singular physiognomy to the modern constellation that my reading of de Burgos's *Poema* seeks to retrace, I want to conclude this programmatic section by returning, from a different angle, to some of the methodological and philosophical questions addressed in my previous discussion of Benjamin's concept of the dialectical image. My goal is to clarify how my attempt to construct the image of de Burgos through the constellation of modernity that attains legibility in the textuality of *Poema* satisfies some of the conditions that Benjamin spells out as necessary for the presentation of an image. Recall that earlier I mentioned that, although the appearance of an image is not something that can be entirely programmed or predicted, it is nonetheless not an entirely aleatory event that would lack any internal structure or be devoid of any a priori features. Quite the contrary: Benjamin himself discusses some of the necessary conditions that must be met for something like an image to, perhaps, appear. At this point, it would be worthwhile to quote again the passage from *Das Passagen-Werk* that I previously commented on:

> To thinking belongs the movement as well as the arrest of thoughts. Where thinking comes to a standstill in a constellation saturated with tensions—there the dialectical image appears. It is the caesura in the movement of thought. Its position is naturally not an arbitrary one. It is to be found, in a word, where the tension between dialectical opposites is greatest. Hence, the object constructed in the materialist presentation of history is itself the dialectical image. The latter is identical with the historical object; it justifies its violent expulsion from the continuum of historical process.[62]

What Benjamin here spells out are the *necessary* (though never *sufficient*) conditions for the legible appearance of a dialectical image in a constellation.[63] The fact that the image requires for its appearance the saturation of a "space" through its configuration in *oppositional* terms makes explicit the dialectical structure that remained somewhat implicit in Benjamin's account of the constellation in entry "N3,1" of *Das Passagen-Werk*, where the conditions for the image's constellated appearance are described solely in "temporal" terms, that is, through the encounter between "the now" and "what has been."[64] With the help of Derrida's claim regarding the *dialectical* nature of Husserlian temporality earlier I suggested that the dialectics of Benjamin's constellation could be described in terms of the young Hegel's conception of the Absolute as the "identity of identity and non-identity": The "now" and the "what has been" are absolutely nonidentical because of their historical singularity or indexicality, yet their very entrance into the constellation spatializes their temporalization, rendering them simultaneous in spite of their persistent radical nonsimultaneity and, thereby, identifying them *in* their radical alterity and singularity.[65] The passage that I just quoted, however, adds another layer to the constellation's dialectics, less linked to its temporal *form* than to its *content*. Indeed, it is not only the case that the constellation requires the dialectical polarization of self/other, now/what has been if it is to appear at all, but what appears in it is equally polarized, equally saturated by the form of an opposition that the dialectical image does not sublate but rather *intensifies* or *heightens*.

Accordingly, my reading of *Poema* lays the groundwork for the construction of the image of de Burgos by paying heed to how the speaker presents her *embodied, gendered* ipseity by saturating the poetic space of the collection with a series of polar oppositions and intractable antagonism. As we will see, the speaker's dialectical procedure throughout *Poema* is completely resonant with the Benjaminian aphorism that I quoted previously: "The political function of utopia: to illuminate the sector of those worthy of destruction."[66] This layer of *Poema*'s historicity marks the moment in which the ambivalent relation to modernity I have just outlined is resolved through the establishment of a violent antagonism. As my reading shows, *Poema*'s poetization of an embodied ipseity that secures its sovereignty and its radical interiority through the feeling of intimacy requires the concomitant production of what Alexander Weheliye calls a "fleshly surplus" as the very inimical figure over and against which the body's pure autoaffectivity can be delineated.[67] De Burgos's reclaiming of the body as the heart of the structure of ipseity entails the production of an improper body, more precisely a *carne*, or *flesh*, whose incapacity to overcome its own viscosity by mounting a challenge to the fungibilizing forces of modern life justifies its destruction, which, in turn, justifies the elimination of all the allegorical figures that the speaker of *Poema* presents as the bearers of an irredeemable flesh.

The production of this fleshly surplus through de Burgos's strategic and novel retrieval of a rather classic sarxophobic schema takes different shapes across the twenty poems that compose *Poema*. Indeed, the violence unleashed by the ipseity that speaks throughout the volume begins by targeting the authorial figure herself: In "1. A Julia de Burgos," the bearer of viscosity is none other than Julia de Burgos, from whom the speaker violently dissociates herself over the course of a memorable poem that has secured for de Burgos a place of honor within Puerto Rican, Caribbean, and Latin American feminism. In "2. Íntima," *la carne* emerges as the essential trait of another allegorical figure, namely, *los hombres* or *el hombre*, "men/Man," which constitutes the major antagonist of the speaker of *Poema* and which becomes the emblem of modernity's determination of human life through the institution of a homogeneous temporality that blocks the advent of a humanity fully appropriated to its own ipseitological essence. And in "12. Ay ay ay de la grifa negra," the abjection of the flesh becomes incarnated in the emblematic figure of the slave-descendant, Afro–Puerto Rican woman, whose abject lament can only find consolation in her embrace of her own elimination as a bearer of raciality through her whitening.

Whenever de Burgos mobilizes *the flesh* in *Poema*, what transpires is the production of *ecstatic* viscosity as the mode of being that characterizes human life under modernity. *Ecstatic* here designates the essence of *la carne* as the being through which what Denise Ferreira da Silva calls "affectability" is ontologically positioned and then understood as the bearer of being-outside-itself. A "form" of life incapable of becoming what Agamben calls "form-of-life," condemned not to be able to achieve the *enstatic* movement of intimacy that alone can turn the flesh into a plastic body in Cathérine Malabou's (not Jackson's) sense.[68] The experience of intimacy alone can restore affectability to its proper mode of being, namely, its being-itself-for-itself, by anchoring the self in the experience of autoaffection, thereby rescuing the "I" from its improper, incarnated being-for-the-other—from its essential determination as a heteroaffected being.

The reinvention of *la carne* characterizes de Burgos's response to the violence of modernity: Fighting fire with fire, her poetics unleashes a counterviolence that necessitates the invention of the *flesh* as that abject, viscous, material substance that bears the seal of what Benjamin calls *bloßes Leben* ("mere life")[69] and whose elimination is required for the emergent gendered ipseity that speaks throughout the volume to accede to the sovereign life that could only be afforded to her by proper embodiment. This is perhaps what is most catastrophic about de Burgos's poetics of ipseity: Claiming to have already overcome modernity's catastrophe, her very overcoming further retrenches the modalities of violence of this catastrophe. And her reception, in an equally catastrophic manner (though this time in Benjamin's narrower sense of the term), turns these poems into the script of a triumphal procession in which de Burgos or the speaker of *Poema* cannot but appear as the messianic figure that has finally vanquished the greatest foe.

In the next three sections, I undertake a closer reading of three key poems of *Poema*—"1. A Julia de Burgos" ("1. To Julia de Burgos"), "2. Íntima" ("2. Intimate"), and "12. Ay ay ay de la grifa negra" ("12. Ay Ay Ay of the Griffe Negress")—with the goal of interrupting this triumphal procession and its totemic reception so that, perhaps, *another* history may attain legibility in the mirror of these poems.

§22. NAMELESSNESS AND HUMANISM: "1. A JULIA DE BURGOS"

Poema opens with a bang whose reverberations are still being felt. Indeed, I would argue that Carl Schmitt's statement that "often the first sentence of a publication already decides its destiny"[70] rings truer for fewer books than it does for de Burgos's first published poetry volume, whose opening poem, "1. A Julia de Burgos," has largely contributed to sealing the fate of her image. This is the case from the poem's very title, whose self-apostrophic character heralds the audacity characteristic of the self that emerges in and through *Poema*'s twenty poems. Let's quote the poem in its entirety, so we may better attune our reading ears to the timbre that distinguishes this voice's self-presentation.

1. A Julia de Burgos	**1. To Julia de Burgos**
Ya las gentes murmuran que yo soy tu enemiga,	Already people murmur that I am your enemy,
porque dicen que en verso doy al mundo tu yo.	for they say that in verse I give to the world your I.
Mienten, Julia de Burgos. Mienten, Julia de Burgos.	They lie, Julia de Burgos. They lie, Julia de Burgos.
La que se alza en mis versos no es tu voz; es mi voz;	Who rises in my verses is not your voice: it is my voice;
porque tú eres ropaje y la esencia soy yo;	for you are the garb and I am the essence;
y el más grande abismo se tiende entre las dos.	and the greatest abyss lies between us.
Tú eres fría muñeca de mentira social,	You are the cold doll of social lies,
y yo, viril destello de la humana verdad.	And I, the virile spark of human truth.
Tú, miel de cortesanas hipocresías; yo no;	You, honey of courtly hypocrisies; not I;
que en todos mis poemas desnudo el corazón.	who in all my poems undress the heart.
Tú eres como tu mundo, egoísta; yo no;	You are like your world, selfish; not I;
que todo me lo juego a ser lo que soy yo.	who bets everything to be what I am.
Tú eres sólo la grave señora señorona;	You are only the somber, haughty lady;
yo no; yo soy la vida, la fuerza, la mujer.	Not I; I am life, strength, woman.

Tú eres de tu marido, de tu amo; yo no;	You are of your husband, your master; not I;
yo de nadie, o de todos, porque a todos, a todos,	I am of nobody, or of all, because to all, to all,
en mi limpio sentir y en mi pensar me doy.	in my limpid feeling and thinking I give myself.
Tú te rizas el pelo y te pintas; yo no;	You curl your hair and dye it; not I;
a mí me riza el viento; a mí me pinta el sol.	I am curled by the wind; I am dyed by the sun.
Tú eres dama casera, resignada, sumisa,	You are a domestic, resigned, submissive lady
atada a los prejuicios de los hombres; yo no;	Bound to the prejudices of men; not I;
que yo soy Rocinante corriendo desbocado	For I am Rocinante running wild
olfateando horizontes de justicia de Dios.	tracking horizons of divine justice.
Tú en ti misma no mandas; a ti todos te mandan;	You do not rule in yourself; you are ruled by all;
en ti mandan tu esposo, tus padres, tus parientes,	in you rule your husband, your parents, your relatives,
el cura, el modista, el teatro, el casino,	the priest, the dressmaker, the theater, the club,
el auto, las alhajas, el banquete, el champán,	the car, the jewels, the banquet, the champagne,
el cielo y el infierno, y el qué dirán social.	heaven and hell, and what society might say.
En mí no, que en mí manda mi solo corazón,	Not in me, in me only rules my heart,
mi solo pensamiento; quien manda en mí soy yo.	my sole thinking; who rules in me is I.
Tú, flor de aristocracia; y yo la flor del pueblo.	You, aristocratic flower; and I the flower of the people.
Tú en ti lo tienes todo y a todos se lo debes,	You have everything in you and you owe it to all,
mientras que yo, mi nada a nadie se la debo.	whereas I owe my nothing to nobody.
Tú clavada al estático dividendo ancestral,	You, stuck to the static ancestral dividend,
y yo, un uno en la cifra del divisor social,	and I, a one in the number of the social divisor,
somos el duelo a muerte que se acerca fatal.	We are the duel to the death that fatally approaches.
Cuando las multitudes corran alborotadas	When the multitudes run amok
dejando atrás cenizas de injusticias quemadas,	leaving behind the ashes of burned injustice,
y cuando con la tea de las siete virtudes,	and when, with the torch of the seven virtues,
tras los siete pecados, corran las multitudes,	after the seven vices run the multitudes,
contra ti, y contra todo lo injusto y lo inhumano,	against you and against all that is unjust and inhumane,
yo iré en medio de ellas con la tea en la mano.	I will be in their midst torch in hand.
Julia de Burgos[71]	Julia de Burgos

A cursory glance suffices to grasp why "A Julia de Burgos" lends itself so well to the "hagiographical impulse" that, according to Lena Burgos-Lafuente, has produced the image of de Burgos as the "heroic and orthodox poet."[72] To the extent that, as Lilliana Ramos Collado suggests, this poem unfolds in the allegorical register of *psychomachy*, or "a war within the soul," of the poet herself, then heroism and orthodoxy would appear to be indissociable.[73] Whereas the orthodox aspect of *Poema* crystallizes in the "poetics of presence and authenticity" that, as Vanessa Pérez Rosario argues, characterizes de Burgos's wager throughout this volume, the heroic dimension of this poetics results from the speaker's ongoing realization that her authentic self-presence to herself can only be won by waging war against herself and ensuring, in the end, the defeat of the inauthentic Julia by the authentic Julia.[74] Which is precisely what the poem appears to stage, from the speaker's opening declaration of war against her addressee—who is presumably herself, Julia de Burgos—to the poem's concluding utopian scene in which the speaker imagines herself among a torch-bearing multitude ready to set fire to de Burgos and to all that is "inhuman."

But what has made this poem truly irresistible for the erection of de Burgos as the totem of the marginal, nomadic, progressive style of Puertoricanness is the way de Burgos's political heroism and moral orthodoxy are here articulated in terms of the *heterodoxic* values of *feminism*, understood as a project of political and indeed metaphysical emancipation. Indeed, at stake in this reputed battle in and for the poet's soul is not just the poet's existential authenticity, unmarked by the normative strictures of gender as a modern technology of anthropogenesis. For the very possibility of her authenticity hinges on what Ivette López Jiménez describes as a "critical confrontation with the morality that controls the lives of women."[75] The psychomachia not only seeks to institute the selfhood of the poetic voice in its propriety but does so by launching an assault against patriarchy and the "sexual contract" that "establishes men's political right over women" and "orderly access by men to women's bodies."[76] The antipatriarchal psychomachy is so radical that it forces de Burgos to enact an absolute dissociation of *her-self* from *herself*, separating the "I" or the ego that speaks throughout *Poema* from the patriarchalized woman who bears the nom de plume Julia de Burgos.

In the first part of this book, I showed how de Burgos's afterlife has been secured through the institution of a catastrophic reception that has turned her life and works into the totem of both hegemonic and counterhegemonic tendencies within Puerto Rican historicity. Reading "1. A Julia de Burgos" allows us to see how this catastrophic tradition has partly taken shape as a response to demands for a type of legibility that, as Burgos-Lafuente has suggested, are *actually* embedded in her poetry, which actively participates in the construction of its own monumental mythologization.[77] From the moment of its initial publication in the newspaper *El Imparcial* until today, this poem has largely functioned as a mirror in which generations of de Burgos's readers have encountered little more than the manifestation of their own desire to *imitate Julia* by being just as authentic as her, that is to say, by also instituting themselves as selves that are ontologically different from the social personas that mark their entrance into the symbolic order. The fact that this poem has also been regarded as one of the foundational texts of Puerto Rican literary feminism has not modified this protocol of symbolic mirroring and totemic mimesis; it has simply expanded the purview of what is demanded of the reader if they are to become, like de Burgos, an authentic self.

This idealized-speculative reading protocol produces a situation in which this poem, certainly among the most discussed and famous in her corpus, remains paradoxically *over-read*, at once submitted to ongoing celebratory *paraphrases* while seldom explicated, let alone interrogated. This is largely the result of the fact that "the underlying assumption of such a paraphrastic reading is itself one of specular understanding in which the text serves as a *mirror* of our own knowledge and our knowledge *mirrors* in its turn the text's signification," to quote Paul de Man.[78] But rather than trying to shatter that mirror, the reading that follows takes a cue from another moment in which de Man, writing about the work of Carol Jacobs, establishes a provisional distinction between *paraphrasing* and what he calls *true reading*, which "is an argument, that is, it has the sequential coherence we associate with a demonstration or with a particularly compelling narrative."[79] My reading will take the form of an explication of "1. A Julia de Burgos" that seeks to demonstrate that this poem unfolds as an allegorical narrative that figures the initial stage in the *genesis of gendered ipseity*.

The two terms that I have selected as the main title of this paragraph—*namelessness* and *humanism*—capture the two aspects of this poem that my reading brings into relief to explore some of the consequences of de Burgos's feminist poetics of ipseity. Expanding and revising Ramos Collado's claim regarding this poem's psychomachy, my reading shows that, instead of a battle within or even for the poet's soul, what unfolds in the poem is the speaker's reenactment of her own presumably successful and necessarily violent disidentification from the patriarchalized, submissive woman who bears the name Julia de Burgos. Namelessness thus emerges in this poem as necessary for the poetic voice to become an "I," which raises the stakes of the antagonism between the self that speaks in this poem and the sedimented patriarchal lifeworld in which her existence unfolds. If "1. A Julia de Burgos" can be rightfully seen as one of the inaugural texts of Puerto Rican antipatriarchal feminism, this is so because the poem ratifies and sediments the institution of a self that *occupies the ontological position of sovereignty and autonomy* while being marked as *feminine*.

At the same time, this poem also *reenacts* the counterviolence that was necessary for the speaker's inventive reclaiming, to paraphrase Hortense Spillers, of "the monstrosity (of being a female with the potential to say *ego ipsa*.)"[80] To understand the grounds of this violence as the speaker re-presents them in this poem, we must contend with another major emblematic polarity that emerges in the poem's closing allegorical scene, namely, the *human/inhuman* distinction. Indeed, our reading must reckon with the speaker's *utopian* dreams of bringing about an end to what we might call with Emmanuel Levinas, Franz Fanon, or Sylvia Wynter "the humanism of Man."[81] The feminism that emerges in this poem attains its properly ontological and historical dimensions when the bearer of the "proper name" Julia de Burgos emerges as the incarnation of modern, inhuman humanity, which must be destroyed if the *proper* humanism that the speaker *already* embodies in her very own ipseity is ever to be instituted in its place.

Only if we pay heed to the depths of the gulf that opens up in this poem could we begin to take measure not only of the ideological nature (in a de Manian sense) of de Burgos's poetics of selfhood but also of the catastrophic implications that her own self-institution as the norm of what a *new humanity* ought to be would carry for *other* women—including that woman who answered to the name Julia de Burgos.

Address and Response: Understanding and Identification

One possible way to begin measuring this poem's audacity while assessing one of its many claims to (literary) modernity would be to attend to what befalls apostrophe in the complicated scene of address that unfolds throughout "1. A Julia de Burgos." Apostrophe has been a privileged trope in the study of the lyric—especially since the advent of de Manian deconstruction and rhetorical reading—because, as Jonathan Culler has argued, it foregrounds a feature without which the very "essence" of the lyric would remain hardly thinkable, namely, lyric address.[82] This is particularly true of the kind that Culler labels as "indirect" or "triangulated address," in which the lyric voice or speaker is figured as "addressing the audience of readers by addressing or pretending to address someone or something else, a lover, a god, natural forces, or personified abstractions."[83] For Culler, indirect address is a conditio sine qua non of the lyric; in triangulating us as readers, address "makes the poem an event in the lyric present rather than the representation of a past event."[84]

But despite its fundamental role within the very genesis and structure of the lyric, address presupposes an even more fundamental structure of lyric poetry, namely, the poetic voice, whose "phenomenalization," as de Man has argued, constitutes "the principle of intelligibility" of lyric poetry: "Our claim to understand a lyric text coincides with the actualization of a speaking voice, be it (monologically) that of the poet or (dialogically) that of the exchange that takes place between author and reader in the process of comprehension."[85] The aesthetic ideology of the lyric presupposes and reactivates a belief that, as Derrida has shown, is constitutive of the history of metaphysics, whose "privilege of presence as consciousness could not have been established . . . except through the excellence of the voice."[86] As the reputed source of what de Man calls the poem's "aesthetic presence,"[87] the voice occupies a metaphysical dimension irreducible to that of any tropological or figurative aspect of the poem in which its voicing happens, since it is this very voicing that is held to constitute and lend phenomenality to every phenomena that may manifest itself in the poem, including our own phenomenalization as the triangulated or direct addressees of the lyric speaker.

To grasp *how* and *why* the apostrophe that opens both "1. A Julia de Burgos" and *Poema* as a whole constitutes an audacious lyric innovation, a comparison with "Au lecteur" ("To the Reader"), the poem that opens Baudelaire's *Les fleurs du mal*, is instructive. This might seem obvious to readers familiar with Baudelaire; after all, both poems share several features in common, beginning with the fact that both rely on the Spanish and French prepositions *a* and *à* (which becomes *au* through the contraction of *à* + *le*, the definite masculine article), whose dative status foregrounds from the get go the poems' apostrophic or invocative quality. At a more thematic level, both poems could also be said to be largely concerned with "epideictic discourse," which Culler, following a tradition that goes back at least to Aristotle's *Rhetoric*, defines as the "discourse of praise or blame."[88] Indeed, in both cases we are confronted with a lyric that is overwhelmingly concerned not so much with the depiction of actions as it is with the presentation of the many sins and vices that afflict the addressees, which both poets depict in language that is explicitly theological, even overtly Catholic: Whereas in the case of de Burgos's poem it's the allegory of the seven capital sins that recurs near the end of the poem, in Baudelaire's case, references to sin are so ubiquitous that pointing to any single instance would be superfluous.

Still, what is truly instructive here are not the similarities between these poems but their formal and thematic differences. Whereas the opening apostrophe of *Les fleurs du mal*, as Benjamin astutely observes in his "Motifs" essay, implies that Baudelaire "dedicated his book to those who are similar to him," that is, readers who are "familiar with spleen" and whose "willpower and also their capacity for concentration leave much to be desired,"[89] the speaker of "1. A Julia de Burgos" addresses this poem to none other than the author of the book that this poem opens. Culler's account of lyric address can help us grasp the difference that this divergence *makes* at the level of form or genre. For, according to Culler, Baudelaire's "Au lecteur" belongs to what we might describe, in turn, as a minor subgenre of the lyric composed of poems whose goal is "to welcome the reader in and to frame the collection" that they inaugurate.[90] The main feature of these poems for Culler appears through their reception: They're "experienced as exceptional, explicitly metapoetic," because, unlike other poems contained in their volumes, they're "dependent on the collection they introduce."[91] These poems, in other words, function like preludes, exordia, or proems not only because of their position in a volume but also because of their semantic function, which is closely linked to the rhetorical technique of the *captatio benevolentiæ*, the "capturing of the audience goodwill," recognized since Cicero as one of the keystones of oratory.[92] The fact that *epideixis* in "Au lecteur" is voiced mostly in the first-personal plural *nous*, or "we," buttresses this point: The lyric voice in *Les fleurs du mal* posits a fraternal community of sinners that abolishes any moral difference between the addressee and the addresser, since the former is ultimately a mirror image of the latter: "—Hypocrite reader, —my likeness, —my brother."[93] Things are otherwise in "1. A Julia de Burgos." By inverting the directionality of address and turning its invective inward, de Burgos's *Poema* subverts the generic expectations of this genre, thereby emerging as even more "exceptional" and "metapoetic" than other poems in this subgenre. On this account, "1. A Julia de Burgos" welcomes us into *Poema* only obliquely, almost as if we had been invited to witness a scene of invective self-interpellation, an intimate conflict that appears not to concern us directly.

But this enigmatic and abyssal self-apostrophe does something more significant; namely, it sharpens the *critical* (from the Greek *krinō*, meaning "I decide") role of apostrophe in the lyric by addressing us indirectly as her readers with the tacit goal that we may ratify the felicitousness of the speaker's claim to be entirely *other than* her addressee, that is, other than Julia de Burgos herself.

That the reading of *Poema* places us from the outset in the site of a decision whose consequences are grave is clear from the poem's first six lines:

Ya las gentes murmuran que yo soy tu enemiga,
porque dicen que en verso doy al mundo tu yo.
Mienten, Julia de Burgos. Mienten, Julia de Burgos.
La que se alza en mis versos no es tu voz: es mi voz;
porque tú eres ropaje y la esencia soy yo;
y el más grande abismo se tiende entre las dos.

Already people murmur that I am your enemy,
for they say that in verse I give to the world your I.
They lie, Julia de Burgos. They lie, Julia de Burgos.

> Who rises in my verses is not your voice: it is my voice;
> for you are the garb and I am the essence;
> and the greatest abyss lies between us.

To begin with, we should note that de Burgos's choice of the plural instead of the singular *la gente* suggests that the subject of this line is not so much the collective singular noun *the people*, with all of its substantial political resonances, but a more diffuse entity: It is not the people gathered in a political assembly and gathered into a body politic but the people as the spectral agent of gossip. Moreover, this nominal phrase could itself be read as an abbreviation of Spanish verbal locutions that idiomatically do take the plural, such as *el dicho* or *el decir de las gentes*, which the Real Academia Española defines precisely as "murmuración o censura pública" ("gossip or public censure").[94]

But perhaps the most crucial aspect of this phrase lies in the way it conditions and determines the scene of address and the apostrophic nature of this poem. As a matter of fact, our initial claim regarding the singularity of this apostrophe as linked to the deviation of the speaker's address from the volume's reader to its author is not precise enough. If apostrophe, as Barbara Johnson argues, is a form of "ventriloquism" that animates whoever or whatever is addressed in and through this trope, then what we have here could not count as a case of apostrophe unless we revise the presential unidirectionality that reputedly structures this trope and turns its turning away into the bringing forth of an absence within the poem's presentation.[95] For instead of bringing into presence an absent addressee, apostrophe here is meant to conjure away Julia de Burgos. This explains the crucial, though barely perceptible, role that the figure of *las gentes* plays in this scene of address. We might even say that the actual target of the speaker's irascible epideixis is not her explicit addressee but the triangulated audience indirectly apostrophized in the allegory of *las gentes*. In other words, apostrophe here conjures away Julia de Burgos by indirectly conjuring up the motley and shapeless crowd of nosy people who keep conjuring up Julia de Burgos by insisting on the *identity* of the *speaker* of the poems and the person who bears that name and functions as their author.

It is at this point of the reading—thus, from the very beginning—that we encounter the decision before which the speaker of this poem places her readers: Will we read *Poema* in such a way that we show ourselves as belonging to *las gentes*, that is, as readers who, perhaps informed by the Romantic notion of the lyric as an *expressive* "representation of subjective experience,"[96] cannot see that whoever speaks in the twenty poems that compose *Poema* does not coincide with Julia de Burgos? Or will we read/hear this poem as the voice herself utters it, that is, as the immediate manifestation of her self-present "I," and not as the externalization of internal mental states and experiences that could be located within the subjectivity of that real person called Julia de Burgos?

Since the critical dimension of this apostrophe has not been explicitly remarked by de Burgos's readers, it is not surprising that most interpreters have read this poem exactly how the speaker demands that it *not* be read, namely, as a poetic mirror that reflects to the author the self-image that the speaker has projected. Perhaps the first textual traces of this type of reading can be found as early as 1938, and they're signed by none other than Trinidad Padilla de Sanz (1864–1957), who at the time was the doyenne of Puerto Rico's elite feminist circles and a prominent figure in the most conservative wing of the Nationalist movement. Less than a month after "A Julia de Burgos" made its first public appearance in the pages of *El Imparcial* (one of the island's major newspapers) on March 5, 1938, Padilla de Sanz published a response in the same newspaper under the equally apostrophic title "De la Hija del Caribe a Julia de Burgos" ("From the Daughter of El Caribe to Julia de Burgos"). A quick glance at this poem affords an occasion to witness the constitution of de Burgos's catastrophic reception as it was being made.

Padilla de Sanz's poem opens with four lines that center on the issue of understanding, affirming unequivocally that she has understood de Burgos's poem:

> Te admiro, Julia de Burgos, he leído tus versos
> Si hay quien no los entienda, los he entendido yo,
> Tus versos tan audaces, y por eso te admiro;
> Si te atacan los necios y censuran, yo no.[97]

> I admire you, Julia de Burgos, I have read your verses;
> If somebody doesn't understand them, I have understood them,
> your audacious verses, and that's why I admire you;
> If the stupid attack you and censor you, not I.

The fact that Padilla de Sanz decides to begin her poem by foregrounding the question of understanding may not be surprising in itself, though I would argue that this gesture is more significant than it might seem at first glance. For in throwing into sharp relief her own status as someone who has not only *read* but *understood* de Burgos's verses, Padilla de Sanz cannot avoid raising the spectral possibility that the poem's message or sense may not be understood, which, in turn, implicitly raises the question concerning the conditions of intelligibility of "1. A Julia de Burgos." Moreover, as these first four lines make clear, what Padilla de Sanz means by understanding here should not be simply characterized as a semantic process in which dead signs are imbued with spiritual meaning; rather, this semantic or cognitive event is itself grounded in an affective, empathetic intentionality that, in turn, depends on and consolidates the circuit of specular identification.

And yet, in a way typical (though seldom examined) of most homage scenes, the play of empathy and identification is ironically inverted: Padilla de Sanz *understands* "A Julia de Burgos" because she *admires* her, but she admires her because de Burgos is *like her*, who also feels disdain for the *necios* who harbor "hypocritical prejudices" and may attack and censor the author of this poem.

> Hembra fuerte y fecunda curtida en mis labores,
> Desdeño los prejuicios hipócritas. . . .
> . . .
> y por eso te admiro, porque eres sana y fuerte,
> y presentas el alma desnuda, como yo.[98]

> Strong and fecund female hardened seasoned by labor,
> I disdain hypocritical prejudices. . . .
> . . .
> and that's why I admire you, because you're strong and healthy,
> and you present the soul naked, like I.

Despite the speaker's multiple declarations regarding the novelty and uniqueness of de Burgos's poetry, these lines, which appear halfway through the poem, draw to a close the circle of identification produced by specularity: Padilla de Sanz admires Julia de Burgos because Julia de Burgos is fundamentally the *same* type of woman as herself. The last two lines of the poem further consolidate this process of mirroring and self-other identifications that boil down to sameness:

> Canta, nueva poetisa, con tu estro sublime
> Porque eres como dices; y como tú soy yo.[99]

> Sing, new poetess, with your sublime muse
> Because you are as you say; and I am like you.

We can now return to the question that Padilla Sanz implicitly poses in her poem, namely, the question regarding what it would mean to understand a poem like "A Julia de Burgos." Could we say that Padilla Sanz's poem reflects an *understanding* of what *happens* in this poem? Recall, in this context, de Man's claim that the condition for the intelligibility of lyric poetry is traditionally held to depend on the phenomenalization of the lyric voice. What are the conditions for the phenomenalization of the voice that speaks in "A Julia de Burgos?" In other words, how are those conditions articulated by the speaker of de Burgos's poem? Paradoxically, by addressing her poem to the person called Julia de Burgos, Padilla Sanz misses the mark; she directs her praise and admiration to that exact persona from whom the "I" or "self" that speaks in de Burgos's poem had to distinguish *her self* in order to become *herself*, in order to secure her ipseity and to establish and remark the radical phenomenological difference that separates her from Julia de Burgos. This produces an ironic situation, which was exacerbated by de Burgos's decision to include Padilla Sanz's poem in the preface to her own book: At the precise moment in which Padilla Sanz sees herself in Julia de Burgos and reestablishes a feminist genealogy in which the mother figure sees herself in her daughter because the daughter mirrors her mother, she has actually stopped hearing the voice that speaks in "A Julia de Burgos." Wanting at all costs to remove herself from the spectral *gentes* that gossip and lie about the identity of Julia de Burgos, conflating the submissive, patriarchalized wife with the speaker of the poems signed by her, Padilla Sanz nonetheless ends up joining those same people by failing to pay heed to the radicality of the split that this poem claims to have established between the lyric voice and the authorial figure—a split that determines the conditions for the phenomenal manifestation of this voice *as such*, that is, as *herself*. Thinking she has passed the test in which "A Julia de Burgos" places her readers and understood the challenge that the poem articulates, Padilla Sanz actually fails to address the central claim that structures this poem, namely, that the proper name constitutes a technology of self-alienation and symbolic inscription that *must be abandoned* in order for the speaker to emerge as her-self, in order to appear in and *as* the pure autoaffectivity of her own voice.

What's in a Name? Pseudonyms and Feminist Allegories

As I have suggested, the question of the proper name occupies a crucial role in this poem, and it therefore deserves closer scrutiny, both theoretically as well as historically. It so happens that the status of the proper name in the history of the publication of this poem and in de Burgos's developments as a poet from 1934 to 1938 constitute an issue in its own right. As it pertains to "A Julia de Burgos," I already noted that the first version of this poem was published in the Puerto Rican newspaper *El Imparcial*, on March 5, 1938. Now, a curious detail of this first version is the fact that there is a discrepancy between the text and paratext of the poem when it comes to what is perhaps the poem's most crucial detail, namely, the poet's "proper" name. Whereas the poem is addressed to Julia Burgos and signed by an author who identifies herself as Julia Burgos, in the actual text of the poem the lyric voice apostrophizes her addressee—that is, the authorial figure, presumably herself—not by using the nom de plume that the author herself had used to publish this poem (namely, Julia Burgos) but rather by using the one that would become known to posterity, Julia *de* Burgos. As part of his meticulous work tracking down the original publications of de Burgos's early poetic output, Cuperes has identified the earliest appearance of the pseudonym Julia de Burgos: It appears for the first time in October 1937, in the pages of the journal *Renovación*, which published the poem "Cortando distancias" ("Cutting Distances")—which de Burgos later included as the seventh poem of *Poema*. In other words, several months before the first publication of "A Julia Burgos," the poet had already begun to appear in public under a different pseudonym. These details might seem insignificant were it not for the fact that even these minor shifts in the poet's self-designation have acquired great significance for the symbolic protocols of interpreting the poet's life and works.

To see both the symbolic significance that has been granted to these shifts in the poet's choice of pseudonym as well as the dimension of historicity that this symbolic reading obfuscates, it is crucial to keep in mind that Julia de Burgos was born as Julia Constanza Burgos García; hence, both Julia Burgos and Julia de Burgos are pseudonyms. Moreover, these two noms de plume belong to a series of names that de Burgos used to appear in public as a writer, which begins with Julia Burgos de Rodríguez, crafted on the basis of her married name. If we position these three names alongside one another, their very succession already yields an allegorical narrative of feminist emancipation: De Burgos launched her publishing career announcing to the world her status as a married woman; then, after her divorce, she used her paternal last name, Burgos, remarking her condition as a divorcée; then, she finally settled on Julia de Burgos, a name that, through the retention of the particle *de* before her paternal last name, suggests a return of the relationship of appropriation, of ownership, or of belonging—but this time exclusively directed to herself. As Pérez Rosario, writing about "A Julia de Burgos," puts it, "around the same time in 1938 when this poem was published, Burgos dropped her married name; rather than reverting to her maiden name, she inserted *de* before her father's last name, which in Spanish indicates marital status or possession. She thus became Julia de Burgos, symbolically taking possession of herself."[100] In becoming Julia *de* Burgos, Julia Burgos would have undergone a transformation not unlike that of marriage, not only enacting something like a self-marriage but also retaining the aspirational, ennobling effects that are still associated in the Spanish-speaking milieu with last names that are preceded by that preposition.

As I mentioned before, the symbolic reading of de Burgos's series of pseudonyms, while more than justified, occludes a deep stratum of *Poema*'s historicity. We can begin to approach this occlusion if we bring this symbolic-allegorical reading protocol to bear on our reading of "1. A Julia de Burgos." Indeed, only if we grasp the significance of de Burgos's prior self-designation after her divorce can we then measure how thoroughgoing is the challenge that "1. A Julia de Burgos" mounts to the baptismal scene of personal appellation as a crucial technology in the ontological process of modern anthropogenesis. For the name that the speaker of *Poema* wishes to set on fire, the name from which this egological voice had to dissociate herself in order to become herself, is none other than *the name that she gave herself*, the name by which she wanted to be identified in public as a poet and organic intellectual of the Puerto Rican left after her divorce, the name that she never publicly disowned—except in the space opened up by the *literary event* of "1. A Julia de Burgos" and, by extension, of *Poema* as a whole.

Here emerges one of the most theoretically challenging aspects of de Burgos's *Poema*, namely, her challenge to a philosophical tradition that regards ipseity as bound up in the bestowal of proper names. Paul Ricœur summarizes this tradition most succinctly when he writes that "the privilege of proper names assigned to *humans* is due to their ulterior role of confirming their *identity* and their *ipseity*."[101] Rather than confirming both human identity and ipseity, the proper name emerges in "1. A Julia de Burgos" as a vector of expropriation whose imposition neutralizes the experience of being an authentic ipseity for the sake of becoming an identifiable *social persona*. After this poem, the act of self-naming implicitly appears as complicit with a historico-metaphysical configuration of social life that reduces the presence of the self to itself to a social ritual of personal identification. The proper name is, at best, only able to secure sameness within a social milieu, guaranteeing the individuality and identity to itself *for others* of the person who bears *this* or *that* name, and it can only do so at the expense of usurping and blocking the possibility of a language that might convey the experience of life at its most *intimate* and *enstatic*, lived in the radical singularity of the first person. The proper name thus stands at the very ground of an understanding of *human* personhood that is properly speaking *inhuman* to the extent that it, paradoxically, serves as a medium of self-alienation through the social reification of selfhood.

Psychomachia: Beyond Enmity?

Let us now return to the text of "1. A Julia de Burgos" and, in particular, to the figure of enmity that emerges from its very opening sequence:

> Ya las gentes murmuran que yo soy tu enemiga,
> porque dicen que en verso doy al mundo tu yo.
> Mienten, Julia de Burgos. Mienten, Julia de Burgos.
> La que se alza en mis versos no es tu voz: es mi voz;
> porque tú eres ropaje y la esencia soy yo;
> y el más grande abismo se tiende entre las dos.
>
> Already people murmur that I am your enemy,
> for they say that in verse I give to the world your I.
> They lie, Julia de Burgos. They lie, Julia de Burgos.
> Who rises in my verses is not your voice: it is my voice;
> for you are the garb and I am the essence;
> and the greatest abyss lies between us.

In one of the most compelling engagements with this poem, Lilliana Ramos Collado astutely retrieves the medieval allegorical genre of the *psychomachia*—literally, a battle of souls or spirits—in order to capture the depths of the *psychic* antagonism that characterizes the poem:

> The figure of enmity guarantees the intelligibility of Julia de Burgos's struggle to the death against herself, a struggle that is forged through an incompatibility that, in turn, assumes the discourse of insult. The fact that we are dealing with a psychomachy, or a war within the soul, in which each of the Julias, being the enemy of the other Julia, is an enemy to herself, is striking. Against the dishonest murmur that emerges from anonymous and cowardly rumors, and against the silence of the equally cowardly, haughty Julia, the hardened Julia "raises" her voice.[102]

As I mentioned before, I want to retain Ramos Collado's interpretation of this poem as a psychomachia, but with some modifications, which are aimed at both raising the stakes of the *polemos* or *makhia* that this poem evokes and sharpening the contours of the selfhood that emerges through this strife. This sharpening becomes necessary because, as the first sentence in the passage just quoted makes clear, something remains barely digested, perhaps undigestible, in this poem, which has to do with the mode of relationship that it posits through its apostrophe. Note the discrepancy between Ramos Collado's claim that enmity emerges as the figure that warrants the *intelligibility* of this poem and the poem itself, which opens precisely by denying the veracity of those who deploy that very figure and thus by rejecting the intelligibility that it would afford. But perhaps Ramos Collado is right after all, and the possibility of understanding this poem necessitates that we tone down the voice's claims regarding her absolute separation from de Burgos as a social persona or authorial figure and accept the view that the conflict between these selves ultimately boils down to a conflict between two possible forms of life or modes of existence—two souls that, in spite their seemingly intractable antagonism, would belong to the same self. Rather than following this ultimately deflationary reading, I want to argue that to measure the radicality of what happened with the publication of *Poema* we must take this voice at her word—and this means that we must resist any effort to psychologize or anthropomorphize the struggle between this nameless I and Julia de Burgos by turning them into two different modes of social being, whether two different personæ that would be at war *within the same soul* or two different souls that would be at war *within the same self*. This explains why the figure of the psychomachy, though helpful to understand the event that happens in and as this poem, can be misguiding if it is understood, as Collado Ramos does, as a war raging *inside* de Burgos's soul. Granting that the speaker of "1. A Julia de Burgos" has so radically disidentified *her self* from the proper name Julia de Burgos is a necessary precondition for the transcendental stakes of this poem's *psychomachia* to come clearly to the fore. For the poem is not a "battle for the soul" of the author or of Julia—quite the contrary. The poem, instead, stages a battle between a voice that is already *all soul* before arriving to the poetic scene and an author who is literally *soulless*, whose incapacity to renounce her proper name and all its wages keeps her from attaining that dimension of intimate animacy that constitutes the embodied ground of the *gendered ipseity* that speaks across the text of *Poema*.

To read this nuance in the poem's polemic unfolding, we should dwell for a bit longer than most readers on the series of oppositions that the poem establishes in what we might call its second part, which is dominated syntactically and rhetorically by the rapid, oppositional oscillation of the "I" and the "you," of the speaking self and Julia de Burgos:

> Tú eres fría muñeca de mentira social,
> y yo, viril destello de la humana verdad.
> Tú, miel de cortesanas hipocresías; yo no;
> que en todos mis poemas desnudo el corazón.
> Tú eres como tu mundo, egoísta; yo no;
> que todo me lo juego a ser lo que soy yo.
> Tú eres sólo la grave señora señorona;
> yo no; yo soy la vida, la fuerza, la mujer.
> Tú eres de tu marido, de tu amo; yo no;
> yo de nadie, o de todos, porque a todos, a todos,
> en mi limpio sentir y en mi pensar me doy.

Tú te rizas el pelo y te pintas; yo no;
a mí me riza el viento; a mí me pinta el sol.
Tú eres dama casera, resignada, sumisa,
atada a los prejuicios de los hombres; yo no;
que yo soy Rocinante corriendo desbocado
olfateando horizontes de justicia de Dios.
Tú en ti misma no mandas; a ti todos te mandan;
en ti mandan tu esposo, tus padres, tus parientes,
el cura, el modista, el teatro, el casino,
el auto, las alhajas, el banquete, el champán,
el cielo y el infierno, y el qué dirán social.
En mí no, que en mí manda mi solo corazón,
mi solo pensamiento; quien manda en mí soy yo.
Tú, flor de aristocracia; y yo la flor del pueblo.
Tú en ti lo tienes todo y a todos se lo debes,
mientras que yo, mi nada, a nadie se la debo.
Tú, clavada al estático dividendo ancestral,
y yo, un uno en la cifra del divisor social,
somos el duelo a muerte que se acerca fatal.

You are the cold doll of social lies,
And I, the virile spark of human truth.
You, honey of courtly hypocrisies; not I;
who in all my poems undress the heart.
You are like your world, selfish; not I;
who bets everything to be what I am.
You are only the somber, haughty lady;
Not I; I am life, strength, woman.
You are of your husband, your master; not I;
I am of nobody, or of all, because to all, to all,
in my limpid feeling and thinking I give myself.
You curl your hair and dye it; not I;
I am curled by the wind; I am dyed by the sun.
You are a domestic, resigned, submissive lady
Bound to the prejudices of men; not I;
For I am Rocinante running wild
tracking horizons of divine justice.
You do not rule in yourself; you are ruled by all;
in you rule your husband, your parents, your relatives,
the priest, the dressmaker, the theater, the club,
the car, the jewels, the banquet, the champagne,

heaven and hell, and what society might say.
Not in me, in me only rules my heart,
my sole thinking; who rules in me is I.
You, aristocratic flower; and I the flower of the people.
You have everything in you and you owe it to all,
whereas I owe my nothing to nobody.
You, stuck to the static ancestral dividend,
and I, a one in the number of the social divisor,
We are the duel to the death that fatally approaches.

Given the tightness of their form and the systematic nature of its rhythmic constitution, it is understandable that these lines have lent themselves primarily to syntactical reading, perhaps best exemplified by the following commentary from Ivette López Jiménez:

> The lyric speaker, identified by the pronoun I, addresses herself to a textual receiver represented by the pronoun you and the name Julia de Burgos.... The grammatical opposition is reiterated through the distribution of metric units: to each person may correspond a hemistich ... two verses ... a whole strophe.... On the axes of the you and the I, the poem unfolds the semantic fields that are identified with each grammatical person (artificial and natural, false and true, immobile and mobile, slave and free, aristocracy and people) until it culminates in the final contradiction, represented by a revolutionary uprising.[103]

As López Jiménez implicitly suggests in this passage, one of the structural aspects of this poem comes to the fore as a privileging of syntax over semantics. The poem performs the demarcation of its two major semantic fields—the group of lines that establish some predicates of the "I" and those that do the same for the "you"—exclusively through syntactical means, that is, through the sheer iteration and exacerbation of the apostrophic I/you relation. The privilege of syntax over semantics—or of "form," if you will, over "content"—is such that the syntactical establishment of the oppositional I/you grammar appears to override and recode any *semantic specificity* of the content that the speaker relies on in order to lend concreteness and substance to this opposition. This explains why it seems to be so easy to construct the oppositional matrix that produces all the different binary permutations that *could* appear in this poem. A quick glance at the series of binary oppositions that López Jiménez isolates in the passage just quoted makes clear that the specific semantic content of these values matters less here than their seeming capacity to saturate a conceptual field by signifying its polar extremities. For every single system of predicates can be deployed at any moment by the speaker, so long as it allows a dialectical polarity to emerge, thereby iterating the distance that she has already established between herself and Julia de Burgos.

As a matter of fact, the poem's opening section already institutes this procedure when the speaker introduces the first binary opposition *essence/garb*, itself a partial metaphor for the metaphysical opposition *essence/appearance*, whose ultimate metaphysical form is the opposition *essence/accident*. This explains why the speaker can both claim to be radically untethered from the *social*—unlike Julia de Burgos, who cowers before "el qué dirán social (what society might say)"—and, later in the poem, put herself on the side of the *social* and (in a true divergence from Pedreira) of *number*, while berating Julia de Burgos for being stuck in the "static ancestral dividend." To be sure, the difference between these two valences of the social can be explained in semantic terms: Whereas in the first case sociality emerges in its oppressive guise as a force that, as Wynter might have put it, "dysselects" antipatriarchal behaviors, in the second the social emerges, in accordance with a more sociological, indeed modernist imaginary, as a force that dissolves the communitarian, stratified lifeworld of the ancien régime; this explains why number, in spite its abstraction and impersonality, emerges here as an ally in the speaker's feminist struggle. What we encounter here is one of the most basic and least explored aspects of what earlier I described as de Burgos's ambivalence with regards to modernity. But even this ambivalence is as much a function of the dialectical antagonism of this poem's syntax as it is a feature of its actual historical semantics.

The primacy of syntax over semantics becomes more pronounced when the poet identifies herself as the *true-natural* person over and against the *false-artificial* persona, while in the same breath identifying herself as both the *master-populist* self over and against the Julia de Burgos who is a *slave-aristocrat*. Whereas associating the values of *truth* with *nature* and *falsehood* with *artifice* feels like an easy and even natural thing to do (Western metaphysics at its most basic, namely, as common sense, could be said to consist in this particular association), linking *mastery* with *populism* and *slavery* with *aristocracy* would require a logical leap if it were not for the sheer positional force of the speaker's language, which is capable of constructing a chain of equivalences distributed along the I/you axes that gather values which, in themselves, appear to be mutually opposed, if not even self-contradictory. This is why, although I agree with Aurea María Sotomayor when she claims that this poem "is equivalent to a poetic and civic autogenesis," I would argue that the binary opposition *public/private* that she identifies as the matrixial form of the poem's oppositional syntax is not the best candidate for the opposition that enacts and presides over this process of self-generation,[104] which I am inclined to understand in the literal sense, that is, as a *genesis of the gendered self itself*, before its opposition into public or private. Opposition functions in such a *pure* way, self-antagonism is so much the ground and source of this voice's emergence, that the poem instead demands to be read as an aberrant quasi-Fichtean allegory that is concerned above all with the (self)-institution of the *I* through the sheer positing of *itself* and of its *other*, the *not-I*. Even the poem's utopian ending could be read as the messianic anticipation of the eventual arrival on this earth of the *normative order* that the speaker already *embodies* and *anticipates* to the extent that the content of her existence is shown throughout the poem to coincide with nothing but her own "activity of *self-determination*," which, as Rocío Zambrana reminds us, takes the form in Fichte's idealism of the self's absolute positing through the positing of the "boundary between the I and not-I."[105]

But, unlike the case of Fichte and other absolute idealisms of identity, the *I* that posits herself here cannot come to terms or reach any form of reconciliation with the *not-I* whose dangerous abjection has infected the reputed site of her highest intimacy, namely, her proper name. It is this unbearable intimacy that explains the implacable necessity of the line that closes the second "part" or sequence of the poem and marks the transition to the third and final sequence, where the psychomachia reaches its apex:

> somos el duelo a muerte que se acerca fatal.
> Cuando las multitudes corran alborotadas
> dejando atrás cenizas de injusticias quemadas,
> y cuando con la tea de las siete virtudes,
> tras los siete pecados, corran las multitudes,
> contra ti, y contra todo lo injusto y lo inhumano,
> yo iré en medio de ellas con la tea en la mano.
>
> we are the duel to the death that fatally approaches.
> When the multitudes run amok
> leaving behind the ashes of burned injustice,
> and when, with the torch of the seven virtues
> after the seven vices run the multitudes,
> against you and against all that is unjust and inhumane,
> I will be in their midst torch in hand.

The psychomachia comes to an end in proper fashion, that is, by recalling the literary memory of its first known instantiation, namely, Prudentius's *Psycho-*

machia, a second-century text that is regarded as one of the inaugural texts in Christian classical literature. As its title suggests, it portrays an allegorical battle of souls that features the allegories of the seven virtues and the seven vices engaged in a mortal combat, from which the virtues emerge victorious.[106] Implicitly evoking the memory of this struggle against vice and immorality, the poem's closing lines presents the speaker in the midst of a multitude that embodies the allegorical image of the seven virtues, torches in hand, in a revolutionary frenzy that will set fire to the authorial figure, Julia de Burgos herself, who has become the emblem and effigy of an inhuman world.

A reader as perceptive as Ramos Collado has suggested that the violence that de Burgos exerts upon herself amounts to a form of internalized misogyny, essentially arguing that in order to disidentify *her-self* from herself, to dissociate the patriarchalized, submissive woman that bears the name Julia de Burgos from the feminine ipseity that speaks throughout *Poema*, de Burgos must paradoxically rehearse the quintessential patriarchal, Abrahamic gesture of blaming women for the introduction of the "seven sins" into the world.[107] In a similar vein, Cuperes has even wondered whether de Burgos here should not be seen as endorsing the same sexist views of women that Pedreira himself espoused and that other, equally conservative members of the Generación del 30 rejected as sexist, such as Margot Arce de Vázquez.[108] Although there is some truth to this argument, my reading suggests that we will not understand the significance of the disidentificatory violence that de Burgos unleashes in this poem if we do not read it as a response to the violence of the patriarchal gender system that is part and parcel of the modern world-system, to which the territory now known as Puerto Rico was conscripted after the Spanish "discovery" and colonization of the island in 1492 and 1508. To simply read the violence that the speaker directs against the persona that bears the name of Julia de Burgos as the result of the poet's internalized misogyny misses what is most crucial about the feminism that emerges in this poem, which is not concerned with advocating for gender equality under the law or merely rehearsing gynophilic views. Instead, the feminism of "1. A Julia de Burgos" attempts to reckon with the fact that women are conscripted by the modern, patriarchal gender system to ensure the perpetuation of male supremacy and that, as a result, within this system the position of women is itself structured by misogyny. The speaker's disidentification of *her-self* from herself thus emblematizes the violence that would be required in order to release women from their conscription by patriarchy, which ensures its stable replication not only by harnessing women's reproductive labor but also by interpellating women as part of the work of reproducing the ideology of male supremacy. The fact that, as the poem concludes, Julia de Burgos herself emerges as the emblem of all that is *inhuman* and deserves to be destroyed reveals the scale at which the feminism that takes shape in this poem is pitched—it entails nothing less than a very redefinition of the humanity of the human.

Indeed, the unfolding of the poem's concluding lines can be read as animated by the insight that the social or existential opposition between authenticity and inauthenticity, or the conflict between a feminist and a patriarchalized woman, cannot find a resolution within the discursive and practical domains in which these conflicts are articulated without at the same time bringing about a radical transformation of what it means to be human. The poem's concluding image, in which the speaker evokes a future revolutionary scenario in which she will set fire—symbolically, but perhaps also literally—to the person who bears the name Julia de Burgos and who emerges as the emblem of all that is inhuman about the current order of things, provides a vivid representation of the messianic dimension that animates the speaker's political project, her awaiting for the moment in which, to quote Fanon, "we would like to light the carcass of man and leave. Perhaps we will arrive at this result: Man tending this fire by self-combustion."[109] Only if we retrieve de Burgos's questioning of the meaning and future of *the human* could we begin to approach the most radical dimension of de Burgos's historico-ontological wager throughout *Poema en veinte surcos*, the place in which her ambivalent relationship to what we might call the *historicity* of *modernity* comes more vividly to the fore.

§23. ENSTATIC IPSEITY, ECSTATIC FLESH: "2. ÍNTIMA" AS PHENOMENOLOGY OF EMBODIED LIFE

At first sight, the poem "2. Íntima" appears to be nothing more than a continuation of the psychomachia that opens *Poema* (this, perhaps, explains why de Burgos placed it immediately after her first poetic salvo). Upon closer inspection, the poem reveals itself as de Burgos's most philosophically exacting attempt to pose a question that, to a large extent, remained unasked in the first poem of the volume: What are the *conditions* under which *ipseity* can be experienced in a historical context marked by what we might call, for lack of a better name, *modernity*? In other words, if "1. A Julia de Burgos" staged an allegorical psychomachia, I argue that "2. Íntima" presents a philosophical allegory whose goal is to pose and answer the problem that this psychomachia presupposed, namely, the question concerning the essence of ipseity. Whereas "1. A Julia de Burgos" has as its function to exclude the person who bears the proper name Julia de Burgos from the lyric space of *Poema*'s enunciation so that only the "pure I" of lyric voice remains, the task of "2. Íntima" is more self-reflexive, if not outright philosophical, namely, to disclose the essence of this "I" by presenting the process whereby the speaker becomes a *Yo misma*, an "I myself," thus attaining the site of her ipseity. This alone goes a long way toward justifying the unheard-of privilege that I place on this poem, which has barely attracted the interest of de Burgos's readers.[110] I would even go as far as to argue that "2. Íntima" holds the key to the architecture of *Poema*; it is the *surco* or "furrow" that gathers all the other *surcos* and lends the volume its strange, seldom remarked "monadological" structure.[111]

To begin retracing that furrow, let me quote the poem in its entirety:

2. Íntima	2. Intimate
Se recogió la vida para verme pasar.	Life gathered itself to see me pass.
Me fui perdiendo átomo por átomo de mi carne	I myself went losing atom by atom of my flesh
y fui resbalándome poco a poco al alma.	and went sliding myself bit by bit to the soul.
Peregrina en mí misma, me anduve un largo instante.	Pilgrim in myself, I walked myself a long instant.
Me prolongué en el rumbo de aquel camino errante	I prolonged myself in the course of that errant path
que se abría en mi interior,	that was opening itself in my interior,
y me llegué hasta mí, íntima.	and arrived myself up to me, intimate.
Conmigo cabalgando seguí por la sombra del tiempo	Riding with myself I continued through the shadow of time
y me hice paisaje lejos de mi visión.	and made myself landscape far from my vision.
Me conocí mensaje lejos de la palabra.	I knew myself message far from the word.
Me sentí vida al reverso de una superficie de colores y formas.	I felt myself life on the reverse side of a surface of colors and shapes.
Y me vi claridad ahuyentando la sombra vaciada en la tierra desde el hombre.	And I saw myself clarity dispelling the shadow emptied upon the earth from man.
***	***
Ha sonado un reloj la hora encogida de todos.	A clock has sounded the shrunken hour of all.
¿La hora? Cualquiera. Todas en una misma.	The hour? Any. All in the same one.
Las cosas circundantes reconquistan color y forma.	Surrounding things conquer again color and shape.
Los hombres se mueven ajenos a sí mismos	Men move alien to themselves

para agarrar ese minuto índice	to grasp that minute-index
que los conduce por varias direcciones estáticas.	that leads them through various static directions.
Siempre la misma carne apretándose muda a lo ya hecho.	Always the same flesh pressing into itself moves to the already-made.
Me busco. Estoy aún en el paisaje lejos de mi visión.	I search for myself. I am still in the landscape far from my vision.
Sigo siendo mensaje lejos de la palabra.	I continue to be message far from the word.
La forma que se aleja y que fue mía en un instante	The form that distances itself and that was mine in an instant
me ha dejado íntima.	has left me intimate.
Y me veo claridad ahuyentando la sombra vaciada en la tierra desde el hombre.[112]	And I see myself clarity dispelling the shadow emptied upon the earth from man.

A mere glance at "2. Íntima" should be enough for us to notice a curious formal feature of this poem, namely, its division in two parts. This is somewhat of an oddity in Burgos's entire corpus—but especially in *Poema*, where this is the only poem that is divided in two halves by asterisks that, ironically, remark and intensify the blank space that separates the first and the second part. And yet, given the abyssal thematic and temporal differences that distinguish the two parts of this poem, de Burgos's choice of this formal device should come as no surprise. I would even argue that the poem could hardly manage to do the philosophical work it actually does without this feature. Indeed, it would even be possible to offer quick, yet insightful, paraphrases of this poem by simply attending to the most obvious ways in which these two parts diverge thematically and temporally.

At the level of theme, perhaps the most striking contrast between these two parts can be located in their different regimes of motion and rest. On the one hand, the first part is exclusively concerned with figuring movements that I would describe as *enstatic*. Popularized in twentieth-century religious studies and philosophy by Mircea Eliade's work on Yoga—who offered the term as a translation of the Sanskrit *samādhi*, often rendered as "contemplation" or "medidative absorption"[113]—the term *enstasis* is a variation of the Ancient Greek term *ekstasis* (*ek* + *stasis*, literally "standing outside"), meaning both "displacement" and "change," hence also "degeneracy," "differentiation," and "standing aside oneself," from which the senses of being "entranced," "astonished," or "raptured" follow. *Enstasis* is thus, quite literally, a "standing within," which, if used adjectively to describe a motion, corresponds only to movements of self-gathering or of self-recollecting, inward or internal motions: a movement within the self towards the self itself. Moreover, the fact that the word *enstasis*, though attested in Ancient Greek, was not used initially to designate the opposite of *ekstasis*, is not irrelevant to our purposes. For the fact that *ekstasis* was initially opposed to *stasis*, without any prefix, suggests a more rigid opposition between motion and rest than what obtains when dealing with *enstasis*, which requires a certain suspension of this polar opposition. The concept of *enstasis* in the Ancient Greek context would have been oxymoronic or, at best, pleonastic, since the quality of inwardness would be analytically contained in the very concept and experience of *stasis*, of standing restfully in one's essential and proper place, of having always-already been erected into an *ousia* or a *substance*. The figures of motion in the first part of the poem—the gathering of life and the speaker's passing (through) in the poem's first allegorical sequence, the speaker's pilgrimage in herself and her arrival into herself, her horseback riding with herself and the series of oxymoronic transmogrifications that obtain in the last four lines of the first part—are en-static precisely because they delineate a motion toward the self's innermost *stasis* for the sake of attaining precisely that state in which rest and motion are no longer opposed. The opposite befalls the theme of motion in the second part of the poem. Indeed, as soon as the speaker awakens at the sounding of a clock telling the time, she's suddenly thrown into what seems like an urban landscape populated by men whose motions betray their self-alienation. The second part of the poem thus features a sort of inverted *katabasis* in which the speaker descends not into an underworld but into *this* world and faces a regime of motion so dominated by *ecstatic temporality* that movement itself emerges as the grounds of a generalized being-outside-oneself in its most devalorized or pejorative sense.

A similarly oppositional difference can be easily remarked at the level of the poem's internal temporality by tracking the way tense shifts between these two parts: Whereas the first half of the poem is overwhelmingly dominated by the simple past (with the sole exception of the verb *abría*, which is conjugated in the imperfect, thus indicating the ongoing aspect of the opening of the internal path in which her enstatic trajectory unfolds), the second part positions the reader in the present of the poem's own lyrical unfolding through its overwhelming use of the present, punctuated only by the appearance of a present perfect construction ("*Ha sonado un reloj la hora . . .*"; "A clock has sounded the hour . . ."), which functions thematically (if not syntactically) like a caesura. This shift from an accomplished past to the present is further emphasized by the poem's last stanza, which repeats three of the last four lines of the first part verbatim, except by changing the tense of these lines from past to the present. The poem thus concludes by repeating the conclusion of the first part, with the speaker reiterating, as it were, the end of her enstatic pilgrimage. In this way, this inward movement loses the character of a past event that the speaker is indirectly reporting to us and becomes an event both in our present as readers and in the present of the poem's own unfolding. This temporal shift has crucial implications for the interpretation of the poem. For the fact that the speaker is able to confirm that her own being-intimate-with-herself persists in spite of her sudden and rough awakening to a social milieu characterized by the very negation of the possibility of intimacy suggests how strong and durable her hold on her own self is. Rather than being an experience that she once had and then lost, ipseity emerges here as the enduring condition of her selfhood, which was attained enstatically and endures despite her fall into an ecstatic social world.

These highly schematic observations already anticipate the broad strokes of what follows. My reading of this underexamined and fascinating poem shows that it constitutes de Burgos's most systematic effort to turn poetry into the medium in which the *experience* of being an "I" or a self can be experienced in its purity, that is, in its innermost intimacy. Moreover, while seemingly committed to understanding the possibility of ipseity in supratemporal and ahistorical terms, the experience that the poem poeticizes is motivated by concerns that are historical through and through. Indeed, I read the poem's concerns with intimacy as being motivated by the challenge that modernity reputedly poses to the sense of self—that is, to the possibility of ipseity. How can the self maintain a proper relation to itself in a social and historical context in which even the most personal mark of identity—that is, the proper name—becomes a vector of ontological expropriation? How could one have an experience of oneself as an *ipseity* within a world that is bent on alienating humanity from its properly ipseitological life?

My working hypothesis is that the poem's very unfolding provides a positive answer to these questions by presenting a felicitous allegory of becoming-an-ipseity. The poem not only narrates the speaker's past attainment of her intimate selfhood but also allegorizes the possibility of retrieving in the present this past experience of self-possession—even as the speaker inhabits a social milieu that would seem to render such recuperation impossible. In this way, the poem not only sets in motion a "method" for both becoming an ipseity and securing this intimate sense of self from the corrosive effects of modernity. Perhaps most importantly, the poem also becomes a vector for the transmission of this method of retrieval to its readers. "2. Íntima" thus offers readers a path to remain inalienably themselves in a world in which even one of the most basic aspects of life—that is, kinesis, animacy, self-movement—reveals or indicates nothing other than human alienation, understood in precise terms as an incapacity for intimacy (and, hence, for ipseity).

"Metaphysics Is Julia's Passion":
"2. Íntima" as Life-Phenomenology

Before turning to the poem itself, then, I would like to clarify the historical stakes of my reading of "2. Íntima" and unpack the philosophical presuppositions that inform my reading. As I previously suggested (see §21), de Burgos's response to modernity takes the form of a phenomenological radicalization of the project of *Lebensphilosophie*, or "Life-Philosophy," as Benjamin understood it. Accordingly, the reading that follows is deeply informed by my previous treatment of Benjamin's engagement with the divergent ways in which Bergson and Baudelaire related to the change in the structure of their readers' experience (see §10). Throughout this section, the Bergson-Baudelaire opposition will thus serve as a model of sorts to take the measure of de Burgos's own ambivalent relationship to modernity.

To explain why this model is fitting, I would like to briefly revisit Benjamin's sui generis definition of *Lebensphilosophie* in "Über einige Motiven bei Baudelaire" ("On Some Motifs in Baudelaire"):

> If conditions for the reception of lyric poetry have become less favorable, it is reasonable to assume that only in exceptional cases does lyric poetry maintain contact with the experience of its readers. This could be because their experience has been altered in its structure. One may perhaps approve this development but only remain even more at a loss when it comes to characterizing what could have changed in it. [*Man wird diesen Ansatz vielleicht gutheißen, aber nur desto verlegener um eine Kennzeichnung dessen sein, was sich in ihr könnte gewandelt haben.*] In this situation, one will ask philosophy. In doing so, one stumbles upon a peculiar state of affairs. Since the end of the previous century, philosophy has carried out a series of attempts to take possession of "true" experience, as opposed to the experience that sediments itself in the normed, denatured existence of the civilized masses. It is customary to categorize these forays under the concept of "Life-Philosophy."[114]

As I discussed in Part I, the crux of the divergence that Benjamin identifies in the comparison of Bergson and Baudelaire is at once historical and philosophical: Whereas Bergson's intuitionist philosophy of duration, memory, and the *élan vital* intensifies the disavowal of the historicity of experience that is the very condition of *Lebensphilosophie*, Baudelaire addresses himself to the "civilized masses" whom modernity has rendered precisely unable "to take possession of 'true' experience." My reading retains the structure of this opposition as a model to approach de Burgos's own *ambivalent* relationship to modernity because I take de Burgos's modernism to be at once Baudelairean and Bergsonian.

On the one hand, de Burgos's poetics of modern life are Baudelairean insofar as she does confront the ongoing transformation of the Puerto Rican lifeworld (which, coincidentally, I take to be a more precise concept for what Benjamin's calls the "structure of experience"), rather than avert her eyes from the historical conditions of her own lyric production. Moreover, unlike Bergsonism, the modernism of *Poema* does not take the form of a project of reenchanting the world through the intuition of its true vital forces. There is no cosmological principle of unification and differentiation at work in *Poema* and no single poem, with the notable exceptions of "3. Río Grande de Loíza" and "8. Amaneceres," presents physical nature as an ontological region in which the self may feel at home, let alone expand the reach of its ipseity. There is also a notable absence in *Poema* of the kind of racialist vitalism that Donna V. Jones has shown is at work in the *Négritude* movement, itself deeply marked by Bergson's racial metaphysics and that found in Puerto Rican poetry a representative in the "Black" poetry of Luis Palés Matos (I will return to this point in the next section).[115] Along the same lines, we should note that experiences that Benjamin would have characterized as "auratic" are largely missing from *Poema*.[116] And when something like aura does appear (as is the case in "2. Íntima," "3. Río Grande de Loíza," and "20. Yo misma fui mi ruta"), it is usually tempered by the recognition that this authentic or proper experience of "true life" in its insurmountable distance from the punctual here and now can only be had within the boundaries of the speaker's ego. The auratic register of *Poema* produces a situation in which the speaker does not restore the world to its sacrality but instead becomes all the more isolated from the world. Indeed, the modernism of *Poema* is largely devoid of the nostalgic or idealistic belief in the possibility of finding some absolute shelter from modern alienation. Hence the intensity of its political wager, which some of her contemporaries bemoaned as propagandistic: The overcoming of modern life can only be achieved through historical means, that is, through the political transformation of the world, and is not at all a matter of philosophical or aesthetic contemplation. This is why I would argue that what Benjamin wrote about the heroism of Charles Baudelaire—whose defining feature, for Benjamin, lies in Baudelaire's commitment "to live in the heart of unreality (semblance)"[117]—can also be said of de Burgos: Her modernist poetics of ipseity remains firmly indexed to the experience of modernity as a catastrophic historico-ontological condition.

On the other hand, by saying that "2. Íntima" represents the clearest, most rigorous, and systematic articulation of de Burgos's Life-Philosophy, I am indeed suggesting, with Benjamin, that the task of this poem (and of *Poema* as a whole) is analogous to Bergson's philosophical attempt to "take possession of 'true' experience." What is more, by claiming for de Burgos's text the status of Life-Philosophy, I am also implicitly suggesting that what is at stake in her modernist poetics is nothing other than the question concerning the very essence and meaning of life itself. De Burgos's modernist poetics remains Bergsonian because it is animated by the task of restoring the self to its ipseity despite modern alienation. Indeed, as we will see, what de Burgos calls *life* in "2. Íntima" and in other crucial moments in *Poema* will turn out to be nothing other than the very principle of ipseity. Hence, for the speaker of *Poema*, to be alive and to be a self are *the same*. And *intimacy* is the name that de Burgos gives to the affect in which the self is able to experience the radical indistinction of life and ipseity in its own experience of itself, that is, in the very immanence of its life, in the sheer "act" of living.

That being said, it is de Burgos's radical restriction of the horizon of Life-Philosophy to the life of the self and the selfhood of life that justifies my characterization of her philosophical wager as a *phenomenological* radicalization of *Lebensphilosophie*. My reading thus shows that this poem's concern with experiencing life in its truth results in the articulation of a *Lebensphänomenologie* that anticipates, by several decades, some of the basic insights of Michel Henry's enstatic phenomenology of life. Indeed, in what follows I will argue that the poem's allegorical unfolding sets in motion nothing short of a poetic, radicalized version of two of the quintessential methods of phenomenology, namely, the transcendental-phenomenological reduction and the *epokhē*. The radicality of this method lies in the scope of its transcendental reduction and, more precisely, in the way it is applied to *the lifeworld* as a whole. This reduction is accompanied by a corresponding reduction to what we may call, with Husserl, the *Eigensphäre*, or "sphere of ownness," of the speaker, which, in turn, requires the application of something like an *epokhē* to bracket anything within the realm of pure experience that falls outside that innermost ego-logical sphere.[118] Access to this sphere is what de Burgos attains and secures through her affective poetics of *intimacy*.

As a result of this reduction to her intimate ego, the essence of human life can no longer be understood in terms of what Husserl calls "the streaming-living present." For even after the application of the *epokhē* and the transcendental-phenomenological reduction to the world, the living present only appears to Husserl in its *world-constitutive* guise, namely, as "*that subjectivity in which all validity-for-me* [Mir-Gelten] is originally accomplished, in which all sense of being is sense for me and is lived by me as a valid, conscious being."[119] At the very moment of its emergence as "originary temporalization," the living present is *eo ipso* reduced to *being* the source of intentionality, which ipso facto restricts life to the role of guaranteeing the a priori correlation of the self and the world. Much less should we understand the phenomenology of embodied ipseity that emerges in de Burgos's poem in terms of a mundane "ontology" of facticity as in the early Heidegger, for whom the self or *Dasein* is constitutively defined by ecstaticness and worldhood, that is, by the necessity of "being-outside-itself-in-the-world."[120] The feeling of intimacy that "2. Íntima" poetizes cannot be lived or experienced if the subject's enstatic unworldliness—its "standing within-itself-and-without-the-world"—is restricted to its almost sovereign power of world-formation. For at stake in the phenomenality of feeling is something akin to what Henry describes as "the auto-revelation that constitutes the essence of life," an autorevelation that reveals nothing other than the self's autoaffection by itself and does so in a way that is nonintentional, hence imperceptible, yet deeply felt by that self itself.[121] This emphasis of autoaffection brings us to what is perhaps the most important result of the reductions that take place in "2. Íntima," namely, the emergence of what I would call an *arche-body* as the very agent and patient of ipseity, as the bearer of life in its unworldly purity and as the living being that lives that life.

Coincidentally, the reading that follows should place us in a better position to finally assess the pertinence of some of the claims that Luis Llorens Torres made when he introduced de Burgos to the broader Puerto Rican reading public in a short essay published in *Puerto Rico Ilustrado* in October 1937, which I briefly mentioned in Part I (see §11). Here's the relevant passage for our purposes:

> Julia de Burgos, Puerto Rican, is today the highest promise of Hispano-American poetry. . . . In those purely metaphysical flights, when thought surpasses the whole plane of sensibility to plumb the depths of pure abstractions, Julia de Burgos is unique, because today there is no poet in our América that can follow her to the heights of her ideological flights. Through her paternal grandmother she is a quarter German, which can be divined in some traits of her rounded face and even more so in her mental propensity for Kantian abstractions. She finds solace in her ironic verses (see the poem *Nada*), where she firmly roots in prose her pure mind (Kant would say her pure reason) disintegrated from all sensibility, from all experimental apprehension, from all intuition of what exists, from all sense data.[122]

If we take Llorens Torres at his word, we would have to conclude that both he and de Burgos interpreted Kant's investment on the purity of reason as entailing a commitment to the radical separation between reason and sensibility. Although this interpretation of Kant's *theoretical* philosophy is deeply flawed, Llorens Torres's identification of de Burgos with transcendental idealism is not entirely misguided. For de Burgos's all-too-modern response to modernity mobilizes an understanding of the transcendentality of the body that, in many ways, could be read in relation to what the noted Kant scholar Angelica Nuzzo has discerned as Kant's theory of "ideal embodiment."[123] While going against the grain of their reported conversations about Kantian philosophy, "2. Íntima" poetizes an experience of selfhood that insists on the irreducibility of embodiment and, hence, of a sensibility radically directed inward, within the *purified* field of transcendental or a priori experience. Not only does this poem show how right Llorens Torres was when he stated that "Metaphysics is Julia's passion"; it also reveals that, after "2. Íntima," the *passion* of the self is precisely the site in which the metaphysics of life resides.

But access to this metaphysical experience of life, as I already suggested, comes at a cost—to the self, and, above all, to the world. To disclose the idealized materiality of the arche-body as the inalienable site of life and ipseity de Burgos must exercise a violence that targets those whose experience of their own body cannot or will not allow itself to be extricated from its modern entanglements. The metaphysical title that captures the (un)essence of those figures "worthy of destruction" is, not surprisingly, *la carne*, "the flesh." And the allegorical figure that emerges as the flesh's bearer, and thus as the poet's major antagonist, is none other than *el hombre*, "Man." It is here that the specific historico-metaphysical tenor of de Burgos's utopian (anti)humanism will attain its most spectacular, almost blinding, legibility. And it is here that the dialectical oppositionality necessary for the taking place of de Burgos's image within the constellation of modernity will resurface again. The reductions that, according to my reading, the speaker of this poem enacts are not simply philosophical operations; they're also, as the poem "8. Amaneceres" makes patently clear, defensive and offensive incursions against an *improper*, fallen and viscous, humanity. In this way, "2. Íntima"'s desire for ipseity is compelled to reenact some of the foundational rituals of ontological violence that characterize modernity, even if the reactivation of this violence is, ironically, brought about by what may appear to some as a radical *transformation* of Cartesian dualism.

The Gathering of Life: A Philosophical Allegory

To track how this transformation occurs in and as the very allegorical unfolding of the poem, I suggest that we pay close attention to what happens to the term *life* in this poem, beginning with its opening line.

Se recogió la vida para verme pasar.

Life gathered itself to see me pass.

But before turning to this line, a word about how I approach de Burgos's allegorical procedures in "2. Íntima " is in order. At the most basic level, I would argue that "2. Íntima" mobilizes or, better, exemplifies at least two different senses of allegory: The first is linked to a certain sequentiality in presentation, itself produced by a reading protocol that foregrounds temporality, and which produces something like a narrative; for convenience's sake, we could designate this allegorical mode as de Manian.[124] The second sense of allegory at work in this poem is closer to the sense of allegory that Benjamin elaborates in his groundbreaking work on the German baroque and on Baudelaire's modernist poetics. The combination of these two allegorical modes and especially de Burgos's penchant for the second one are aspects of her poetics that await more careful scrutiny. For the purpose of my reading, in what follows I will limit myself to unpacking some of Benjamin's insights into the relationship between ideality and allegorical presentation because they can shed light on this crucial, though still underexamined, aspect of this poem—and of de Burgos's poetics more generally. Then, I will make some general observations about how the poem weaves together two modes of allegorical presentation, and what implications this has for my reading of "2. Íntima" as a philosophical allegorization of a transcendental reduction to the self's embodied "sphere of ownness."

First, recall that, in the *Trauerspiel*, and while accounting for the ways in which late Roman theater served as a precursor to medieval and, especially, modern Baroque allegory, Benjamin outlines the basic effect that allegorical presentation has on the very onto-theological status of ideas or, as he also calls them, *Wesenheiten*, or "essentialities": Allegory, according to Benjamin, transposes ideas into the realm of representations or concepts, thereby enacting something like an immanentization of the transcendental.[125] Such, I would argue, is the lot of the nonempirical objects or ideas, such as *life*, *flesh*, *soul*, *time*, *Man/men*, that populate the poetic space of the "2. Íntima": They're brought down from what some might regard as their reputed *topos ouranos* into the mundane or secular theater of poetic writing. And yet, Benjamin's insistence that modern allegory as a mode of presentation or as a linguistic form of expression cannot be simply reduced to the procedure of personification characteristic of late Roman allegory also finds an echo in de Burgos's poem. For the *end* of this allegorization of life as *idea* or *essentiality* does not simply lie in its reduction to a concept or a representation. Quite the contrary: The dialectics implicit in allegory as a form can only be grasped if we understand allegorical intentionality as determined by the goal of re-presenting the idea's "survival [*Fortleben*] in a milieu [*Umwelt*] that is unsuitable, indeed is hostile, to it."[126] This same goal is, precisely, what I argue animates the allegorization of life that occurs in "2. Íntima."

Second, I would argue that in order to understand how the allegorical unfolding of the poem (that is, allegory understood in its de Manian sense, or allegory as tropological narrative) is woven together with the poem's allegorical intention (that is, allegory in Benjamin's sense), we must pay heed to the "dialectical" procedure at the heart of this process of allegorization. In other words, to read the logic of the poem's own narrative or allegorical unfolding, we must attend to the poem's paradoxical and violent attempt to immanentize the transcendental; destroy any semblance of organic nature or life as a theosophical, Romantic transcendentality; and, at the same time, render eternal that which its allegorical intention has "brought down to earth" and reduced to a form of prosaic mechanicity. For, as we will see, the poem's tropological narrative is animated by the task of presenting both the antagonism between these different allegories—between life and life, between the self and Man, etc.—and the end of this antagonism through the overcoming of their opposition. This overcoming, I contend, is the result of the series of reductions that the poem allegorizes. It is to these reductions that I now turn, beginning with the reduction that announces itself in the first line through the figure of the gathering of life:

Se recogió la vida para verme pasar.

Life gathered itself to see me pass by.

From the very first line, the poem presents the first stage in this allegorical conflict, which is centered around the dialectical polarities of *life* as such and the speaker's *self*. As we will see, this polarity already contains within itself all the dialectical tensions that the poem's allegorical movement will unfold until the very semblance of a conflict will be finally removed.

Moreover, note that what sets in motion the poem's first allegorical sequence (lines 1–3) is the trope of personification: The speaker presents *la vida* as having already carried out a process of self-gathering, which, as the particle *para* ("to" "for," in some cases, "for the sake of") suggests, created the condition for the poet's self-presentation before it, that is, before life itself, which is thus doubly allegorized as both an agent of self-gathering and as endowed with vision. But how should we read, rather than simply paraphrase, this *self*-gathering of life? And what is at stake in this strange allegorical motion?

In order to pursue this line of inquiry, it is important to note from the outset that this opening verse, with its use of a reflexive form of the verb *recoger* in relation to life as the subject of that gathering action, could be read as a play on an idiomatic phrase of Puerto Rican Spanish, *recogerse a buen vivir*, a literal translation of which would read: *to gather oneself to good living*. The *Tesoro lexicográfico del español de Puerto Rico* glosses this verbal locution in the following way: "Después de una etapa de gran agitación, dedicarse a la vida tranquila, hogareña" ("To devote oneself to a quiet, domestic life after a period of great agitation").[127] Such a reading would find support in the bipartite structure of the poem, whose first part is dominated by an ambiance of quietness that contrasts greatly with the second part, where the speaker suddenly finds herself in the midst of a bustling urban landscape.

This more semantic reading of the opening line as a play on this idiom could find further support in the syntactical quasi-parallelism that can be discerned between the two phrases, which renders the poem's subtle inversion of the idiom's terms all the more significant. For notice that, unlike the case with the idiom, the poem does not present us with a speaker who, after having led a dissolute life or being too dispersed or agitated, must gather herself so as to come into her own, get a grip on her life, and secure its goodness. Rather, it is *life* as such that here has to gather itself in order to see the poet's self pass by.

Moreover, it is important to note that this verbal phrase, *verme pasar* ("see me pass"), entails another complication, which can be fruitfully explored through translation. I am referring to the fact that the infinitive verb *pasar* in the Spanish phrase *verme pasar* ("see myself pass by") has a polysemic quality that is difficult to render with a single, elegant formula in English. To be sure, *ver pasar algo* ("to see something pass") can be used to designate the action of seeing an object move across space in the most general, i.e., physical or mechanical, sense. But the phrase can also be used in Spanish in a more general or even ontological register in order to denote the fact that one has witnessed a happening or an occurrence, regardless of whether the event that *came to pass* did so in the mode of *passing by* (i.e., as spatio-temporal motion). In order to read thoughtfully this opening line, we should keep these two senses in play and hear them together, so that what is at stake when the speaker's self *passes by* in front of life's "eyes" is precisely the *coming to pass* of her *self—the event of her ipseity*.

Still, the question as to what this gathering of life entails remains open. If the self-gathering of life is the condition for the movement in and through which the speaker's self *comes to pass* in *passing by*, then what kind of event is at stake in life's self-gathering, self-retracting, or self-withdrawing? And what relationship can be discerned between these two ipseities, that is, between life's *self-*gathering and the speaker's *self-*passing? Is the relationship purely oppositional, so that if the former does not obtain then the latter also can't take place? If this were the case, then what would be the ontological status of the self's eventful passage? To wit, is it an event within life, or is it outside of life? If so, could it be that what the poem allegorizes is the event of ipseity as something that can only take place at the moment of death, once life has folded in on itself? Perhaps we should now reread the poem's opening line and the self's passage with an ear for its English translation, which would help us discern in the original the workings of a third mode of *passing* that is barely legible in the original Spanish, namely, passing as another way of designating *death*.

The plausibility of this reading appears to be buttressed by the other two lines that compose the poem's opening allegorical sequence, which set in motion a second allegorical polarity that mobilizes one of the oldest conceptual pairs in Western onto-theology, namely, *la carne* ("the flesh") and *el alma* ("the soul"):

Me fui perdiendo átomo por átomo de mi carne
y fui resbalándome poco a poco al alma.

I myself went on losing atom by atom of my flesh
and went on sliding myself bit by bit to the soul.

The near-complete parallelism of these two lines paradoxically accentuates their differences, in particular the barely conspicuous, though decisive, difference in the determiners that precede the appearance of the words *carne* and *alma*: Whereas the flesh appears as the speaker's *own*, presented in the mode of a possession, the soul is preceded by *al*, a Spanish contraction of the preposition *a* ("to") and *el* ("the," though in Spanish the definite article *el* is gendered as masculine). Hence, the poem not only figures the soul as the *terminus* of the speaker's sliding or slipping movement but also presents the soul, unlike the *flesh*, as *not belonging* to the speaker. There is a somewhat predictable irony at work in this iteration of the speaker's ipseitological passing: She must be expropriated of the thing that is most immediately *hers*, namely, her flesh, if she is to attain the impersonal abode of the soul and thus reach the place of her *actual* self-appropriation. The irony is predictable because it answers to a Western metaphysico-theological script that, though acutely at work in hegemonic strands of Christianity, cannot be circumscribed to the Christian cultural milieu alone, since it is at work everywhere in which a notion of "mere life," usually anchored in the "flesh," is positioned as that which must be sacrificed in order to ensure that the self will gain access to the experience of spiritedness or ensoulment that alone constitutes its ipseity.[128]

The syntactic parallelism of these lines also has another crucial implication, since it engenders a movement that is anything but twofold, let alone parallel. The textual operator at work here is chiasmus, which entangles these two lines in such a way that their apparently linear movement gives way to a cyclical, if not circular motion. For the loss, *atom by atom*, of the self's flesh, this process of excarnation, is also *at once* the speaker's progressive gliding, *bit by bit*, into the soul. The more her flesh is neutralized or destroyed, the closer the speaker is to reaching the soul, which is the destination of her sliding movement. In other words, these two lines do not describe two movements that will never intersect but two radically opposite aspects of a *single movement*, namely, of excarnation-cum-ensoulment. This movement, in turn, can be read as a repetition that develops, unfolds, or explicates what was enveloped, enfolded, or implied in the poem's inceptual movement, that is, life's self-gathering and the self's passing by/coming to pass. The withdrawal into itself of life is the event that opens up the space-time in which the speaker's self can reach itself and thus happen as ipseity, and this twofold event requires the total and literal *mort*ification of her flesh. For only thanks to its absolute *reduction* or neutralization is the speaker able to accede to that ipseitological abode, that sphere of ownness, in which it exists in the mode of *ensouled animacy*.

Does this mean that "2. Íntima" poeticizes life as thoroughly reducible to the materiality of the flesh? Before pursuing this question in more detail, and at the risk of further slowing down the pace of my reading to truly glacial levels, I want to take a step back and quickly gather the threads I have teased out so far. To do so, I want to return to my initial hypothesis, namely, that this poem of de Burgos enacts a thoroughgoing transformation of the structure of selfhood that locates the self's essence in the realm of embodied autoaffection. From the poem's initial sequence, this hypothesis appears to make little sense. On the contrary, the self that emerges in this poem seems to be completely in step with the platonic-Christian tendencies that determine the hegemonic, somatophobic strand in Western ontology—a somatophobia that presumably was only intensified by the advent of modern notions of the subject and the invention of life as a biological process and of nature as a realm either entirely separated from or at the very least subordinated to culture, history, in short, *spirit*. From a Wynterian perspective, we might say that the conclusion of this poem's opening allegorical sequence seems deeply imbued in the *biocentricism* that characterizes modernity at least insofar as it establishes an absolute opposition between fleshly existence, qua the bearer of life understood as an objective, real, purely physiological or biological entity, and an ensouled selfhood whose essence can only be properly experienced on the condition of its wholesale excarnation.[129] Such a reading would find support in de Burgos's own thoughtful redeployment of the language of *atomism* to characterize the process of the flesh's reduction. If the speaker can lose her flesh *atom by atom*, it is because the flesh exists in the mode of exteriority as such: It is the body *regarded* in its pure extensivity or as *partes extra partes*.[130] The flesh constitutes a complex mereology whose parts exist in a relation of separability from one another. Its form is thus devoid of any simplicity; its boundedness and atomistic discreteness pale in comparison with the holistic unity that could only obtain if the parts of this fleshly matter were to compenetrate one another. In da Silva's terms, the poem's self would amount to another instantiation of the foundational presupposition of modernity, namely, the separation of interiority and an affectable exteriority and the subordination of the former to the latter.[131]

Enstatic Ipseity; or, the Trials of Self-Reflection

Is this de Burgos's last word on the relation between life, the self, and the *soma*? This seems hardly to be the case since, as a matter of fact, life makes a crucial reappearance near the end of the poem's first part:

> Me sentí vida al reverso de una superficie de colores y formas.
>
> I felt myself life on the reverse side of a surface of colors and shapes.

The trajectory of the first part of the poem is thus bookended by two processes that at first sight appear to be contradictory: on the one hand, life's removal from the space poeticized in the poem in favor of the speaker's passing manifestation; on the other hand, life's reappearance within the milieu of that very speaker's affected-sensible ipseity, that is, within the very immanent dimension for whose sake life initially had to gather itself and the flesh be thoroughly eliminated. How is this return of life to be accounted for? How does the poem's own allegorical movement achieve this sudden reconciliation, removing the radical opposition between life and selfhood that constitutes the poem's abstract and indeed biocentric point of departure so that life can be disclosed as something other than a fleshly, anatomical, or biological process, becoming instead the mark of the self's own realization of its own selfhood as a concrete, *embodied* essence?

But before we can track the emergence of this *arche-body* we must first register how the poem unfolds what is enfolded in the speaker's self's passing, that is, we must see how "2. Íntima" presents the speaker as finally arriving to herself and thus attaining her innermost intimacy. To do so, we must turn to the second allegorical sequence that unfolds in the first part and read *what* happens when the speaker's self is released from its fleshly life:

> Peregrina en mí misma, me anduve un largo instante.
> Me prolongué en el rumbo de aquel camino errante
> que se abría en mi interior,
> y me llegué hasta mí, íntima.

> Pilgrim in myself, I walked myself a long instant.
> I prolonged myself in the course of that errant path
> that opened itself in my interior,
> and arrived myself up to me, intimate.

The second allegorical sequence gravitates around the *topos* of a pilgrimage, with the speaker figuring herself as a *peregrina en mí misma* ("pilgrim in myself"). De Burgos's choice of this term recasts the *terminus* of the first sequence by making even more explicit the theological, or, better, mystical sediments which the poem is, as it were, secularizing through the redeployment of the image of an enstatic journey as the movement whose *end* is precisely the self's "standing within" itself. We can now better understand what was at stake in the gathering of life and the analogous mortification of the speaker's flesh: The intensive diminution of these two allegories must reach their zero degree if the speaker is to be all-soul. But, as the etymology of the word *peregrina* suggests (from the Latin *per-egre*, meaning "to or from abroad," itself derived from the Proto-Italic *pere-agro*, which literally means "what lies beyond the land") the state of ensoulment that coincides with the self's passing before life is not yet the *event of ipseity*. Even after attaining a dimension of pure ensoulment, the poet remains a foreigner in her own soul. It is this foreignness, her own status as migrant in and from herself, that will be presumably removed over the course of the second sequence, which concludes with the speaker finally arriving *herself* to *her-self* and attaining her intimacy. It is only at this point that the allegorical movement of the poem presents what the opening sequence had only anticipated, namely, the coming-to-pass of *her-self* itself, the event of ipseity.

This event is remarked throughout this sequence through a procedure that, among other formal aspects of this poem—such as its almost total lack of rhyme, its free-verse form—indexes its belonging to a modernist/avant garde mode that privileges formal experimentation. I am referring to the poem's peculiar ungrammaticality, which is the result of the poem's excessive use of both possessive and reflexive anaphoric personal pronouns. Although reflexive constructions are more common and more easily accommodated in Spanish than in English, this poem pushes this accommodation to a limit, forcing the translation of these lines to be even clunkier than the original already is (case in point: *me llegué hasta mí* / arrived myself up to me). To unpack this aspect of the poem, I want to return for a moment to the last two lines of opening sequence, since De Burgos's insistence on remarking the place of the self at the expense of grammar is already at work there in ways that merit a quick examination:

Me fui perdiendo átomo por átomo de mi carne
y *fui resbalándome* poco a poco al alma.

I *myself* went on *losing* atom by atom of my flesh
and went on *sliding myself* bit by bit to the soul.

Notice the quasi *antimetabole*, that is, the abc/bca pattern, which opens these two lines, where *a* stands for the clitic pronoun *me* (enclitic in the second line), *b* stands for the verb *fui*, and *c* for the gerundive verbals *perdiendo/resbalandome*. When isolated, this repetitive schema produces a spatiality that literally bookends the poem's opening between two *Me*s or *myself*s. This reiterative inscription of the personal pronoun is compounded by de Burgos's decision to not pay heed to some of the possibilities afforded by Spanish grammar. I am referring specifically to the fact that as a null-subject language Spanish admits dropping the subject in phrases such as these. This is even truer for a phrase whose direct object, namely, *la carne* ("the flesh"), is already inscribed as belonging to the speaker via the personal possessive pronoun *mi* ("my").

Rather than follow grammar and custom, de Burgos reinscribes the speaker's self or "I" by placing the personal pronoun *me* in the canonical place of the grammatical subject. To be sure, this gesture could be interpreted as de Burgos's attempt to mimic aspects of the speech patterns proper to Puerto Rico's peasantry—the class to which de Burgos belonged. More specifically, the excessive remarking of the personal pronoun in "2. Íntima" evokes a peculiarity of the Spanish of Puerto Rico's peasantry attested by linguists, namely, the tendency to invert the order of the object pronouns by either turning enclitic pronouns into proclitics (e.g., instead of *Heme aquí*, which means "Here I am," *Me he aquí*) or by placing the proclitic before the reflexive pronoun (e.g., instead of *Se me cayó el sombrero*, which means "My hat fell," *Me se cayó* . . .).[132] Bringing to bear this sociolinguistic dimension on de Burgos's poem actually adds a more explicitly referential layer to our reading of this poem's allegorical unfolding, suggesting that speaker's pilgrimage in herself could also be read as a movement of return to the countryside landscape of her natal Santa Cruz, away from the incipient modernity of San Juan, the epicenter of the island's budding urbanization efforts in the late 1930s. Moreover, such a reading would recast in even stronger terms the urban shock that the speaker experiences in the second part of the poem when she suddenly wakes up in the middle of a bustling crowd and is forced to again engage in an exercise of enstatic soul-searching in order to secure her recently acquired grip on her ipseity.

While keeping this reading in play, I want to insist on another approach to de Burgos's gesture of remarking again and again the first-person anaphoric personal pronoun in ways that are not only ungrammatical and semantically superfluous but also diverge ever so slightly from the uses of these pronouns to convey emphases in Spanish. Let us quote this opening and closing lines of this sequence again:

Peregrina en mí misma, *me* anduve un largo instante.

. . .

y *me* llegué hasta mí, íntima.

Pilgrim in myself, I walked *myself* a long instant.

. . .

and arrived myself up to *me*, intimate.

My suggestion is that the repetition of these pronominal marks should be read as de Burgos's attempt to remark the absolute place of the *myself* or the *mi misma/o/e* as the ground of ipseity. The iterations of all these nonsemantic and, from that perspective, gratuitous *mes* and *mi mismas* inscribe in the poem the purely *autoreferential* relation that establishes the law of personal ipseity as self-sameness, that is, as the structure whereby anything that can say "I" *is* an "I" insofar as it *is* always in an intimate relation with itself prior to entering into any other form of relation.

We can see now the extent to which these four lines carry out an even more radical form of reduction than the one figured in the first three lines of the poem. Recall that the initial reduction took the form of a "shutting down" of natural life, indeed of the lifeworld itself, understood as a transcendent, natural reality in which the self would always-already find itself. Concomitant to this reduction was what I would call a *carnal epokhē*, which, in neutralizing the flesh as the material essence that binds the speaker's soul to *this life*, opens and delivers the ensouled-excarnated self to the sphere of its innermost ownness. And yet, the reduction allegorized through the topos of an enstatic pilgrimage reduces even the soul, taken as the purely ideal or, more precisely, metaphysical principle of the self's enstatic motion, in favor of disclosing an experience in which the "I" experiences itself not as a soul-without-a-body but in its pure ego-logical essence, attained through the equally pure *feeling* of the self's intimacy with itself.

Intimate Reduction: Disclosing the Living/Lived Archi-Body

If the poem's second sequence carries out the allegorical movement through which the speaker reaches the abode where she can finally attain and secure a grip on her ipseity, the poem's third sequence discloses how the experience of being-a-self that is at stake in "2. Íntima" entails the retrieval of *the lived body* after the elimination of *the flesh*, with the concomitant relocation of that dimension of *ideal embodiment* at the very core of ipseity. The movement of these lines should thus be read as a further explication of the essence of intimacy. What these lines progressively reveal is that the self is capable of relating to itself and constituting its self into an ipseity only in the mode of embodied autoaffection. But, as we will see, what unfolds in these lines should not be simply described as the poem's *addition* of autoaffection to the basic structure of autoreferentiality established in its opening lines. In other words, the goal of this last phase in the philosophical allegory is to show that the experience of life-as-selfhood coincides entirely with the *feeling of somatic intimacy*:

> Conmigo cabalgando seguí por la sombra del tiempo
> y me hice paisaje lejos de mi visión.
> Me conocí mensaje lejos de la palabra.
> Me sentí vida al reverso de una superficie de colores y formas.
> Y me vi claridad ahuyentando la sombra vaciada en la tierra desde el hombre.

> Riding with myself I continued through the shadow of time
> and made myself landscape far from my vision.
> I knew myself message far from the word.
> I felt myself life on the reverse side of a surface of colors and shapes.
> And I saw myself clarity dispelling the shadow emptied upon the earth from man.

Note that the third sequence (lines 8–12) opens with the speaker describing her pilgrimage not in terms of walking but as a horseback riding. To be sure, the sudden appearance of the figure of the horse lends support to the more explicitly referential reading mentioned earlier, which would discern throughout this poem an oblique or indirect allegory of returning to the countryside as a response to modernization. This referential reading would be strengthened by a curious fact of de Burgos's biography, namely, her fondness for horses and love of horseback riding, instilled by her father from an early age.

Besides taking this figure as an index of a rurality or country life that could perhaps be constructed as a source of resistance to the forces of modernization, I want to remark on the more significant fact that this sequence opens with a reflexive construction—*conmigo cabalgando* ("riding with myself")—that is even stranger than the ones we encountered before. The oddity of this phrase, however, conveys eloquently the strange zone of indistinction in which the speaker finds herself vis-à-vis the polarity activity/passivity after finally reaching the end of her enstatic movement and arriving to her intimate ipseity. For the self-reflexivity of this verbal phrase makes it impossible to determine who is the horse and who is the rider—or, better, it suggests that at this point the speaker is her own rider and her own horse, being both rider and ridden. In so doing, the poem upends the deeply sedimented Platonic metaphor of the horse as the irrational, unbridled, pathos-driven body that the rider, as the emblem of the rational agent, must conduct properly and with discipline so as to prevent his soul from being derailed.[133] The same indistinction between agent and patient, between rider and horse, between body and soul or matter and spirit, becomes progressively more pronounced as the rest of the first part of the poem unfolds. That said, the intensification of this undecidability does not entail something like the return of *la carne*, which before had been eliminated. The indistinction between body and soul is instead predicated on the *absolute distinguishability* between the self's proper embodiment and the always-abjectable, hence already-eliminated flesh: It is because the body and the flesh are *toto cælo* apart that the living/lived body can *be* ipseity.

The "intimate reduction" to the speaker's living/lived body unfolds in the four verses that begin with the personal pronoun *Me*. When read on their own terms, these verses present the reader with various oxymoronic, or, to be more precise, paradoxical scenarios, with the speaker first *becoming* a landscape that is somehow at odds with vision, then *knowing* herself as a wordless message, then *feeling* herself as life itself, but a life that is radically foreign to the mundane geometry of surfaces and colors, and finally *seeing* herself *as* clarity itself. How should we read these lines and the activities they present?

Rather than dissolve their paradoxical semblance, my reading will try to justify the rigor and, indeed, the necessity of this paradoxical mode of presentation. For what these paradoxes convey is the strenuous change in attitude that is required to convey in language the experience of intimacy, which cannot bear the gap that language necessarily institutes between what it says and what it means and between what it means and it refers to. These paradoxes push language against itself in order to represent a reductive process far more radical than the ones carried out in the first and second allegorical sequences. If the first one reduced *life as viscosity* and the second reduced the soul in favor of ipseity, then the third sequence carries out a reduction *to* the kinaesthetic, autoaffective, or living body. But this reduction transforms the very structure of the self's experience of its own kinaesthesia, which ceases to be put in relation with perception and hence located back in the world, instead becoming attuned solely to the self's feeling of itself in its proper invisibility.

To trace these reductions, let us turn to the first verse in this sequence:

y me hice paisaje lejos de mi visión.

and made myself landscape far from my vision.

What the speaker is describing here is a process of transmogrification that concludes with a certain interruption of visuality. This process results in a paradox: As the meaning of the Spanish word *paisaje* indicates, landscapes not only belong to the field of the scopic but also, and perhaps more importantly, are usually understood to be objects of aesthetic contemplation. Indeed, what distinguishes a landscape from any other framed space within geographical reality is the visual-aesthetic intentionality that demarcates it and determines its constitution. In other words, landscapes *are* insofar as there are aesthetic-eidetic "eyes" that behold them *as such*; they exist only within the "correlational space" that is afforded by the intentionality of the subject who constitutes them as aesthetic objects in the very act of beholding them. And yet (and this is what is paradoxical about this transformation), the distance that emerges in the speaker's becoming-landscape is precisely a distance from *mi visión* ("my vision"). But how could this transformation be produced at the expense of visuality? How is it possible for a "landscape" to appear at a distance from the eyes of the beholder? And how should we understand this distance?

As a way to approach this question, in what follows I interrogate this distance from the vantage point of its implications for the phenomenal status of this landscape. Doing so, however, requires that we unpack some of the possible ways in which this line can be read. The distance that emerges in this line could be read as referring to this landscape's peculiar invisibility, that is, its unavailability to her sense of sight in general. In other words, distance here would figure her ironic subtraction from the field of *her* vision—a subtraction that would be ironic because it happened as soon as she became a landscape, that is, an object presumed to be thoroughly made *for the sake* of being beheld or contemplated. A different, though not incompatible, reading of this line could take the speaker to be referring not to her sense of sight *in general* but to the possibility of *seeing herself*, that is, of having the ipseitological landscape that she herself has become as a possible object of perception. In both cases, distance here appears to acquire a qualitative, rather than a quantitative, determination, since, by being located beyond what her eyes can see, her self-landscape is located beyond the limit of the visible, whether visibility here is generalized or restricted to her own autoscopy.

A third possible reading, however, would seem to remove us from the scopic context in which this line appears to unfold, at least prima facie. For the Spanish nominal phrase *mi visión* may also refers to vision in a more "metaphorical" sense of the term, closer to insight or, better, foresight than to optics as a physical or psychophysiological phenomenon. This sense can be attested from the use in phrases such as *Mi visión de los hechos es la siguiente* ("This is my take on the facts") or *¿Cuál es tu visión para con este proyecto?* ("What are your expectations with regard to this project?"). But even if we were to determine that the vision at stake here is not a physical phenomenon that refers to the muscular eyes of the head but the theoretical eyes of the mind, the distance that emerges between her becoming-landscape and her own capacity for (in)sight would not be diminished; rather, they would be intensified, with her transformation being out of reach not only of her physical but also of her eidetic eyes.

This development might be construed as a deviation from the ipseitological trajectory of this poem—as if the speaker could not constitute herself as both the object and subject of her landscape vision in a moment of pure visual autoreferentiality. I would argue, however, that something else is happening here: It is actually because of her own becoming-ipseity that she cannot and indeed must not relate to her own self in the mode of vision, contemplation, or intuition—be it understood as a psychophysical or metaphysical mode of *sight*. The suspension of sight, the reduction of *her vision* would thus be necessary in order for her life to *appear as such*, that is, *in* and *as* its proper embodied immanence.[134]

This *reductio* reaches another milestone in the next line in this sequence:

Me conocí mensaje lejos de la palabra.

I knew myself message far from the word.

A "message that is far from the word" might strike some as a logocentric fantasy, but it is one admittedly more intuitive than a becoming-landscape that entails an interruption of visibility. For the experience poetized here is that of attaining a form of self-knowledge whose cognitive or eidetic purity is such that it either can dispense entirely with the mediation of the spoken or written word or, at the very least, take some distance from its own *incarnation* in the linguistic *dead letter*. Recall Paul's famous words: "For the letter kills but the spirit gives life." (2 Corinthians 3:4–6). The term "incarnation" here is not only justified but crucial to understanding how this second line sheds light on the previous one—as is also suggested by their strong parallelism. For what underlies and enables the possibility of conceiving of a message that is not mediated by words or signs of any kind is the very opposition between the flesh and the embodied self. The same holds for the speaker's becoming landscape and the eyes that would behold it. What is crucial, however, is that, in decoupling *being* a landscape from *seeing* herself as such, just as in decoupling *knowing* herself as message from *reading/hearing* herself as such, the speaker is delineating a zone of embodied immanence whose ontological concreteness does not admit of any separation or mediation—not even the basic mediation whereby a self requires its mirroring representation in order to cohere into its identity. As a result, the speaker *is* already a landscape without needing to see herself in order to become such, just as she is already a message without needing any words to know herself as such.

So far, these two lines have figured the relation between "ipseity" and "the flesh," between a "landscape" and "vision," and between a "message" and "the word" as a form of nonrelation, remarked in the text by the Spanish word *lejos* "far," which simply refers to an undetermined form of distance. The third verse in this sequence, however, lends determinacy to this distance, which is significantly complicated by the logical space in which the poem unfolds:

Me sentí vida al reverso de una superficie de colores y formas.

I felt myself life on the reverse side of a surface of colors and shapes.

Before turning to what happens to unspecified distance when it becomes topologically specified as the "reverse side" of a surface, it is crucial to note that this leap occurs at the precise moment in which the poem comes full circle and *life* reappears after its initial self-gathering. This time around, however, life no longer manifests itself as a transcendent reality whose allegorical figuration was buttressed by the use of the feminine definite article *la*, or "the," in the opening verse of the poem, i.e., *la vida* or "the life." Rather, life now presents itself *within* the very core of the self's immanence and *as* this very immanence. This event is syntactically remarked by life's grammatical position in this verse as a subject complement that specifies the very modality of sensation characteristic of the arch-experience of intimacy as the name for ipseity in its autoaffection: *me sentí vida*, "I felt myself life." To feel oneself life is to live, and life itself is nothing but the self's feeling of itself, the mode of autoaffection in which being-affected and affecting qua activity coincide absolutely. Accordingly, the shift in the terms of this distance is not coincidental. It is only at the precise moment in which the *flesh* (as the site of both vision and of the emission, hearing, writing, and reading of words) has been thoroughly reduced that the distance between the *felt ipseitological body* (as a gazeless landscape or a wordless message) and the flesh crosses a threshold and gains qualitative determinacy, becoming a pure, rather than an intensive, quality.

Such a decisive crossing unfolds through the speaker's deployment of a different spatial figure, namely, her use of *al reverso* ("on the reverse side") to redescribe the distance that separates the experience of *feeling herself as life* from the modes of affect that are linked to the perception of *surfaces, colors, and shapes*—to wit, the experience of what Husserl already in 1924 calls "pure physical experience," which can only be thematized through *Abbau* or deconstruction, understood as abstractive reduction that suspends all the sedimented layers of meaning that inform and determine this experience.[135] Recall that, in previous lines, the speaker had relied on the Spanish word *lejos* ("far") to mark the distance between her embodied self and the fleshly modes that she has now left behind. In spite of its indeterminacy, or rather because of it, this distance marker does not exclude in principle that what was "far away," *lejos*, might be brought *más cerca*, "nearer." A different situation is at work when two things lie *al reverso* or "on opposite sides" of each other: Undetermined distance becomes determined through its figuration in terms of a rudimentary topology, consisting of a two-sided figure—on one side, there is "a surface of colors and shapes," on the other, the embodied ipseity of the speaker—which, if it does not altogether exclude, at least complicates the possibility of bringing the speaker's ecstatic flesh closer to her enstatic body. A simple demonstration would make this clear: If we mark at random two different sets of points on each side of a two-sided figure, the distance between the points on side A or B would not be commensurate to the distance between points that lie *across* these two sides, since the latter also entails crossing the edge of the figure, passing, as it were, to the other side. The topology that this line presents would thus appear to be wholly different from the Möbius strip, that figure which Jacques Lacan famously held as the very topological structure of the *objet a* because, though initially two-sided, its complete traversal demonstrates that it is "a surface with one side," which, as such, "cannot be turned over."[136] To be "on the reverse side of a surface of colors and shapes" entails an exacerbation of the distance between the embodied self and the flesh that effectively crosses the limit separating intensity and quality. Indeed, after this line, an impossible threshold would have to be crossed for *the* distance between the embodied self and the flesh to be removed—impossible since, in order to cross to the other, *viscous* side, the self would have to renounce its ipseity and relinquish the absolutely ontological difference that it *feels* between its own *lively* autoaffection and the being-outside-itself of fleshly sensuousness.

The movement of intensifying intimacy reaches its apex in the last line of the first part of the poem, which retrieves the possibility of sight and insight for this enstatic body after the reduction of ocular vision that took place in the very first step of this sequence of transformations:

Y me vi claridad ahuyentando la sombra vaciada en la tierra desde el hombre.

And I saw myself clarity dispelling the shadow emptied upon the earth from man.

Paradoxically, this moment of sight is not really one, at least if by sight we still have in mind something like perception. For what is seen in this moment of self-vision is not the self's body understood as a surface, a shape, or a color, not even the landscape into which she had already been transmogrified at the beginning of this sequence. Rather, what the speaker now contemplates is her own self transformed into "clarity" (*claridad*). At the end of this sequence, she emerges both as the pure phenomenon of phenomenality and as the pure phenomenality of all phenomena. The speaker now appears invisibly to her own "vision"—invisibly, since she offers *no-thing* to her own vision, not even a vision of herself as an object of self-contemplation and thus of self-objectification. What she gives herself to see is the invisible ground of sight itself, a clarity that can never be seen as such since it is that which the world of perception necessarily presupposes for any thing or being to appear to any subject.

But this becoming-diaphanous and, above all, her own self-contemplation as this diaphaneity not only bring to an end the speaker's movement of enstatic ipseity and her retrieval of a sense of life as an ontological ground that, in turn, can itself only be grounded in the immanence of her embodiment; they also constitute a historical force in its own right. For it is only once her intimate revolution has reached an end that we encounter the allegorical figure of everything that the speaker herself has left behind and ceased to be, namely, *el hombre*, or "Man."

Time in the Flesh: Modernity, Temporality, Humanism

In the last verse of the first part of "2. Íntima," *el hombre,* or "Man," appears as the very *incarnation* of modern life, as the emblem of a historico-ontological form of life that remains bound to the atomistic construction and experience of the living body in its viscosity. Thus understood, humanity emerges in its modern light, that is, as a hetero-affected entity whose sensibility, perception, and being are ontologically structured along the *partes extra partes* model of *res extensa*. But more crucial than the mere appearance of "Man" in the poem's allegory is the mode in which this allegorical figure appears. In this respect, it is significant, indeed crucial, that the figure of man and its attendant humanism emerges in the phenomenal guise of *shadows*. To grasp the significance of this figure, we need to reckon with the fact that the semantic purview and import of this trope exceeds the immediate agonistic context in which it appears in the line discussed previously, namely, the conflict between the speaker and Man, which is allegorized (in a rhetorical language that respects the strictures of the psychomachia) as a struggle between clarity and shadows, between light and darkness—a conflict thus laden with theological, Manichean, if not even Marcionite, resonances.[137] Here, it is crucial to note that, if the last line construes *la sombra* as the emblem of the anthropogenetic agency of Man on this earth, this shadow also communicates with the shadows that, earlier in the poem, the voice had to traverse as part of her pilgrimage toward her ipseity:

> Conmigo cabalgando seguí por la *sombra* del tiempo
>
> Riding with myself I continued through the *shadow* of time

When read with this line in mind, the concluding verse of both the first and second part of "2. Íntima" acquires an entirely different meaning. For now it is *time itself* that appears to be inscribed as an effect of what I referred to earlier as Man's modern anthropogenetic agency. If time is an effect of a particular mode of being-human, if time is so indissociable from that style of humanity that its own transcendental or ontological role should be seen as radically contextualized or historicized, that is, located within the bounds of Man's agency, does the experience of life that emerges through the self's attainment of her ipseity signal to the advent of *another* time than the time that was "emptied" upon the earth by Man? Or is this experience *other* than temporal *in general*, that is, entirely outside of time, hence timeless, perhaps even eternal?

My reading of this philosophical allegory as establishing a structural link between temporality and the inhuman humanism of Man is further reinforced by the fact that the second part of "2. Íntima" begins with both Man and time taking the poem's center stage:

> Ha sonado un reloj la hora encogida de todos.
> ¿La hora? Cualquiera. Todas en una misma.
> Las cosas circundantes reconquistan color y forma.
> Los hombres se mueven ajenos a sí mismos
> para agarrar ese minuto índice
> que los conduce por varias direcciones estáticas.
>
> Siempre la misma carne apretándose muda a lo ya hecho.
>
> A clock has sounded the shrunken hour of all.
> The hour? Any. All in the same one.
> Surrounding things conquer again color and shape.
> Men move alien to themselves
> to grasp that minute-index
> that leads them through various static directions.
>
> Always the same flesh pressing into itself moves to the already-made.

Note the drastic change of setting, tone, and even voice that occurs between the first and the second parts of the poem. Until this point, the poem has been overwhelmingly dominated by the speaker's ipseitological compulsion, which manifested linguistically through her excessive remarking of the position of her ipseity through the equally excessive deployment of anaphoric reflexive pronouns. But now the voice speaks in the third person, describing processes that are not only foreign to her own self but that also present a vivid image of foreignness as such, that is, of the kind of alienation that stands as the polar opposite to her own condition after her attainment of ipseity. To the change in voice corresponds also a change in tone: Whereas the first part of the poem, though somewhat cryptic, appears to be voiced in all earnestness, we begin to encounter here signs of sarcasm, if not even of irony. I will return to this in a moment, but first, it is important to remark on the change of setting, which is perhaps the most immediately palpable change that happens between the first and the second part of the poem.

In a gesture that evokes the bipartite movement of Baudelaire's prose poem "La chambre double" ("The Double Room"), the enstatic pilgrimage to the site of intimacy and its horseback prolongation is suddenly interrupted by a clock that sounds the hour.[138] All of a sudden, the speaker returns to the world of the flesh, the very same world that she had left behind through the intimate reduction to the living sphere of her pure embodied ipseity. Though the poem remains rather austere in its description of the scene to which she awakes, from the few elements that compose it we can deduce that she's in the middle of an urban setting in a context in which the shape and movements of life are ruled by what we might call, after Bergson and Heidegger, the time of the clocks.

It is at this point that we encounter the first explicit instance of sarcasm or perhaps irony in the speaker's voice. To see this, we should pay attention to the Spanish phrase that the voice mobilizes to mark the moment of the emergence of clock-time in the poem. The saying *ha sonado la hora* literally means that a clock has sounded the hour, and yet, just as its English cognate, "the hour has sounded," this phrase has a more apocalyptic, if not even eschatological tone, closer to the dramatic and heavily Christological phrase *the time has come*. The very manner in which time reemerges in the poem suggests a proximity to *kairos* over *chronos*: The time that has sounded is not time as an endless flow of moments but the right time of a singular event or decision. The decisive character of this time perhaps explains why, in all subsequent editions of this poem—except the *editio princeps* and the original poem, published on July 16, 1938, in *Puerto Rico Ilustrado*—editors have modified this verse so that instead of reading "Ha sonado un reloj la hora *encogida* de todos" ("The clock has sounded the *shrunken* hour of all"), the line says "Ha sonado un reloj la hora *escogida* de todos" ("A clock has sounded the time *chosen* of all.") In the absence of any critical edition of de Burgos's manuscripts, which may reveal that the original publications of the poem were themselves erroneous or later revised by the poet, I have chosen to retain the original version of this line, which was published twice while de Burgos was alive. And yet, the alternative, now-dominant version could easily be mobilized in support of my attempt to demonstrate a shift in the speaker's tone as soon as the second part begins. For the fact that the selection of this hour would have been the result of a unanimous choice made by "all" lends a certain democratic flair to this kairological, messianic moment, undercutting, if not even secularizing, its theological resonances.[139] And yet, it is the very quality of an instant that would not only be qualitative but also eschatological that is immediately dispelled by the speaker's own rhetorical question—"¿La hora?" ("The hour?")—which she immediately follows by an answer that precisely denies any singularity to the hour that the clock has just sounded and that everybody had chosen: "Cualquiera. Todas en una misma" ("Any. All in the same one"). Rather than the result of an exercise in popular sovereignty, the decisive nature of this choice of time as well as its singularity turn out to be a farce: The hour that has been chosen is entirely *homogenous* to *any* other hour, containing all of them of in one, and as a result it is devoid in principle of any singularity and could be therefore substituted by any other hour.

It is important to note that de Burgos's characterization of this temporal totality as contained in one single unit of time betrays the philosophical rigor of her understanding of what has come to be known as "homogeneous time." Indeed, her characterization of the time whose emergence marks the end of her ipseitological experience tracks closely with Immanuel Kant's "Axioms of Intuition" in the first *Critique*, where Kant famously lays out that "all intuitions are *extensive* magnitudes," by which he means the type of magnitudes that construct a continuity through a "successive synthesis (from part to part)," so that "the representation of a part makes possible the representation of the whole."[140] Moreover, de Burgos's characterization of this temporal regime—in which not only is any hour ultimately equal to any other hour but men are also forced to be constantly reckoning with time—evokes one of the key passages in Bergson's groundbreaking *Essai sur les données immédiates de la conscience*, where Bergson relies on the example of two different ways of relating to the sixty oscillations of a pendulum that would constitute a minute to show that, in order to think of the very idea of *durée*, or *duration*, it is necessary to abandon the linear analogy that constructs the duration of the minute through the juxtaposition of sixty oscillations, instead positing the idea that duration unfolds in a way that cannot be arrested and decomposed in discrete succeeding parts without losing precisely its "*durée*" character.[141] But de Burgos's implicit critique of clock-time perhaps evokes even more explicitly a crucial aspect of Heidegger's treatment of "*Uhrzeit*" in *Sein und Zeit*, namely, Heidegger's insistence on the clock as a particularly powerful form of "vulgar time," of time understood in accordance with the Aristotelian definition that restricted the destiny of all metaphysical explorations of time within the horizon of measurement.[142] It is only in becoming a measurable being that time is able to *regulate* the way in which the average life of *Dasein* unfolds in its public facticity, in its irreducible being-with-other-*Daseins*, alienating *Dasein* from the possibility of having a *proper* experience of its own being and of its own authentic temporality.[143] The major differences that separate these two thinkers when it comes to the question of time notwithstanding, we could say that de Burgos is on their side insofar as she also doubts that life can be lived in its propriety, authenticity, or ipseity within the temporal milieu of clock-time and its homogenizing ontological agency. Which returns us to the same question that I posed earlier: Is there a *time* that is *proper to* the experience of intimate ipseity that de Burgos poetizes in "2. Íntima?" Or is this experience of life in its embodied autoaffection outside of time?

But in order to approach this question, we must return to the original version of this line ("The clock has sounded the *shrunken* hour of all") and grapple with yet another nonintuitive image. For what could a shrunken time mean here? Especially when this shrunken time contains *all* the hours, the "totality" of homogeneous or vulgar clock-time within it?

One way to approach this image requires that we step outside the boundaries of this poem and turn briefly to other poems in which de Burgos figures time by recourse to this peculiar, allegorical, locution of *la hora*, or "the hour." Fortunately, we already encountered two such cases. Recall that in my previous discussion of "8. Amaneceres"—a poem intimately related to "2. Íntima"—we already encountered a series of lines that appear to figure precisely the opposite allegory of *the hour* to "2. Íntima":

El hombre aburguesado
de cuerpo,
de mente
y de energía.
El hombre desviado
huyendo ferozmente de sí mismo.
A ese hombre burgués
hay que destruirlo,
ahora,
en la hora presente,
en la hora robusta,
en la hora universal.

¡Amanece en el mundo!
Cuando se abre la puerta íntima
para entrar a una misma,
¡qué de amaneceres![144]

Bourgeois man
of body,
mind,
and energy.
Deviant man
furiously escaping from himself.
That bourgeois man

must be destroyed,
now,
in the present hour,
in the robust hour,
in the universal hour.

The world dawns!
When the intimate door opens
to enter into oneself,
What dawns!

Unlike the hour whose sounding opens the second part of "2. Íntima," the hour that sounds throughout the text of "8. Amaneceres" is "present," "universal," and, above all, "robust." Since "present" and "universal" are qualities that could be plausibly ascribed to the hours marked by clock-time, it stands to reason that robustness is the adjective that can better help us get a hold of what the speaker is trying to say when she describes the clock-time as having been "shrunken of all." Indeed, the passive nature of this verbal construction is crucial, since it suggests that the shrinking of time is the result of the agency of the poet's main antagonist throughout this philosophical allegory, namely, *el hombre/los hombres*, or "Man/men." The fact that "8. Amaneceres" describes "the robust hour" as the now-time of the destruction of *bourgeois Man* sheds light negatively on the reasons why clock-time is, for the speaker, a shrunken, diminished time. For the clock here functions precisely as the emblem of the mode of humanity that bourgeois Man has instituted through what we may describe, with Wynter, as its progressive "overrepresentation."[145] The figure of a shrunken time hence does not primarily refer to the speed at which time is measured but signals radically incompatible qualities of time—incompatible, because one refers to a time that is structurally deprived of any quality, of any distinction, since it is nothing but the time in which the modern leveling of time stretches itself over the totality of temporal determinations and, in the process, narrows enormously the temporal horizon of humanity.

(Before pursuing this line of inquiry further, I want to open a parenthesis to say a word on the relation between these two poems, which, I'd argue, resembles how de Man saw the relation between Baudelaire's poems "Correspondances" and "Obsession," with "2. Íntima" playing the role of the former and "8. Amaneceres" the latter.[146] There is, indeed, a "specular symmetry" between these poems, whose most obvious symptom is the crucial reappearance of the language of intimacy in the opening and closing quartets of "8. Amaneceres." But notice that the latter, as it were, *externalizes* what remained in "2. Íntima" a name for the innermost interiority of the embodied self, with the adjective *íntima*, or "intimate," modifying not the self that has arrived to itself but the door that will presumably lead to such arrival. This movement of externalization is perhaps most pronounced when it comes to the transcendental aesthetics of the Burgosian self. What in "2. Íntima" remained radically unworldly, absolutely withdrawn or abstracted from the realm of perception, in "8. Amaneceres" is externalized in the mode of a *naturalization* and, by extension, of a *becoming-mundane*, with the self's kinaesthesia firmly anchored in a natural earth that emerges as the figure of the lifeworld (see my discussion of "8. Amaneceres" in §22). This *worldification* of ipseity is intensified by the *politicization* of intimacy that occurs in "8. Amaneceres" and that is totally absent from "2. Íntima." Whereas the former precisely identifies the destruction of bourgeois man as the task—at once ontological and political—of de Burgos's utopian countermodernism, "2. Íntima" articulates a task of existential rescue that could be described as "infrapolitical," in the sense that Alberto Moreiras and others have given to this term.[147] Within the economy of *Poema*, there is a definite hierarchy between these two poems, with "2. Íntima" functioning as what de Man calls the "infratext" or "hypogram" not just of "8. Amaneceres" but of most of the poems that compose the quasi-monadological textuality of *Poema*.)

Another perspective on this shrunken time can be obtained if we focus on a different figuration of *the hour*, namely, the hour of the speaker's fallen, viscous, erotic encounters. As I already argued, this motif appears for the first time in "4. Dame tu hora perdida," whose opening couplet suffices for our purposes:

De tu existencia múltiple, dame tu hora perdida
cuando vacío de todo, no sientas ni la vida.

From your multiple existence, give me the lost hour
when, empty of all, not even life you may feel.

Although the erotic context of the speaker's possible future encounter with a man seems *toto cælo* different from the speaker's *katabasis* into modern life, the *lost hour* that she demands from her possible future lover shares a crucial feature with the hour that gathers the totality of clock-time, namely, that in both cases we are dealing with empty time. Indeed, its emptiness is such that what characterizes this hour, that is, its singular quality, is the quality of having no qualities, of being a time that is radically empty of all sensation, an hour that is not even filled by the sensation of *mere life*. The lover thus finds himself in exactly the opposite ontological condition as the poet-speaker of *Poema* after "2. Íntima"; that is, he is incapable of the enstatic journey that alone would allow him to enter into himself and feel himself life, *sentirse vida*.

Coincidentally, this poem is perhaps the best place to grasp why Luis Llorens Torres's characterization of de Burgos's Kantianism was not just erroneous but misguided, precisely because de Burgos's thinking about empty time and the relationship between life and the transcendental is more radically phenomenological than Kant's. To grasp this, it is worth recalling Kant's way of distinguishing between "a filled or an empty time" in the paragraph from "On the schematisms of pure concepts of the understanding" that corresponds to the "Anticipations of Perception." Not surprisingly, this distinction hinges on precisely the same concept as the empty time of the speaker's lover in the poem we're examining, namely, *sensation*, which is what makes empirical consciousness precisely *empirical*, that is, consciousness *of* a reality that is necessarily external to consciousness.[148] Although, for Kant, time is in principle empty, since its status as the pure form of inner intuition is prior to and independent of the possibility of empirical intuition, empirical consciousness necessarily experiences time in some degree of fullness because what it experiences necessarily contains some sensation, that is, a reality that affects the subject from without, beyond the subject's autoaffective temporal agency. Time itself may be nothing but a name for the subject's pure autoaffection, but that autoaffection alone cannot produce the appearance of this intense shade of red, this bright light, or this sharp toothache.

This brief detour can help us see why de Burgos's poetics of empty and full time are more complicated than this Kantian schema. As I suggested in my previous commentary of "4. Dame tu hora perdida" (see §22), the problem with the lover's emptiness is not something that can be simply addressed by the speaker's filling up his time with her own sensation of life. For the sensation of life that "2. Íntima" poetizes is something that cannot be imparted, since it is the very ground and existence of ipseity-as-life: Each ipseity must enter through the intimate door and undergo their own enstatic journey to arrive to themselves. Moreover, "4. Dame tu hora perdida" is deeply aware of the impossibility of allowing her male lover to gain access to his own ipseity through their erotic intercourse. When, later in the poem, the speaker says

> Yo te daré verdades de todo lo tangible
> para pesar la nada de tu vida insensible.
>
> I will give you truths of all that is tangible
> to weigh the nothing of your insensible life.

it becomes clear that the one-sided exchange that is happening here will not result in the bestowal of the feeling of life to the lover. Indeed, the poem concludes with the following two couplets:

> Y alzaremos en ritmo vibrante y alocado
> la sublime mentira de habernos encontrado.
>
> Yo, en la nada de tu hora perdida,
> y tú, en la también nada de mi frívola vida.[149]
>
> And we will raise in vibrant and frenzied rhythm
> the sublime lie of having found each other.
>
> I, in the nothing of your lost hour,
> And you, in the also nothing of my frivolous life.

The speaker may have furnished some tangible sensations to fill the empty time of her lover's lost hour, and the truth of the tangible world may have lent weight and density to the insensibility of her lover's purely formal time. But the life that she exchanged for his deadening non-being is itself "frivolous," as she admits in the last line. Frivolity here does not simply or merely indicate the speaker's own moral judgment of herself; it also has a deeply phenomenological dimension. For what is frivolous about her life is precisely its mundaneness, that is, its viscosity, its willful descent into the realm of the flesh—which, presumably, only irony, in the ultimately dubious form of self-knowledge, can mitigate.

This erotic version of the antagonism between the speaker and Man/men is such a structural element of the architectonics of *Poema* that there is a hardly a poem in which it fails to resurface. The *locus classicus* of this dialectical motif is to be found in "10. Nada," which could be read as the continuation of "4. Dame tu hora perdida." Consider its first two verses:

> Como la vida es nada en tu filosofía
> brindemos por el cierto no ser de nuestros cuerpos.
>
> Since life is nothing is your philosophy
> let us toast for the certain non-being of our bodies.

Note how the speaker ironically greets the addressed lover prior to their encounter with a rather surprising accusation, turning a toast that perhaps would have been the prelude to a moment of erotic intimacy into an ironic debate about the place of life in her lover's philosophy. Note also how life is again intimately bound up *not with the flesh* but with the body, so much so that the affirmation that their bodies are marked by a "certain non-being" follows from the lover's philosophical declaration of the nothingness of life in a quasi-syllogistic fashion. The lover's empty hour is the time in which the living body is non-being and all there is is either flesh or a disembodied cogito.

But there is at least one more temporal image that we must briefly bring to bear on the image of the "shrunken hour," since it is perhaps the closest in figural quality to the time in question in "2. Íntima." I am referring to another crucial poem, "16. Soy en cuerpo de ahora" ("I am in the now-body"), where the antagonism between Man/men and the speaker is allegorized by the conflict between the different times that each of them represents, with the "burden of centuries" standing as the emblem of a temporality that anchors humanity in the "ancestral dividend" and the "Now," which, naturally, figures the speaker's time:

> —Tengo miedo de lo alto de tus miras —me dice—;
> el ayer que me nutre se doblega en lo interno
> de tu vida sencilla, que no admite pasado,
> y que vive en lo vivo desplegada al momento;
> . . .
> mira a un lado y a otro: jorobados, mediocres;
> son los míos, los que abrevan mi vacío siempre lleno;
> sé uno de ellos; destuerce tu vanguardia; claudica:
> es tan fácil volcarse de lo vivo a lo muerto.[150]

> —I'm afraid of the heights of your aims —he tells me—;
> yesterday, which nourishes me, yields within
> your simple life, that admits no past,
> and that lives in the living unfolded to the moment;
> . . .
> look at both sides: hunchbacked, mediocre;
> they are mine, those who water my always full void;
> be one of them; untwist your avant-gardism; surrender:
> is so easy to turn over from the living to the dead.

These mediocre men who are perpetually inclined before each other, as in Paul Klee's famous etching *Two Men Meet, Each Believing the Other to Be of Higher Rank* (1903), reiterate the men in "2. Íntima." Their hunchbacks, which are the result of their fleshly mediocrity, have also produced a hunchback time, a time of a diminished humanity.

After this excursus, we are perhaps in a better position to approach the question that I posed earlier: Is there a *time* that is *proper to* the experience of intimate ipseity that de Burgos poetizes in "2. Íntima?" Or is this experience of life in its embodied autoaffection outside of time?

To begin to approach this question, it would be important to return to the second sequence in the first part of the poem. This sequence opens with a verse that I have already commented on, in which the poet recasts her slippery movement toward her soul as a form of autopilgrimage—she was a "pilgrim in myself." What I did not thematize in my earlier reading of this passage is that, presumably, like any pilgrimage, this one took time, and yet the measure of this time is so hard to *quantify* that the poet can only do so by recurring to an oxymoronic formulation, "un largo instante" ("a long instant"), which contravenes commonsense conceptions of the instant as the indivisible, nonextended limit that marks at the same time the end and the beginning of two distinct temporal periods. Anticipating Derrida's famous claim in *La voix et le phénomène* (*Voice and Phenomenon*) that "*l'instant a sa durée*" ("the instant has its duration"), the poet brings into play a paradoxical, if not aporetic, form of "extension," a stretching out of time that would not amount to the negation of the instant but instead constitute its very instantaneity.

Moreover, the bizarre duration of this prolonged yet instantaneous pilgrimage is not only a feature of its time. For this "time" cannot be separated from the very "space" in which this pilgrimage unfolds, which the next line introduces when the speaker refers to "el rumbo de aquel camino errante / que se abría en mi interior," ("the course of that errant path / that was opening in my interior"). The link between the temporality and the spatiality of this pilgrimage are not only reinforced by the rhyme that obtains between "*inst*ante" and "*err*ante"—the sole case of consonant rhyme in the entire poem—but also by the chiasmus formed through the inversion of the order of the adjectives in these nominal phrases, "largo instante" and "camino errante," which allows us to read the path as the spatial correlate to the temporal instant and the path's errancy as the correlate to the instant's length. There is a sui generis becoming-space of time and a becoming-time of space at work in this allegory, which can be read as an attempt to capture the more-than-authentic and more-than-durational time-space in which the self becomes intimately itself.

Still, this process of becoming ipseity, and the time-space that is suited to it, comes to an *end* in the poem, and this end, understood both as limit (*peras*) and goal (*telos*), signals a shift in the temporal and spatial stakes of the poem. If, as I suggested earlier, "2. Íntima" ups the ante on the critiques of vulgar or homogeneous time that we find in Bergson's Life-Philosophy and Heidegger's existential analytic, this is because the poem not only opposes an authentic time to an inauthentic time (Heidegger) or an experience of qualitative duration to the quantitative (spatialization) of time as measurable (Bergson); it also opposes an understanding of the finite essence of time *as* ecstatic—that is, as the ontological ground for a *proper* understanding of life or of existence as being-outside-oneself—to a temporality that is barely thinkable *as such*, since it is indissociable from an experience of life as embodied ipseity—an experience whose *enstatic* quality and radical interiority entails precisely the erasure of time understood as the general ontological title for being-cum-exteriority.

Here, we touch on the deepest sediment of de Burgos's psychomachia, which finds allegorical expression in the speaker's last confrontation with the flesh, incarnated this time not in her own alter-ego, that is, in the Julia de Burgos of "1. A Julia de Burgos," but in the allegorical figure of men:

Los hombres se mueven ajenos a sí mismos
para agarrar ese minuto índice
que los conduce por varias direcciones estáticas.

Siempre la misma carne apretándose muda a lo ya hecho.
Me busco. Estoy aún en el paisaje lejos de mi visión.
Sigo siendo mensaje lejos de la palabra.

La forma que se aleja y que fue mía un instante
me ha dejado íntima.
Y me veo claridad ahuyentando la sombra vaciada en la tierra desde el hombre.

Men move alien to themselves
to grasp that minute-index
that leads them through various static directions.

Always the same flesh pressing into itself moves to the already-made.
I search for myself. I am still in the landscape far from my vision.
I continue to be message far from the word.

The form that distances itself and that was mine in an instant
has left me intimate.
And I see myself clarity dispelling the shadow emptied upon the earth from man.

Note the remarkable economy of expression that de Burgos achieves in the first four lines quoted here, which condense into a single emblem all the allegorical figures that the psychomachia of the *Poema*'s first poem had marked for elimination. This process of allegorical condensation begins, not surprisingly, with the figures of humanism that de Burgos singles out for elimination. This time, however, it is not *el hombre*, "Man," but *los hombres*, or "men," whose movements and agency are presented by the speaker as incarnating the very fleshly substance that the speaker had to leave behind precisely in order to retrieve a sense of her own body as the very fertile soil for life's reappropriation of itself, for becoming ipseity. And yet, there is no gap between "Man" and "men" here: The latter *are* the former insofar as they incarnate humanity through their feverish race to seize time, represented synecdochically through the allegory of the *minuto índice*, the "minute-index" that measures time by the seconds, minutes, and hours. Just as that *minuto índice* is the part that presents the whole of *ecstatic time*, *los hombres* appear as the part that encapsulates the whole of modern humanity.

Note also that, just as we saw before in our analyses of the time-space of the speaker's pilgrimage, here as well de Burgos coordinates time and space in her depiction of the modern humanity as a temporal ontology: To the temporal determination of said humanity in terms of the indexical minute corresponds a spatial determination—what the speaker calls *direcciones estáticas*, "static directions"—that is just as sterile and stagnant as the minute that measures men's motions. The irony of this process is that, in trying to capture time, it is men who become captured by time: Their entire lives are consigned to be lived in the shadows that they themselves qua Man have emptied upon the earth, and so they're condemned to remain viscous, consigned to their timely flesh. Thus, it is not at all surprising that the flesh reappears as the allegorical emblem that ultimately gathers all of these allegories, emerging as the speaker's polar opposite.

The line in which the flesh reappears, however, deserves a closer analysis, since it holds the key to the possibility of retrieving that *other* sense of time— which is almost *other than time*—that opens up in the intimate experience of being-a-self:

Siempre la misma carne apretándose muda a lo ya hecho.

Always the same flesh pressing into itself moves to the already made.

As is the case in this dense and difficult poem, each one of the words in this line is crucial. Take, for instance, the adverb that begins the line: *Siempre*, "Always." To its grammatical status as a modifier of a verb—hence as a modifier of the grammatical term that is canonically held to be responsible for introducing *time* in a phrase—this line adds a semantic function of grave ontological import, namely, that of asserting that there is *no time* in which men-cum-viscosity *will not* "move to the already made," thereby enacting the mode-of-being that corresponds to their constitution as temporal beings in the flesh. This ontological role becomes more emphatic if we read this adverb against the grain of its normative grammatical function as part of an adverbial phrase composed of itself and the other adverb that appears in this line, namely, *ya*, "already." If we do so, then it becomes possible to read this line as mobilizing the powerful temporal rethinking of the a priori that characterizes Heidegger's inventive use of the expression *immer schon*, "always already," or, in Spanish, *siempre ya*.[151] Not unlike the case of Heidegger's *always-already*, de Burgos's *siempre . . . ya* denotes a determination of Being that inheres and holds in advance of anything that might happen to those human beings whose ontological constitution is ruled by viscosity. But unlike Heidegger's *always-already*—which, qua determination of *Dasein*, entails the possibility that *Dasein* might temporalize itself authentically or inauthentically, properly or improperly, vulgarly or ecstatically—the *always-already* that de Burgos pre-imposes on the flesh leaves no possibility of an outside, no *other becoming* than that of always-already becoming *being-in-the-time-of-the-flesh*. This is why the *siempre ya* that emerges in this line is determined or accompanied by another adjective or adverb, the participle, *hecho*, "made." The *fact* of *viscous facticity* admits no transformation: The *flesh* is neither immanent to itself, since it lacks ipseity, nor transcendent, since it lacks the dimension of distance in which alone something like transcendence, and the attendant alterity that constitutes it, can unfold. De Burgos's flesh thus marks a being so indissociable from viscous abjection that it cannot *be* without ceasing to be *itself* entirely.

And yet, the *self* that belongs to the flesh is precisely the negation of the ipseity that becomes available through the elimination of the flesh. In this respect, it is significant that de Burgos also relies on the adjective *misma*—which, depending on the context, could be translated in English as "same" or "it-her/him-self"—to modify *la carne*. Unlike the ipseity of the self whose intimate ideal embodiment secures both an unassailable self-belonging and the capacity of transformation, the *flesh* is *always-already* condemned to remain *the same as it is*, that is, to be viscosity, which, qua viscosity, is precisely devoid of ipseity and thus of *self*-sameness. The sense of this ontological condemnation, which constitutes the peak of "2. Íntima"'s own psychomachia, is reinforced by the barely perceptible yet extremely thoughtful use of the verb *mudar* that de Burgos chose for this line. The thoughtfulness of this verb lies in the fact that it oscillates undecidably between two major philosophical concepts of motion, namely, *kinēsis* and *metabolē*, motion in the sense of spatial movement or change of location and motion in the sense of alteration, change, transformation. Whether the line is read as presenting the flesh as always moving to the already made or mutating into it, the effect is the same, since the flesh will remain the same as it will have always already been.

Finally, after this reading we are in a better position to approach the most enigmatic term in this line, namely, the reflexive verb *apretándose* ("pressing itself") that accompanies the movement or mutation of the flesh into itself. The verb *apretar*, which could be translated as *to tighten, to squeeze, to press together, to apply pressure*, conveys the sense of suffocation, of constriction that is produced when one is enclosed within an exceedingly tight covering or casing; for instance, the term is used colloquially in Spanish to describe the feeling of discomfort generated by wearing articles of clothing or shoes that are too tight. In the context of this line, however, the action of the flesh "pressing into itself" delineates a parallel movement to the shrinking of time that opens the poem's second part, consolidating the poem's allegorization of the impossibility of both immanence and transcendence that characterizes the "being" of the flesh. As such, this motion of self-pressurization constitutes the flip side of the flesh's movement or mutation into the already-made: If the latter appears—though this is mere semblance—to move outward or centrifugally, the flesh's pressing into itself emphasizes that the flesh's motion, however hyperactive it may be, remains a motion-*within* that is paradoxically barred from all intimacy, emerging as a sameness without ipseity—a motility with no movement. One is tempted to bring physics to bear on this image; for it is almost as if the flesh, in its motile self-pressurizing, constituted something like a *black hole* in de Burgos's humanist ontology—a point at which matter attains infinite density under the pressure of its own collapse.

Moreover, the fact that something like a *black* hole—a point of enormous density without inwardness—emerges here should alert us to another possible valence of the term *apretándose*, this time linked with racial Blackness. As a matter of fact, this valence is remarked unavoidably in the history of the Spanish verb *apretar*, from which the adjective *prieto* is derived, which is attested since the fourteenth century by Spanish lexicographers as synonymous with black but which acquired a more explicitly racial meaning in the Spanish Caribbean, where it is used to this day at once euphemistically and derogatorily as a colorist term to designate Black or Afro-descendent people of the darkest complexion. The fact that Spanish etymologists have confirmed the causal link between a verb that refers primarily to density or tightness and a term that refers to racial Blackness suggests that this linguistic development is grounded in a pretheoretical, sedimented perceptive regime that associates density, thickness, and tightness with opacity, obscurity, or Blackness—a regime that, as Black feminist science scholars remind us, continues to harbor murderous implications for the Blackened bodies compelled to occupy the position of the *flesh* that is supposed to be *only* flesh. Indeed, de Burgos's operation in this line recalls Zakiyyah Iman Jackson's demonstration of the role played by "the 'evacuated and overfull' appearance of the Black(ened) body with respect to ontologized and ontologizing polarities, such as human-object, human-animal, for example, where the manifestation of Black(ened) bodies clears the way for a plasticization and potential fluidification of embodied minds and the fleshly matter of existence."[152] Such a reading of de Burgos's execration of the flesh as a racializing script will be pursued in more detail when we turn our attention to "12. Ay ay ay de la grifa negra" ("12. Ay Ay Ay of the Griffe Negress") in the next section.

It should be no surprise, then, that it is right at the moment in which the speaker confronts the spectacle of this human-all-too-human *fleshly black hole* that she is forced to return, again, to herself, to the intimate abode of her ipseity.

> Me busco. Estoy aún en el paisaje lejos de mi visión.
> Sigo siendo mensaje lejos de la palabra.
>
> La forma que se aleja y que fue mía un instante
> me ha dejado íntima.
> Y me veo claridad ahuyentando la sombra vaciada en la tierra desde el hombre.
>
> I search for myself. I am still in the landscape far from my vision.
> I continue to be message far from the word.
>
> The form that distances itself and that was mine in an instant
> has left me intimate.
> And I see myself clarity dispelling the shadow emptied upon the earth from man.

In this return to herself, we are finally exposed to that *other* time that is radically other to both the time of the clocks and the proper time of futural ecstasy. Time here emerges as the ontological dimension of what remains and persists in its ipseity, so immanent to the life that feels itself in the immediacy of its ideal body that it cannot admit any separation, any horizonality, any distance. The poem conveys this sense of temporality—which is properly speaking inexpressible— through the interplay of tense, more specifically, through the deployment of the present, especially via its combination with the gerund, and the *pretérito perfecto*, which corresponds to the English present perfect. The time of the persistence of the speaker in her ipseity recalls what Marcia Sa Cavalcante Schuback has written recently about the "gerundive time" that is at work in the writing in neuter of Clarice Lispector, which she characterizes as an attempt to show "the impossible grammar of 'life being seen by life.'"[153] Turning inward, the speaker confirms her persistence in that dimension in which life is lived, that is, felt as life, which means that the past of her ipseitological pilgrimage, in spite of its interruption, was not past, but is rather *present*, and thereby belongs to a regime of presence that cannot be understood according to any durational, phenomenological, or existential model of time. Ironically, perhaps the closest thing in the philosophical tradition to the time that emerges here—a time in which the present and the preterite perfect are so intimately bound that every moment, every instant presents itself in its perfective aspect as the lived time of ipseity—would be something like the famous end of Hegel's *Phänomenologie des Geistes*, where Absolute Spirit, erasing the time of its negativity and history, is able to remember its previous forms while remaining infinitely proximate to itself.[154] Indeed, the last line of the term, when read in relation to the last line of the first part, evokes something of the concluding scene of Hegel's magnum opus. For the only divergence between these two lines is a minor shift in tense: Whereas the first verse is in the simple past or preterite, the second is in the present, marking the transformation of the past experience through its integration as both past and present, as an essence that, having been, nonetheless remains. But de Burgos's thinking of the essence of interiority is infinitely more immediate than Hegel's, and the time of intimacy is accordingly devoid of negativity and even of passage: In the continuity between past and present, what emerges is a time closer to that which Henry has described as "a temporality without difference, an immanent movement moving itself in itself that never separates itself from itself."[155] This is the time of life after the self has experienced the mystical visitation of what de Burgos, in a nod to the Platonic tradition in philosophy, does not hesitate to call by that oldest of names, *Forma*, a "Form" whose instantaneous possession nonetheless attunes the life of her selfhood in an enduring manner to the autoaffective rhythms of intimate ipseity.

Recovering through poetry a life capable of surviving and living in the midst of modernity's catastrophe, the poet who speaks throughout *Poema* secures her access to an experience of intimacy that can deliver each time the (un)timely experience of a life untarnished by modern life, untouched by its viscosity.

Although one of my goals in this section was to show that de Burgos's *Lebensphänomenologie* does not constitute a nomadic line of flight from the ideology that animated the leaders of the Generación del 30, de Burgos's somatophilic sarxophobia clearly has implications beyond the confines of Puerto Rican intellectual history. Indeed, on this account, "2. Íntima" presents us with a scenario that is often elided in contemporary debates about coloniality and European modernity as a historico-metaphysical catastrophe.[156] In the work of thinkers as varied as Walter Mignolo or da Silva, there is a tendency to identify the Cartesian splitting of *res cogitans* from *res extensa* as one of the key ontological matrices responsible for the institution of coloniality, itself understood in onto-epistemic terms through the institution of a racialized boundary that separates interiority from exteriority, differentiating those human beings endowed with rational sovereignty from those regarded as too affectable and hence too close to nature.[157] Although this claim is at a certain level irrefutable, it is also deeply flawed, both as an interpretation of the history of philosophy and of the historicity of the raciality that is constitutive of the metaphysics of modernity.[158] De Burgos's *Poema* can help us approach the problems with this narrative, since, on this account, her first poetry volume stages an alternative that is seldom contemplated by these thinkers; namely, it discloses how affectability may always enable the reconstitution of a sovereign ipseity that is not exempt from the violent reinvention of ever more racialized/(un)gendered others, since it is actually instituted and buttressed by this violence.[159] *Poema* institutes the possibility that sovereignty may be attained and secured thanks to, and not in spite of, affectability, through the production of a somatic split at the heart of affectability, which allows ipseity to disavow its viscosity.

In this way, "2. Íntima" reenacts some of the foundational rituals of ontological violence that characterize modernity, even if the reactivation of this violence is, ironically, brought about by a *transformation* of the Cartesian schema that announces, if not already brings about, the dissolution of what is often held (however erroneously) as the most insidious and pervasive legacy of Cartesian modernity, namely, the radical dissociation between interiority and exteriority. "2. Íntima" *alters* the very structure of interiority, which a thinker such as da Silva has singled out as one of the key racial technologies of Western imperial modernity. In her historico-philosophical engagement with modern European ontology as a racializing apparatus, da Silva claims that interiority emerged as "the private holding man has always occupied in Western thought";[160] as such, the category designates the main feature that the mind or consciousness must possess in order to be able to attain and secure "self-determination" or, as she also puts it, "sovereignty."[161] According to da Silva, buttressing the fortress of Western rational man required the concomitant invention of another ontological figure, namely, the "affectable I," shorthand for "the scientific construction of non-European minds" as ontologically incapable of interiority and thus as irremediably exposed to both the heteronomous power of natural forces and the autonomous activity of rational (i.e., Western) agents.[162]

De Burgos's poetization of *intimacy* as the very cipher of the experience of *ipseity* radically upends this highly influential, though reductive, interpretation of Cartesian modernity. For what unfolds *in* and *as* this poem is the disclosure and institution of an "affectable I" that, paradoxically, emerges *as the true site of sovereignty*. In other words, although her poem recasts the self's interiority in terms of *intimacy*—that is, in terms of a radically embodied, sensible mode of autoaffection—this transformation *does not bring about the undoing of the self's sovereignty*. Quite the contrary, the invention of an ipseity for which even life as such can only be if it is *felt* within the radical immanence of the self's intimate life, its being-with-itself, demonstrates that affectability can be retrieved from its "modern" racialized, abjected disavowal and be repurposed as the very source of a self who remains vested with sovereignty. In other words, although the ipseity that emerges as the very essence of the "I" or of the "self" in de Burgos's poem cannot be said to be isomorphic to the *dominant* (and largely limited, if not even mistaken) interpretations of the Cartesian cogito or of Hegelian Spirit, this discrepancy does not diminish at all the sovereign violence that informs the very position occupied by the self that finds expression in "2. Íntima." Instead, this poem demonstrates that the political and metaphysical investments in sovereignty can well accommodate a theory of radical embodiment and turn even *affect* into the medium for an attempt to secure sovereignty's hold on its own autonomous power.

The fact that an embodied and gendered ipseity is possible and that, for the sake of its possibility, an anti-Black script needs to be reinstituted indexes a possibility whose structural effects must be reckoned with. Insisting that the reclamation of the lived body—especially when that body is (un)gendered/racialized—brings about ipso facto the undoing of Cartesian coloniality is one way of avoiding the problem that de Burgos's sovereign script poses for thought. This possibility, I would also argue, should question the facility with which the motif of *autopoiesis* is held as the solution to the problem posed by biocentrism, especially in the wake of Wynter's influential engagement with the work of Humberto Maturana and Francisco Varela.[163] In the wake of de Burgos's intimate revolution and its catastrophic iterations throughout *Poema*, it is not the subject and its disembodiment but the very (im)position of an embodied-cum-excarnated sovereign *ipseity* as the normative form that human *life* must take if it is to produce itself *properly* that stands in need of deconstruction.

§24. BLACK MASQUERADES, WHITENED EXCORIATIONS: "12. AY AY AY DE LA GRIFA NEGRA"

My reading of "2. Íntima" in the previous section captured the most salient aspect of Burgos's ambivalence with regards to modernity. For it is only through her destructive inheritance of this most canonically modern of *topoi*—the *cogito* as the essence of the "I" or the self—that the speaker of *Poema* is able to found her own ipseity, instituting herself as the sole being whose own sovereign essence grants her the power to resist modernity's expropriating fungibility. And yet, de Burgos's undoing of standard accounts of modern subjectivity as entailing a privilege of the mind over the body or of interiority over exteriority paradoxically produces a countermode of affectability, which finds expression in the allegorical figure that de Burgos, throughout *Poema*, calls *la carne* (the flesh). De Burgos's reinvention of *la carne* indexes a process akin to that which produces what Alexander Weheliye calls a "fleshly surplus"[164] in his original rearticulation of Hortense Spillers's distinction between "the flesh" and "the body."[165] Weheliye coins the term "fleshly surplus" to designate the viscous, racialized substance or the material substrate engendered through the brutal technologies of domination that undergird social and political life in a post-1492, (post)plantation global context. In a way not unlike how Weheliye's centering on the flesh rewrites genealogies of biopolitics, I argue that de Burgos's retrieval of the *flesh* in *Poema* provides the key to understanding the *phenomenological* philosophy of life that is inchoately articulated throughout this volume—a *Lebensphänomenologie* indexed to the experience of intimate ipseity as the ontological ground that anchors the political task of overcoming modernity's capture of life.

But for the *flesh* to function as this biopolitical substance it must be incarnated allegorically. We have already analyzed how the speaker's (counter)modernist political utopia requires the production of at least two major avatars of this allegorical flesh: first, Julia de Burgos herself, who stands as the effigy of patriarchalized femininity and thus incarnates a historico-metaphysical epoch structured by the impossibility for womanhood and ipseity to coincide; second, the figure of Man/men, who embody the ecstatic temporality that provides the rule for modern life's carnal, sensualistic sensibility that is unable to experience embodiment in all its transcendental glory. But, as I already anticipated, the speaker's institution of her embodied/gender ipseity also *reactualizes modernity's constitutive raciality*, breathing, as it were, *new/old life* into the structural positioning of Blackened life as an enduring problem for an equally Whitened ontology.[166] Nowhere does the emergence of modern raciality inflect the phenomenology of life that *Poema* poetizes more than in the volume's twelfth poem, "12. Ay ay ay de la grifa negra":

12. Ay ay ay de la grifa negra

Ay ay ay, que soy grifa y pura negra:
grifería en mi pelo, cafrería en mis labios;
y mi chata nariz mozambiquea.
Negra de intacto tinte, lloro y río
la vibración de ser estatua negra;
de ser trozo de noche, en que mis blancos
dientes relampaguean;
y ser negro bejuco
que a lo negro se enreda
y comba el negro nido
en que el cuervo se acuesta.
Negro trozo de negro en que me esculpo,
ay ay ay, que mi estatua es toda negra.

Dícenme que mi abuelo fue el esclavo
por quien el amo dio treinta monedas.
Ay ay ay, que el esclavo fue mi abuelo
es mi pena, es mi pena.
Si hubiera sido el amo,
sería mi vergüenza;
que en los hombres, igual que en las naciones,
si el ser el siervo es no tener derechos,
el ser el amo es no tener conciencia.
Ay ay ay, los pecados del rey blanco
lávelos en perdón la reina negra.

Ay ay ay, que la raza se me fuga
y hacia la raza blanca zumba y vuela
a hundirse en su agua clara;
o tal vez si la blanca se ensombrará en la negra.
Ay ay ay, que mi negra raza huye
y con la blanca corre a ser trigueña;
¡a ser la del futuro
fraternidad de América![167]

12. Ay Ay Ay of the Griffe Negresse

Ay ay ay that I am griffe and pure Black;
nap in my hair, *cafrería* in my lips
and my flat nose mozambiques.
Black of intact tint, I cry and laugh
the vibration of being a Black statue;
of being a slice of night, in which my white
teeth flash;
and being the Black liana
that twines around the Black
and curves the Black nest
in which the crow lies.
Black slice of Black in which I sculpt myself
Ay ay ay that my statue is all Black.

They tell me that my grandfather was the slave
For whom the master gave thirty pieces.
Ay ay ay that the slave was my grandfather
is my pain, is my pain.
If it had been the master,
it would be my shame;
for among men, just as among nations,
if being the servant is having no rights,
being the master is having no conscience.
Ay ay ay the sins of the White king
the Black queen wash them in forgiveness.

Ay ay ay that race escapes me
And toward the White race buzzes and flies
to sink itself in its clear water;
or perhaps if the White will shade itself in the Black.
Ay ay ay that my Black race flees
And with the White runs to become Brown;
to be the future race
of American fraternity!

Folkloric Blackness and the Pain of Slavery's Afterlife: de Burgos as *Poeta Negrista*?

Given the totemic nature of de Burgos's reception and the protocols of idealistic specularity that are required to continue to erect her totemic figure, it is not surprising that this poem has been largely "read" within parameters that reduce its historicity to the question of ethnic or racial identity, which is further reduced by being approached almost exclusively under the anthropologistic lenses of *folklorism* and *heritage*. We already saw one of the paradigmatic cases of this operation in Gelpí's claim that this poem mounts "a defense of African heritage and a celebration of racial miscegenation in the Americas."[168] Similar gestures can be found in many of de Burgos's biographers and scholarly readers who evoke de Burgos's "Ay ay ay" in order to argue for de Burgos's commitment to defend the presence and centrality of Blackness in Puerto Rican culture against the Hispanophilia that dominated the island's lettered city in the 1930s. López Jiménez summarizes this position when she claims that this poem offers "a celebration of Blackness and *mestizaje* which responds to the Hispanophilia and the racism of the authorized discourses of cultural nationalism, at the same time as it rejects the terms in which Palés figures Black men (and women)."[169]

The reference to the figure of Luis Palés Matos here is crucial to understanding the importance that is implicitly granted to de Burgos's "12. Ay ay ay" whenever it is evoked in the terms laid out by Gelpí and López Jiménez, among others. For Palés Matos—who belongs to that select group of "national poets" alongside de Burgos, Llorens Torres, and Corretjer—is not only the controversial founder of the Puerto Rican tradition of *poesía negrista* (also known by its earlier racialist and pejorative title of *poesía negroide*) but was also one of the main protagonists of a public debate that unfolded in some of the most prominent newspapers of the island during the mid-1930s concerning the place of Blackness in Puerto Rican culture.[170] In keeping with his investment in depicting "Black" themes and tropes in his poetry, Palés Matos—who was a White man from an elite, though somewhat financially insecure, background—defended the view that Puertoricanness is irreducibly bound to *mulataje* and that, as a result, the Puerto Rican ethnic-cultural type cannot be understood, as Pedreira argued in *Insularismo*, as a Caribbean extension of Hispanicity with some Black and Indigenous epiphenomenal elements.[171] A crucial element in this dossier was the publication in 1937 of Palés Matos's *Tuntún de pasa y grifería* (translated into English as *Tom-Toms of Kinky Hair and All Things Black*), the long-awaited collection of his decade-long production of *negrista* poems, which received the award by the Institute of Puerto Rican Literature for best book of poetry that same year. Given the proximity in the publications of *Tuntún* and *Poema* and the prestige that Palés Matos already enjoyed among Puerto Rican intellectuals, it is quite possible that de Burgos conceived of "12. Ay ay ay de la grifa negra"—which, after all, is her only poem written in the voice of a Black speaker and explicitly concerned with slavery's afterlife—as an attempt to enter into the debate about Blackness in Puertoricanness launched, in part, by Palés Matos's poetics.

The controversy surrounding Palés Matos's poems remains alive to this day, and this is not the place to weigh in on the matter. But to understand the interpretive strand that López Jiménez's captures in the passage quoted earlier we could turn briefly to Isar P. Godreau's summary of the positions advanced by those who take a critical side on the ongoing debate about the place of Negrophobia/Negrophilia in Palés Matos's poetry:

> Critiques of *negroide* poetry have also condemned its gendered representations, arguing that its focus on large black hips and buttocks hypersexualizes black women's bodies in a caricaturesque way that renders them erotically primitive and less than human. In effect, if signifiers of "*negroide* culture" point to deep urges that emerge from within, these are dynamically channeled through the black woman's body. As the repository par excellence of black folklore, the black woman's alleged corporeal exuberance is often transformed into magical, erotic, or prohibited dimensions in *negroide* aesthetics.[172]

A quick glance at "12. Ay ay ay de la grifa negra" suffices to see why many of de Burgos's readers are quick to insist, in what effectively amounts to an expansion of Gelpí's nomadic-subject thesis, that de Burgos also effectively challenges not only the White supremacy of Pedreira but also the vitalist Negrophilia of Palés Matos. For one can hardly find any traces in de Burgos's poem of the reified props that Palés Matos mobilizes in order to put on poetic stage a folklorized "*negroide* culture" for the consumption of his mostly Whitened audience: Drums, fetishes, voodoo, and the mythologized figure of Tembandumba are all absent from this poem. More importantly, absent from "12. Ay ay ay de la grifa negra" are any explicit references to the Black feminine figure as the bearer of a boundless sensuality that nonetheless acquires a paradoxically nonthreatening aspect in the poetics of Palés Matos and other pro-*mestizaje* Caribbean male writers—in a move that should be seen as indissociable from *mestizaje* as a biocultural project. Instead, as Pérez Rosario has pointed out, "The woman in these opening stanzas is described in dehumanizing stereotypes and has no agency. She does not speak; rather, she is described as a statue, and neither her feelings nor her humanity are ever revealed to the reader. Her hair is: 'grifería,' her lips are 'cafrería,' and her nose is 'chata,' while the whiteness of her teeth is so bright, its contrast to her black skin is a lightning flash, 'relampaguean.' "[173] Indeed, it would be possible to read the speaker's self-fashioning as a *statue* as de Burgos's ironic attempt to unmask what we may call, with Donna V. Jones, the *racialist vitalism* that characterizes Palés Matos's *negrista* poems, where Blackness (and especially Black femininity) is figured as endowed with a quasi-Bergsonian racial *élan vital* that echoes some of the racial-metaphysical claims put forward by *Négritude*'s founder Leopold V. Sénghor in essays such as "L'esprit de la civilisation ou les lois de la culture négro-africaine" ("The Spirit of Civilization and the Laws of Negro-African Culture").[174] Whereas Palés Matos's "Majestad Negra" ("Black Majesty") features an unnamed Black woman who becomes the incarnation of the legendary queen-warrior Temba Ndumba of the Kasanje People as she sensually dances by moving her generous posterior against the backdrop of a sugarcane plantation, the Black woman who speaks in de Burgos's poem is precisely characterized by her lamenting voice, with her "ay ay ay" foregrounding not just the world-shattering dimension of her pain but also the historico-metaphysical grounds of this suffering in the transatlantic slave trade and the centuries-old enslavement of peoples of African descent in the "New World."

In this respect, de Burgos's poem does configure what we may provisionally describe as a line of flight from the racist/racialist discourse of the Generación del 30, but not in the way that Gelpí and López Jiménez suggest: Rather, the first two stanzas of de Burgos's poem depart from the folkloric treatment of Blackness that still characterizes Puerto Ricans' broadly shared romance with their own reputed "racial democracy" and felicitous miscegenation by recognizing that the genesis of Blackness in a post-1492 context entailed the production of what Frank Wilderson calls a "new ontology," one whose cornerstone was the generation of "an entire race," a "people who, a priori, that is prior to the contingency of the 'transgressive act' (such as losing a war or being convicted of a crime), stand as socially dead in relation to the rest of the world."[175]

Finally, to measure more precisely the historical depths of de Burgos's pessimistic figurations of Black femininity, we should attend to another crucial intertext of "12. Ay ay ay de la grifa negra," namely, the first chapter of Pedreira's *Insularismo*, which is devoted to the "biological" constitution of *homo portoricensis*. One possible aspect of this poem that, to my knowledge, remains to this day unexplored is the possibility that de Burgos is departing not only from the poetics of Palés Matos but also from the racialist/racist discourse of Pedreira.

This lacuna in her reception is somewhat puzzling, since the racial terminology that structures de Burgos's poem—beginning with the crucial term of *grifa*, or "griffe"—is closer to Pedreira's already antiquated reactivation of the colonial *casta* system than to the largely folkloric use of *grifería* that we encounter in Palés Matos. We should recall that, for Pedreira, the figure of the *grifo*—which both in the Spanish and French colonial racial categorization systems designated a child who was presumed to be the offspring of Black and mulatto or mixed-Black parents—harbored a threat that needed to be contained or carefully navigated by the cultural and political authorities of any future Puerto Rican republic organized under the principles of White supremacy.

To grasp this threat, we must remark on the basic principle that grounds Pedreira's account of Puertoricanness as racial formation, which he articulates in the following pithy formulation: "The Spanish element founds our people and blends with the other races. From this fusion begins our con-fusion."[176] For Pedreira, *mestizaje* leads to *con-fusion* both in the putatively neutral and descriptive sense of a "blending-with" and in the more normative register that distinguishes what is murky, ill-defined, not yet properly bound, and thus not yet self-determined from what is clear, transparent, self-evidently itself. But this programmatic maxim of Pedreira's thinking, from which even Puerto Rico's ongoing colonial situation will be derived, rests on at least two more fundamental principles, which constitute his biocultural metaphysics of racial life or being: The first is Pedreira's belief in the superiority of pure racial types over mixed ones, and the second is his belief in the superiority of the White Europeans over the Black Africans: "In the *mestizo* two antagonistic races which are difficult to conjugate, with opposite cultures, struggle. Caught between the superior and the inferior, the *mulato* will always remain a borderline element, participating in both racial tendencies that will become more or less pronounced depending on the type chosen for a second coupling: the mestizo, white, or black."[177] On the opposite side of this antagonistic racial mapping of the island lies, for Pedreira, the figure of the *criollo*, "born out of the crossing of pure Spanish people that, against all odds, struggled with illnesses and the climate" and, above all, its descendant figure, the mythologized Whitened peasant or *jíbaro* that, to this day, remains the default standard-bearer of Puertoricanness.[178] One of the offshoots of Pedreira's intervention is to place the *jíbaro* at the center of any future project of nation building by Puerto Rican anticolonial elites, since, as the rightful descendant of the Spanish founders of the island, the *jíbaro* is the racial formation among the Puerto Rican population in which Whiteness presumably predominates.

But to defend the interests of the poor Whitened peasants, Pedreira needs to put the *mulato* population in its place, a task that becomes considerably difficult once the figure of the *grifo* enters the equation:

> The *criollo*, then, and the *mulato* have perfectly acclimated to our soil. The latter, who carries in the blood African resistance, upon coupling again with a Black person, produced an intermediary type, the *grifo*, of stronger complexion and more daring than any other Puerto Rican ethnological production, who has increasingly made the harshest tasks of our coasts and plantations his own. Lively and active, in him predominate the strength of the Black and the intelligence of the White, never well-balanced. . . . In him there is a subconscious revindication of the slave: the *mulato* is not as decisive: he's too harmonious to fall on either side. The *grifo*, on the contrary, because of the small amount of White blood that fertilizes his claim to rights [*abona su derecho*], aspires and has ambitions, and his resentment finds an escape valve in democracy. Thus, he amounts to an animating element in some cases, disturbing in others.[179]

We can now reconstruct better the bizarre a-logical, because rigorously racist, logic that finds in the *grifo* a sort of ontological wild card that is both "animating and disturbing" to Pedreira's nation-building agenda. To the extent that the *grifo* represents the willful embrace of hypodescendency, it constitutes a catastrophically wrong step in the right direction. For, despite all of Pedreira's empty gestures about his lack of interest in fanning the flames of racial tension, the ultimate *telos* of *Insularismo* is to be done with the "con-fusion" that was born(e) out of Puerto Rican racial "fusion"; hence the *grifo* constitutes this step through which Black Puerto Ricans approximate the reputed purity of their racial type, as a result producing the paradox of a type of Afro-descendant that is "superior," because it is presumably "purer," but *without having to undergo whitening*. This, alone, explains why Pedreira devotes so much time and effort to construct this racist fantasy of Black domination, taking careful steps to associate *grifos* with proletarianization and democracy, that is, indicating their complicity with two of the main drivers of modernity and "civilization" as the historical-ontological agent of cultural and spiritual expropriation. Hence the *grifo* needs to be put under strict surveillance by the White *criollo* elites whose historico-metaphysical task is to construct a nation with the Whitened peasants of the mountain range at its hegemonic center.

Unpacking the strange logic of this threat is crucial to grasp the depths of de Burgos's pessimistic, if you will, rendition of the *grifa* figure. The first stanza of the poem is more than eloquent in this respect:

> Ay ay ay, que soy grifa y pura negra:
> grifería en mi pelo, cafrería en mis labios;
> y mi chata nariz mozambiquea.

Negra de intacto tinte, lloro y río
la vibración de ser estatua negra;
de ser trozo de noche, en que mis blancos
dientes relampaguean;
y ser negro bejuco
que a lo negro se enreda
y comba el negro nido
en que el cuervo se acuesta.
Negro trozo de negro en que me esculpo,
ay ay ay, que mi estatua es toda negra.

Ay ay ay that I am a griffe and pure Black;
nap in my hair, *cafrería* in my lips
and my flat nose mozambiques.
Black of intact tint, I cry and laugh
the vibration of being a Black statue;
of being a slice of night, in which my white
teeth flash;
and being the black liana
that twines around the Black
and curves the Black nest
in which the crow lies.
Black slice of Black in which I sculpt myself,
Ay ay ay that my statue is all black.

De Burgos's *grifa* retains the Palésian insistence on the continuity between Afro-Caribbean and African cultural forms, which is remarked through the allegorical inscription of stereotypes of Africa on those parts of her face-statue on which race and Blackness is most commonly read: her hair, her lips, and her nose, for which de Burgos even coins a verb on the basis of the African country of Mozambique. And from Pedreira, de Burgos retains the legacy of the New World caste systems of racial classification according to which the *grifo* in postslavery contexts embodies the failure of the protocols of Whiteness instituted by the dominant culture to contain the danger of the Blackening of Puerto Rico. The coup de force of this first stanza, however, lies in the way the poem removes even the semblance of this danger or, rather, discloses the racist fantasies that produce the specter of an abundantly lively Blackness as the grounds for what we may call, with Calvin Warren, its ongoing "onticide."[180] For *grifería* is here depicted not simply as the loss of agency and humanity, as Pérez Rosario describes it, but as the bearer of a *life* that is no life at all, as a form-of-life radically cut off from the ontological vitalistic fantasies projected onto the Blackened body, albeit for radically different ends, by both Pedreira and Palés Matos.

After mapping the first three racist-Eurocentric emblems of Africanness onto the Blackened body of the *grifa*, the poem reinforces the positional effect of its incipit by producing a poetic surface that is saturated with Blackness. This procedure, achieved at once through semantic and syntactic means, constitutes the counterimage of what unfolds in the first part of "2. Íntima." Whereas in that poem the speaker, after losing all the atoms of her flesh, begins to voice her arrival to her ipseity in a poetic language in which almost every word is either a possessive or reflexive anaphoric personal pronoun, here the speaker's entire language is limited to the exhibition of her atomistic flesh (which could never be *her own*, even if it is the thing that completely overdetermines her entire being), which emerges as the cipher of an inert, dead matter that is all the more dead because of its hypodescendent *grifería*. We begin to see now the configuration of the most subtle yet more extreme version of all the antagonisms that characterize the textuality of *Poema*. The speaker of the volume, endowed with both the *power of ipseity* granted by her pure embodiment gained through the experience of intimacy and with the possibility of affirming that ipseity while embodying the norm of a postpatriarchal femininity, now puts on a *blackened mask* in order to speak in the first person *as if* she were a *grifa negra* and voice the claim of an impossible self. The speaker will thus manage to appropriate for herself even a "*logos*" that presents itself as constitutively incapable of securing the (no doubt phantasmatic) closure of the "circuit" of self-reference. The speaker's voice will now become the bearer of a counter-Heideggerian ironic *mineness*, one solely appropriated to the cry of an enduring expropriation—*ay ay ay*—as she voices her perverse openness to being-plundered by a White(ned) world.

Before addressing in detail the thorny question of the status of this poem's speaker, we must first contend with another layer of de Burgos's defolklorization of Afro-Puertoricanness that occurs in the first several lines of the second stanza:

Dícenme que mi abuelo fue el esclavo
por quien el amo dio treinta monedas.
Ay ay ay, que el esclavo fue mi abuelo
es mi pena, es mi pena.

They tell me that my grandfather was the slave
For whom the master gave thirty pieces.
Ay ay ay that the slave was my grandfather
is my pain, is my pain.

Note that de Burgos here establishes a different type of continuity between Africanness and Afro-Caribbeanness, a continuity that reckons with the discontinuity of the Middle Passage and thus could be seen as a contemporary version of apposite moments in Aimé Césaire's *Cahier d'un retour au pays natal* or the later versions of an Afro-Caribbean poetics in authors like Derek Walcott and Édouard Glissant, who insist on the interruption of genealogy that the process of enslavement entailed for the enslaved Africans who survived their deportation and made it to the "New World."[181] There are no references in her sorrowful song to Mackandal, Temba Ndumba, no allusions to African kingdoms, not even to *bomba y plena*, the two Afro-Caribbean rhythms par excellence within Puerto Rican culture. Her sole inheritance, received from grandfather to granddaughter, is the enduring pain of what Saidiya Hartman calls "the afterlife of slavery." In one of the few readings that engages at a deeper level with the complicated textuality of this poem, Aurea María Sotomayor has remarked that this sense of an imposed racial inheritance is explicitly poetized by the speaker's use of the unusual verb *Dícenme*, instead of the more common construction *Me dicen*, which for Sotomayor is figured "as if it were an imposed burden, a brand with which the poetic voice is stigmatized."[182] I would expand this reading by remarking on the fact that this constitutes the sole appearance in the poem of the anaphoric personal pronoun, which was so pervasive in "2. Íntima." At the only moment in which the speaker utilizes this pronoun to speak of herself in the accusative, the subject that addresses her *is not herself* but a spectral alterity that simply tells her that she's not only Black but a descendant of slaves—an important distinction given the relatively large population of *pardos libres* or "freed Blacks" throughout Puerto Rico's colonial history.

We can now see why readers such as Gelpí and López Jiménez, who insist on interpreting this poem as a folkloric celebration of Afro-Rican heritage, are not reading the poem at all. At the same time, it is not enough to bemoan or condemn, as Pérez Rosario does, the lack of agency and dehumanization to which this figure succumbs under the seemingly unassailable forces of anti-Blackness and Hispanophilic White supremacy. For the emphasis on agency and denied or excluded humanity implicitly upholds the belief in the eventual attainment or bestowal of agency and humanity as the *telos* whose arrival would finally mark the undoing of the damaging effects of anti-Black racism. Such a reading traffics in the liberal imaginaries that, as da Silva has pointed out, rely on the "sociohistorical logic of exclusion" to explain the workings of raciality in the modern world.[183] But the logic of exclusion fails to account for the historico-ontological mechanisms that produced "New World" Blackness-cum-enslaved life as what

Jackson has called a form of plasticization in which *"the African's humanity is not denied but appropriated, inverted, and ultimately plasticized in the methodology of abjecting animality."*[184] Such interpretations also fail to pay heed to the questions that, as Saidiya Hartman has powerfully shown, the afterlife of slavery poses: "What if the endowments of man—conscience, sentiment, and reason—rather than assuring liberty or negating slavery acted to yoke slavery and freedom?"[185] I would argue that these are some of the questions that "12. Ay ay ay de la grifa negra" poses in its initial two stanzas, even if they are quickly covered over by the second half of the second stanza and the last two stanzas of the poem, which figure the speaker both mimicking the liberal-abolitionist discourse of Puerto Rican elites that reduced slavery to a matter of civil rights and embracing *mestizaje* ideology.

Will the Real Julia de Burgos Please Stand Up?

Before turning to the second half of the poem, I want to return to the question of the status of the speaker of "12. Ay ay ay de la grifa negra" broached in the previous section. Pulling this thread will unravel a whole series of questions that touch upon de Burgos's biography and that cannot be dealt with adequately in the space of this reading, even though a provisional engagement with these questions is still required if we are to track and project a more thorough desedimentation of the totemic protocols that have overdetermined the reception of this poem.

I began my reading showing how two of de Burgos's most established readers, driven by their investment in de Burgos's totemic configuration, misread the textuality of this poem and misconstrue the nature of its departure from the racial ideologies that dominated Puerto Rican discourse in the 1930s. On my reading, de Burgos's challenge to this racist formation does not reside in her celebration of Afro-Puerto Rican heritage, let alone in her embrace of *mestizaje* ideology; rather, the sole aspect of de Burgos's poem that perhaps breaks with the strictures of Puertoricanist racial discursivity is her sobering and pessimistic resituating of Afro-Puertoricanness within the longue durée of slavery.

There is, however, another reading of this poem that exacerbates even more the totemic investments that determine this tradition. Torres Santiago and Yolanda Ricardo Garcell are paradigmatic of a more explicitly *referential* version of this celebratory reading that relies on the positing of two overlapping continuities between the author of *Poema* and the speaker of its twenty furrow/poems and between the speaker of the other nineteen poems in the collection and the speaker of "12. Ay ay ay de la grifa negra."[186] What is particularly pernicious about this procedure is that the first claim, which even the most cursory reading of "1. A Julia de Burgos" should render, at the very least, suspect, is not only affirmed as true but also transformed into the first premise of a syllogism that goes as follows: Since the speaker of *Poema* and de Burgos are the same person, and since the speaker of *Poema* is the same across all twenty poems, then the speaker of "Ay ay ay" is not a generic Black female voice celebrating Afro-ricanness in general but de Burgos herself, reclaiming her *own* status as an Afro-Puertorican or an Afro-Latina. Given the increasing dissemination of this interpretation, rendered nearly irresistible by the demand for ever more transparent representations of Afro-Latinos within a United States marked by the death of George Floyd and the threat of an increasing realignment of Latinos with the White supremacism of the Republican Party, a quick foray into de Burgos's biography and her complicated relationship to Whiteness and Blackness cannot be avoided.

De Burgos's ambiguous status as a *mestiza* has contributed significantly to her totemization. As we have seen, de Burgos came to prominence as a poet at a time when leading figures of the Puerto Rican intelligentsia began to spouse a renewed sense of racial destiny through the embrace of Latin-Iberian scripts of whiteness, inspired by intellectuals such as Oswald Spengler, José Ortega y Gasset, and José Vasconcelos, among others. Likewise, a racialist metaphysics was not absent from the discourse of Pedro Albizu Campos, the main leader of the Puerto Rican Nationalist Party, who not only was personally close to Vasconcelos but also saw Puerto Rico's struggle for independence as a key chapter in an ongoing racial war between the Iberian and Anglo-Saxon Americas.[187] Given the well-attested intensification of Whitening as a project of nation building during the first half of the twentieth century, it stands to reason that de Burgos, who was already from a poor, landless background, was quite likely submitted to some forms of Whitening as she gained admission to the most elite literary and intellectual institutions in the island.

It is in this direction that I'm inclined to interpret the role that de Burgos's reputed Germanness plays in Luis Lloréns Torres racialist explanation-cum-boutade of de Burgos's propensity for "Kantian abstractions."[188] De Burgos's legendary Teutonicity found support in her father's use of the last name Hans, instead of Hance/Yance, in some official documents. That being said, the exhaustive genealogical study of de Burgos's family tree done by Neftalí García Martínez casts some doubts on de Burgos's reputed Germanness. García shows that her third great-grandfather, Matthias Yance, who arrived in Puerto Rico at some point in the eighteenth century and founded the so-called German "Hans" side of her family, married a *parda libre* (a "free woman of color," or *mestiza*), Rafaela de

Castro Pabón.[189] When we turn to the question of the racial background of de Burgos's mother, Paula García Marcano, we find an analogous, though diametrically opposed, situation. Although de Burgos's mother appears listed as "white" both on the poet's birth and baptism certificates, García Martínez's research has shown that the poet's mother was registered in the 1910 census as a "mulata," along with her entire family.[190] What is more, his genealogical reconstruction shows that the poet descended, through her mother's Marcano side, from a line of *pardos libres*, or "free people of color," that extends all the way back to the poet's third great-grandparents, Juan Antonio Marcano and María Ramona Pérez.[191] García Neftalí even goes as far as to hypothesize that the discrepancies in official documents in the race given for de Burgos's mother and maternal grandparents are the result of a willful decision by Francisco Burgos Yance to Whiten his family—a plausible hypothesis that reinforces my impression that the reputed Germanness of the Hans last name may also be an attempt to lay claim to a more prestigious White genealogy for himself and his children.

If de Burgos's initial reception framed the poet as a light-skinned, near-White mestiza, this hasn't prevented other scholars from treating de Burgos as a privileged example of the felicitous results of Puerto Rican "racial democracy" and its longstanding ethnonationalist romance with *mestizaje*. For instance, according to Rodríguez Pagán, de Burgos's most exhaustive biographer, de Burgos was "a beautiful and delicate woman in whom the three captive races of the human type of our islands are mixed, in an accomplishment of racial *mestizaje*."[192] Not surprisingly, most recent attempts to appropriate the figure of de Burgos have tended to emphasize her Afrodescendancy, both to undo the Whitening to which her figure was subjected in the initial stages of her canonization and, in the case of Afro–Puerto Rican writers and activists like Yolanda Arroyo Pizarro, to reclaim de Burgos's as a major figure of Afro-Puertoricanness.[193] The reconstruction of de Burgos as a Black poet is also in full swing in the United States, where de Burgos is quickly emerging as a totemic figure within the incipient efforts to construct a countercanon of Afro-Latino aesthetics and literature. Perhaps the most remarkable landmark in this posthumous process of Blackening has been the inclusion of de Burgos in Kevin Young's monumental anthology *African American Poetry: 250 Years of Struggle and Song*, published by the Library of America. Ironically, among the five poems of de Burgos selected by Young, "12. Ay ay ay de la grifa negra" is included.

But just as there is ample evidence to prove that de Burgos's claim to Whiteness was at best tenuous—even in a milieu as colorist as Puerto Rican society, in which the category of Whiteness is still to this day astonishingly elastic—a similar situation can be said about her Blackness. Perhaps there is no better place to examine this matter than de Burgos's *Cartas a Consuelo*, which contains at least two letters that are crucial to this matter. The first letter is dated April 9, 1940. De Burgos has been living for a couple of months in New York City after leaving Puerto Rico, and, to make ends meet, she has taken a job at the US Census Bureau, which has assigned her to Central Harlem, affording de Burgos a window into the living conditions of the neighborhood's mostly Black immigrant population:

> Imagine, I've been assigned to the middle of the Harlem district, the central gathering place of North American blacks, who, by the way, remain near-savage. These Blacks don't even know how to speak English. They speak a bad slang, mumble, and don't know their own names, or where they were born. It is hard to work in this place. But I couldn't find another job in the end. In my district—of about 1,000 people—I haven't found a single Latino, nor a single White North American. The majority of these blacks are from the Virgin Islands and Bermuda, Martinique, etc.—*cocolos*, as they are called. They live with their savage rites, practicing witchcraft and burning incense, lighting candles, etc. I've seen all of this with my own eyes, for I've had to go into their homes, sit with them, and hear and see their lifestyle. It is interesting, but bothersome and dangerous. They are very angry with the White man who humiliates them and they continue to live in a spoiled and brutal manner.[194]

We find here a univocal display of racism directed largely against other fellow Caribbean migrants. What is more, this letter also records de Burgos's own disidentification from what she perceives as an excessive, bestialized Blackness, which she describes in stereotypical White supremacist terms as characterized by the lack of dominion of language (in this case English) and the practice of non-Western forms of spirituality and religiosity. Indeed, at times this letter reads like a page taken straight out of Pedreira's book; this is particularly the case of her description of their "resentment" vis-à-vis the White man, which evokes precisely Pedreira's anxieties about the *grifo*'s desire for equality stemming from an indocility that seeks to revindicate their enslaved past.

The second letter is dated May 15, 1940. De Burgos is in Washington, DC, where she is spending some time with the family of José Lanauze Rolón—an Afro-Puertorican physician who graduated from Howard University and who was one of the main founders of Puerto Rico's Communist Party—on her way down south to embark on the ship that will take her to La Habana, Cuba, to join her lover, Juan Isidro Jimenes Grullón. While in Washington, DC, de Burgos experienced for the first time a social space explicitly cut across by state-sanctioned racial segregation. The following anecdote illustrates some of the calculations that she had to make in order to navigate such a space:

> They wanted me to stay in their home for a week and organize me a reading in the University of colored people, but after I observed the tremendous situation of racial prejudice that exists there, I decided not to give the reading, because then I would not be able to go to any public space that would not be for Blacks, not even parks, etc.[195]

The least we may say about this letter is that it reveals the ambiguous racial positionality of de Burgos. Roque Salas Rivera describes this positionality succinctly when, commenting on a prior letter that de Burgos sent to her sister from Washington, DC, he writes that "she clearly isn't white, though she often passes for white, and does not pass as black."[196] To which I would add that perhaps she did pass a bit as Black, given her concerns with being identified as such by dint of doing a poetry reading at Howard, which would not have been the case if she was firmly anchored in US Whiteness as constructed at the time. What remains true is that the sharper contours around the Black/White racial divide that de Burgos experienced in Washington, DC, cast her racial image in starker relief, and what emerges is a non-White figure that passes as White because she is by default regarded as non-Black, but, depending on the circumstances, could face the adverse consequences of being identified with Blackness. But perhaps the aspect of this letter that offers the strongest insight into de Burgos's racial identifications is her own decision to disidentify with Blackness, even at the risk of alienating her hosts. What is more, since the letters from this period do not narrate any other cultural events that other figures in Washington, DC, may have organized to disseminate her work, we must conclude that de Burgos effectively decided to pass on the opportunity to share her poetry at the most prestigious institution of Black higher education in the United States for the sake of keeping her options open in case an invitation from a White institution were to materialize.

Shouldn't these letters, among other aspects of de Burgos's dossier, lead us to reconsider the status of the racial, identitarian projections that are close to sedimenting into yet another totemic image of Julia de Burgos, now reconfigured as the symbol of Afro-Latinidad? I have undertaken this brief foray into the thorny issue of de Burgos's racial identity not because I am interested in setting the record straight, let alone because I believe that there is such a thing as the "real" race of de Burgos that we must try to discover. Moreover, even if we were to grant the first premise of the hermeneutical syllogism that undergirds these readings—namely, that the speaker of *Poema* and the historical individual Julia de Burgos are one and the same—the ambivalent, complicated, and conflicting scripts of racialization that overdetermine her racial identity cannot yield any definitive reading of this poem as an expression of her reputed "racial truth."

Beyond the highly questionable nature of their biographic interpretive mode, the fact that these different constructions of de Burgos's race do not seem to withstand scrutiny yet continue to hold sway should give us pause. Again, in pointing out these inconsistencies, my goal is not so much to correct the historical record as to register the enduring hold that these cohesive yet contradictory scripts of racial identification have on her reception today. As Derrida once wrote, "coherence in contradiction expresses the force of a desire," and this case is no exception:[197] The desire for de Burgos's to serve as both mirror and totem, and the pleasures granted by the idealized reflections that her monumental specularization affords, are virtually unassailable. Although it is my hope that the attempt to interrupt this play of mirrors might open *other* historical possibilities for de Burgos, and for ourselves, I am under no illusion about the guaranteed effectiveness of this critical or deconstructive procedure, especially when faced with the historicist desire to appropriate historical images for the sake of reconstituting ourselves into historical ipseities by confirming the stories that we already know about ourselves. At a certain point an "unconditional renunciation to sovereignty finds itself required *a priori*" in order to take a step outside of this circle—and no power, let alone the power of rigorous argumentation, can elicit such a renunciation from a reader.[198]

Black(ened) Masquerades, Nomadic Territorializations

Let us now pick up the reading of the poem where we left it to track how de Burgos's poetics of *grifería* amounts less to an identification with her ancestors than to the articulation of a dialectical antagonism in which the figure of the *grifa negra* will come to incarnate all the categories and qualities that de Burgos associates with modern life at its most alienated and abject. As I noted earlier, already by the second half of the second stanza, de Burgos's line of flight from the racialist/racist discourses of Palés and Pedreira begins to territorialize itself around a familiar cartography. This shift occurs in the second stanza when the speaker, after having evoked the effective specter of her enslaved grandfather, changes the register of her voice from an "intimate" lamentation to a public discourse that is closer to a political pronouncement, only to return later to the "ay ay ay" that marks each of the poem's stanzas:

> Si hubiera sido el amo,
> sería mi vergüenza;

que en los hombres, igual que en las naciones,
si el ser el siervo es no tener derechos,
el ser el amo es no tener conciencia.
Ay ay ay, los pecados del rey blanco
lávelos en perdón la reina negra.

If it had been the master,
it would be my shame;
for among men, just as among nations,
if being the servant is having no rights,
being the master is having no conscience.
Ay ay ay the sins of the white king
the black queen wash them in forgiveness.

As Pérez Rosario has pointed out, the speaker's counterfactual scenario attests to a radical choice on the part of the speaker, who "rejects any association with the colonizing power and clearly locates herself among the enslaved race."[199] No matter how painful being a descendant of slaves who has not moved up in the racial hierarchy through whitening may be, the speaker finds that pain preferable to dealing with the shame of being the descendant of a slave owner. What I find more interesting about this passage, however, is not this rejection of Whiteness per se—a rejection that, though it certainly takes place, only lasts for a moment and holds only for the past, not for the future that the *grifa negra* will forge when she becomes the Black *mater* of the mestizo race—but the terms in which this rejection is framed. These terms are profoundly moral and legal, with slavery being figured as a matter of civil rights and as a violation of the moral dignity of the human person. This understanding of the "peculiar institution" resonates with how the Puerto Rican tradition of elite liberal thought—to which Pedreira, in spite his conservative views, belongs—constructed what César Salgado has called a "liturgy of exceptionality" around the abolition of slavery in Puerto Rico that presents the island as the sole "territory in which the gordian knot of slavery is dissolved through public, reasonable debate and balanced legislation, rather than through insurrections fueled by resentment."[200] I would like to suggest that there is an intimate, structural bond between de Burgos's sudden embrace of a legalistic, modern, liberal language to recode what appeared in the first stanza as a pessimistic poetics of Blackness and the last two lines in this second stanza, whose gendered reference to White sin and Black forgiveness sets the stage for the third stanza. Indeed, one of the ways in which the Black queen has already forgiven the White king for his sins is by embracing the dominant culture's interpretation of slavery. Rather than unfolding her lament that refracts the survival in a postabolition moment of what Orlando Patterson describes as the "social death" and "natal alienation" of the slave, the speaker reduces slavery to a condition of rightlessness that can be redressed through the extension of rights and that, at bottom, is *more desirable* than bearing the shame of being the descendant of slave owners.[201]

We reach here a middle point in which the lament that opens the poem gives way to a moral-juridical language of duty, an obligation that reaches a paradoxical point in the poem's fourth "ay ay ay," by far the most enigmatic of all, given the sudden change in speaker.

> Ay ay ay, los pecados del rey blanco
> lávelos en perdón la reina negra.
>
> Ay ay ay the sins of the white king
> the black queen wash them in forgiveness.

Assuming, as I suggest we do, that the Black queen is none other than the speaker, then how should we approach this line? Unlike the other five ay ay ays in the poem, this one doesn't feature a voice that speaks in the first person; rather, it is as if the speaker of the poem had an experience of splitting its very fleshy "ego," which affords her enough distance to finally relate to herself *as* herself but only through the sudden invasion of another's voice that assigns from above a command that the speaker cannot but reiterate and obey. If the second stanza opens with the sole appearance of the personal pronominal enclitic particle *-me* in a way that actually deprived any possibility of self-reflexion, it closes with the disclosure of a mode of self-reflexion that paradoxically produces heteronomy, rather than autonomy, as the speaker is condemned to act in accordance to a law that does not constitute the source of her autonomy and freedom.

The third stanza of the poem then completes the transition from lament to the celebration of *mestizaje* to which this poem is often reduced:

> Ay ay ay, que la raza se me fuga
> y hacia la raza blanca zumba y vuela
> a hundirse en su agua clara;
> o tal vez si la blanca se ensombrará en la negra.
> Ay ay ay, que mi negra raza huye
> y con la blanca corre a ser trigueña;
> ¡a ser la del futuro
> fraternidad de América!

> Ay ay ay that race escapes me
> And towards the white race buzzes and flies
> to sink in its clear water;
> o perhaps if the white will shade itself in the black.
> Ay ay ay that my black race flees
> And with the white runs to become brown;
> to be the future race
> of American fraternity!

Given the strength of her catastrophic reception, it should not come as a surprise that even this stanza has provided occasions for critics to erect yet another totemic figure. Sotomayor, for instance, has taken the speaker's mobilization of figures of water, and especially her use of the chain of verbs *fuga-zumba-vuela-huye-corre*, as an occasion to argue for this stanza as another instance of de Burgos's poetics of nomadism: "The dispossessed ... turns to the weapon of alterity to reject a too-solid antithesis ... between slave and master and, paradoxically, affirm herself in a futural hybridity. The surface on which she contemplates herself is liquid and fleeting."[202] But can we say that the speaker is here contemplating herself? Within the strictures of *Poema*, self-contemplation is a characteristic of the speaker-cum-embodied/gendered-ipseity, who remains the polar opposite of the *grifa negra* precisely to the extent that she will only be able to reach something resembling self-contemplation through the mediation of her coupling with the White king, that is, through her embrace of the Whitening task that she has been assigned by the dominant sense-configurations of Puerto Rican historicity *to this day*. Rather than configuring a line of flight that may deterritorialize the racial binary, the speaker here is instead reenacting what Judy Rodríguez calls a "poetics of *blanqueamiento* that emerges from the structural collusion of ethnonationalism and antiblackness."[203] The fact that so many readers of de Burgos seem to have problems seeing this reveals how deeply sedimented the romance with racial democracy and *mestizaje* remains within dominant scripts of Puertoricanness.

But this romance with *mestizaje* is ultimately grounded in a more atavistic, and seemingly paradoxical, romance with racial purity. As Jared Sexton has argued,

> White supremacy and anti-blackness ... emerge in the interplay between miscegenation and the forms of resistance to it. An important claim follows from this reasoning: rather than establishing themselves in vulgar opposition to miscegenation, *white supremacy and antiblackness produce miscegenation* as a precious renewable resource, a necessary threat against which they are constructed, a loyal opposition, a double exposure.[204]

Following Sexton, we can begin to understand the extent to which the supposed overcoming of the color line that "12. Ay ay ay de la grifa negra" appears to poetize through its racial utopia of Brownness amounts to a ruse that ensures the survival of the color line under transformed historical and social conditions. For the so-called threat that miscegenation may pose to White supremacy is in fact part of the very movement through which racial purity produces the phantasm of its own substantial referentiality, by positing itself retroactively as the natural origin that miscegenation threatens.

What this poem rehearses in the unfolding of its three stanzas is a trajectory analogous to what Franz Fanon had painfully anticipated as the destiny of Black people in the introduction to *Peau noire, masques blanques*: "For the Black, there is but one destiny. And it is White."[205] By celebrating the utopian effacement of Blackness through its accession to Whiteness in the form of the constitution of a multiracial formation, de Burgos's poem reveals to what extent her political utopia necessarily traffics in the epistemic and ontological arsenal of modern raciality as a technology of domination. Nowhere is raciality more at work in *Poema* than when this poem announces the overcoming of racial differentiation under the aegis of a *mestizo fraternity*, since for the sake of that fraternity Blackness itself must be excoriated. The place of Black femininity as figured by de Burgos under her Blackened masquerade thus appears in the guise of what Jackson calls the "Black *mater*": The *grifa* both enters the scene only as an "abject representation" of what has no place within the alternative modernity projected by *Poema*'s retrieval of ipseity as the essence of life and being, and she will have exited the scene by literally giving birth to "to an imperial Western humanist conception of *the* world *as such*," which here takes the form of a world *without* raciality—a world in which all the reputed bearers of viscosity will have finally assumed a body by emancipating themselves from raciality, that is, by becoming White.[206]

§25. CODA: HOMAGE *EN SOUFFRANCE*

Poema en 20 surcos concludes with a poem that contains perhaps the clearest figure of the will to modernity that animates de Burgos's pursuit of a poetics of ipseitological intimacy:

20. Yo misma fui mi ruta	20. I Myself Was My Own Path
Yo quise ser como los hombres quisieron que yo fuese:	I wanted to be like men wanted me to be:
un intento de vida;	an attempt at life;

un juego al escondite con mi ser.	a game of hide-and-seek with my being.
Pero yo estaba hecha de presentes;	But I was made of presents,
y mis pies planos sobre la tierra promisoria	and my flat feet on the promissory earth
no resistían caminar hacia atrás,	could not bear to walk backwards,
y seguían adelante, adelante,	and kept going forward, forward,
burlando las cenizas para alcanzar el beso de los senderos nuevos.	evading the ashes to reach the kiss of the new paths.
A cada paso adelantado en mi ruta hacia el frente	At each advanced step in my route towards the front
rasgaba mis espaldas el aleteo desesperado de los troncos viejos.	the desperate flapping of the old trunks would tear into my back.
Pero la rama estaba desprendida para siempre,	But the twig was forever detached,
y a cada nuevo azote la mirada mía	and with each new lash my own gaze
se separaba más y más y más de los lejanos horizontes aprendidos;	separated itself more and more and more from distant acquired horizons:
y mi rostro iba tomando la expresión que le venía de adentro,	and my face began to take the expression that came from within,
la expresión definida que asomaba un sentimiento de liberación íntima;	the defined expression that manifested a feeling of intimate liberation;
un sentimiento que surgía	a feeling that was emerging
del equilibrio sostenido entre mi vida	from the sustained equilibrium between my life
y la verdad del beso de los senderos nuevos.	and the truth of the kiss of the new paths.
Ya definido mi rumbo en el presente,	Already defined my path in the present,
me sentí brote de todos los suelos de la tierra,	I felt myself the sprout of all the soils of the earth,
de los suelos sin historia,	of the soils without history,
de los suelos sin porvenir,	of the soils without to come,
del suelo siempre suelo sin orillas,	of the soil always soil without borders,
de todos los hombres, y de todas las épocas.	of all men and of all epochs.
Y fui toda en mí, como fue en mi la vida . . .	And I was wholly in me, as was in me life . . .
Yo quise ser como los hombres quisieron que yo fuese:	I wanted to be like men wanted me to be:
un intento de vida;	an attempt at life;
un juego al escondite con mi ser.	a game of hide-and-seek with my being.
Pero yo estaba hecha de presentes;	But I was made of presents;
cuando ya los heraldos me anunciaban en el regio desfile de los troncos viejos;	Already when the heralds announced me in the regal parade of the old trunks;
se me torció el deseo de seguir a los hombres	my desire to follow men was bent
y el homenaje se quedó esperándome.[207]	and the homage was left waiting for me.

Note how the poem gathers almost all of the threads and images that *Poema* mobilizes, beginning with the allegory of "men/Man," which the poem overwrites allegorically through the figure of the "parade of old trunks" and which reemerges here as the speaker's major antagonist: It is men/Man who have imposed their trajectory on the speaker's desire, and it is against them and the desire that they have autotellically determined that the speaker will unleash the force of her modernist ipseity. This ipseity, in turn, is allegorized through a plethora of figures, beginning with the temporal mode of a present whose spontaneity and self-presence the poem figures in terms so radical that we are forced to conclude that this present is radically liberated from the burden of retention. To further emphasize the relationship between temporality, desire, and man/Men, the speaker presents this liberation through the figure of the "detached branch," yielding an ironic inversion of synecdoche: Whereas the old trunks figured the calcified, sedimented tradition that constitutes the historicity of man/Men, the speaker is not a branch that belongs to and may even stand in as the whole of which it is a part but is "forever detached" from those trunks and their inhuman humanity. Perhaps more crucial for our purposes is the reappearance of intimacy as the affective modality in which this liberation of the present from the past can be lived, a liberation that, as the image of the speaker's autoaffective transmogrification into the very *soil* of *life itself* suggests, is radically ahistorical, being solely oriented toward the horizon of a future whose newness does not place the speaker perpetually outside or beyond herself but rather further deepens her sense of ipseitological intimacy, the *life-philosophical* certainty that life in its totality is holistically contained within her unbounded self.

Among these figures, it is on the concluding image of an homage *en souffrance*, left waiting or suspended in abeyance, that I want to dwell for a moment as I gather some of the threads of my reading of *Poema*. The allegorical context in which this suspension unfolds is particularly important, since it returns us to the willful embrace of anonymity or namelessness that characterizes the speaker's efforts in "1. A Julia de Burgos" to establish her ego in its purity, by separating the "I" of ipseity from the "I" that recognizes its egoity when hailed by its proper name. *Poema* thus begins and ends by presenting a speaker whose proper voice requires a radical form of disidentification. In refusing to answer to her call, the speaker of the poem turns away from the homage that awaited her, which here stands in synecdochally for more than the total network of social relations that require the proper name as the technology of substantial identification that allows a self to accrue social, cultural, and economic capital over time. For, as I have argued in more detail elsewhere, both the very etymology of homage and the inscription of this term in this last stanza suggest the possibility of reading this *homenaje* as standing in for the process of modern anthropogenesis—a becoming-Man from which the speaker is able to extricate herself, given her attainment of an ipseity that harbors in its own essence the destiny of a humanness beyond the humanity of Man.[208] But what is perhaps most puzzling about this allegory of homage *en souffrance* is the affective atmosphere in which it is couched. This becomes especially salient if we compare this poem's call for another humanity with the analogous moment in "1. A Julia de Burgos." Whereas *Poema* opens with the futural projection in which the speaker joins a multitude ready to set fire to Man/men, the authorial figure named Julia de Burgos included, no multitude accompanies the speaker on her revolutionary gesture in "20. Yo misma fui mi ruta." On the contrary, it is the speaker who ends up extricating herself from the space of a crowd and going her way, presumably in solitude, after reckoning with the event that bent her "desire to follow Man/men," altering her existential trajectory in favor of an ever-more intimate direction.

Facing this will-to-solitude, manifested in the speaker's desire to end homage as the social ritual that sustains a determination of desire as being always the "desire of the other," to speak with Jacques Lacan, de Burgos's readers by and large have only been able to respond with the very thing that the speaker of this poem rejected, namely, an homage.[209] De Burgos's reception has mostly taken shape in willful or unconscious ignorance of this audacious moment. This is in itself not surprising. For to respond adequately to a poetic voice that rejects homage would require an entirely different grammar of reception, indeed a different historical *idiom*.

The reading of *Poema* sketched here constituted an attempt to find such a nonhomagistic idiom. Rather than paying tribute to de Burgos as the Messianic incarnation in whose destiny my own destiny, as a member of many of the communities that she supposedly symbolizes, is inscribed, my engagement with *Poema* sought to displace the monumental protocols that have presided over this volume's reception. I have tried to set in place a nonhistoricist protocol of historical reading in order to expand the realm of what is legible in these poems by rescuing all those less-than-ideal elements that are also present in the Burgosian mirror but that her idealistic reading protocols must necessarily minimize or altogether ignore in order to continue to organize their own liturgies to the totem, their own parades of old trunks. Key among these elements is the way de Burgos's poem indexes anti-Blackness as a constitutive feature not only of

Puerto Rican modernization in the crucial decade of the 1930s but in Puerto Rico's present.

My interpretation of the catastrophic modernity of de Burgos's first poetry volume argues that her commitment to instituting an embodied, gendered ipseity in the medium of intimate autoaffection betrays a utopian desire for attaining a form-of-life that would be impervious to the more damaging aspects of modernity-cum-catastrophe, beginning with the radical loss of self and the fall into inauthenticity that the speaker of *Poema* presents as one of the major symptoms of the massive expansion of bourgeois ways of life under ongoing conditions of modernization. Not surprisingly, this desire for historical invulnerability has greatly contributed to her own catastrophic traditionalization, which has frozen her image into the eternal symbol of authenticity and resistance against everything deemed inhuman or inhumane. But this desire also evinces the extent to which the speaker of *Poema* remains conscripted by the very modern historicity that she in part wishes to escape. Indeed, my reading suggested that the violence that the speaker directs toward the persona that bears the name Julia de Burgos, toward all the men who are the incarnated bearers of the humanity of Man, and toward the emblematic figure of what Jackson calls "the Black mater"—all figures that belong, in different ways, to the sector of those marked for elimination by de Burgos's political utopia—is a necessary violence, one required by the imperative to sustain the dissociation between the sovereign body and the abject flesh, without which the sovereignty and ontological purity of the speaker's embodied/gendered ipseity would be compromised.

Without ceding an inch to the judgmental moralism that might take these conclusions as an occasion to condemn de Burgos for failing to live up to the very ideals that she continues to emblematize within the Puerto Rican cultural and political imaginary, my reading of *Poema* made the case that the aporias and double binds that mark de Burgos's attempts to imagine the overturning of modern life remain very much our own. If the catastrophic reception of de Burgos turned her life and works into the mirror in which generations of Puerto Ricans would always see themselves reflected in the poet's *imago* and thus see themselves in the best possible light, my reading has sought to endanger this specular complacency without purporting to shatter the mirror or without claiming that we can easily break away from the specular scene of reading and from the irreducibility of some residue of self-reflection. To read de Burgos's egological drive, her anti-Blackness camouflaged by utopian scripts of mestizaje, and the violence necessary to maintain an intimate sovereignty is also to read ourselves. But the text that emerges in this reading is quite different from that which the tradition has imposed in order to read itself in de Burgos's totemic reflection. The result is that historical features that constitute our now may finally begin to emerge from out of this encounter with this exceptional work. In this way, *Poema* itself *may* become an *image* in whose constellation our very historicity is *dangerously* entangled.

Quisiera bregar con lo peligroso. Lo que aún no tiene alba.

I would like to handle the dangerous. What has yet no dawn.
—Francisco Matos Paoli

EPILOGUE: AFTER SOVEREIGNTY?

Although it was not conceived as a book of what is nowadays called "autotheory," *Catastrophic Historicism* remains an auto-bio-graphical book in more ways than one. First of all, because it could not be otherwise. As Jacques Derrida reminds us in *L'animal que donc je suis* (*The Animal That Therefore I Am*), the auto-bio-graphical is ultimately grounded in the fact that the "I," this "minimal phenomenological structure," must position itself as "a sign of life, of life in presence" if it is to be at all, and thus the very possibility of an "I" or a "self" is intimately bound to the institution of ipseity as the very phenomenological-metaphysical essence of life.[1] At this most general level, the autobiographical dimension of this and any other book rests on the necessary fact that, without an "I" positioning or presenting itself as the authorial life-source of any book, no book would ever manifest itself. This structure of self-presentation is so pervasive that it covers the entire surface of any book, including those pages in which no authorial ipseity is explicitly remarked through first-person deixis.

This "autobiographicality" may hold for all books, but in the case of *Catastrophic Historicism* it produces a specific ironic effect that is worth unpacking. For the inevitable reinscription of ipseity within the very *poesis* of a book whose ultimate goal is precisely to track the onto-epistemic effects of the desire for ipseity in the terrains of the philosophy or theory of history and Puerto Rican studies cannot but destabilize its own mise en scène, compromising its self-presentation as a site of *critique*. Put otherwise, even a book that thematizes ipseity as the matrixial form of the ontological idea(l) of sovereignty and insists on the necessity of drawing a closure to ipseity's unbridled hegemony over the field of the historical cannot free itself entirely from this ultratranscendental commitment to the "minimal phenomenological structure" that posits the "I," however passively construed, as the source of the *graphein*, as the origin and telos of the *writing of life*. Without trying to recuperate what seems like a critical failure by transmuting it into success, I would like to nonetheless remark that this complicated situation, in which the possibility of exceeding a historico-metaphysical closure remains paradoxically retained by and contained within the dominant terms of that closure, provides an apt illustration of what I take to be the most rigorous aspect of deconstruction. More than showing binary oppositions to be undecidable or rejecting a priori the stability of meaning, I regard deconstruction as a way of vigilantly inhabiting the very house that one is trying to dismantle. Such an inhabitation necessarily involves the experience of enduring the intractability of aporia. In this case, the aporia in question can be articulated as the experience of not yet (and perhaps never) being *able* to say that I or we are finally done with sovereignty, that we have finally instituted ourselves as *selves without ipseity*, and that, therefore, we are finally done deconstructing history, that we have once and for all freed the realm of historical representation from its ipseitological capture. Deconstruction is often unbearable not because it is too difficult or too abstract but because it demands a patience greater than Job's and a zealotry more militant than Paul's. For, to acquire a taste for deconstructive tasks, one must abandon the belief in the very possibility of an ultimate instance as a position that one may ever *live* to see, let alone occupy. Only then can one truly devote oneself, without teleological subterfuges and eschatological guarantees, to the urgent work of earthly, institutional alteration.

But there are other ways in which *Catastrophic Historicism* could be regarded as not just autobiographical but as being *about* autobiography. Indeed, given its attempt to redefine historicism by foregrounding its transcendental source in the appropriating agency of ipseity, my meditations on the possibility of a nonhistoricist (literary) history could be read as an attempt to *transform* what Derrida suggests is the autobiography of all autobiographies, namely, *History itself*, that "autobiographical story" which "anthropo-centric subjectivity" has always already told itself in order to reappropriate its human life:[2] "As concerns history, historicity, even historiality, these motifs belong precisely to *this* self-definition, to *this* self-apprehension, to *this* self-situation of Man or the human *Dasein* with regards to the living and to animal life, they belong to Man's autobiography."[3] The task of reopening historicism beyond its ipseitological closure remains necessarily unfinished, but I hope that my effort to spell out some of the formal conditions that would be required to articulate a concept of historicity irreducible to the determination of history as "Man's autobiography" has restored some degree of question-worthiness to the problem of historicism in the eyes of my reader. Likewise, I hope that my reading of de Burgos's twofold historical catastrophes has contributed to this urgent theoretical task. If there is a lesson to be learned from de Burgos's ambivalent modernism, it is perhaps that any attempt to ground autonomy, freedom, liberation, or emancipation in ipseity will necessarily reinscribe capitalist/colonial commodification, alienation, and fungibilization. Against the intentions of its lyrical I, de Burgos's *Poema* constitutes another chapter that does not alter but instead extends "Man's autobiography" by reproducing the modes of ontological violence necessary to secure the possibility of ipseitological autopoiesis as the very essence of the humanity of the human, as the *arkhē* and *telos* of History.

Finally, *Catastrophic Historicism* is also an autobiographical book in a much more self-evident manner. Since I am myself Puerto Rican, my efforts to intervene in the sedimentations that structure Puerto Rican historicity as it crystallizes in the catastrophic tradition of de Burgos inevitably engage my own historicity. As such, this book could (and perhaps should) be read as a critical attempt at *self-clarification*. The term *critical* becomes particularly apposite in this context if it is read as a nod to Friedrich Nietzsche's concept of the "critical historian," whom Nietzsche explicitly describes as both *dangerous* and *endangered*: dangerous, because they threaten the sedimented institution of a continuous, genealogical tradition; endangered, because they belong to the very tradition that they're taking apart, so their own critical activity cannot but bring their historical identities—and the ipseity that subtends them—into a crisis.[4] Any effort to interrupt the specular constitution of a historical ipseity may always appear as an unwelcome and even violent attempt to deconstruct the house of history, especially to those most habituated to their historical dwellings. In the case of Puerto Rican historicity, the fact that the country is not only the world's oldest colony but also a colony of the US empire—which has ceased for generations to understand itself as such—intensifies the stakes of this critical exercise. Indeed, since the becoming-totem of de Burgos provides a crucial infrastructure for several scripts of Puertoricanness that, regardless of their differences, not only share a commitment to anticoloniality but also cherish de Burgos as an anticolonial hero, my attempt to interrupt her heroic monumentalization could always be registered as an assault on Puertoricanness itself, if not even as proof that I'm siding with the colonizer. This is a risk that must be taken and a price that must be paid if, to quote Hortense J. Spillers, "rigor is our dream."[5]

Indeed, perhaps the most urgent task for Puerto Rican studies today is to dare to dream dreams that are no longer determined by sedimented political grammars that have produced that particular mode of historicity that Juan Carlos Quintero Herencia has recently described with the apt title of *queda(era)*. A colloquial term that could be translated as "stuck(ery)" or, even more precisely, as "stuck(age)," *quedaera* describes the particular modality of *stasis* institutionalized by the discursive and political strategies of the Puerto Rican left (and not just of the left and certainly not just in Puerto Rico): "To un-cover the operativity of stuck(age) might clear up where and when the bottom falls out from Puerto Rican political existence and political eventhood as a consequence of this pact with *the same*."[6] Within the compact with *sameness* that, for Quintero Herencia, characterizes Puerto Rican historicity in its *queda(era)*, the totemic or talismanic reading of de Burgos's image as the very symbol of resistance and the totem of the marginalized has played a not insignificant role.[7] But what no doubt has played an even larger role in the "stuck(age)" that finds expression in de Burgos's reception are the dreams of sovereignty that continue to animate the Puerto Rican political imagination in most of its permutations. My attempt to expand what can be read in de Burgos's poetics of sovereignty and ipseity was precisely an attempt to awaken to such a dream. What modalities of *political independence* might we be able to (de)construct if we were to actually pay heed to Yarimar Bonilla's recent call for "unsettling sovereignty?"[8] How would our political imaginary be transformed if we were to acknowledge the extent to which our own desire for sovereignty cannot be extricated from the production and dissemination of the very forms of abjection that sovereignty promised to, precisely, abject, thereby restituting Puerto Rican subjectivities to their proper humanity? What modes of Puertoricanness might be able to reckon with the specific modalities of anti-Black violence that have historically troubled the island of racial democracy, without having recourse to culturalist subterfuges of a universalizable Afro-Caribbean heritage or to the identitarian alibi of a generalized mestizaje?

As Walter Benjamin writes, "in each epoch, the attempt must be made to reclaim tradition from the conformism that is about to overpower it."[9] To do so, we must relearn again how to think *dangerous* thoughts.

ACKNOWLEDGMENTS

In *What Calls for Thinking?*, Heidegger famously wrote that *Denken ist danken*, "to think is to thank." It is in this spirit that I would like to acknowledge some of the people who, in different ways, have given me the gift of thinking the thoughts inscribed in this book—for whose maladroitness I nonetheless take full responsibility.

I must begin by thanking those intellectual companions without whose constant support this book would not have been written. All the thoughts—especially the most dangerous ones—consigned in this book were thought out loud in dialogue with Christina León, whose friendship during the past fifteen years I could only describe as a constant yet effortless attempt to rescue from meaninglessness the word *world*. It is my hope that this book joins Christina's exemplary work in demanding that Caribbean aesthetic and literary production be *read*, rather than mined for biographical or sociological evidence. I also hope to have finally committed to writing some thoughts on danger and ipseity that may live up to Christina's instigations. Likewise, this book is in many ways the product of my friendship with Rocío Zambrana, whose philosophical rigor, ethical integrity, and political commitment continuously redefine what thinking philosophically with and from Puerto Rico can look like. My ongoing conversations with María del Rosario Acosta about Continental philosophy, trauma studies, and the perils of historical memory in Latin America can be remarked across this book, from its earliest layers (which hark back to my dissertation project) to its current iteration. Axelle Karera's friendship continues to serve in my life as a model for what philosophy, and deconstruction in particular, may yet do—take thought to its limits and maintain an exemplary form of vigilance. In more recent years, I have had the honor of counting on the intellectual and amical interlocution of two exemplary Caribbeanists, Ren Ellis Neyra and Dixa Ramírez D'Oleo; our conversations about Caribbean literature, Critical Black studies, and Puerto Rico's reputed exceptionality in the region have deeply informed this book, as has their constant moral support. I also must thank Matías Bascuñán for the past decade of intense philosophical interlocution and for his careful reading of portions of the manuscript. Thanks also to John Kelleher—model doctoral student and friend—whose interlocution accompanied the book's gestation from its initial stages. He also read the entire manuscript and gave me invaluable feedback about how to restructure it. I also want to thank my colleague Zakiyyah Iman Jackson, whose intellectual interlocution and institutional mentorship have been invaluable during my time at the University of Southern California. Likewise, I want to thank Natalie Belisle and Veli Yashin for their friendship and companionship during these years in the tenure track.

Many other people have been responsible for the very existence of this book, but I would be remiss if I didn't thank several friends and colleagues who modeled a critical disposition to the figure of Julia de Burgos that has deeply marked this book. In 2015, while still in the midst of the euphoric celebrations of de Burgos's centenary, I had the opportunity to have a conversation with the Puerto Rican poet Nicole Cecilia Delgado about the status of de Burgos's use of the *alma,* or *soul,* in *Poema en 20 surcos.* Nicole's impatience with de Burgos's theological language stuck with me, so much so that this book could be read as an attempt to continue that conversation about de Burgos's *alma.* Later in 2017, I had the chance to present a talk on de Burgos's *Poema* at the Annual Meeting of the Southern California Working Group on Hispanism/Critical Thought (SoCrit), which later became my first publication on this aspect of de Burgos's corpus. Jaime Rodríguez Matos asked me a critical question that, in an uncanny way, echoed Nicole's query about de Burgos's *Poema*, which unsettled some of the claims regarding temporality and the metaphysics of presence that I made in that talk. In many ways, this book is also an attempt to reckon with some of the consequences of Jaime's critical engagement with my earlier attempts to read the constellation of modernity in the textuality of *Poema*. Likewise, I would be remiss if I didn't thank Roque Salas Rivera for turning his Facebook wall into a site for an earnest conversation about de Burgos's openly racist letters; for conversations about the limits of current interpretations of de Burgos poetry, in particular of "Ay ay ay"; and for sharing his unpublished dissertation with me. Along the same lines, I want to thank Judith Rodríguez for sharing her unpublished work on de Burgos as well as acknowledge her track record of work centering anti-Blackness as a constitutive aspect of the cultural ethnonationalist discourses about Puerto Rican identity. Finally, for their interlocution on de Burgos and Caribbean modernist literature more broadly, and for reading some of the work published in this book, I would like to give special thanks to Vanessa Pérez Rosario, as well as to Lena Burgos-Lafuente and Arnaldo Cruz Malavé. I would also like to thank Edwin Cuperes for making available the archive of primary materials he gathered as part of his dissertation on Julia de Burgos.

Since the genesis of this book predates my decision to center de Burgos's *Poema* as the main case study for an attempt to both theorize and practice a nonhistoricist literature history, I would like to take a moment to acknowledge the people who nurtured this project before I even suspected that it would crystallize into a book of Puerto Rican studies. The roots of this project go way back to my undergraduate years as a philosophy major at Boston College, where, unbeknownst to me, I had the luck of stumbling upon one of the leading centers of Continental philosophy in the Anglophone world. I would like to thank Vanessa Rumble, my first philosophy teacher, who saw potential in me from the moment I arrived at BC and enrolled in her exhilarating and daunting "Freud and Philosophy" course. Soon after that experience, and thanks to Vanessa's recommendation, I was taking graduate courses with Richard Kearney, John Sallis, and David Rasmussen, whom I would like to thank for their rigorous and generous philosophical teaching. In the Romance Languages department I was also fortunate to have had a remarkable French teacher, Andrea Javel, and to continue to enjoy the enduring friendship and mentorship of Debbie Rusch. But it is above all Kevin Newmark whom I must acknowledge as the teacher who set me on the path to a career as a scholar. Kevin not only introduced me to literary theory—he taught me how to read and think while providing a mentorship that remains for me the model of intellectual rigor, personal integrity, and generosity.

After graduating from BC, I had the privilege of doing my doctoral work in comparative literature at Emory University, where I was part of a truly unique community of interdisciplinary researchers in which theoretical scholarship was the norm and not the exception. In particular, I would like to thank Cathy Caruth, Deborah Elise White, Jill Robbins, Hernán Feldman, Elizabeth Goodstein, Lynne Huffer, Elizabeth Wilson, Ursula Goldenbaum, María Mercedes Carrión, and, especially, Elissa Marder for expanding my theoretical and scholarly horizons with their teaching and research. My thinking also benefited from the interlocution of so many brilliant fellow graduate students. Besides Christina, I would like to thank Ania Kowalik, Adam Rosenthal, Tze-Yin Teo, Taylor Schey, Lucas Donahue, Armando Mastrogiovanni, Perry Guevara, Aaron Goldsman, and, especially, Melinda Robb. In one way or another, their presence can be felt in these pages. I also want to thank especially Andrew J. Mitchell, for his outstanding mentorship and ongoing friendly interlocution on Heidegger, phenomenology, and German thought, as well as my two dissertation advisors, Geoff Bennington and José Quiroga, without whose support I would not have been able to craft a book that, for all its flaws, is as intensely anchored in Caribbean and Puerto Rican studies as it is committed to philosophical questions.

In the academic year 2012–2013, I was fortunate enough to start the research that eventually led to my dissertation under the auspices of a DAAD fellowship, which took me to Goethe Universität-Frankfurt am Main to do research under the guidance of the late Werner Hamacher, who unfortunately passed away in 2017. Attending the five seminars that Werner gave during his last year as a professor remains the intellectual highlight of my life. During that year, I also made friends and colleagues whose interlocution has remained a constant in the last decade and whose input has decisively shaped this book. I would like to give special thanks to Mauricio González Rozo and Nassima Sahraoui. The composition of this book would have also not been possible without the intense conversations that took place in the various initiatives that Alberto Moreiras has organized around the idea of "infrapolitics," with which I have been associated since 2014. Besides Alberto, I would like to thank Sergio Villalobos Ruminott, Jaime Rodríguez Matos, Maddalena Cerrato, and Gerardo Muñoz for the years of interlocution, whose traces can be read in these pages even if the word "infrapolitics" is barely mentioned in them.

Luckily, after leaving Emory I came to USC, which has provided an ideal climate to foster the development of a book as interdisciplinary as this one. This is largely the result of two main factors. First, Peggy Kamuf's intellectual and institutional leadership in the department of Comparative Literature and the Comparative Studies in Literature and Culture doctoral program. This book would not have been written without Peggy's enduring intellectual and moral encouragement; I am fortunate enough to count her as not only a senior mentor but also a dear friend. Second, I could have not asked for a more idyllic and intellectually stimulating home department than USC's Latin American and Iberian Cultures department, where my colleagues Julián Gutiérrez Albilla, Sherry Velasco, Sam Steinberg, Roberto Ignacio Díaz, Natalia Pérez, and Natalie Belisle have been a constant source of support throughout this process. Special thanks go to Erin Graff Zivin, whose mentoring has been invaluable throughout the last several years. At USC, I have also had the privilege of working with various colleagues from other departments who have also been a source of intellectual provocation and moral support. In particular, I would like to thank Neetu Khanna, Olivia Harrison, Edwin Hill, and Lydie Moudileno. I would also like to thank the graduate students whose thoughts and interlocution have nourished directly or indirectly the writing of this book. Besides John Kelleher, whom I have already mentioned, I would like to thank Noraedén Mora Méndez, Carlos Colmenares Gil, Javier Pávez, Sarah Skillen, César Pérez, Brieuc Gérard, Edith Adams, Jane Kassavin, Nayla Ramalho, Pascual Brodsky, Franchesca Rotger, Nisarg Patel, Jacon Goldman, Michael Zalta, and Miguel Morales Pulgar. I would also like to thank the students of my undergraduate Spanish course "Sovereignty and Its Discontents: Puerto Rico in the American Century."

During my time at USC, I have also made a second intellectual home in Chile. Many Chilean friends and colleagues have played a major role in the composition of this book. In particular, I would like to thank Gustavo Bustos and Niklas Bornhauser for their invitation to give a series of lectures on Hamacher, where I tested out a preliminary version of some of the work included in Part II of this book. Likewise, I would like to thank Mauro Senatore, Miriam Jerade, and Diego Rosello for their interlocution. Besides Matías Bascuñán, special thanks are due to Valeria Campos Salvaterra and Iván Trujillo, arguably the two main culprits for my own intense case of reinfection with the "transcendental philosophy" bug, some of whose effects can be felt in these pages. A very special thanks is due to Francesco Vitale, whose invitation to Salerno in 2019 gave me the opportunity to finally commit to writing my interpretation of Benjamin's dialectical image as a "phenomenology of history." I would be remiss if I didn't point out that Francesco was the first friend to understand the ultimate stakes of this project as necessitating nothing other than a Deconstruction of History. And a very special thanks to Tom Lay, Jacques Lezra, and Paul North for believing in this project and for going the extra mile to see it through; I am incredibly lucky to be able to count on their editorial support.

Last, but not least, I want to turn to the deepest layer of grace and give thanks to my friends and relatives in Puerto Rico who have made this book possible. Beatriz Navia and Orlando Planchart have been enthusiastic about this project from its inception. Likewise, I thank Mara Pastor for her intellectual friendship and poetic brilliance. I want to thank my mother, Angie; my stepdad, Ricardo; my siblings Natalia, Juan Carlos, and Ricardo Jesús; my nephews; my aunts Carmen and Zilkya; and my cousins Arnaldo and Katherine for their patience over the last couple of years of intense work in the research and composition of the book. I hope it makes them proud, even if it won't give us back the time we didn't spend together. I also want to mark the memory of my godfather, Amado Arnaldo, *Padrino*, whose absence is felt every single day.

Finally, this book is dedicated to my partner-in-life-and-thought, Benjamin H. Brewer. He discussed every argument and went over every idea for a close reading with me. He also read every single word of this book and even edited the endnotes. But, above all, he kept me calm when I thought that I had bitten off more than I could chew. I simply would not have been able to finish this book without the life we have built with our furry friends Rocky and Naya.

NOTES

INTRODUCTION: READING DANGER

1. For recent critiques of historicism that have influenced this book, see Eric Hayot, *On Literary Worlds* (Oxford: Oxford University Press, 2012), 8; "Manifesto of the V21 Collective," http://v21collective.org/manifesto-of-the-v21-collective-ten-theses/; Ethan Kleinberg, Joan Wallach Scott, and Gary Wilder, "Theses on Theory and History." *History of the Present* 10, no. 1 (2020): 157–65.

2. Ranke coins the formula "wie es eigentlich gewesen" in the foreword to part 1 of his *Geschichten der romanischen und germanischen Völker von 1494 bis 1535* (*History of the Latin and Teutonic Nations from 1494 to 1535*): "History has been ascribed the function of rectifying the past, of teaching contemporaries to be useful to future generations: the present attempt is not devoted to such lofty tasks: it merely wants to say how it really [has] been." Ludwig von Ranke, *Geschichten der romanischen und germanischen Völker von 1494 bis 1535* (Leipzig: G. Reimer, 1824), v–vi. Passages in languages other than English are quoted only in English translation in the body of the text or in footnotes, except for the writings of Julia de Burgos, which will be quoted in Spanish and in English translation. All translations are my own unless stated otherwise. To facilitate consultation, reference will be made first to the original publication, then to existing English translations.

3. I take the motif of the *Schritt zurück*, or the "step back," from Martin Heidegger. See Martin Heidegger, *Gesamtausgabe 11: Identität und Differenz*, ed. Friedrich-Wilhelm von Herrmann (Frankfurt am Main: Klostermann, 2006), 58–60 (hereafter quoted as *GA* 1–101); Heidegger, *Identity and Difference*, trans. Joan Stambaugh (Chicago: University of Chicago Press, 2002), 49–51.

4. See Jacques Derrida, *L'écriture et la différence* (Paris: Seuil, 1967), 11, 314; Derrida, *Writing and Difference*, trans. Alan Bass (London: Routledge, 2001), 3, 266. For a helpful take on this motif in Derrida, see Stephen Thomson, "Derrida Somnambule," *Angelaki: Journal of the Theoretical Humanities* 26, no. 5 (2021): 103–6.

5. Walter Benjamin, *Gesammelte Schriften 5: Das Passagen-Werk*, ed. Rolf Tiedemann (Frankfurt am Main: Suhrkamp, 1982), N9,4, 591 (hereafter cited as *GS* 1–7); Benjamin, *The Arcades Project*, trans. Howard Eiland and Kevin McLaughlin (Cambridge, MA: Harvard University Press, 1999), 473. Subsequent citations of *Das*

Passagen-Werk refer only to the original, followed by the cited entry (e.g., N9,4) and the page numbers in both the German and the English editions, separated by a virgule.

6. I borrow the language of sedimentation and desedimentation from the late work of Husserl, in particular the *Krisis* (*Crisis*) and related texts. See the important §15 in Edmund Husserl, *Husserliana 6: Die Krisis der europäischen Wissenschaften und die transzendentale Phänomenologie*, ed. Walter Biemel (The Hague: Martinus Nijhoff, 1976), 71–74 (hereafter quoted as *Hua* 1–42); Husserl, *The Crisis of European Sciences and Transcendental Phenomenology*, trans. David Carr (Evanston, IL: Northwestern University Press, 1970), 70–73. That being said, my use of the lexicon of desedimentation is heavily inflected by Derrida's own appropriation of this conceptual metaphor, which, as Nahum Dimitri Chandler reminds us, Derrida often used as a substitute for the metaphorics of deconstruction. See Jacques Derrida, *De la grammatologie* (Paris: Seuil, 1967), 21; Derrida, *Of Grammatology*, trans. Gayatri Chakravorty Spivak (Baltimore, MD: John Hopkins University Press, 2016), 11. See also Nahum Dimitri Chandler, "Paraontology: Or, Notes on the Practical Theoretical Politics of Thought," Society for the Humanities Annual Culler Lecture in Critical Theory, Cornell University, October 15, 2018, https://vimeo.com/297769615.

7. See chapter 1 of Nahum D. Chandler, *X: The Problem of the Negro as a Problem for Thought* (New York: Fordham University Press, 2014). For an elaboration of Chandler's phrase in the context of the problem that Blackness poses to the project of ontology, see Calvin Warren, "Improper Bodies," *Palimpsest* 8, no. 2 (2019): 35.

8. Gilles Deleuze and Félix Guattari, *Qu'est-ce que la philosophie?* (Paris: Minuit, 1991), 21–38; Deleuze and Guattari, *What Is Philosophy?*, trans. Hugh Tomlinson and Graham Burchell (New York: Columbia University Press, 1994), 15–34.

9. Frank Ankersmit, *Meaning, Truth, and Reference in Historical Representation* (Ithaca, NY: Cornell University Press, 2012), 14.

10. See Jacques Derrida, *Voyous. Deux essais sur la raison* (Paris: Galilée, 2003), 30–32; Derrida, *Rogues: Two Essays on Reason*, trans. Pascale-Anne Brault and Michael Naas (Stanford, CA: Stanford University Press, 2005), 10–12.

11. Hans Michael Baumgartner, "Thesen zur Grundlegung einer Transzendentalen Historik," in *Geschichte und Theorie: Umrisse einer Historik*, ed. Hans Michael Baumgartner and Jörn Rüsen (Frankfurt am Main: Suhrkamp, 1982), 279.

12. Louis O. Mink, *Historical Understanding* (Ithaca, NY: Cornell University Press, 1987), 60.

13. For an excellent overview of this debate, see the prelude to László Tengelyi, *The Wild Region in Life-History*, trans. Géza Kallay (Evanston, IL: Northwestern University Press, 2004), xiii–xxxvi.

14. The Husserlian motif of *Sinngebilde* ("sense-configuration") and the broader theme of *Sinnbildung* ("sense-formation") are characteristic of his later work, which is often described in terms of a shift from a static to a genetic and eventually a "histori-

cal" phenomenology. Husserl's understanding of the dynamic interplay between *Gebilde* and *Sinnbildung* in his famous text known as the "Origin of Geometry" has been of crucial importance for my attempt to sketch out a deconstruction of history. See Husserl, *Hua*, 6:365–86; Husserl, *Crisis*, 353–78.

15. Husserl, *Hua*, 6:380; Husserl, *Crisis*, 371.

16. Ethan Kleinberg, *Haunting History: For a Deconstructive Approach to the Past* (Stanford, CA: Stanford University Press, 2017), 1, emphases mine.

17. Jacques Derrida, *Le problème de la genèse dans la philosophie de Husserl* (Paris: Presses Universitaires de France, 1990), 2n2.

18. Michel Foucault, "Entretien inédit entre Michel Foucault et quatre militants de la LCR, membres de la rubrique culturelle du journal quotidien Rouge (juillet 1977)," *Question Marx?* (February 2, 2014), https://questionmarx.typepad.fr/question-marx/2014/02/un-document-inedit-sur-le-site-de-question-marx.html.

19. Frederick C. Beiser, *The German Historicist Tradition* (Oxford: Oxford University Press, 2014), 25–26. Beiser is using the term "science" in the German sense of *Wissenschaft*, which refers to any scholarly endeavor endowed with disciplinary protocols, methodologies, foundational concepts, etc.

20. Beiser, *The German Historicist Tradition*, 26.

21. Ankersmit, *Meaning*, 4.

22. Jacques Derrida, *La voix et le phénomène* (Paris: Presses Universitaires de France, 1967), 115; Derrida, *Voice and Phenomenon*, trans. Leonard Lawlor (Evanston, IL: Northwestern University Press, 2011), 88.

23. My use of the terms *modal* and *modality* throughout this book hews closely to the Continental reception of Kant's transcendental approach to the canonical modal categories of *possibility*, *actuality*, *necessity*, and *impossibility*, as outlined in the "Postulates of Empirical Thinking in General" and the "Table of the Nothing" sections of the First Critique. See Immanuel Kant, *Kritik der reinen Vernunft*, ed. (Berlin: De Gruyter, 1968), A218–226/B266–274, A290/B346 (hereafter quoted as *KrV*); Kant, *Critique of Pure Reason*, trans. Paul Guyer and Allen W. Wood (Cambridge: Cambridge University Press, 1998), 321–26, 382–83 (hereafter quoted as *CPR*). Within this reception, I privilege the engagements with this broad Kantian modal framework in the work of the early, more explicitly phenomenological Heidegger (up to *Sein und Zeit*) and the quasi-transcendental thinking of possibility and impossibility elaborated by Derrida throughout his entire career.

24. Martin Heidegger, *GA* 2:38/51–52, 262/348; Heidegger, *Being and Time*, trans. Joan Stambaugh and Dennis Schmidt (Albany: SUNY Press, 2010), 36, 251. Page references to the German edition of *Being and Time* first mention the pagination of the 1927 Niemeyer *princeps* edition, followed by the pagination of the *GA* edition, separated by a virgule.

25. On Dilthey's concept of the *Zusammenhang des Lebens* or "life-nexus," see Wilhelm von Dilthey, *Gesammelte Werke*, vol. 7: *Der Aufbau der geschichtlichen Welt*

in den Geisteswissenschaften, ed. Bernhard Groethuysen (Stuttgart: Teubner, 1958), 191–204. Dilthey, *Selected Works*, vol. 3: *The Formation of the Historical World in the Human Sciences*, ed. Rudolf Makkreel and Frithjof Rodi (Princeton, NJ: Princeton University Press, 2002), 213–25.

26. My engagement with de Burgos's biography is informed by the following book-length studies of de Burgos: Yvette Jiménez de Baez, *Julia de Burgos: Vida y poesía* (San Juan, PR: Editorial Coquí, 1966); Juan Antonio Rodríguez Pagán, *Julia en blanco y negro* (San Juan, PR: Sociedad Histórica de Puerto Rico, 2000); José Manuel Torres Santiago, *Julia de Burgos, poeta maldita* (San Juan, PR: Los Libros de la Iguana, 2014); Edgardo Rodríguez Masdeu, *Carta de presentación: Julia de Burgos* (San Juan, PR: Los Libros de la Iguana, 2014); Vanessa Pérez Rosario, *Becoming Julia de Burgos: The Making of a Puerto Rican Icon* (Chicago: University of Illinois Press, 2014); and Edwin Cuperes, "*Poema en 20 surcos*: Enfrentamiento dialéctico a la crítica doxográfica, ético/moral e ideológica desde el materialismo filosófico como teoría de la literatura," PhD diss., Centro de Estudios Avanzados de Puerto Rico y el Caribe, 2020. Both in this brief biographical vignette and in the longer version (see § 10), I refer to specific passages from the texts mentioned here, as well as to other secondary sources, only whenever necessary. Finally, I would like to acknowledge my debt to Cuperes's painstaking archival work on de Burgos, which has greatly facilitated my own work. Notwithstanding my strong disagreements with both Cuperes's philosophical commitments to Gustavo Bueno's brand of philosophical materialism and the ideological underpinnings that motivate his work on de Burgos, I would be remiss if I didn't note the remarkable level of documentary evidence that Cuperes has gathered and made available to all scholars of de Burgos.

27. See José Emilio González, "Algo más sobre la vida y la poesía de Julia de Burgos," qtd. in Torres Santiago, *Poeta maldita*, 39–40.

28. See Juan Antonio Rodríguez Pagán, *En blanco*, 45–46.

29. Hayden White, *The Practical Past* (Evanston, IL: Northwestern University Press, 2014), x–xi.

30. White, *The Practical Past*, xiii.

31. Lena Burgos-Lafuente, "Untendered Eyes: Literary Politics of Julia de Burgos—Introducción," *CENTRO Journal* 26, no. 2 (Fall 2014): 23n1.

32. Benjamin, *GS* 5:N9,4, 591/473.

33. Benjamin, *GS* 5:N3,1, 578/463.

34. Bolívar Echevarría, *Modernidad y blanquitud* (Mexico City: Ediciones Era, 2010), 13; Echevarría, *Modernity and "Whiteness,"* trans. Rodrigo Ferreira (Cambridge: Polity, 2019), 1.

35. Zakiyyah Iman Jackson, *Becoming Human: Matter and Meaning in an Antiblack World* (New York: New York University, 2020), 83–85. See also Jackson, "'Theorizing in a Void': Sublimity, Matter, and Physics in Black Feminist Poetics," *South Atlantic Quarterly* 117, no. 3 (July 2018): 621–22.

36. Alexander Weheliye, *Habeas Corpus: Racializing Assemblages, Biopolitics, and Black Feminist Theories of the Human* (Durham, NC: Duke University Press, 2014), 2.

37. See the second chapter in Reinhart Koselleck, *Vergangene Zukunft. Zur Semantik geschichtlicher Zeiten* (Frankfurt am Main: Suhrkamp, 1979), 38–66; Koselleck, *Futures Past: On the Semantics of Historical Time*, trans. Keith Tribe (New York: Columbia University Press, 2004), 26–42.

38. Derrida, *La voix*, 115; Derrida, *Voice*, 88.

39. See chap. 5 in Kleinberg, *Haunting History*, 134–49.

40. Marc Nichanian, *The Historiographic Perversion*, trans. Gil Anidjar (New York: Columbia University Press, 2009), 1.

41. See the preface to Cathy Caruth, *Literature in the Ashes of History* (Baltimore, MD: John Hopkins University Press, 2013), ix–xii.

42. María del Rosario Acosta García, "From Aesthetics as Critique to Grammars of Listening: On Reconfiguring Sensibility as a Political Task," *Journal of World Philosophies* 6 (Summer 2021): 148.

43. Saidiya Hartman, "Venus in Two Acts," *Small Axe* 26, no. 2 (June 2008): 11.

PART I. CATASTROPHIC TRADITIONS: READING THE IMAGE OF JULIA DE BURGOS, *DANGEROUSLY*

1. See Julia de Burgos, "20 de noviembre de 1952," in *Cartas a Consuelo* (San Juan, PR: Folium, 2014), 209–10. Subsequent references to de Burgos's correspondence with her sister will only mention the date of the letter and the page number of the quoted passage.

2. de Burgos, "28 de junio de 1953," 222, emphases mine.

3. de Burgos, "17 de mayo de 1953," 221.

4. de Burgos, "14 de mayo de 1945," 192.

5. de Burgos, "25 de septiembre de 1940," 69.

6. Maira Garcia, "Overlooked No More: Julia de Burgos, a Poet Who Helped Shape Puerto Rico's Identity," *New York Times*, May 2, 2018, https://www.nytimes.com/2018/05/02/obituaries/overlooked-julia-de-burgos.html.

7. Bridget Fowler, *The Obituary as Collective Memory* (London: Routledge, 2007), 40.

8. Amisha Padnani and Jessica Bennett, "Overlooked," *New York Times*, March 8, 2018, https://www.nytimes.com/interactive/2018/obituaries/overlooked.html.

9. The entry on Julia de Burgos on the page from the official website of Leonard Bernstein dedicated to Songfest exposes, as it were, the tokenizing logic that animates this gesture, as well as its political limits. "The poet qualifies as an American citizen since she was from the Commonwealth of Puerto Rico. In angry words (sung in Spanish) she expresses her self-conflict about the dual role she plays as a conventional woman and as a liberated woman poet. (Her poem antedates by two decades

the so-called women's liberation movement.) The music is sharply rhythmic, almost a dance." "Songfest (1977)," https://leonardbernstein.com/works/view/61/songfest. Citizenship—a citizenship that de Burgos, a committed supporter of Puerto Rican independence, vehemently rejected—becomes the lever that justifies inclusion within this epical song cycle that proclaims the intention of "a comprehensive picture of America's artistic past."

10. See the introduction to Rocío Zambrana, *Colonial Debts: The Case of Puerto Rico* (Durham, NC: Duke University Press, 2021), 1–19.

11. Jacques Derrida, *L'Université sans condition* (Paris: Galilée, 2001), 74; Derrida, *Without Alibi*, ed. and trans. Peggy Kamuf (Stanford, CA: Stanford University Press, 2002), 234.

12. For a useful general history that addresses this historical amnesia from a US-centered perspective, see the introduction to Daniel Immerwahr, *How to Hide an Empire: A History of the Greater United States* (New York: Picardo/Farrar, Strauss and Giroux, 2019), 3–19.

13. For a critique of the liberal insistence on Puerto Ricans' status as American citizens in the context of Hurricane María, see Francés Negrón-Muntaner, "Our Fellow Americans: Why Calling Puerto Ricans 'Americans' Will Not Save Them," *Dissent*, January 10, 2018, https://www.dissentmagazine.org/online_articles/our-fellow-americans-puerto-rico-hurricane-maria-colonialism-rhetoric.

14. Frank B. Wilderson III, *Afropessimism* (New York: Liveright, 2020), 202. These different articulations of politics and culture were already addressed in Wilderson's earlier work: "I am calling for a different conceptual framework, predicated not on the subject-effect of cultural performance but on the structure of political ontology, a framework that allows us to substitute a culture of politics for a politics of culture." Frank B. Wilderson III, *Red, White, and Black: Cinema and the Structure of US Antagonisms* (Durham, NC: Duke University Press, 2010), 57.

15. On da Silva's thinking of transparency, see chapter 1 in Denise Ferreira da Silva, *Towards a Global Idea of Race* (Minneapolis: University of Minnesota Press, 2007), 1–16. Gayatri Chakravorty Spivak, *Can the Subaltern Speak? Reflections on the History of an Idea*, ed. Rosalind C. Morris (New York: Columbia University Press, 2010), 43.

16. da Silva, *Towards*, xxiv.

17. *Downes v. Bidwell*, 182 U.S. 244 (1901), 287.

18. We can see why, as Zambrana puts it, debt "is an apparatus of capture . . . through which race/gender/class hierarchies are deepened, intensified, posited anew." Zambrana, *Colonial Debts*, 10.

19. Julia de Burgos, *Poema en 20 surcos* (San Juan, PR: Imprenta Venezuela, 1938). As a rule, I will cite *Poema* in the *editio princeps*. I have made this decision because there are numerous, and shockingly significant, discrepancies between the versions of the poems that were published in periodicals and newspapers and then gathered

in the first edition of *Poema* and the versions of those poems gathered in anthologies and the multiple editions of de Burgos's collected works. In the absence of both a critical edition of de Burgos's works and of the possibility of consulting her extant manuscripts, working with the *editio princeps* seemed like the best compromise. For poems not published in *Poema*, I will refer to the Spanish edition of her complete poetry, *Obra poética*, vols. 1–2 (Madrid: La Discreta, 2009). Occasionally, I also refer to the first publication of poems in newspapers and periodicals. All English translations of de Burgos's poems are mine. For the most complete and accessible English edition of de Burgos's poems, see Julia de Burgos, *Song of the Simple Truth: The Complete Poems of Julia de Burgos*, ed. and trans. Jack Agüeros (Evanston, IL: Northwestern University Press, 2008).

20. See Walter Benjamin, *Gesammelte Schriften* 1, ed. Rolf Tiedemann and Hermann Schweppenhäuser (Frankfurt am Main: Suhrkamp, 1991), 607–8 (hereafter cited as *GS* 1–7). Benjamin, *Selected Writings*, vol. 4, 1938–1940, ed. Howard Eiland and Michael Jennings (Cambridge, MA: Harvard University Press, 2006), 313–14 (hereafter cited as *SW*).

21. Eugen Fink, "Operative Begriffe in Husserls Phänomenologie," *Zeitschrift für Philosophische Forschung* 11, no. 3 (1957): 321–37; Fink, "Operative Concepts in Husserl's Phenomenology," in *A Priori and World*, ed. and trans. W. McKenna, R. M. Harlan, and L. E. Winters (Springer: Dordrecht, 1981), 56–70.

22. This explains why I earlier invoked Fink's distinction between *thematic* and *operative* concepts. Unlike thematic concepts, which obtain whenever "philosophy intentionally aims at those concepts in which thinking *fixes* and preserves its thought," operative concepts constitute, for Fink, *"the shadows of a philosophy"*; they designate a conceptual zone of relative opacity that informs the very movement of thought without being explicated by the thinker and fixed through explicit discursive articulation. See Fink, "Operative Begriffe," 324, 325; Fink, "Operative Concepts," 59.

23. Benjamin, *GS* 5:N10a,3, 595; Benjamin, *The Arcades Project*, trans. Howard Eiland and Kevin McLaughlin (Cambridge, MA: Harvard University Press, 1999), 475. Subsequent citations of *The Arcades Project* refer only to the original, followed by the cited entry (e.g., N9,4) and the page numbers in both the German and the English editions, separated by a virgule.

24. Benjamin, *GS* 1:607–8.

25. Benjamin, *GS* 1:608–9; Benjamin, *SW* 4:314.

26. Benjamin, *GS* 1:608–9; Benjamin, *SW* 4:314.

27. Benjamin, *GS* 1:609; Benjamin, *SW* 4:315.

28. Henri Bergson, *Matière et mémoire: Essai sur la relation du corps et l'esprit*, ed. Frédéric Worms (Paris: Presses Universitaires de France, 2012), 93–94; Bergson, *Matter and Memory*, trans. Nancy Margaret Paul and W. Scott Palmer (New York: Zone, 1991), 87–88.

29. Benjamin, *GS* 1:609; Benjamin, *SW* 4:315.

30. Elissa Marder, *Dead Time: Temporal Disorders in the Wake of Modernity (Baudelaire and Flaubert)* (Stanford, CA: Stanford University Press, 2001), 81.

31. Benjamin, *GS* 1:208; Benjamin, *Origin of German Trauerspiel*, trans. Howard Eiland (Cambridge, MA: Cambridge University Press, 2019), 2.

32. Benjamin, *GS* 1:609; Benjamin, *SW* 4:315.

33. Benjamin, *GS* 5:N3,1, 578/463.

34. Charles Baudelaire, *The Flowers of Evil*, trans. Nathan Brown (Zagreb: MaMa, 2021), 9.

35. Benjamin, *GS* 5:N10a3, 595/475.

36. Benjamin, *Werke und Nachlaß* 19: *Über den Begriff der Geschichte*, ed Gérard Raulet (Frankfurt am Main: Suhrkamp, 2009), 104 (hereafter cited as *WuN*); Benjamin, *SW* 4:395.

37. Henri Bergson, *Essai sur les données immédiates de la conscience*, ed. Frédéric Worms (Paris: Presses Universitaires de France, 2007), 74–75, emphases mine; Bergson, *Time and Free Will: An Essay on the Immediate Data of Consciousness*, trans. F. L. Pogson (Mineola, NY: Dover, 2001), 100.

38. Bergson, *Matière*, 204; Bergson, *Matter*, 184.

39. Benjamin, *GS* 1:337; Benjamin, *Origin*, 166.

40. Benjamin, *GS* 1:337; Benjamin, *Origin*, 166.

41. For the *locus classicus* of Benjamin's concept of aura, see Benjamin, *WuN* 16:215; Benjamin, *SW* 3:105. On Bergson's concept of *élan vital*, see Bergson, *L'évolution créatrice*, ed. Frédéric Worms (Paris: Presses Universitaires de France, 2021), 88–98.

42. Benjamin, *WuN* 19:98; Benjamin, *SW* 4:392.

43. Benjamin, *WuN* 19:94; Benjamin, *SW* 4:390.

44. Kevin Newmark, "Traumatic Poetry: Charles Baudelaire and the Shock of Laughter," *American Imago* 48, no. 4 (Winter 1991): 519.

45. Moreover, as we will see, the ultimate gist of Benjamin's theory of history is precisely to remove this opposition and to make the case for a concept of philosophical speculation where the transcendental, if not even the Absolute, is necessarily contaminated by historical actuality, affected by an indexical moment.

46. Benjamin, *GS* 5:N3,1, 578/463.

47. For the formulation of this principle, see G. W. Leibniz, *Discours du métaphysique*, in *Monadologie und andere Schriften*, ed. Ulrich Johannes Schneider (Hamburg: Meiner, 2002), 20; Leibniz, *Discourse on Metaphysics*, trans. Gonzalo Rodríguez-Pereyra (Oxford: Oxford University Press, 2020), 13.

48. Ethan Kleinberg, *Haunting History: For a Deconstructive Approach to the Past* (Stanford, CA: Stanford University Press, 2017), 1, emphases mine.

49. Benjamin, *GS* 5:N3,4, 578/463.

50. Immanuel Kant, *Kritik der reinen Vernunft*, ed. (Berlin: De Gruyter, 1968), Bxiv–vi, (hereafter quoted as *KrV*); Kant, *Critique of Pure Reason*, trans. Paul Guyer

and Allen W. Wood (Cambridge: Cambridge University Press, 1998), 109–11 (hereafter quoted as *CPR*).

51. Benjamin, *GS* 5:K1,1, 490/388–89.

52. Kant, *KrV*, B197; Kant, *CPR*, 283.

53. The military metaphors present in Benjamin's Copernican turn actually echo Kant's own formulation: "In metaphysics we have to retrace our path countless times, because we find that it does not lead where we want to go, and it is so far from reaching unanimity in the assertions of its adherents that it is rather a battlefield, and indeed one that appears to be especially determined for testing one's powers in mock combat; on this battlefield no combatant has ever gained the least bit of ground, nor has any been able to base any lasting possession on his victory. Hence there is no doubt that up to now the procedure of metaphysics has been a mere groping, and what is the worst, a groping among mere concepts." Kant, *KrV*, Bxiv; Kant, *CPR*, 109–10.

54. In his tour de force essay on Benjamin's theory of history, Werner Hamacher had already made this suggestion: "The 'Copernican turn' in historical intuition that Benjamin wants to bring about is thus more than a transcendentalist turn. For this Copernican turn, what-has-been no longer offers any fixed point, nor can 'historical intuition' be considered as substantial quantity or as a continuum founded upon transcendental forms. History can be missed. That means, however, that it, and therefore also the happiness to which it refers, are never experienceable except in the danger of being missed; and that means, furthermore, that history is only possible in the danger of not being history." Werner Hamacher, "Jetzt. Walter Benjamin zur Historischer Zeit," in *Perception and Experience in Modernity*, ed. Helga Geyer-Ryan, Paul Koopman, and Klass Intema (Leiden: Brill, 2002), 156; Hamacher, "Now: Walter Benjamin on Historical Time," trans. N. Rosenthal, in *The Moment: Time and Rupture in Modern Thought*, ed. Heidrun Friese (Liverpool: Liverpool University Press, 2011), 169. Although I follow Hamacher on this point, my own approach to Benjamin's "more than a transcendentalist [Copernican] turn" dwells longer on the transcendental dimension of Benjamin's theory of history in order to clarify more precisely than Hamacher does here why a Kantian or Husserlian transcendental cannot do justice to the radicality of Benjamin's attempt to bring about a revolution in the theory of history. As we will see, at stake in the dialectical image is a form of a priori correlation that cannot be described strictly speaking as transcendental since what this correlation enables is the very dialectical genesis of the correlata within it. Since the image itself has the seemingly paradoxical character of both an event that befalls the historian and something that the historian constructs (and thus necessarily intends), a dialectics or, better, a *différance* necessarily emerges at the heart of the (de)constitution of historical time for Benjamin, since the image does not exist prior to the correlated constellation that it schematizes and the times within the constellation do not exist prior to their violent collision in the space-time of the image.

55. G. W. F. Hegel, *The Difference between Fichte's and Schelling's System of Philosophy*, trans. H. S. Harris and Walter Cerf (Albany: SUNY Press, 1977), 156.

56. Jacques Derrida, *Marges—de la philosophie* (Paris: Minuit, 1972), 63; Derrida, *Margins of Philosophy*, trans. Alan Bass (Chicago: University of Chicago Press, 1982), 55.

57. Edmund Husserl, *Husserliana* 6: *Die Krisis der europäischen Wissenschaften und die transzendentale Phänomenologie*, ed. Walter Biemel (The Hague: Martinus Nijhoff, 1976), 161–63 (hereafter quoted as *Hua* 1–42); Husserl, *The Crisis of European Sciences and Transcendental Phenomenology*, trans. David Carr (Evanston, IL: Northwestern University Press, 1970), 159–60.

58. Stefano Marchesoni, "Pour une archéologie de l'image dialectique: La rencontre de Walter Benjamin avec Proust et les surréalistes," *Lendemains: Études comparés sur la France* 184 (2021): 84.

59. Benjamin, *GS* 5:N3,1, 578/463.

60. Benjamin, *Gesammelte Briefe*, vol. 4, ed. Christoph Gödde and Henri Lonitz (Frankfurt am Main: Suhrkamp, 2000), 19 (hereafter cited as *GB*).

61. Benjamin, *WuN* 19:94; Benjamin, *SW* 4:390.

62. Frank Ankersmit, *Meaning, Truth, and Reference in Historical Representation* (Ithaca, NY: Cornell University Press, 2012), 14.

63. Benjamin, *WuN* 19:124; Benjamin, *SW* 4:405.

64. That such an event could have never been "written" in the historical—objective, empirical, or positive—record is a strict consequence of the fact that the process whereby the structure of experience changes historically must necessarily remain inaccessible to empirical experience in general and to historical experience in particular. This explains why Benjamin's historical methodology necessarily entails a *speculative* moment that requires taking what is historically or indexically given while going beyond its mere factuality in order to project or reconstruct the sense-formations that alone grant historical reality and significance to those indexical facts. For the phenomenological or "idealist" (rather than realist) concept of speculation that informs my use of this term here, see chap. 5 in Alexander Schnell, *Was ist Phänomenologie?* (Frankfurt am Main: Klostermann, 2019), 137–62.

65. On Benjamin's metaphorics of crystallization in his theory of historical time, see Nassima Sahraoui, "A Crystal of Time," *Discontinuous Infinities*, special issue of *Anthropology & Materialism* (2017), http://journals.openedition.org/am/796.

66. Benjamin, *GS* 5:K1,2, 491/388–89.

67. Hayden White, *The Practical Past* (Evanston, IL: Northwestern University Press, 2014), 9.

68. See Julia de Burgos, *Diario*, ed. Edgardo Martínez Masdeu (San Juan, PR: Los Libros de la Iguana, 2014).

69. White, *The Practical Past*, xiii.

70. The *locus classicus* of Benjamin's concept of the symbol—be it theological

or aesthetic—can be found in the opening pages of the second part of his failed *Habilitation* dissertation. See Benjamin, *GS* 1.1:336–44; Benjamin, *Origin of German Trauerspiel*, trans. Howard Eiland (Cambridge, MA: Harvard University Press, 2019), 165–75. For the analogous *locus* of de Man's conception of the symbol, which is informed by Benjamin's, see Paul de Man, "The Rhetoric of Temporality," in *Blindness and Insight: Essays in the Rhetoric of Contemporary Criticism*, 2nd ed. (Minneapolis: University of Minnesota Press, 1983), 187–228.

71. This phrase is an explicit reference to Benjamin's discussion of the image of Baudelaire's life in *Zentralpark* ("Central Park"); see Benjamin, *GS* 1:665; Benjamin, *SW* 4:168.

72. María Consuelo Sáez Burgos, qtd. in Garcia, "Overlooked No More: Julia de Burgos," May 2, 2018.

73. Benjamin, *GS* 5:N9,4, 591/473.

74. Benjamin, *GS* 5:N3,1, 578/463.

75. Benjamin, *WuN* 19:102; Benjamin, *SW* 4:395.

76. Benjamin, *GS* 5:K1,2, 491/399.

77. Edmund Husserl, *Hua* 6:72; Husserl, *Crisis*, 71.

78. Husserl, *Hua* 6:366, 377; Husserl, *Crisis*, 354, 367.

79. Husserl, *Hua* 6:52; Husserl, *Crisis*, 52.

80. Benjamin, *GS* 1:659; Benjamin, *SW* 4:163.

81. This opposition is borrowed from Derrida, who himself borrowed it from Ernst Cassirer. See Jacques Derrida, *La voix et le phénomène* (Paris: Presses Universitaires de France, 1967), 20; Derrida, *Voice and Phenomenon*, trans. Leonard Lawlor (Evanston, IL: Northwestern University Press, 2011), 17.

82. Marcos Reyes Dávila, "Julia de Burgos, 'poeta maldita' y barroca," *80 grados* (November 7, 2014): https://www.80grados.net/julia-de-burgos-poeta-maldita-y-barroca.

83. For the most exhaustive study to date of the "militarization" of the Partido Nacionalista under Albizu Campos's leadership, see José Manuel Dávila Marichal, *Pedro Albizu Campos y el ejército libertador del Partido Nacionalista de Puerto Rico, 1930–39* (San Juan, PR: Laberinto, 2022). For his account of the foundation of the Hijas de la República, see 103–11.

84. See Margarita Aurora Vargas Canales, "La revuelta también vino de la caña: el caso de Puerto Rico," *Latinoamérica. Revista de Estudios Latinoamericanos* 50 (enero–junio 2010): 81–101. For a general overview of Puerto Rico's economy and politics during the 1930s, see chap. 5 in Rafael Bernabe and César Ayala, *Puerto Rico in the American Century* (Chapel Hill: University of North Carolina Press, 2007), 95–116.

85. The exception to this consensus is Cuperes, who asserts on several occasions that "de Burgos was never a member of the Nationalist Party," basing this claim on de Burgos's deposition to the FBI while being investigated under the Hatch Act in 1945.

Edwin Cuperes, "Poema en 20 surcos: Enfrentamiento dialéctico a la crítica doxográfica, ético/moral e ideológica desde el materialismo filosófico como teoría de la literatura," PhD diss., Centro de Estudios Avanzados de Puerto Rico y el Caribe, 2020, 91, 115. On this chapter in de Burgos's life, see Harris Feinsod, "Between Dissidence and Good Neighbor Diplomacy: Reading Julia de Burgos with the FBI," in *CENTRO Journal* 26, no. 2 (Fall 2014): 98–127.

86. See appendix B in Dávila Marichal, *Pedro*, 293, 295. Dávila Marichal mentions two press notes published in *El Mundo* (31 de marzo de 1933, 30 de mayo de 1933), the most important newspaper in Puerto Rico during that time, as proof that de Burgos's was significantly involved in the cadres and organizations of the Nationalist Party reserved for women. On the Daughters of Liberty, see Dávil Marichal, *Pedro*, 103–11.

87. See Torres Santiago, *Julia de Burgos: poeta maldita* (San Juan: Los Libros de la Iguana, 2014), 56–97.

88. See chap. 2 in Roberto Véguez and Tom Woodward, *En las montañas de Vermont: Los exiliados en la escuela española de Middlebury College* (Digital Book, 2019): https://schoolofspanish.middcreate.net/centenario/libro/chapter2.

89. Yvette Jiménez de Baez, *Julia de Burgos: Vida y poesía* (San Juan, PR: Editorial Coquí, 1966), 20.

90. See Benigno Trigo, "Anorexia as Idealization: Clemente Pereda's Protest Fast (Puerto Rico 1934)," *Hispanic Review* 83, no. 1 (Winter 2015): 47–75.

91. Julia de Burgos, *Obra poética*, ed. Juan Varela-Portas de Orduña (Madrid: Ediciones de la Discreta, 2009), 2:171. The original appeared in *Alma Latina* 51 (October 1934).

92. All English translations of de Burgos's poems are mine. For an extant English translation, see de Burgos, *Song of the Simple Truth*, 485.

93. Roland Barthes, *La chambre claire: Note sur la photographie* (Paris: Cahiers du Cinéma Gallimard, 1980), 49; Barthes, *Camera Lucida: Reflections on Photography*, trans. Richard Howard (New York: Hill and Wang, 1981), 27.

94. de Burgos, *Obra poética*, 2:117/495. The original appeared in *Alma Latina* 55 (February 1935). I quote the original, since the published versions of this poem in *Obra Poética* and *Song of the Simple Truth* contain a key erratum that also affects Agüeros's translation. The fifth line of the first strophe does not read *verte*, as in "to see you," but the infinitive *verter*, meaning "to pour." This mistake distorts the sense of the first strophe in its entirety.

95. See Juan Antonio Corretjer, "Como persona y como poetisa. Recordando a Julia de Burgos," *Claridad: Suplemento en Rojo* (May 4, 1963). Portions of this text are reproduced in Juan Antonio Rodríguez Pagán, *Julia en blanco y negro* (San Juan, PR: Sociedad Histórica de Puerto Rico, 2000), 94–95.

96. According to Jiménez de Báez, the earliest document known that mentions the

existence of this missing poetry volume was published in the poetry journal *Bayoán* 4, no. 5 (enero 1951). See Jiménez de Báez, *Vida y poesía*, 22.

97. For the most careful study of Albizu Campos's Catholicism and its effects on the increasingly conservative turn within the Nationalist Party throughout the 1930s, see Luis A. Ferrao, *Pedro Albizu Campos y el nacionalismo puertorriqueño, 1930–1939* (San Juan, PR: Editorial Cultural, 1990), 257–91.

98. Pedro Albizu Campos, "Carta a la Presidente [sic] del Frente Unido Femenino Pro Convención Constituyente," qtd. in Rodríguez Pagán, *En blanco*, 121.

99. de Burgos, "La mujer ante el dolor de la patria," *La Acción* (November 7, 1936), 7. A transcription of the speech, with some notable discrepancies and errata, can be found in Rodríguez Pagán, *En blanco*, 131–34.

100. Tertullian, *Apology*, in Tertulian, Minucius Felix, *Apology. De Spectaculis. Minucius Felix: Octavius*, trans. T. R. Glover and Gerald H. Rendall, Loeb Classical Library 250 (Cambridge, MA: Harvard University Press), 1931.

101. de Burgos, "La mujer," 7.

102. This actualization occurs through the implicit assumptive logic of heterosexual gendering that underpins de Burgos's fantasies of feminine martyrdom. The calculation at the basis of de Burgos's claim is that it is only when women begin to die for the cause of independence that the Puerto Rican home—and especially Puerto Rican fathers, brothers, and sons—will revolt. Given the enduring exposure of female-identifying bodies (especially racialized/Blackened ones) to gratuitous forms of violence, de Burgos's argument only makes sense if we assume an idealized view of the protections that the distribution of gender along race/class lines are supposed to afford. Even on this account, de Burgos's gendered fantasies are perhaps more telling in that they index the operations of a universalized presumption of gender in a milieu in which such universality cannot be taken for granted, given the persistence of what Hortense Spillers calls "ungendering." Hortense J. Spillers, *Black, White, and in Color* (Chicago: University of Chicago Press, 2003), 206–7. On the logic of actualization with respect to the modern gender/race system characteristic of coloniality, see Rocío Zambrana, *Colonial Debts*, 9–11. On compulsory heterosexuality and the heterosexual matrix, see chap. 2 in Judith Butler, *Gender Trouble: Feminism and the Subversion of Identity* (London: Routledge, 1999), 45–100.

103. Albizu Campos, *Obras escogidas*, ed. J. Benjamín Torres (San Juan, PR: Editorial Jelofe, 1981), 2:108.

104. Jacques Derrida, *Séminaire: La peine de mort*, vol. 1, *1999–2000*, ed. Geoff Bennington, Marc Crépon, and Thomas Dutoit (Paris: Galilée, 2012), 376–77: Derrida, *Death Penalty I (1999–2000)*, trans. Peggy Kamuf (Chicago: University of Chicago Press, 2014), 279.

105. Benjamin, *GS* 1:659; Benjamin, *SW* 4:163.

106. Perhaps the most eloquent proof that de Burgos's increasing fame is due to

her legendary status as the antibourgeois emblem par excellence within Puerto Rican historicity is furnished by Torres Santiago's biography, *Julia de Burgos: Poeta maldita*, which relies on the historical persecution of Puerto Rico's Nationalist movement to recast the aspects of de Burgos's life and works most determined by the logic of martyrdom as emblematic of her challenge to bourgeois norms.

107. Antonio Coll y Vidal, "Poema en Julia de Burgos," qtd. in Rodríguez Pagán, *En blanco*, 262–3.

108. de Burgos, *Obra poética*, 2:147.

109. de Burgos, *Obra poética*, 2:119.

110. de Burgos, *Obra poética*, 2:194.

111. Cuperes, "Enfrentamiento," 148.

112. Benjamin, *GS* 1:608–9; Benjamin, *SW* 4:314.

113. See Ferrao, *Pedro*, 303–27.

114. Albizu Campos, "Carta a Laura Meneses (December 24, 1937)," qtd. in Ferrao, *Pedro*, 327.

115. As a matter of fact, in the same letter from 1937 cited earlier (note 114) Albizu Campos describes the dictatorship of the proletariat as "the most modern of personal tyrannies." Albizu Campos, "Carta a Laura Meneses," qtd. in Luis A. Ferrao, *Pedro*, 326.

116. de Burgos, *Obra poética*, 2:173–76. The original was published in *La Acción* (September 12, 1936).

117. de Burgos, *Obra poética*, 2:223–24.

118. Chiqui Vicioso, *Julia de Burgos en Santo Domingo* (San Juan, PR: Editorial Patria, 2018), 24–25.

119. For more details of de Burgos's professional engagements during the 1930s, see Rodríguez Pagán, *En blanco*, 92–103.

120. See Ferrao, *Pedro*, 53–54.

121. Corretjer, "Como persona," *Claridad* (May 4, 1963).

122. Luis Lloréns Torres, "Cinco poetisas de América," in *Luis Lloréns Torres: Antología verso y prosa*, ed. Arcado Díaz Quiñones (San Juan, PR: Ediciones Huracán, 1986), 160. This text was originally published in *Puerto Rico Ilustrado* (13 de noviembre de 1937).

123. For a transcription of these poems, see Rodríguez Pagán, *En blanco*, 107–14. They were first published in *Mester* 2, nos. 10–11 (February–May 1969): 16–17.

124. Roberto Ramos Perea, ed., *Tuya siempre; Julita: Los amores entre Julia de Burgos y Luis Lloréns Torres* (San Juan, PR: Ediciones Le Provincial, 2017).

125. de Burgos, *Obra poética*, 1:67–68. Published originally in *El Imparcial* (December 4, 1937). This poem is included as poem 9 in *Poema en 20 surcos*. "A Julia de Burgos" was published originally in *El Imparcial* (March 5, 1938) and was included as the poem that opens *Poema en 20 surcos*. This poem will be the center of an extensive reading in Part III (see §22).

126. Vanessa Pérez Rosario, *Becoming Julia de Burgos: The Making of a Puerto Rican Icon* (Chicago: Illinois University Press, 2014), 47–48.

127. Nilita Vientós Gastón, "Al margen de un libro de Julia de Burgos," *Puerto Rico ilustrado* (April 8, 1939).

128. José Emilio González, "Julia de Burgos: intensa, siempre viva," *Asomante* 9, no. 4 (October–December 1953): 23.

129. See Sigmund Freud, *Gesammelte Werke 9: Totem und Taboo* (Frankfurt am Main: Fischer, 1999), 169–76 (hereafter quoted as *GW*); Freud, *The Standard Edition of the Complete Psychological Works of Sigmund Freud*, vol. 13: *Totem and Taboo and Other Works (1913–1914)*, trans. James Strachey (London: Hogarth Press, 1958), 140–46.

130. Claude Levi-Strauss, *Œuvres*, ed. Vincent Debaene, Frédéric Keck, Marie Mauzé, and Martin Rueff (Paris: Pléiade, 2008), 544; Levi-Strauss, *Totemism*, trans. Rodney Needham (Boston: Beacon, 1963), 101.

131. José Emilio González, "Julia de Burgos: intensa, siempreviva," 25–26.

132. Pérez Rosario, *Becoming*, 3.

133. See Benjamin, *GS* 1:608–9; Benjamin, *SW* 4:314.

134. José Emilio González, "La poesía de Julia de Burgos," in de Burgos, *Obra Poética*, ed. Consuelo Burgos and Juan Antonio Pagán (San Juan, PR: Instituto de Cultura Puertorriqueña, 2014), xxxvii.

135. Pérez Rosario, *Becoming*, 4.

136. Lena Burgos-Lafuente, "Untendered Eyes: Literary Politics of Julia de Burgos—Introducción," in *CENTRO Journal* 26, no. 2 (Fall 2014): 23n1.

137. Gilles Deleuze and Félix Guattari, *Mille Plateaux* (Paris: Minuit, 1980), 34.

138. Juan G. Gelpí, *Literatura y paternalismo en Puerto Rico* (San Juan, PR: Editorial de la Universidad de Puerto Rico, 2005), 36, 38, 39, 48.

139. Benjamin, *WuN* 19:98; Benjamin, *SW* 4:392.

140. Sylvia Wynter, "The Ceremony Must Be Found: After Humanism," *On Humanism and the University I: The Discourse of Humanism*, special issue of *Boundary 2* 12/13, nos. 3–1 (Spring–Autumn 1984): 42.

141. Wynter, "The Ceremony," 26.

142. Wynter, "Unsettling the Coloniality of Being/Power/Truth/Freedom: Towards the Human, After Man, Its Overrepresentation—An Argument," *New Centennial Review* 3, no. 3 (2003): 267.

143. Wynter, "Unparalleled Catastrophe for Our Species? Or, to Give Humanness a Different Future: Conversations," in *Sylvia Wynter: On Being Human as Praxis*, ed. Katherine McKittrick (Durham, NC: Duke University Press, 2015), 24.

144. Wynter, "Beyond Miranda's Meanings: Un/Silencing the 'Demonic Ground' of Caliban's 'Women,'" in *Out of the Kumbla: Caribbean Women and Literature*, ed. Carole Boyce-Davies and Elaine Savory Fido (Trenton, NJ: Africa World, 1990), n54.

145. Wynter, "Unparalleled," 22.

146. Áurea María Sotomayor, "El delito de Julia, la *outsider*," in *CENTRO Journal* 26, no. 2 (Fall 2014): 69.

147. See the introduction to Ángel Rodríguez, *Julia de Burgos. FBI File: Estudio crítico (1943–1956)* (San Juan, PR: Editorial Nuevo Mundo, 2020), iii–iv.

148. José Quiroga, "Review of *Obra poética completa*," in *CENTRO Journal* 26, no. 2 (Fall 2014): 314.

149. Juan Carlos Quintero-Herencia, "Aquí se puede hacer eso: Nido prohibido, casa familiar y banquete de Julia de Burgos. Lectura de *Cartas a Consuelo*," *Revista Iberoamericana* 82, no. 257 (October–December 2016): 874.

150. Burgos-Lafuente, "*Yo, múltiple*: Las cartas de Julia de Burgos," in *Cartas a Consuelo*, xxix.

151. Derrida, *Dire l'événement, est-ce possible? Séminaire de Montréal* (Paris: L'Harmattan, 2001), 109.

152. Friedrich Nietzsche, *Unzeitgemäße Betrachtungen*, in *Kritische Studienausgabe*, vol. 1, ed. Giorgio Colli and Mazzino Montinari (Berlin: de Gruyter, 1980), 270 (Hereafter *KSA*); Nietzsche, *Unfashionable Observations*, trans. Richard T. Gray, in *The Complete Works of Friedrich Nietzsche* (Stanford, CA: Stanford Univeristy Press, 1995), 2:107.

153. Derrida, *Spectres de Marx* (Paris: Galilée, 1993), 94. Derrida, *Specters of Marx: The State of the Debt, the Work of Mourning and the New International*, trans. Peggy Kamuf (London: Routledge, 1994), 67.

154. Benjamin, *WuN* 19:95–96; Benjamin, *SW* 4:390–91.

155. Hamacher, "Jetzt," 174; Hamacher, "Now," 187.

156. Benjamin, *GS* 5:N3,1, 578/463.

PART II: THE CLOSURE OF HISTORICISM; OR,
HISTORY IN DECONSTRUCTION

1. Juan Carlos Quintero-Herencia, "Aquí se puede hacer eso: Nido prohibido, casa familiar y banquete de Julia de Burgos. Lectura de *Cartas a Consuelo*," *Revista Iberoamericana* 82, no. 257 (October–December 2016): 874.

2. Jacques Derrida, *Voyous: Deux essais sur la raison* (Paris: Galilée, 2003), 198; Derrida, *Rogues: Two Essays on Reason*, trans. Pascale-Anne Brault and Michael Naas (Stanford, CA: Stanford University Press, 2005), 143.

3. By using the language of synthesis, I am implicitly taking distance from Samuel Weber's commentary on the dialectical image, which he regards as a form of "nonsynthesis." Samuel Weber, *Benjamin's-abilities* (Cambridge, MA: Harvard University Press, 2008), 49. Although he grounds this claim on Benjamin's earlier work on Kant, Weber's designation of this synthesis as nonsynthetical seems more guided by a certain allergy to the metaphysical resonances of synthesis than by an attempt to pay heed to Benjamin's own conceptual choices. For, in *Das Passagen-Werk*, Benjamin

does refer to the image on several occasions as a synthesis. See Walter Benjamin, *Gesammelte Schriften*, 5: *Das Passagen-Werk*, ed. Rolf Tiedemann (Frankfurt am Main: Suhrkamp, 1982), N,9a,4, 592 (hereafter quoted as *GS* 1–7); Benjamin, *The Arcades Project*, trans. Howard Eiland and Kevin McLaughlin (Cambridge, MA: Harvard University Press, 1999), 474. Subsequent citations of *The Arcades Project* refer only to the original, followed by the cited entry (e.g., N9,4) and the page numbers in both the German and the English editions, separated by a virgule. Evidently, to the extent that this synthesis does not entail a reconciliation of opposites but rather an intensification of their antagonistic oppositionality, Benjamin's synthesis is no regular synthesis. But to call it a nonsynthesis is precisely to sidestep the difficulty at stake here. Moreover, I maintain the term "synthesis" because I want to make Benjamin's dialectical image communicate with Derrida's thinking of *différance*, which is anything but a traditional, Hegelian synthesis but which Derrida himself nonetheless describes it as an "irreducible arch-synthesis, opening in one and the same possibility, temporalization, the relation to the other, and language." Jacques Derrida, *De la grammatologie* (Paris: Minuit, 1967), 88; Derrida, *Of Grammatology*, trans. Gayatri Chakravorty Spivak (Baltimore, MD: John Hopkins University Press, 2016), 65. To the extent that the image itself opens temporalization as a relation between times that are radically other and is *given* in the medium of language as a legible configuration, it is something close, though not entirely analogous to, the arch-synthetic "capacity" of *différance*.

4. Walter Benjamin, *Werke und Nachlaß* 19: *Über den Begriff der Geschichte*, ed. Gérard Raulet (Frankfurt am Main: Suhrkamp, 2009), 94 (hereafter cited as *WuN*); Benjamin, *Selected Writings*, vol. 4: *1938–1940*, ed. Howard Eiland and Michael Jennings (Cambridge, MA: Harvard University Press, 2006), 390 (hereafter cited as *SW*).

5. Benjamin, *GS* 1:1175. On the motif of the past's intentionality in Benjamin's theory of history, see Werner Hamacher, "Jetzt. Walter Benjamin zur Historischer Zeit," in *Perception and Experience in Modernity*, ed. Helga Geyer-Ryan, Paul Koopman, and Klass Intema (Leiden: Brill, 2002), 147–50; Hamacher, "Now: Walter Benjamin on Historical Time," trans. N. Rosenthal, in *The Moment: Time and Rupture in Modern Thought*, ed. Heidrun Friese (Liverpool: Liverpool University Press, 2011), 161–64.

6. For a more sustained version of this claim, I take the liberty of referring the reader to my essay, Ronald Mendoza-de Jesús, "Index and Image: Benjamin, Héring, Heidegger, and the Phenomenology of History," *Qui Parle* 30, no. 2 (December 2021): 293–335.

7. Benjamin, *WuN* 19:97; Benjamin, *SW* 4:392. Hamacher, "Jetzt," 150; Hamacher, "Now," 164.

8. Here I depart from Quintero-Herencia's critique of de Burgos's becoming-mirror and the narcissistic criticism it enables. See Juan Carlos Quintero-Herencia, "Aquí," 875.

9. Derrida, *Points de suspension. Entretiens*, ed. Elisabeth Weber (Paris: Galilée,

1992), 212, emphasis mine; Derrida, *Points . . . Interviews* (1974–1994), trans. Peggy Kamuf et al. (Stanford, CA: Stanford University Press, 1995), 199.

10. Derrida, *L'écriture et la différence* (Paris: Seuil, 1967), 188; Derrida, *Writing and Difference*, trans. Alan Bass (London: Routledge, 2001), 160.

11. Derrida, *Voyous*, 31; *Rogues*, 11.

12. On Husserl's genetic turn, see Alexander Schnell, *Husserl et les fondements de la phénoménologie constructive* (Grenoble: Millon, 2007), 197–206.

13. Edmund Husserl, *Husserliana* 17: *Formale und transzendentale Logik*, ed. Paul Janssen (The Hague: Martinus Nijhoff, 1974), 243–44 (hereafter cited as *Hua* 1–42); Husserl, *Formal and Transcendental Logik*, trans. Dorion Cairns (The Hague: Martinus Nijhoff, 1969), 237.

14. Husserl, *Hua* 17: 243; Husserl, *Formal*, 237.

15. Sigmund Freud, *Gesammelte Werke* X (1913–1917), ed. Anna Freud et al. (Frankfurt am Main: Fischer, 1999); 138–39; Freud, *The Standard Edition of the Complete Psychological Works of Sigmund Freud* 14 (1914–1916): *On the History of the Psycho-Analytic Movement, Papers on Metapsychology, and Other Works*, ed. and trans. James Strachey (London: Hogarth, 1957), 73–74.

16. Jean Laplanche and J.-B. Pontalis, *Vocabulaire de la psychanalyse* (Paris: Presses Universitaires de France, 1967), 264.

17. Derrida, "Une lecture de Droit de regards," in Marie-Françoise Plissart, *Droit de regards* (Les impressions nouvelles, 2010), xxxvii.

18. Ranjana Khanna, *Dark Continents: Psychoanalysis and Colonialism* (Durham, NC: Duke University Press, 2003), 83.

19. Pleshette DeArmitt, *The Right to Narcissism: A Case for an Im-possible Self-Love* (New York: Fordham University Press, 2014), 1–21, 39–40.

20. Benjamin, *WuN* 19: 124; Benjamin, *SW* 4: 405.

21. Derrida, *Voyous*, 198; Derrida, *Rogues*, 143.

22. Walter Benjamin, *WuN* 19:124; Benjamin, *SW* 4:405.

23. Gilles Deleuze and Félix Guattari, *Qu'est-ce que la philosophie?* (Paris: Minuit, 1991), 21–38; Deleuze and Guattari, *What Is Philosophy?*, trans. Hugh Tomlinson and Graham Burchell (New York: Columbia University Press, 1994), 15–34.

24. Adi Ophir, "Concept," in *Political Concepts: A Critical Lexicon*, ed. J. M. Bernstein, Adi Ophir, and Ann Laura Stoler (New York: Fordham University Press, 2018), 71.

25. Ophir, "Concept," 72, emphases mine.

26. See Walter Benjamin, *Gesammelte Briefe*, vol. 6: *1938–40*, ed. Christoph Gödde and Henri Lonitz (Frankfurt am Main: Suhrkamp, 2000), 399–401 (hereafter cited as *GB*).

27. See Frank R. Ankersmit, *Meaning, Truth, and Reference in Historical Representation* (Ithaca, NY: Cornell University Press, 2012).

28. See Werner Hamacher, "Über einige Unterschiede zwischen der Geschichte

literarischer und der Geschichte phänomenaler Ereignisse," in *Texte zur Theorie und Didaktik der Literaturgeschichte*, ed. Marja Rauch and Achim Geisenhanslücke, 163–82 (Stuttgart: Reclam); Hamacher, *On the Brink: Language, Time, History, Politics*, trans. Jan Plug (London: Rowman and Littlefield, 2020), 29–41.

29. Jacques Derrida, *La voix et le phénomène* (Paris: Presses Universitaires de France, 1967), 115; Jacques Derrida, *Voice and Phenomenon*, trans. Leonard Lawlor (Evanston, IL: Northwestern University Press, 2011), 88.

30. Benjamin, *GB* 6:400.

31. On these crucial motifs in Benjamin's thinking, see Daniel Weidner, "Fort-, Über-, Nachleben: Zu einer Denkfigur bei Benjamin," *Benjamin-Studien* 2 (2011): 161–78. My own thinking of Benjamin's powerful, though often quite classic or traditional, if not even spiritualist, understanding of the concept of life is strongly inflected by Derrida's readings of Benjamin. For Derrida's engagement with Benjamin's thoughts about life, history, nature, and translation, see Jacques Derrida, "Des tours de Babel," in *Psyche: Inventions of the Other*, vol. 1, (Paris: Galilée, 1987), 213–14; Derrida, *Psyche I*, ed. Peggy Kamuf and Elizabeth Rottenberg (Stanford, CA: Stanford University Press, 2007), 202–3.

32. Benjamin, *WuN* 7:13; Benjamin, *SW* 1:254.

33. Benjamin, *GS* 2:468; Benjamin, *SW* 3:262.

34. Benjamin, *WuN* 19:96; Benjamin, *SW* 4:391.

35. See Frank R. Ankersmit, *History and Tropology: The Rise and Fall of Metaphor* (Berkley: University of California Press, 1994); and Frank R. Ankersmit, *Sublime Historical Experience* (Stanford, CA: Stanford University Press, 2005).

36. Ankersmit, *Meaning*, 1.

37. Ankersmit, *Meaning*, 4.

38. Ankersmit, *Meaning*, 11.

39. Richard Rorty, *Philosophy and the Mirror of Nature* (Princeton, NJ: Princeton University Press, 2009), 6.

40. Ankersmit, *Meaning*, 27.

41. For Ankersmit's remarks on why this order matters, see Ankersmit, *Meaning*, 67.

42. See Saul Kripke, *Naming and Necessity* (Cambridge, MA: Harvard University Press, 1980).

43. Ankersmit, *Meaning*, 78.

44. Ankersmit, *Meaning*, 112.

45. Richard Evans, *In Defense of History* (London: Granta, 1997), 14.

46. See Benjamin, *GS* 1:226–27; Benjamin, *Origin of German Trauerspiel*, trans. Howard Eiland (Cambridge, MA: Harvard University Press, 2019), 24–25.

47. See Weber, *Benjamin's -abilities*, 134; and Hans Heinz Holz, "Idee," in *Benjamins Begriffe*, ed. Michael Opitz and Erdmut Wizisla (Frankfurt am Main: Suhrkamp, 2000), 2:477–78.

48. Ankersmit, *Meaning*, 4.

49. Derrida, *Voyous*, 198; Derrida, *Rogues*, 143.

50. Ankersmit, *Meaning*, 13.

51. Ankersmit, *Meaning*, 99–100, emphases mine.

52. See Ankersmit, *Narrative Logic: A Semantic Analysis of the Historian's Language* (The Hague: Martinus Nijhoff, 1983), 131.

53. G. W. Leibniz, *Confessio Philosophii: Papers Concerning the Problem of Evil*, trans. Robert C. Sleigh Jr. (New Haven, CT: Yale University Press, 2005), 45.

54. Ankersmit, *Meaning*, 14.

55. Carl Schmitt, *Politische Theologie. Vier Kapitel zur Lehre von der Souveranität* (Berlin: Duncker and Humblot, 2015), 43; Schmitt, *Political Theology: Four Chapters on the Concept of Sovereignty*, trans. George Schwab (Cambridge, MA: MIT Press, 1985), 36.

56. Benjamin, *WuN* 19:124; Benjamin, *SW* 4:405.

57. G. W. F. Hegel, *Gesammelte Werke* 18: *Vorlesungsmanuskripte* II (1816–31), ed. Walter Jaeschke (Hamburg: Meiner, 1995), 192 (hereafter quoted as *GW*); Hegel, *Lectures on the Philosophy of World History* 1: *Manuscripts of the Introduction and the Lectures of 1822-3*, ed. and trans. Robert F. Brown and Peter C. Hodgson (Oxford: Clarendon, 2011), 115.

58. Hamacher, "Über einige Unterschiede," 165; Hamacher, *On the Brink*, 30.

59. Hamacher, "Über einige Unterschiede," 165; Hamacher, *On the Brink*, 30.

60. See Paul de Man, "Phenomenality and Materiality in Kant," in *Aesthetic Ideology*, ed. Andrzej Warminski (Minneapolis: University of Minnesota Press, 1996), 70–90.

61. Hamacher, "Über einige Unterschiede," 166–67; Hamacher, *On the Brink*, 31.

62. Hamacher, "Über einige Unterschiede," 169; Hamacher, *On the Brink*, 33.

63. Hamacher, "Über einige Unterschiede," 173–74; Hamacher, *On the Brink*, 35–36.

64. Hegel, *GW*, 18:140 Hegel, *Lectures on the Philosophy of World History*, 1:79.

65. This opposition is borrowed from Derrida, who borrowed it from Ernst Cassirer. See Derrida, *La voix*, 20; Derrida, *Voice*, 17.

66. Aristotle, *Metaphysics*, trans. Joe Sachs (Santa Fe, NM: Green Lion Press, 1999), 1020a, 94.

67. Aristotle, *Poetics*, trans. Joe Sachs (Newburyport, MA: Focus Publishing, 2006), 1451b1–6, 32.

68. Aristotle, *Poetics*, 1451a20–30, 31.

69. Wilhelm von Humboldt, "Über die Aufgabe der Geschichtschreibers" in *Werke 1: Schriften zur Anthropologie und Geschichte*, ed. Andreas Flitner and Klaus Giel (Darmstadt: Wissenschaftliche Buchgesellschaft, 1960), 591; Humboldt, "On the Historian's Task," *History and Theory* 6, no. 1 (1967): 61.

70. Hamacher, "Über einige Unterschiede," 177–8; Hamacher, *On the Brink*, 37–38.

71. Per se modalities are introduced by Leibniz for the first time in his 1672–

1673 philosophical dialogue *Confessio Philosophii* in order to deal with the classic theodical problem of how to reconcile the absolute goodness of God with the existence of evil in the world. See Leibniz, *Confessio*, 49.

72. Within the history of modern philosophy, the term *nihil negativum* is often associated with Kant's "Table of Nothing," which brings the Transcendental Analytic of Kant's *Kritik der reinen Vernunft* (*Critique of Pure Reason*) to an end. There, Kant posits this concept in paradoxical and almost proto-Hegelian terms as an "empty object without concept," which he also calls an *"Unding"* (that is, an "un-thing," or "non-thing") by virtue of it being "opposed to possibility insofar as even the concept cancels itself out." Immanuel Kant, *Kritik der reinen Vernunft*, ed. (Berlin: De Gruyter, 1968), A292/B349 (hereafter quoted as *KrV*); Kant, *Critique of Pure Reason*, trans. Paul Guyer and Allen W. Wood (Cambridge: Cambridge University Press, 1998), 383 (hereafter quoted as *CPR*).

73. Derrida, *De la grammatologie*, 25; Derrida, *Of Grammatology*, 14.

74. Jacuqes Derrida, "La phénoménologie et la clôture de la métaphysique," *Alter: Revue de Phénoménologie* no. 8 (2000): 84.

75. Derrida, *La voix*, 115; Derrida, *Voice*, 87–88.

76. Ankersmit, *Meaning*, 22n57.

77. Derrida, "La phénoménologie," 84.

78. The most elegant version of this basic deconstructive "principle" that I know of was formulated by Henry Staten: "If essence is always exposed to the possibility of accidents, is this not then a necessary, rather than a chance, possibility, and if it is always and necessarily possible, is it not then an essential possibility?" Henry Staten, *Wittgenstein and Derrida* (Lincoln: University of Nebraska Press, 1986), 16. In the wake of the work of scholars such as Chantal Mouffe, Ernesto Laclau, Judith Butler, and Gayatri Chakravorty Spivak, this principle became known as "the constitutive outside." A more precise formulation would be to speak of "the de-constitutive outside," placing the emphasis on the ways the outside not only constitutes but also undoes the fixed boundaries of any sense-configuration.

79. Jacques Derrida, *Marges de la philosophie* (Paris: Éditions de Minuit, 1972), viii; Derrida, *Margins of Philosophy*, trans. Alan Bass (Chicago: University of Chicago Press, 1982), xvi.

80. See, in particular, the following passage: "When metaphysics thinks beings in view of its ground, which is common to each being as such, then it is logic as onto-logy. When metaphysics thinks beings as such as a whole, that is, in view of the highest being that grounds all, then it is logic as theo-logy." See Martin Heidegger, *Gesamtausgabe*, vol. 11: *Identität und Differenz*, ed. Friedrich-Wilhelm von Herrmann (Frankfurt am Main: Klostermann, 2006), 76, (hereafter quoted as *GA 1–101*); Heidegger, *Identity and Difference*, trans. Joan Stambaugh (Chicago: University of Chicago Press, 2002), 72.

81. Derrida, *Marges*, 383; Derrida, *Margins*, 322.

82. Ankersmit, *Meaning*, 115.

83. Ankersmit, *Meaning*, 117, emphases mine.

84. Ankersmit, *Meaning*, 246.

85. Derrida, *Marges*, 370, 375; Derrida, *Margins*, 311, 316.

86. Derrida, *Marges*, 375; Derrida, *Margins*, 316.

87. Derrida, *Marges*, 375; Derrida, *Margins*, 316.

88. Derrida, *Marges*, 375, 376; Derrida, *Margins*, 316.

89. Heidegger, *GA* 2:262; Heidegger, *Being and Time*, trans. Joan Stambaugh and Dennis Schmidt (Albany: SUNY Press, 2010), 251. Future page references to the German edition of *Being and Time* first mention the pagination of the 1927 Niemeyer *princeps* edition, followed by the pagination of the *GA* edition, separated by a virgule.

90. Derrida, *Marges*, 374; Derrida, *Margins*, 315.

91. Geoffrey Bennington, *Scatter 1: The Politics of Politics in Foucault, Heidegger, and Derrida* (New York: Fordham University Press, 2016), 274.

92. Jacques Derrida, *Force de loi* (Paris: Galilée, 1994), 38; Derrida, "Force of Law," in *Acts of Religion*, ed. Gil Anidjar (New York: Routledge, 2002), 244.

93. Derrida, *La voix et le phénomène*, 115/87–88.

94. Jacques Derrida, *Voyous*, 197, emphases mine; Derrida, *Rogues*, 143.

95. Derrida, *L'Université sans condition* (Paris: Galilée, 2001), 75; Derrida, *Without Alibi*, ed. and trans. Peggy Kamuf (Stanford, CA: Stanford University Press, 2002), 234.

96. See Barnaby Nelson, Josef Parnas, and Louis A. Sass, "Disturbance of Minimal Self (Ipseity) in Schizophrenia: Clarification and Current Status," *Schizophrenia Bulletin* 40, no. 3 (2014): 479–82.

97. See Jean-Paul Sartre, *Être et néant: essai d'ontologie phénoménologique* (Paris: Gallimard, 1943), 140; Sartre, *Being and Nothingness: An Essay of Phenomenological Ontology*, trans. Sarah Richmond (New York: Washington Square, 2018), 160.

98. See, for instance, Heidegger's famous lapidary statement near the end of the introduction to *Sein und Zeit*, "Higher than actuality stands *possibility*," or his formal characterization of the ways of being of Dasein in terms of *Seinkönnen*, literally, "being-possible." Martin Heidegger, *GA* 2:38/51–52, 143/191; Heidegger, *Being and Time*, 36, 139.

99. Sartre, *L'être et le néant*, 218, emphases mine; Sartre, *Being and Nothingness*, 257.

100. For Levinas's thinking of ipseity as "hostage," see "La substitution," the crucial fifth chapter in Emmanuel Levinas, *Autrement qu'être ou au-delà de l'essence* (The Hague: Martinus Nijhoff, 1974), 167–218; Levinas, *Otherwise than Being or beyond Essence*, trans. Alphonso Linguis (Dordrecht: Kluwer, 1991), 99–129.

101. See Paul Ricœur, *Soi-même comme un autre* (Paris: Seuil, 1990), 13–14 ; Ricœur, *Oneself as Another*, trans. Kathleen Blamey (Chicago: Chicago University Press, 1992), 3.

102. See chapter 2 in Michel Foucault, *Histoire de la séxualité*, vol. 3: *Le souci de soi* (Paris: Gallimard, 1984), 53–94; Foucault, *History of Sexuality*, vol. 3: *The Care of the Self*, trans. Robert Hurley (New York: Patheon Books, 1986), 37–68.

103. In Romano's recent philosophical work, ipseity has acquired an even more central role than in his earlier work on eventhood and temporality. This is particularly the case in *Être soi-même: une autre histoire de la philosophie* (*Being Oneself: Another History of Philosophy*), where Romano offers a history of philosophy that claims to be "non-metaphysical (in the Heideggerian sense of the term)" to the extent that it demonstrates that ipseity is not only at the basis of modern subjectivity but is also prior and irreducible to it. See the introduction to Romano *Être soi-même: une autre histoire de la philosophie* (Paris: Folio, 2019), 19–44.

104. See Dan Zahavi, *Subjectivity and Selfhood: Investigating the First-Person Perspective* (Cambridge, MA: MIT Press, 2005).

105. For Heidegger's thinking of *das Selbe*, see Heidegger, *GA* 9:187; Heidegger, *Poetry, Language, Thought*, trans. Albert Hofstadter (New York: HarperCollins, 1971), 216–17. On Heidegger's thinking of differential identity and unity, see the sixth chapter of Jussi Backman, *Complicated Presence: Heidegger and the Postmetaphysical Unity of Being* (Albany: SUNY Press, 2015), 215–38.

106. Consider the following passage from Henry's *Phénoménologie matérielle* (*Material Phenomenology*): "The essence of ipseity is not an ideal essence, the correlate of an eidetic intuition. It is not such except in our representation, in irreality. As real essence, on the contrary, as effective and living life, it is each time an effective self, the identity of the affecting and the affected in an auto-affection that radically individuates, that imparts the seal of individuality on everything that autoaffects itself in it." Michel Henry, *Phénoménologie matérielle* (Paris: Presses Universitaires de France, 1990), 163; Henry, *Material Phenomenology*, trans. Scott Davidson (New York: Fordham University Press, 2008), 121. I am grateful to Nathan Brown for bringing to my attention the importance of Henry's philosophical wager for an understanding of the stakes of thinking ipseity within contemporary philosophy.

107. See Jean Luc-Nancy, *Être singulier pluriel* (Paris: Galilée, 1996), 53; Nancy, *Being Singular Plural*, trans. Robert D. Richardson and Anne E. O'Byrne (Stanford, CA: Stanford University Press, 2000), 33.

108. It is not difficult to show that ipseity underlies and structures from within the central concept of Agamben's towering Homo Sacer project, namely, the motif of *forma-di-vita* or "form-of-life." In this respect, the fact that Agamben brings the last volume of the Homo Sacer series to a close by turning Spinoza's thinking of joyful ipseity in the *Ethics* in order to describe the mode of being of *forma-di-vita*—"Satisfaction in oneself is a joy borne out of the fact that man contemplates itself as well as its own potency to act"—is telling. Spinoza, *Éthique*, ed. Fokke Akkerman and Piet Steenbakkers, trans. Pierre-François Moreau (Paris: Presses Universitaires de France, 2020), 328. III, prop. 53. See Giorgio Agamben, *L'uso dei corpi* (Vicenza:

Peri Nozza, 2014), 351; Agamben, *The Use of Bodies*, trans. Adam Kotsko (Stanford, CA: Stanford University Press, 2016), 278. Agamben explicitly addresses the motif of ipseity in the central essay of *Che cos'è la filosofia? (What Is Philosophy?)*, where he links ipseity to the Platonic theory of the ideas and their givenness in language in the proper name. Giorgio Agamben, *Che cos'è la filosofia?* (Macerata: Quodlibet, 2016), 80–81; Agamben, *What Is Philosophy?*, trans. Lorenzo Chiesa (Stanford, CA: Stanford University Press, 2017), 54.

109. Although the language of ipseity is not common in Malabou's work, it would be possible to show that her signature concept of plasticity constitutes an attempt to think ipseity as the condition of being or as the principle of an ontology of absolute convertibility or exchangeability. Indeed, the following definition of plasticity attests to the structuring force of ipseity in her thinking: "Plasticity characterizes a regime of systematic *auto-organization* that rests on the capacity that an organism has to integrate the modifications that it undergoes and to modify them in turn." Cathérine Malabou, *La plasticité au soir de l'écriture: dialectique, destruction, déconstruction* (Paris: Léo Scheer, 2005), 113; Malabou, *Plasticity at the Dusk of Writing: Dialectics, Destruction, Deconstruction*, trans. Carolyn Shread (New York: Columbia University Press, 2010), 61.

110. See Edmund Husserl, "§ 13. Generalisierung und Formalisierung," in *Husserliana*, vol. 3: *Ideen zu einer reinen Phänomenologie und phänomenologischen Philosophie I: Allgemeine Einführung in die reine Phänomenologie*, ed. Walter Biemel (The Hague: Martinus Nijhoff, 1950), 32–34 (hereafter quoted as *Hua* 1–42); Husserl, "§13. Generalization and Formalization," in *Ideas for a Pure Phenomenology and a Phenomenological Philosophy I: General Introduction to Pure Phenomenology*, trans. Daniel O. Dahlstrom (Indianapolis, IN: Hackett, 2014), 27–28.

111. Derrida, *Voyous*, 30; Derrida, *Rogues*, 11.

112. Derrida, *Voyous*, 31; *Rogues*, 11.

113. Derrida, *Voyous*, 31; *Rogues*, 11.

114. Husserl, *Hua* 19.1:95; Husserl, *Logical Investigations*, trans. J. N. Findlay (London: Routledge, 2001), 223.

115. Walter Benjamin, *WuN* 19:98; Benjamin, *SW* 4:392.

116. Benjamin, *GS* 5:N3,1, 578/463.

117. Benjamin, *GS* 5:N10a,3, 595/475.

118. See Hamacher, "Jetzt"; Hamacher, "Now." See Rebecca Comay, "Benjamin's Endgame," in *Walter Benjamin's Philosophy*, ed. Andrew Benjamin and Peter Osborne (London: Routledge, 1993).

119. Take, for instance, the following passage from Christopher Fynsk's otherwise compelling chapter on the dialectical image: "In 'N7,2' . . . Benjamin writes that 'the dialectician can't see history as anything other than a constellation of dangers.' This constellation is formed by the threat posed by the reigning ideologies to the constellation of past and present offered by the dialectical image. But the moment is also

dangerous in that it is critical for the past: if the present does not read the past (and *itself* as implicated in this past)—if it fails to read and write itself—the constellation of past and present will simply flit by." Christopher Fynsk, *Language and Relation: That There Is Language* (Stanford, CA: Stanford University Press, 1996), 221. Note how the last sentence of this passage tacitly posits an equivalence between the "flitting by" of the constellation or the image and the "critical danger" of its legibility, which makes it so that the danger of the image lies in the possible actualization of its capacity to evade the historian's grasp. This, in turn, assumes that *averting this danger* is another name for the actual *reading* of the image, which precisely fails to do justice to Benjamin's insistence in "N3,1" that danger "underlies all reading" and to his claim, in thesis V, that the "the true image of the past flits by" (*WuN* 19:95; *SW* 4:390), which suggests that the flitting by of the image is not the negation of its historicization but an essential element or moment within its historicity.

120. Benjamin, *GS* 5:N7,2, 587/470.

121. Benjamin, *GS* 5:N3,1, 578/463.

122. Benjamin, *WuN* 19:94; Benjamin, *SW* 4:390.

123. Hamacher, "Jetzt," 156, emphases mine except for *in* and *out of*; Hamacher, "Now," 169.

124. Hamacher, "Jetzt," 176; Hamacher, "Now," 189.

125. Hamacher, "Jetzt," 179; Hamacher, "Now," 192.

126. I take the terms ultra- and quasi-transcendental from Derrida. See Derrida, *La voix*, 14; Derrida, *Voice*, 13.

127. Kant, *KrV*, A219/B266; Kant, *CPR*, 322.

128. Kant, *KrV*, A219/B265; Kant, *CPR*, 322–23.

129. Kant, *KrV*, A291/B348; Kant, *CPR*, 382.

130. Kant, *KrV*, A221/B268; Kant, *CPR*, 323.

131. Benjamin, *GS* 5:N3,1, 578/463, passage slightly modified.

132. See *Early Greek Philosophy: Western Greek Thinkers*, ed. André Laks and Glenn W. Most (Cambridge, MA: Harvard University Press, 2016), part 2, D6, 39.

133. See the translator's introduction in Barbara Cassin, *Parménide. Sur la nature ou sur l'Étant. La langue de l'être* (Paris: Éditions de Seuil, 1998), 30–48.

134. "For the same thing to hold good and not to hold good simultaneously of the same thing and in the same respect is impossible." Aristotle, *Metaphysics*, 1005b18–21.

135. See Plato, *Theaetetus and Sophist*, trans. H. N. Fowler (Cambridge, MA: Harvard University Press, 1921), 241d, 355.

136. Ludwig Wittgenstein, *Tagebücher 1914–1916*, in *Werkausgabe* (Frankfurt am Main: Suhrkamp, 2006), 1:15.11.14, 120; Wittgenstein, *Notebooks 1914–1916*, trans. Elizabeth Anscombe (Oxford: Blackwell, 1979), 30.

137. Jean-François Lyotard, *Le différend* (Paris: Minuit, 1983), §130, 120; Lyotard, *The Differend: Phrases in Dispute*, trans. by Georges Van der Abbeele (Minneapolis: University of Minnesota Press, 1988), 78.

138. See the remarks on Heidegger's *Ereignis* near the conclusion to the note on Aristotle in Lyotard, *Le différend*, 3.4, 116/75.

139. See, for instance, the following programmatic moment in Irad Kimhi's groundbreaking work: "I wish to propose that the contradictory judgments "*S* is *F*" and "*S* is not-*F*" are to be understood as the positive and negative acts of a single two-way logical capacity—which, as we shall see, can be specified through its positive act: "*S* is *F*." The capacity is *asymmetrical*, since the positive act is prior to the negative. This means that the only predicative determination in a simple contradictory pair is the *positive* predication. Yet even the positive case is essentially one of a *pair* of acts." Irad Kimhi, *Thinking and Being* (Cambridge, MA: Harvard University Press, 2018), 20.

140. Friedrich Nietzsche, *Kritische Studienausgabe*, vol. 5: *Jenseits von Gut und Böse, Zur Genealogie der Moral*, ed. Giorgio Colli and Mazzino Montinari" (Berlin: DTV/de Gruyter, 1999), 17 (hereafter quoted as *KSA*); Nietzsche, *Collected Works*, vol. 8: *Beyond Good and Evil, On the Genealogy of Morals*, trans. Adrián del Caro (Stanford: Stanford University Press, 2014), 6 (hereafter quoted as *CW*).

141. Nietzsche, *KSA* 5:17; Nietzsche, *CW* 8:7.

142. Jean-Luc Nancy, *Une pensée finie* (Paris: Galilée, 1990), 33. Nancy, *A Finite Thinking*, ed. by Simon Sparks (Stanford: Stanford University Press, 2003), 17.

143. See Martin Heidegger, *GA* 2:51–2; Heidegger, *Being and Time*, 36.

144. Heidegger, *GA* 2:263/257.

145. Bennington, *Scatter 1*, 281, 275.

146. Derrida, *L'Université*, 75; Derrida, *Without Alibi*, 235.

147. Benjamin, *WuN* 19:95–96; Benjamin, *SW* 4:390–91. For both theses, I base my translation on the "Posthume Abscrift" ("Posthumous Draft"), which corresponds to the typescript that Gretel Adorno transcribed.

148. Holz, "Idee," 445.

149. Benjamin, *WuN* 19:105; Benjamin, *SW* 4:397.

150. See Jürgen Habermas, "Consciousness-Raising or Redemptive Criticism: The Contemporaneity of Walter Benjamin," trans. Philip Brewster and Carl Howard Buchner, *New German Critique* 17 (Spring 1979): 38.

151. Benjamin, *GS* 2:204; Benjamin, *SW* 3:305.

152. See Jacques Derrida, *Monolinguisme de l'autre* (Paris: Galilée, 1996), 32. Derrida, *Monolingualism of the Other*, trans. Patrick Mensah (Stanford, CA: Stanford University Press, 1998) 14.

PART III. READING NOW: THE CATASTROPHIC MODERNITY OF JULIA DE BURGOS

1. See Geoff G. Burrows, "The New Deal in Puerto Rico: Public Works, Public Health, and the Puerto Rico Reconstruction Administration, 1935–1955," PhD diss., Graduate Center, City University of New York, 32.

2. See James L. Dietz, *Historia económica de Puerto Rico* (San Juan, PR: 2018),

140. On coffee's role in Puerto Rico's economy before US colonization, see César Ayala and Laird Bergard, *Agrarian Puerto Rico* (Cambridge: Cambridge University Press, 2020), 41–60.

3. Canario y su Grupo, "Lamento Borincano," track 1, *Early Puerto Rican Music, 1916–1939*, CD (Arhoolie Records, 1930).

4. See Rexford Tugwell, *The Stricken Land: The Story of Puerto Rico* (New York: Doubleday, 1947).

5. See César Ayala and Rafael Bernabe, *Puerto Rico in the American Century: A History since 1898* (Chapel Hill: University of North Carolina Press, 2007), 34.

6. Although in contemporary Puerto Rican Spanish the word *criollo/a* is most often associated with food—where it serves to distinguish culinary traditions that are regarded as autochthonous or folklorically "Puerto Rican"—the term was initially used as an ethno-racial category to distinguish the descendants of Spanish or European settlers in the colonies of the Spanish empire from colonial settlers who were born in the Iberian Peninsula or in Europe.

7. Ayala and Bernabe, *Puerto Rico in the American Century*, 139.

8. For the classic study of the Puerto Rican nineteenth-century economy, see Fernando Picó, *Libertad y servidumbre en el Puerto Rico del siglo XIX*, 2nd ed. (Ediciones Huracán, 1982).

9. On this process and the intensification of the proletarianization of the countryside peasantry it produced, see César Ayala, "The Decline of the Plantation Economy and the Puerto Rican Migration of the 1950s," *Latino Studies Journal* 7, no. 1 (1996): 61–90.

10. See Karl Marx, "The Results of the Direct Production Process," in *Capital: A Critique of Political Economy*, vol. 1, trans. Ben Fowkes (London: Penguin, 1992), 1035.

11. The concept of lifeworld, of Husserlian provenance, is here used in a way that closely tracks Bolívar Echevarría's inventive redeployment of this crucial motif in genetic or historical phenomenology as part of his theory of modernity. Bolívar Echevarría, *Modernidad y blanquitud* (Mexico City: Bolsillo Era, 2016), 13; Echevarría, *Modernity and "Whiteness,"* trans. Rodrigo Ferreira (Cambridge: Polity, 2019), 1.

12. César Ayala and Rafael Bernabe, *Puerto Rico in the American Century*, 35.

13. "The capital-relation is a relation of compulsion, the aim of which is to extract surplus labor by prolonging labor time. . . . This capital-relation as a relation of compulsion is common to both modes of production, but the specifically capitalist mode of production also possesses other ways of extracting surplus value. If, in contrast to this, the basis is an existing mode of labor, hence a given level of development of the productive power of labor and a mode of labor which corresponds to this productive power, surplus value can only be created by prolonging labor time, hence in the manner of absolute surplus value. Therefore, where this is the sole form of production

of surplus value, we have the formal subsumption of labor under capital." Karl Marx, *Economic Manuscript of 1861–63*, in *Marx and Engels, Collected Works*, ed. Jack Cohen et al. (Lawrence & Wishart, 2010), 34:426 (hereafter *MECW*).

14. Lauren Berlant, *Cruel Optimism* (Durham, NC: Duke University Press, 2011), 95–102.

15. See Walter Benjamin, *Gesammelte Schriften* 1: *Abhandlungen*, ed. Rolf Tiedemann and Hermann Schweppenhäuser (Frankfurt am Main: Suhrkamp, 1982), 464 (hereafter cited as *GS* 1–7); Benjamin, *Origin of German Trauerspiel*, trans. Howard Eiland (Cambridge, MA: Harvard University Press, 2019), 45–46 (hereafter cited as *Origin*).

16. As the author himself explains in a note published with the 1962 revised edition of *Tiempo muerto*, the play's ending did not initially contemplate Juana's suicide; the author added that action before the play's debut and subsequently decided to remove it, thus restoring the play's original design. Manuel Méndez Ballester, *Tiempo muerto*, in *El clamor de los surcos y Tiempo muerto* (Barcelona: Ediciones Rumbos, 1963), 287.

17. Méndez Ballester, *Tiempo muerto*, 257.

18. Gilles Deleuze, *L'île déserte. Textes et entretiens, 1953–1974*, ed. David Lapoujade (Paris : Èditions de Minuit, 2002), 15–16; Deleuze, *Desert Islands and Other Texts, 1953–1974*, ed. David Lapoujade, trans. Michael Taormina (Los Angeles: Semiotext(e), 2002), 9–10.

19. Méndez Ballester, *Tiempo muerto*, 221.

20. On the Marxist critique of Robinsonades, see Marx, *MEW* 34:19; Marx, *MECW* 28:17.

21. Jacques Derrida, *Voyous. Deux essais sur la raison* (Paris: Galilée, 2003), 30; Derrida, *Rogues: Two Essays on Reason*, trans. Pascale-Anne Brault and Michael Naas (Stanford, CA: Stanford University Press, 2005), 11.

22. Mercedes López-Baralt, ed., *Sobre ínsulas extrañas: el clásico de Pedreira anotado por Tomás Blanco* (San Juan, PR: Editorial de la Universidad de Puerto Rico, 2001), 190–91.

23. Juan G. Gelpí, *Literatura y paternalismo en Puerto Rico* (San Juan, PR: Editorial de la Universidad de Puerto Rico, 2005), 29–48.

24. In a footnote to "Beyond Miranda's Meanings," Wynter introduces the term "canonism" as a particular version of her own concept of the "totemic set": "The attack on the master canon, and the thrust to devise new canons by hitherto marginalized intelligentsia groups allow us to speak of canonism, as one of the ordering '*isms*.'" Sylvia Wynter, "Beyond Miranda's Meanings: Un/Silencing the 'Demonic Ground' of Caliban's 'Women,'" in *Out of the Kumbla: Caribbean Women and Literature*, ed. Carole Boyce Davies and Elaine Savory Fido (Trenton, NJ: Africa World, 1990), 370n49. For a lengthier discussion of Wynter's understanding of *isms* as isolated

totemic sets that encode "governing behaviour-regulatory codes of symbolic 'life' and 'death'" (365), see §10.

25. Although it bears some affinities to the method that Wynter calls "decipherment," the reading that follows could be characterized more precisely as a desedimentation or deconstruction of Wynterian decipherment, at least to the extent that it questions the *teleology* that undergirds this Wynterian methodological concept, which she identifies as that of "realizing, at long last, the autonomy of human cognition with respect to the reality of the social universes of which we are always already discursively instituted speaking/knowing/feeling subjects, and, therefore, with respect to the processes which govern our modes of being/behaving." Wynter, "Rethinking 'Aesthetics:' Notes Towards a Deciphering Practice," in *Ex-iles: Essays on Caribbean Cinema*, ed. Mbye B. Cham (Trenton, NJ: Africa World, 1992), 239.

26. Walter Benjamin, *Werke und Nachlaß* 13.1: *Kritiken und Rezensionen*, ed. Heinrich Kaulen (Frankfurt am Main: Suhrkamp, 2011), 312 (hereafter cited as *WuN* 1–21); Benjamin, *SW 2:*464.

27. Frederic Jameson, *A Singular Modernity: Essay on the Ontology of the Present* (London: Verso, 2012), 14.

28. Christina León, "Risking Catachresis: Reading Race, Reference, and Grammar in 'Women,'" *diacritics* 49, no. 2 (2021): 66.

29. See Saul Kripke, *Naming and Necessity* (Cambridge, MA: Harvard University Press, 1981). For a more Continental-friendly engagement with Kripke's semantics of proper names, see Jean-François Lyotard, "Le référent, le nom," in *Le différend* (Paris: Minuit, 1983), 56–92; Lyotard, "The Referent, the Name," in *The Differend: Phrases in Dispute*, trans. Georges Van Den Abbeele (Minneapolis: University of Minnesota Press, 1988), 32–58.

30. Echevarría, *Modernidad y blanquitud*,13; Echevarría, *Modernity and "Whiteness,"* 1.

31. For Husserl's most canonical account of the *lifeworld*, see part 3, section A of Edmund Husserl, *Husserliana 6: Die Krisis der europäischen Wissenschaften und die transzendentale Phänomenologie*, ed. Walter Biemel (The Hague: Martinus Nijhoff, 1976), 93–105 (hereafter quoted as *Hua* 1–42); Husserl, *The Crisis of European Sciences and Transcendental Phenomenology*, trans. David Carr (Evanston, IL: Northwestern University Press, 1970), 90–103.

32. Benjamin, *GS* 1:607–8; Benjamin, *SW* 4:313–14. On Husserl's thinking of the *Ur-historicity* of the *lifeworld*, see Husserl, *Hua* 39:53–59.

33. See chap. 3 in Rafael Bernabe, *La maldición de Pedreira (Aspectos de la crítica romántica-cultural de la modernidad en Puerto Rico)* (San Juan, PR: Huracán, 2002), 38–57.

34. See the intermezzo in López-Baralt, ed., *Sobre ínsulas extrañas*, 217–35.

35. See López-Baralt, ed., *Sobre ínsulas extrañas*, 219.

36. López-Baralt, ed., *Sobre ínsulas extrañas*, 221.

37. Benjamin, *GS* 1:608–9; Benjamin, *SW* 4:314.

38. Julia de Burgos, *Poema en 20 surcos* (San Juan: Imprenta Venezuela, 1938). The original edition lacks page numbers.

39. Derrida, *De la grammatologie* (Paris: Minuit, 1967), 208; Derrida, *Of Grammatology*, trans. Gayatri Chakravorty Spivak (Baltimore, MD: John Hopkins University Press, 2016), 157.

40. Derrida, *De la grammatologie*, 208; Derrida, *Of Grammatology*, 157.

41. Benjamin, *WuN* 19:133.

42. Martin Heidegger, *Gesamtausgabe* 58: *Grundprobleme der Phänomenologie* (1919/20), ed. Hans-Helmuth Gander (Frankfurt am Main: Klostermann, 2010), 33–34 (hereafter quoted as *GA*).

43. Husserl, *Hua* 6:145; Husserl, *Crisis*, 142.

44. Derrida, *Voyous*, 178; Derrida, *Rogues*, 127.

45. Husserl, *Hua* 6:51–2; Husserl, *Crisis*, 51.

46. Husserl, *Hua* 6:163; Husserl, *Crisis*, 161.

47. See Husserl, *Hua* 6:49; Husserl, *Crisis*, 48–49.

48. Husserl, *Hua* 37:290.

49. For a helpful discussion of Bergson's philosophy, see Suzanne Guerlac, *Thinking in Time: An Introduction to Henri Bergson* (Ithaca, NY: Cornell University Press, 2006).

50. Michel Henry's thinking of ipseity is both apposite to yet radically opposed to Derrida's. Even a cursory comparison of a text such as the passage from *Phénoménologie matérielle* that I quoted earlier (see Part II, n. 106) with a text such as *La voix et le phénomène* would suffice to show just how proximate yet how infinitely distant Derrida and Henry are on this key point. See chap. 6 in Jacques Derrida, *La voix et le phénomène* (Paris: Presses Universitaires de France, 1967), 78–97; Derrida, *Voice and Phenomenon*, trans. Leonard Lawlor (Evanston, IL: Northwestern University Press, 2011), 60–74.

51. See Giorgio Agamben, *L'uso dei corpi* (Vicenza: Peri Nozza, 2014), 351; Agamben, *The Use of Bodies*, trans. Adam Kotsko (Stanford, CA: Stanford University Press, 2016), 278.

52. Luis Lloréns Torres, "Cinco poetisas de América," in *Luis Llorens Torres: Antología verso y prosa*, ed. Arcado Díaz Quiñones (San Juan, PR: Ediciones Huracán, 1986), 160.

53. de Burgos, *Poema*.

54. For a different approach to de Burgos's erotic poetics in *Poema*, see Nannette Portalatín Rivera, *Julia de Burgos y la tradición de poesía erótica femenina en Puerto Rico* (San Juan, PR: Ediciones Callejón, 2015), 83–97.

55. Hortense J. Spillers, *Black, White, and in Color* (Chicago: University of Chicago Press, 2003), 229.

56. For Zambrana's discussion of the system of race/gender as a key technology of colonial governmentality and, in particular, for her use of the language of "actualization" to describe the historical reinstallation of racial/gendered hierarchies in neoliberal coloniality, see Rocío Zambrana, *Colonial Debts: The Case of Puerto Rico* (Durham, NC: Duke University Press, 2021), 35–44.

57. See Rita Segato, "Colonialidad y patriarcado moderno," in *La guerra contra las mujeres* (Madrid: Traficantes de sueños, 2016), 109–26.

58. See Spillers, *Black, White, and in Color*, 229. Zakiyyah Iman Jackson, "'Theorizing in a Void': Sublimity, Matter, and Physics in Black Feminist Poetics," *South Atlantic Quarterly* 117, no. 3 (July 2018): 635.

59. See Celenis Rodríguez Montero, "La metamorfosis del género," forthcoming.

60. See Saidiya Hartman, *Scenes of Subjection: Terror, Slavery, and Self-Making in Nineteenth-Century America* (Oxford: Oxford University Press, 1997).

61. Zakiyyah Iman Jackson, *Becoming Human: Matter and Meaning in an Antiblack Form* (New York: New York University Press, 2020), 83–85. See also, Jackson, "'Theorizing,'" 621–22.

62. Benjamin, *GS* 5:N10a3, 595/475.

63. These conditions would never be *sufficient*, since a constellation cannot "appear" except in a moment of *dangerous* reading that not only remains unpredictable and nonprogrammable but remains nonarrived even at the moment of its arrival.

64. Benjamin, *GS* 5:N3,1, 578/463.

65. G. W. F. Hegel, *The Difference between Fichte's and Schelling's System of Philosophy*, trans. H. S. Harris and Walter Cerf (Albany: SUNY Press, 1977), 156.

66. Benjamin, *WuN* 19:133.

67. Alexander Weheliye, *Habeas Viscus: Racializing Assemblages, Biopolitics, and Black Feminist Theories of the Human* (Durham, NC: Duke University Press, 2014), 3.

68. See Jackson, *Becoming Human*, 3. See Cathérine Malabou, *La plasticité au soir de l'écriture. Dialectique, destruction, déconstruction* (Paris: Léo Scheer, 2005), 113; Malabou, *Plasticity at the Dusk of Writing: Dialectics, Destruction, Deconstruction*, trans. Carolyn Shread (New York: Columbia University Press, 2010), 61.

69. Benjamin, *GS* 2:201; Benjamin, *SW* 1:250.

70. Carl Schmitt, *Der Begriff des Politischen: Text von 1932 mit einem Vorwort und drei Corollarien* (Berlin: Duncker & Humboldt, 1963), 9.

71. de Burgos, *Poema*. I reproduce this poem exactly as published in the first book edition. The poem appeared with slight variations in *El Imparcial* on March 5, 1938.

72. Lena Burgos-Lafuente, "Untendered Eyes: Literary Politics of Julia de Burgos—Introducción," *CENTRO Journal* 26, no. 2 (Fall 2014): 9.

73. Lilliana Ramos Collado, "Julia de plata," *CENTRO Journal* 26, no. 2 (Fall 2014): 32.

74. Vanessa Pérez Rosario, *Becoming Julia de Burgos: The Making of a Puerto Rican Icon* (Chicago: University of Illinois Press, 2014), 38.

75. Ivette López Jiménez, *Julia de Burgos: La canción y el silencio* (San Juan, PR: Fundación Puertorriqueña de las Humanidades, 2002), 68.

76. Carole Pateman, *The Sexual Contract* (Stanford, CA: Stanford University Press, 1988), 2.

77. See Burgos-Lafuente, "Yo, múltiple: Las cartas de Julia de Burgos," introduction to *Cartas a Consuelo*, ed. Lena Burgos-Lafuente (San Juan, PR: Folium, 2014), xxix.

78. Paul de Man, *The Rhetoric of Romanticism* (New York: Columbia University Press, 1984), 112, emphases mine. On de Man's distinction between paraphrase and reading, see also de Man, "Preface: The Task of the Interpreter," in Carol Jacobs, *Dissimulating Harmony: The Image of Interpretation in Nietzsche, Rilke, Artaud, and Benjamin* (Baltimore, MD: Johns Hopkins University Press, 1978), ix–xii.

79. Paul de Man, "Preface: The Task of the Interpreter," xii.

80. Spillers, *Black, White, and in Color*, 229.

81. See Frantz Fanon, *Peau noire, masques blanques* (Paris: Éditions du Seuil, 1952), 6; Fanon, *Les damnés de la terre* (Paris: Éditions La Découverte, 2002), 302; Emmanuel Levinas, *Humanisme de l'autre homme* (Paris: Fata Morgana, 1987), 9; see also Katherine McKittrick, ed., *Sylvia Wynter: On Being Human as Praxis* (Durham, NC: Duke University Press, 2016), 42–43.

82. Jonathan Culler, *Theory of the Lyric* (Cambridge, MA: Harvard University Press, 2015), 8.

83. Culler, *Theory of the Lyric*, 8.

84. Culler, *Theory of the Lyric*, 8.

85. de Man, "Lyrical Voice in Contemporary Theory: Rifaterre and Jauss," in *Lyric Poetry: Beyond New Criticism*, ed. Chaviva Hošek and Patricia E. Parker (Baltimore, MD: John Hopkins University Press, 1985), 55.

86. Derrida, *La voix*, 16, quotation modified for syntactical purposes; Derrida, *Voice*, 14.

87. de Man, "Lyrical Voice in Contemporary Theory," 55.

88. Culler, *Theory of the Lyric*, 7.

89. Benjamin, *GS* 1:607; Benjamin, *SW* 4:313.

90. Culler, *Theory of the Lyric*, 191.

91. Culler, *Theory of the Lyric*, 191.

92. Cicero, *De oratore* (Cambridge, MA: Harvard University Press), 2:115.

93. Charles Baudelaire, *Œuvres complètes*, ed. Claude Pichois (Paris: Pléiade, 1975), 1:6; Baudelaire, *The Flowers of Evil*, trans. Nathan Brown (Zagreb: MaMa, 2021), 8.

94. s.v. "dicho, cha," *Diccionario de la lengua española*, https://dle.rae.es/dicho#K1fW7Ux.

95. Barbara Johnson, "Apostrophe, Animation, and Abortion," in *The Surprise of Otherness: A Barbara Johnson Reader*, ed. Melissa Feuerstein et al (Durham, NC: Duke University Press, 2014), 218.

96. Culler, *Theory of the Lyric*, 2.

97. Trina Padillo de Sanz, "De la Hija del Caribe a Julia de Burgos," quoted in Rodríguez Pagán, *En blanco*, 183.

98. de Sanz, "De la Hija," quoted in Rodríguez Pagán, *En blanco*, 183.

99. de Sanz, "De la Hija," quoted in Rodríguez Pagán, *En blanco*, 184.

100. Pérez Rosario, *Becoming Julia de Burgos*, 39.

101. Paul Ricœur, *Soi-même comme un autre* (Paris: Seuil, 1990), 42; Ricœur, *Oneself as Another*, trans. Kathleen Blamey (Chicago: Chicago University Press, 1992), 29.

102. Ramos Collado, "Julia de plata," 32.

103. Ivette López Jiménez, *Julia de Burgos: La canción y el silencio* (San Juan, PR: Fundación Puertorriqueña de las Humanidades, 2002), 68.

104. Áurea María Sotomayor, "El Delito de Julia, la outsider," *CENTRO Journal* 26, no. 2 (Fall 2014): 70.

105. Zambrana, *Hegel's Theory of Intelligibility* (Chicago: University of Chicago Press, 2015), 30.

106. See Prudentius, "The Fight for Mansoul," in *Prudentius I*, trans. H. J. Thomas (Cambridge, MA: Harvard University Press, 1949), 274–343.

107. Ramos Collado, "Julia de plata," 35.

108. Edwin Cuperes, *"Poema en 20 surcos*: Enfrentamiento dialéctico a la crítica doxográfica, ético/moral e ideológica desde el materialismo filosófico como teoría de la literatura," PhD diss., Centro de Estudios Avanzados de Puerto Rico y el Caribe (2020), 482–83.

109. Fanon, *Peau noire*, 7.

110. Although this poem remains astonishingly underread by de Burgos's commentators, I want to mention the following two brief but compelling recent engagements with *Poema* and, specifically, with "2. Íntima" that have marked my own reading: Gaddiel Francisco Ruiz Rivera, "Metapoesía y desdoblamientos por los caminos de la mujer del mar," in *Hablan sobre Julia: Reflexiones en su centenario*, ed. Carmen M. Rivera Villegas and Lydia Pagán Tirado (Ponce, PR: Casa Paoli/Publicaciones Gaviota, 2015), 121–28; and Luis Othoniel Rosa, "Los cuentos antes que las cuentas. Parte II: Julia de Burgos," *Puerto Rico Review* 2 (March–September 2018): 19–34. Although there are many affinities between Othoniel Rosa's essay and my reading of de Burgos, our approaches diverge on fundamental points. Othoniel Rosa's essay, though rigorously constructed, is committed to the reactivation of de Burgos's totem along political lines. His excellent essay, in this respect, stands in continuity with Gelpí's reading of de Burgos as a nomadic figure. This explains why Rosa opens his essay arguing that "Intimacy, in Julia's poetry, has nothing to do with a private place, a psychic interiority, a comfortable, bourgeois refuge" (19). Although I agree with all of these statements, my approach to de Burgos's intimacy does not seek to continue the lionization of this figure but instead seeks to inquire into the essence of de Burgos's intimacy by interrogating the historical conditions of its emergence and the modes

of violence that subtend its production. To anticipate my answer to this question, I would say that intimacy is not a "psychic interiority" precisely because it is a *pure* phenomenological interiority—an interiority far more internal, innermost, indeed intimate, than one's own mindedness could ever be. Likewise, I must confess my puzzlement at Othoniel Rosa's claim that the poem "2. Íntima" is the favorite of critics; in my own research, I have seldom come across a sustained reading of this rather unlyrical, prosaic, and enigmatic poem.

111. By "monadological structure," I am referring to a motif that Benjamin introduces in "Zentral Park" ("Central Park") in order to pose the question of the unity of Baudelaire's *Les fleurs du mal*. See Benjamin, *GS* 1:658; Benjamin, *SW* 4:162.

112. de Burgos, *Poema*.

113. See Mircea Eliade, "Les problèmes des origines du Yoga," in *Yoga. Science de l'homme integral*, ed. Jacques Masui (Paris: Les Cahiers du Sud, 1953), 19; Eliade, *Yoga: Immortality and Freedom*, trans. Willard D. Trask (New York: Routledge, 1958), 37. On the concept of *samādhi*, see Stuart Ray Sarbacker, *Samādhi: The Numinous and the Cessative in Indo-Tibetan Yoga* (Albany: SUNY Press, 2005). Sarbacker's work on Indo-Tibetan Yoga engages affirmatively with Eliade's work and renders *samādhi* as "meditative absorption."

114. Benjamin, *GS* 1:607–8; Benjamin, *SW* 4:313–14.

115. See chapter 3 in Donna V. Jones, *The Racial Discourses of Life-Philosophy: Négritude, Vitalism, and Modernity* (New York: Columbia University Press, 2010), 77–128.

116. For the *locus classicus* of Benjamin's concept of aura, see Benjamin, *WuN* 16: 215; Benjamin, *SW* 3:105.

117. Benjamin, *GS* 1:673; Benjamin, *SW* 4:175.

118. On Husserl's motif of the "sphere of ownness," see Husserl, *Hua* 1:124–30; Husserl, *Cartesian Meditations*, trans. Dorion Cairns (The Hague: Martinus Nihjoff, 1960), 92–99.

119. Husserl, *Hua* 34:187.

120. McKittrick, ed., *Sylvia Wynter: On Being Human as Praxis*, 16–17.

121. Henry, *Incarnation: Une philosophie de la chair* (Paris: Seuil, 2000), 90.

122. Lloréns Torres, "Cinco poetisas de América," in *Luis Llorens Torres: Antología verso y prosa*, ed. Arcado Díaz Quiñones (San Juan, PR: Ediciones Huracán, 1986), 160. This text was originally published in *Puerto Rico Ilustrado* (13 de noviembre de 1937).

123. See Angelica Nuzzo, *Ideal Embodiment: Kant's Theory of Sensibility* (Bloomington: Indiana University Press, 2018).

124. I am here thinking, of course, of de Man's most famous essay, "The Rhetoric of Temporality," which distinguishes allegory and irony as tropological systems precisely on the basis of the different temporal schemas to which they give rise. See

de Man, *Blindness and Insight: Essays in the Rhetoric of Contemporary Criticism*, 2nd ed. (Minneapolis: University of Minnesota Press, 1983), 206–8. That being said, de Man's thinking of allegory developed significantly from the publication of this essay until his death, and this development could also be construed in terms of de Man's increasing proximity to, or reliance on, Benjamin's work on allegory in the *Trauerspiel* book, as can best be seen in de Man's discussion of Hans-Robert Jauss's engagement with allegory in the essay "Reading and History." See de Man, *The Resistance to Theory* (Minneapolis: University of Minnesota Press, 1986), 68–70.

125. Benjamin, *GS* 1:397; Benjamin, *Origin*, 243.

126. Benjamin, *GS* 1:397; Benjamin, *Origin*, 243.

127. s.v., "recogerse a buen vivir," *Tesoro lexicográfico del español de Puerto Rico*, https://tesoro.pr/lema/recogerse-a-buen-vivir.

128. On the notion of mere life (*bloßes Leben*), see Benjamin, *GS* 2:200; Benjamin, *Toward the Critique of Violence: A Critical Edition*, ed. Peter Fenves and Julia Ng (Stanford, CA: Stanford University Press, 2021), 57.

129. McKittrick, ed., *Sylvia Wynter: On Being Human as Praxis*, 17.

130. It is worth recalling that Spillers's theorization of the "divided flesh" against which the "high crimes" of the Black slave trade was committed also insists on the atomistic quality of the body. Spillers, *Black, White, and in Color*, 209.

131. See chapter 1 in Denise Ferreira da Silva, *Toward a Global Idea of Race* (Minneapolis: University of Minnesota Press, 2007).

132. I am grateful to Nicole Cecilia Delgado for this observation. For a discussion of this linguistic phenomena in the context of Puerto Rican speech patterns, see Manuel Álvarez Nazario, *El habla campesina del país: Orígenes y desarrollo del español en Puerto Rico* (Río Piedras, PR: Editorial de la Universidad de Puerto Rico, 1990), 174.

133. See Plato, *Phaedrus* 246a–249d.

134. The idea of life as phenomenological immanence is the core insight of Henry's material phenomenology. My claim is that this particular moment in de Burgos's life tracks closely with how Henry understands precisely invisibility as the very phenomenality of life itself: "Now, this non-seeing or this non-seen, this invisible, is not the unconscious, the negation of phenomenology but its first phenomenalization; not a presupposition but our life itself in its incontestable pathos: affect in its passion." Henry, *Phénoménologie matérielle* (Paris: Presses Universitaires de France, 1990), 111.

135. Husserl, *Hua* 37: 296.

136. Jacques Lacan, *Le séminaire. Livre X: L'angoisse* (Paris: Éditions du Seuil, 2004), 114.

137. On Marcion, in relation to Benjamin, see the classic study of Jacob Taubes, "Walter Benjamin—A Modern Marcionite? Scholem's Benjamin Interpretation Reexam-

ined," in *Walter Benjamin and Theology*, ed. Colby Dickinson and Stéphane Symons (New York: Fordham University Press, 2016), 164–78.

138. See Charles Baudelaire, "La chambre double," in *OC* 1:280–82. For a perceptive reading on this poem apposite to my reading of this moment in "2. Íntima," see Elissa Marder, *Dead Time: Temporal Disturbances in the Wake of Modernity* (Stanford, CA: Stanford University Press, 2001), 40.

139. On the concept of *Kairos*, see Manfred Kerkhoff, "Zum antiken Begriff des Kairos," *Zeitschrift für philosophische Forschung* 27, no. 2 (April–June 1973): 256–74.

140. Immanuel Kant, *Kritik der reinen Vernunft* (Berlin: De Gruyter, 1968), A162/B203, (hereafter quoted as *KrV*); Kant, *Critique of Pure Reason*, trans. Paul Guyer and Allen W. Wood (Cambridge: Cambridge University Press, 1998), 287 (hereafter quoted as *CPR*).

141. Henri Bergson, *Essai sur les donées immédiates de la conscience*, ed. Frédéric Worms (Paris: Presses Universitaires de France, 2007), 74, emphases mine; Bergson, *Time and Free Will: An Essay on the Immediate Data of Consciousness*, trans. F. L. Pogson (Mineola, NY: Dover), 100.

142. For Heidegger's most thorough engagement with Aristotle's treatise on time in his *Physics*, see Heidegger *GA* 24:108–69; Heidegger, *Basic Problems of Phenomenology*, trans. Albert Hofstadter (Bloomington, IN: Indiana University Press, 1985), 77–119.

143. Heidegger, *GA* 2:546; Heidegger, *Being and Time*, trans. Joan Stambaugh and Dennis Schmidt (Albany: SUNY Press, 2010), 293–94.

144. de Burgos, *Poema*.

145. Wynter, "Unsettling the Coloniality of Being/Power/Truth/Freedom: Towards the Human, After Man, Its Overrepresentation—An Argument," *New Centennial Review* 3, no. 3 (2003): 267.

146. See de Man, *Rhetoric of Romanticism* (New York: Columbia University Press, 1984), 262.

147. Alberto Moreiras, *Infrapolitics* (New York: Fordham University Press, 2021).

148. Kant, *KrV*, A166/B207–8; Kant, *CPR*, 290.

149. de Burgos, *Poema*.

150. de Burgos, *Poema*.

151. See Rodolphe Gasché, *Of Minimal Things: Studies on the Notion of Relation* (Stanford, CA: Stanford University Press, 1999), 265.

152. Zakiyyah Iman Jackson, "'Theorizing,'" 635.

153. Marcia Sa Cavalcante Schuback, *Time in Exile: In Conversation with Heidegger, Blanchot, and Lispector* (Albany: SUNY Press, 2021), 106.

154. G. W. F. Hegel, *Hauptwerke 2: Phänomenologie des Geistes*, ed.Wolfgang Bonsiepen and Reinhard Heede (Hamburg: Felix Meiner, 2018), 433–34.

155. Henry, *Entretiens* (Paris: Éditions Sulliver, 2005), 118.

156. See Nelson Maldonado Torres, "Afterword: Critique and Decoloniality in the Face of Crisis, Disaster, and Catastrophe," in *Aftershocks of Disaster: Puerto Rico*

before and after the Storm, ed. Yarimar Bonilla and Marisol LeBrón (Chicago: Haymarket, 2019).

157. See chap. 2 in Walter D. Mignolo, *The Darker Side of Western Modernity: Global Futures, Decolonial Options* (Durham, NC: Duke University Press, 2011), 77–117. See part 1 in da Silva, *Toward a Global Idea of Race*, 17–90.

158. To be sure, that the split between *res cogitans* and *res extensa* belongs to the arsenal of epistemic weapons mobilized in and through the institution of modern coloniality is irrefutable; what is questionable, however, is that the Cartesian text can or should be interpreted solely in this light. Indeed, Derrida's gesture with regards to Foucault's reading of Descartes in *Histoire de la folie à l'age classique* remains paradigmatic in my eyes of the problems that assail decolonial philosophy as a project of thinking. Jacques Derrida, "Cogito et histoire de la folie," in *L'écriture et la différence* (Paris: Seuil, 1967), 51–99; Derrida, "Cogito and the History of Madness," trans. Alan Bass (London: Routledge, 2002), 36–77. A similar but even more intense gesture as Derrida's also informs the work of Henry, whose own thinking of ipseity led him to produce an *affective* Descartes that is unrecognizable when compared to the Cartesian punching bag to which philosophers of all stripes—not just decolonial ones, of course—have had recourse for quite some centuries. See the essays gathered in Henry, *Phénoménologie de la vie II. De la subjectivité*, ed. Paul Audi (Paris: Presses Universitaires de France, 2003). That being said, I want to clarify that my ultimate concern is not with whether the decolonial reading of Descartes is correct, generous, or even interesting. My concern is rather that, in restricting the purview of the metaphysical meaning of modernity to a mind/body dualism that would determine the structure of coloniality as both a system of power and an onto-epistemology, decolonial thought is constantly running the risk of simply upholding *alternatives* to the West that upon closer inspection are not alternative at all to Western coloniality and could have only been held to be such because of the limited purview of (and in this sense false) false exits from the intractable historico-metaphysical problem that we face.

159. The motif of "(un)gendering" is one of the central concepts that Hortense J. Spillers theorizes in her foundational intervention in Black feminist theory. Spillers, *Black, White, and in Color*, 207.

160. da Silva, *Toward a Global Idea of Race*, xxxix.

161. da Silva, *Toward a Global Idea of Race*, xxxviii.

162. da Silva, *Toward a Global Idea of Race*, xv.

163. See Wynter, "Human Being as Noun? Or Being Human as Praxis? Towards the Autopoetic Turn/Overturn: A Manifesto," unpublished essay.

164. Weheliye, *Habeas Viscus*, 3.

165. Spillers, *Black, White, and in Color*, 207.

166. For the conceptual language of reactualization as a way of describing the constant renewal of the onto-epistemic conditions of coloniality in a Caribbean, and indeed Puerto Rican context, I am indebted to Rocío Zambrana's work. See the introduction to Zambrana, *Colonial Debts*, 1–20.

167. de Burgos, *Poema*.

168. Gelpí, *Literatura y paternalismo*, 39.

169. López Jiménez, *Julia de Burgos*, 73.

170. Palés Matos Afrophilic essays and the Hispanophilic responses of his friend and collaborator José de Diego Padró were included as an appendix to Diego Padró's short memoir of his friendship with Palés Matos. See José de Diego Padró, *Luis Palés Matos y su trasmundo poético* (San Juan: Editorial Puerto, 1973).

171. For a helpful overview of the debates about Blackness and *mulataje* in the 1930s and the role of Palés Matos therein, see chap. 4 in Isar P. Godreau, *Scripts of Blackness: Race, Cultural Nationalism, and US Colonialism in Puerto Rico* (Chicago: University of Illinois Press, 2015), 121–46.

172. Godreau, *Scripts of Blackness*, 193.

173. Pérez Rosario, *Becoming Julia de Burgos*, 35.

174. See chaps. 3 and 4 of Jones, *The Racial Discourses of Life Philosophy*, esp. 121–50.

175. Frank B. Wilderson III, *Red, White, and Black: Cinema and the Structure of US Antagonisms* (Durham, NC: Duke University Press, 2010), 18.

176. López Baralt, ed., *Sobre ínsulas extrañas*, 140.

177. López Baralt, ed., *Sobre ínsulas extrañas*, 142.

178. López Baralt, ed., *Sobre ínsulas extrañas*, 143.

179. López Baralt, ed., *Sobre ínsulas extrañas*, 145.

180. Calvin Warren, *Ontological Terror: Blackness, Nihilism, and Emancipation* (Durham, NC: Duke University Press, 2018), 27.

181. See Édouard Glissant, "La barque ouverte" in *Poétique de la relation* (Paris: Gallimard, 1990), 17–21. See also Derek Walcott, "The Muse of History," in *What the Twilight Says* (New York: Farrar, Straus and Giroux, 1998), 36–64.

182. Sotomayor, "El Delito de Julia, la outsider," 72.

183. da Silva, *Toward a Global Idea of Race*, xxiv.

184. Jackson, *Becoming Human*, 23.

185. Hartman, *Scenes of Subjection*, 5.

186. José Manuel Torres Santiago, *Julia de Burgos, poeta maldita* (San Juan, PR: Los Libros de la Iguana, 2014), 24; Yolanda Ricardo Garcell, *Más allá del tiempo: Julia de Burgos* (San Juan, PR: Editorial Patria, 2016), 82.

187. For a study of the "racialist underpinnings of the ideology of the [Puerto Rican] Creole intelligentsia" during the 1930s, see Magali Roy-Féquière, *Women, Creole Identity, and Intellectual Life in Early Twentieth-Century Puerto Rico* (Philadelphia: Temple University Press, 2004), 202–29. For a summary of his compelling account of the advent of racialist thought among the elite Puerto Rican intellectuals and politicians before the 1930s, see Rubén Nazario Velasco, *Historia de los derrotados: Americanizacón y romanticism en Puerto Rico, 1898–1917* (San Juan, PR: Ediciones Laberinto, 2019), 259–80. For an excellent historical study outlining the

material and cultural processes of whitening in the first decades of US colonial rule in the island, with a special focus on the racialist ideology of the island's liberal elite, see chap. 2 in Ileana Rodríguez Silva, *Silencing Race: Disentangling Blackness, Colonialism, and National Identities in Puerto Rico* (New York: Palgrave, 2012), 59–90. On Pedro Albizu Campos's conception of race, see Pedro Albizu Campos, *Obras escogidas*, vol. 2: *1923–1936*, ed. J. Benjamín Torres (San Juan, PR: Editorial Jelofe, 1981), 118–19.

188. Luis Lloréns Torres, "Cinco poetisas de América," 160.

189. García Martínez, "Geografía histórica," 37.

190. García Martínez, "Geografía histórica," 7–8;

191. García Martínez, "Geografía histórica," 24. On the racial, demographic category of *pardo libre*, see Jay Kinsbrunner, *Not of Pure Blood: The Free People of Color and Racial Prejudice in Nineteenth-Century Puerto Rico* (Durham, NC: Duke University Press, 1996), 1.

192. Rodríguez Pagán, *En blanco*, xix.

193. For instance, see Yolanda Arroyo Pizarro, "Bembetrueno o el nombre del racismo en Puerto Rico" (July 27, 2017), https://afrofeminas.com/2017/07/27/bembetrueno-o-el-nombre-del-racismo-en-puerto-rico-yolanda-arroyo-pizarro. Arroyo Pizarro, one of the leading Afro–Puerto Rican writers and activists, includes in her discussion of the system of cultural effects of anti-Blackness in Puerto Rico her own ignorance of de Burgos's reputed racial pride in her Blackness. It is telling that this blog was posted three years after de Burgos's letters to her sister Consuelo were published, which contain eloquent evidence of de Burgos's own strategies at passing and her own anti-Blackness.

194. de Burgos, "Martes 9 de abril," in *Cartas a Consuelo* (San Juan, PR: Folium, 2014), 27; translation modified from Roque Raquel Salas Rivera, "The Fetish of the Self-Translator: Self-Translation in the Work of Sotero Áviles and Ángela María Dávila," PhD diss., University of Pennsylvania, 2019.

195. de Burgos, *Cartas a Consuelo*, 38.

196. Roque Raquel Salas Rivera, "The Fetish of the Self-Translator: Self-Translation in the Work of Sotero Áviles and Ángela María Dávila," PhD diss., University of Pennsylvania, 2019, 43.

197. Derrida, *L'écriture et la différence*, 410; Derrida, *Writing and Difference*, 352.

198. Derrida, *Voyous*, 13; Derrida, *Rogues*, xiv.

199. Pérez Rosario, *Becoming Julia de Burgos*, 35.

200. César Salgado, "Sotero Figueroa y las dos aboliciones," *80 grados*, March 26, 2021, https://www.80grados.net/sotero-figueroa-y-las-dos-aboliciones/.

201. See Orlando Patterson, *Slavery and Social Death* (Cambridge, MA: Harvard University Press, 2018).

202. Sotomayor, "El delito," 85.

203. Judy Rodríguez, "Poetic Stasis: Staging Ethnonationalism in Puerto Rico,"

forthcoming manuscript. My thinking about Puerto Ricans' romance with *mestizaje* and racial-democracy discourses is also deeply inflected by Ren Ellis Neyra's work on the pitfalls of the category of Brownness articulated mostly by Latinx studies scholars working in the wake of José Esteban Muñoz. See Ren Ellis Neyra, "The Question of Ethics in the Semiotics of Brownness" *SX Salon* 35 (October 2020): http://smallaxe.net/sxsalon/discussions/question-ethics-semiotics-brownness. On the persistence of anti-Blackness within hegemonic constructions of Latinx identity, see also Yomaira C. Figueroa, "Your Lips: Mapping Afro-Boricua Feminist Becomings" in *Frontiers: A Journal of Women Studies* (41.1, 2020): 4. That said, if the past century could be described as the century of Puerto Rican (colonial) state-sponsored whitening, recent work by Yarimar Bonilla and Isar Godreau suggests that Puerto Rico's intensifying political crisis in the last decade is bringing about a shift away from Whiteness in the construction of racial identities on the island. See Yarimar Bonilla and Isar Godreau, "Nonsovereign Racecraft: How Colonialism, Debt, and Disaster are Transforming Puerto Rican Racial Subjectivities," *American Anthropologist* 123: 509–25. https://doi.org/10.1111/aman.13601.

204. Jared Sexton, *Amalgamation Schemes: Antiblackness and the Critique of Multiracialism* (Minneapolis: University of Minnesota Press, 2008), 25. I want to thank Axelle Karera for bringing Sexton's crucial work on multi-racialism and anti-Blackness to my attention.

205. Fanon, *Peau noire*, 6. For a powerful reading that seeks to suspend and interrupt the reputed certainty of this destiny, see the foreword to David Marriot, *Whither Fanon? Studies in the Blackness of Being* (Stanford, CA: Stanford University Press, 2018), ix–xix.

206. de Burgos, *Poema*.

207. On Jackson's reformulation of the *black mater* in terms of an "abject representation" and the Kantian sublime, see Jackson, "Theorizing," 622. For her thinking of the *black mater* as condition of possibility of Western notions of worldhood, see Jackson, *Becoming Human*, 39. For a discussion of "*the* world *as such*," see also her important footnote 32 to chapter 2 of *Becoming Human*, 233–34. To the extent that the speaker of "Ay ay ay" must undergo a form of death precisely in order to function as the *mater* of a mestizo-cum-whitened world, we may also say that the speaker of this poem exhibits an astonishing capacity to revel in her own becoming *compost*, to borrow a conceptual figure from Dixa Ramírez D'Oleo: "Compost is an eerily apt metaphor for blackness: that which issues from death to yield life for something else." See Dixa Ramírez D'Oleo, *This Will Not Be Generative* (Cambridge: Cambridge University Press, 2023), 12.

208. I take the liberty of referring the reader to my essay "Desire, Bent: Temporal Ruptures in Two Poems of Julia de Burgos," *diacritics* 46, no. 2 (2018): 125–27.

209. Jacques Lacan, "The Place, Origin and End of My Teaching," in *My Teaching*, ed. Jacques Alain-Miller, trans. David Macey (London: Verso, 2008), 38.

EPILOGUE: AFTER SOVEREIGNTY?

1. Jacques Derrida, *L'animal que donc je suis*, ed. Marie-Louise Maillet (Paris: Galilée, 2006), 83–84; Derrida, *The Animal That Therefore I Am*, ed. Marie-Louise Maillet, trans. David Wills (New York: Fordham University Press, 2008), 56.

2. Derrida, *L'animal*, 53; Derrida, *The Animal*, 31.

3. Derrida, *L'animal*, 44–45; Derrida, *The Animal*, 24.

4. See Friedrich Nietzsche, *Unzeitgemäße Betrachtungen*, in *Kritische Studienausgabe*, vol. 1, ed. Giorgio Colli and Mazzino Montinari (Berlin: de Gruyter, 1980), 270; Nietzsche, *Unfashionable Observations*, trans. Richard T. Gray, in *The Complete Works of Friedrich Nietzsche* (Stanford, CA: Stanford University Press, 1995), 2:107.

5. Hortense J. Spillers, *Black, White, and in Color* (Chicago: University of Chicago Press, 2003), 208.

6. Juan Carlos Quintero Herencia, *De la queda(era): Imagen y detención en Puerto Rico* (Lajas, PR: Editorial El Cangrejo, 2022), 35, emphases mine.

7. Quintero Herencia, *De la queda(era)*, 35, emphases mine.

8. Yarimar Bonilla, "Unsettling Sovereignty" *Cultural Anthropology* 32, no. 3 (2017): 330–39.

9. Walter Benjamin, *Werke und Nachlaß* 19: *Über den Begriff der Geschichte*, ed. Gérard Raulet (Frankfurt am Main: Suhrkamp, 2010), 95–96; Benjamin, *Selected Writings*, vol. 4: *1938–1940*, ed. Howard Eiland and Michael Jennings (Cambridge, MA: Harvard University Press, 2006), 390–91.

INDEX

"1. A Julia de Burgos" (de Burgos), 181–82, 184, 192–200, 203, 240, 258, 269; "12. Ay ay ay de la grifa Negra" and, 178; apostrophe in, 186–90, 195; feminism of, 201; namelessness in, 185, 268; psychomachia of, 185, 195–96, 200, 202, 239
"2. Íntima" (de Burgos), 174, 181–82, 202–36, 244–47, 315n110, 318n138; "12. Ay ay ay de la grifa negra" and, 255–56; "16. Soy en cuerpo de ahora" and, 237; the flesh/la *carne* in, 181, 211–12, 215–22, 225–27, 229, 236–37, 239–43, 255; ipseity in, 232, 238; psychomachia of, 202, 241; Spanish language in, 219
"12. Ay ay ay de la grifa negra" (de Burgos), 88–89, 178–79, 181–82, 248–51, 253–59, 262–66; the flesh/la *carne* in, 243

Abbau, 8, 172–73, 226. *See also* Husserl, Edmund
absolute, the, 47, 290n45; German idealist schema of, 48; Hegel's conception of, 180; as the messianic, 53
La Acción, 14, 67, 78, 296n116
Afro-Puertoricanness, 255, 257, 259
Agamben, Giorgio, 138, 174, 181, 305n108
Agüeros, Jack, 28, 294n94
Albizu Campos, Pedro, 64–66, 72–73, 77, 258, 293n83; Catholicism of, 295n97; on dictatorship of the proletariat, 296n115; on race, 320–21n187
Anglo-Saxonness, 32, 170
Ankersmit, Frank, 4–6, 52, 121–22, 127–28, 131, 133–35, 301n41; idealism of, 5, 119; *Meaning, Truth, and Reference in Historical Representation*, 9, 110, 115–20, 129; *Narrative Logic*, 120
anti-Blackness, 21, 179, 256, 265, 269–70, 278, 321n193

antifascism, 16, 93
appropriation, 16, 106–7, 193; of geometry, 62; historical, 4, 20, 98; of the past, 21, 102; self-, 215; of selfhood, 12; of the Third World, 31; transcendental, 60
Aristotle, 111, 125–29, 146, 187, 307n134; Heidegger on, 318n142; Lyotard on, 308n138
Arroyo Pizarro, Yolanda, 259, 321n193
Ateneo Puertorriqueño, 17, 65, 81–82
authenticity, 17–18, 184, 202, 231, 270
autoaffectivity, 44, 180, 192
autobiography, 274–75
autopoiesis, 246, 275
Ayala, César, 158, 293n84, 308–9n2, 308n9

Baudelaire, Charles, 19, 33, 37–44, 48, 53–54, 63, 112, 207–8, 233, 293n71; Benjamin's, 64, 74; "La chambre double," 229, 318n138; *Les fleurs du mal*, 34, 36, 41, 43, 187–88, 316n111; modernist poetics of, 212. *See also* fame
Baumgartner, Hans Michael, 5–6
Beauchamp, Elías, 65, 75
being, 11–12, 21, 32–33, 58, 123, 126, 138–41, 143, 146–48, 170, 176, 227, 255, 267, 311n25; of *Dasein*, 304n98; as exteriority, 239; flesh/*carne* and, 181, 241–42; form-of-life and, 305–6n108; geometrical, 62; great chain of, 120; historical, 52, 111, 124, 133, 148; history of, 8, 131–33; humanity and, 228; inheritance and, 95; ipseity and, 112, 140, 266, 306n109; meaning of, 117; metaphysics and, 303n80; phenomenal actuality of, 125, 127; as presence, 10, 131; presentation of, 136; racial, 252; sense of, 210; social, 196; structure of, 43; subjectivity as essence of, 174; time and, 231
being-possible, 12, 138, 140, 304n98

325

Beiser, Frederick, 9, 11, 285n19
Benjamin, Walter, 2–3, 12, 18–19, 23, 45–46, 48–54, 93, 96–97, 113–14, 121–22, 150–52, 159, 172, 180, 276, 301n31; on allegory, 212–13, 316–17n124; aura, 208, 290n41, 316n116; on Baudelaire, 33–44, 63–64, 74, 187, 207–8, 212, 293n71, 316n111; on Bergson, 36–42, 207, 209; *bloße Leben*, 181; Copernican turn of, 47, 55, 291nn53–54; Hamacher on, 143; historical methodology of, 292n64; letter to Horkheimer, 110, 112–13, 115, 129; Marcion and, 317–18n137; on modernity, 167; *Das Passagen-Werk*, 18, 35, 39–40, 44, 46, 49, 58–59, 97, 141, 179, 283n5; symbol and, 57, 292–93n70; theory of historical time of, 292n65; theory of history of, 101–2, 118, 142, 144, 151, 290n45, 291n54, 299n5; *Über den Begriff der Geschichte*, 52, 59, 110, 112–14, 141, 149–52, 298n154, 308n147. *See also* catastrophe; catastrophic tradition; constellation; danger; dialectical image; image; index; indexicality; *Lebensphilosophie*; materialism; messianic, the; rescue; tradition of the oppressed
Bennington, Geoffrey, 136, 148, 280
Bergson, Henri, 36–44, 174, 207, 209, 230, 238–39, 312n49; *Essai sur les données immédiates de la conscience*, 231; legibility of, 53; racial metaphysics of, 208. *See also durée; élan vital; Lebensphilosophie*
Bernabe, Rafael, 158, 167, 293n84
Bernstein, Leonard, 28–29, 287–88n9
Black *mater*, 20, 178, 263, 266, 270, 322n207
Blackness, 242, 249–51, 254–56, 258, 260–61, 263, 266; de Burgos's pride in her, 321n193; *mulataje* and, 320n171; ontology and, 284n7
Bosch, Juan, 15, 78
bourgeoisie, 172–73; de Burgos as terrorizer of, 63, 74, 79–80; liberal monohumanist Man2 and, 90
Burgos, Consuelo, 23–26, 321n193
Burgos-Lafuente, Lena, 17, 87–88, 94–96, 183–84, 279

capitalism, 157; agrocapitalism, 158
catastrophe, 2, 56, 58–59, 92, 98; conformism as, 114; continuity of, 43; modernity's, 181, 244–45, 270; temporality of, 62

catastrophic tradition (Benjamin), 17–18, 20, 43, 58–62, 91–92, 96, 162, 164, 184; de Burgos's, 18, 59, 61, 63, 82, 89, 92–93, 97–99, 102–3, 108, 164, 270, 275. *See also* traditionalization
catastrophic traditionality: de Burgos's, 59; grammar of, 164
causality, 13; schema of, 59
Chandler, Nahum Dimitri, 3, 109, 284nn6–7
closure, 111–12, 130–33, 137, 255; of historicism, 10, 12, 22, 114, 128–30, 133–35; of history, 136; ipseity and, 140–41, 274–75
coloniality, 73, 89–90, 244–45, 295n102, 319n158; Cartesian, 246; neoliberal, 313n56; onto-epistemic conditions of, 319n166
colonization, 29–31, 157, 161, 167–68, 177, 201, 308–9n2
compulsory heterosexuality, 177, 295n102
conformism, 96, 114, 150, 276
constellation, 40, 49–50, 52–53, 59, 151, 164, 179–80, 271, 313n63; of dangers, 142, 306–7n119; of the image, 100, 291n54; of legibility, 39; of modernity, 19–20, 34, 165, 179, 211
contingency, 21, 122, 128, 150, 153; historical, 167; of historicity, 95; of history, 12; reading danger and, 13; of transgressive acts, 251
continuity, 13, 231, 244, 254, 256; of catastrophe, 43; catastrophic, 64; of catastrophic tradition, 20; of genealogy, 95; schema of, 60, 62
correlation, 5, 51, 55, 100; appropriative mode of, 99; a priori, 46, 48, 53, 153, 210, 291n54; transcendental, 4, 46, 53, 102
correlationism, 48, 111; transcendental, 4
Corretejer, Juan Antonio, 67, 71–73, 78–79, 162, 249
criollo 252–53, 309n6; elites, 157, 167, 253; *Lebensphilosophie*, 168; national consciousness, 156
Culler, Jonathan, 186–88
Cuperes, Edwin, 76, 78, 193, 201, 279, 286n26, 293–94n85

danger (Benjamin), 2, 12, 50, 60, 62, 96–97, 99, 111, 122, 128, 136–37, 140–44, 146–53, 164, 306–7n119; of being missed, 291n54; of the Blackening of Puerto Rico, 254; historical, 144, 146, 149, 151; reading, 13,

135; of reflexivity, 108. *See also* historicity: nonhistoricist
Dasein, 210, 231, 241, 274; being of, 138, 304n98; existential analytic of, 11
Dávila Marichal, José Manuel, 66, 294n86
De Burgos, Julia: "4. Dáme tu hora Perdida," 168, 175, 234–36; "8. Amaneceres," 80–81, 168, 171, 173, 211, 232–34; "10. Nada," 176, 236–37; "20. Yo misma fui mi ruta," 32–33, 208, 266–69; afterlife of, 18, 31–32, 34, 63, 88, 99, 102–3, 165, 184; alcoholism of, 15–16, 23, 79; "A plena desnudez," 75–76, 80; becoming-totem of, 275; bohemian lifestyle of, 13, 15, 79, 81; *Canción de la verdad sencilla*, 14, 26, 81; canonization of, 27–28, 259; *Cartas a Consuelo*, 56, 94, 260–61; catastrophic reception of, 108, 164, 181, 184, 190, 265, 270; critical reception of, 88; death of, 26–27, 29, 57, 82, 84–85; fame of, 33, 43, 54–55, 63–64; FBI investigation of, 15, 56, 93, 293–94n85; as feminist icon, 74, 89; "Gloria a ti," 67–69, 72; historical reception of, 16; historicist reception of, 99, 102–3; image of, 17, 35, 44, 54, 57, 62, 64, 68, 80, 82, 85, 87, 91, 93, 97, 99, 162–63, 165, 211, 276; initial reception of, 259; lacuna in reception of, 162, 252; "La mujer ante el dolor de la patria," 71–73, 295n99; *New York Times* obituary of, 27–33; as nomadic subject, 17, 87–88, 163–64, 184, 250, 315–16n110; over-reading of, 54–55, 57; *Poemas exactos a mí misma*, 26, 71; political militancy of, 15–16, 66, 73; as progressive totem, 91, 262; promiscuity and, 15, 79–80; pseudonyms of, 193–94; psychomachia of, 239; reception of, 19–20, 27–28, 33, 57, 63, 79, 84, 86–87, 89, 92–94, 262, 269, 276; reception history of, 58, 60–62; self-imposed exile of, 16, 84; totem of, 17–18, 20, 62, 86–87, 91–92, 315–16n110; as totem of the marginalized, 276; as totem of Puertoricanness, 54, 184; totemic reception of, 17–18, 92, 249; traditional reception of, 62; US academic reception of, 56; "Yo quiero darme a ti," 69–71, 73, 77. *See also* "1. A Julia de Burgos;" "2. Íntima;" "12. Ay ay ay de la grifa negra;" catastrophic tradition; fame; *imitatio Iuliæ*; *Poema en 20 surcos*
deconstruction, 8, 131–32, 134, 148–50, 172–73, 226, 274; de Manian, 186; desedimentation and, 284n6; of historicism, 121; of history, 21–22, 108, 111, 132–33, 135, 284–85n14; ipseity and, 246; of Wynterian decipherment, 311n25. See also *Abbau*; desedimentation; *Destruktion*
Deleuze, Gilles, 3, 87–89, 109, 160
De Man, Paul, 3, 114, 123, 185–87, 233, 234; on allegory, 316–17n124; conception of the symbol, 57, 292–93n70; on distinction between paraphrasis and reading, 314n78; on lyric poetry, 191
democracy, 253; racial, 251, 259, 265, 276
Derrida, Jacques, 2–3, 5, 8, 12, 21, 30, 45, 47, 93–95, 99, 103–8, 111, 114, 119, 133–34, 136–40, 148–49, 152–53, 160, 172, 180, 187, 262, 285n22, 293n81, 302n65, 307n126; arche-writing, 133–34; on autobiography, 273–74; on Benjamin, 301n31; *De la grammatologie*, 130, 132; desedimentation and, 284n6; *différance*, 298–99n3; on the essence of the religious, 73; on Foucault, 319n158; iterability, 135, 172; supplementarity, 171; "Violence et métaphysique," 103, 105; *La voix et le phénomène*, 10, 131, 238, 312n50. *See also* closure; deconstruction; *différance*; Henry, Michel; ipseity; narcissism; somnambulism; writing
desedimentation, 3, 9, 17, 62, 64, 257, 284n6; of de Burgos's catastrophic tradition, 99; of historicism, 108–9, 130; of Wynterian decipherment, 311n25
Destruktion, 8, 172
dialectical image (Benjamin), 18–19, 35, 39–40, 43–45, 53, 59, 92, 100–2, 108, 110, 118, 141, 163, 165, 179, 291n54; Baudelaire as, 39; constellation and, 180; de Burgos's, 54, 164; Fynsk on, 306–7n119; indexicality of, 48; legibility of, 49–50; as non-synthesis (Weber), 298–99n3. *See also* image
différance, 8, 104, 106, 291n54, 298–99n3
Dilthey, Wilhelm von, 12, 36–37
durée (duration), 38–41, 174, 231, 238

Echeverría, Bolívar, 19, 166–67, 309n11
élan vital, 42, 174, 207, 290n41; racial, 251
Eliade, Mircea, 204, 316n113
embodiment, 19–20, 80, 181, 222, 227, 247, 255; ideal (Kant), 211, 221, 241; radical, 246
empiricism, 2–3, 20, 99, 118, 130, 152
endangerment, 18, 141

enstasis, 204–5
epokhē, 173, 209, 220
ergontology, 123–28, 131
event, 12, 30, 45, 58, 93, 99, 108, 119, 121, 132, 179, 191, 214–16; absolute knowledge as, 131; deconstruction and, 148–49; historical, 19, 51, 53–54, 146; image and, 291n54; of ipseity, 214–15, 218; literary, 124–25, 194; modernity as, 167; phenomenal, 123; poem as, 186; time of, 230
evidence, 105, 134; empirical, 1, 64

fame: Baudelaire's, 34–35, 38–39, 41–44, 53, 63; de Burgos's, 17, 33–35, 43, 54–55, 58, 63–64, 73–74, 92, 295–96n106
Fanon, Frantz, 86, 186, 202, 266
femininity, 176; Black, 20, 251, 266; patriarchalized, 247; postpatriarchal, 255
feminism, 90–91, 181; anti-patriarchal, 16; de Burgos's, 176–79, 184–86, 201–2; of respectability, 15
field, 3, 109; of the composible, 135; conceptual, 198; of experience, 147; historical, 10, 130; of the historical, 22, 114, 133, 274; of historical mimesis, 128; of historical representation, 133; of historical temporality, 45; of history, 131; of legibility, 54; of the scopic, 223; of transcendental/a priori experience, 211
Fink, Eugen, 34, 289n22
flesh, the (*la carne*), 73, 180, 215, 247, 270; mortifications of, 71; in *Poema en 20 surcos*, 19, 181, 247. *See also* "2. Íntima;" "12. Ay ay ay de la grifa negra"
formal subsumption, 157–58, 309–10n13
Foucault, Michel, 3, 8, 114, 138; histories of the present, 164; reading of Descartes, 319n158
Frente Unido Femenino Pro Convención Constituyente de la República de Puerto Rico, 14, 71–72
Freud, Sigmund, 82–83, 105–7

Gelpí, Juan, 88–89, 163–64, 167, 175, 249–51, 256, 315–16n110; "El sujeto nómada en la poesía de Julia de Burgos," 17, 87, 91
gender, 44, 65, 176–78, 295n102, 313n56; de Burgos's outlook on, 80–81; hierarchies, 177, 288n18; ipseity, 247; modern system of, 73, 177; normative strictures of, 184; oppression, 28; roles, 79, 176; patriarchal system of, 201
Generación del 30, 66, 87, 93, 161–62, 201, 244; racist/racialist discourse of, 251
geometry, 61–62, 222
González, José Emilio, 17–18, 82–85, 87
Great Depression, 77, 155–56, 158
Guattari, Félix, 3, 87–89, 109

Hamacher, Werner, 96, 101, 109, 141; "Jetzt: Benjamin zur historischen Zeit," 143–44, 291n54, 299n5; "Über einige Unterschiede zwischen der Geschichte literarischer und der Geschichte phänomenaler Ereignisse," 110–11, 122–29. *See also* ergontology
Hartman, Saidiya, 22, 178, 256–57
Hegel, G. W. F., 124–25, 131; conception of the Absolute, 180; conception of history, 122–23; *Phänomenologie des Geistes*, 244
Heidegger, Martin, 3, 8, 11–12, 51, 114, 117, 119, 133, 135, 172, 174, 210, 230, 285n23, 318n142; always already, 241; *Ereignis*, 308n138; inauthentic time, 239; *Sein und Zeit*, 11, 138, 148, 231, 238, 285nn23–24, 304n98; *das Selbe*, 138–39, 304n105; step back, 283n3. *See also* being; being-possible; *Dasein*
Henry, Michel, 138, 174, 209–10, 244, 312n50, 317n134, 319n158; *Phénoménologie matérielle*, 305n106
Hernández, Rafael, 155–56
Las Hijas de la Libertad, 65–66
Hispanicity, 170, 249
historians, 9, 16, 22, 52, 55–56, 60, 102, 110, 136; critical, 95–96; danger and, 142; deconstruction and, 134; historicist, 4, 6, 135, 153; historicity of, 100–1; normative, 7
historical idea, 6, 110, 115–21, 128–29, 131, 166
historical indexicality, 45–46, 52
historical knowledge, 6, 34, 47–48, 50–52, 111, 149, 153; danger and, 140–41, 143; reading and, 122
historical representation, 2, 10, 102, 114, 116–18, 128–29, 131–33, 153; mastery and, 108; reference and, 120; sovereignty and, 274
historical time, 10, 45, 50, 53, 59–60, 98, 130, 152; (de)constitution of, 291n54; dialectics

INDEX

of, 49; historicity of, 101; image and, 100; ipseity and, 48; theory of (Benjamin), 46, 292n65
historicity, 8, 13, 34–38, 43, 54, 58, 60, 95, 107, 122–23, 142, 153; aestheticization of, 42; of Baudelaire's readers, 41; dangerous, 21–22, 98, 125, 144–45, 149, 271; de Burgos's, 18–19, 62, 92, 99, 103, 164; of experience, 207; finitude and, 148; of the historian, 51–52, 93, 100–1; historicism's, 10; of historicism's history, 7; of history, 141; of human life, 170–72; idealist foreclosure of, 121; of the image, 306–7n119; internal, 130, 132; of man/Men, 268; of modernity, 34–35, 53, 202, 245; nonhistoricist, 6, 11–12, 102, 108, 111, 136, 143; originary, 166–67, 173; phenomenality and, 146; of *Poema en 20 surcos*, 164–65, 174, 176, 180, 194, 270; of the present, 33, 50; rethinking of, 119; of trauma, 22; of violence, 104. *See also* Puerto Rican historicity
historiography, 21–22, 115–16, 125, 128, 136; historicist, 96, 124; materialist, 142; modern, 150; Puerto Rican, 19, 86; transcendental approach to, 5; Western, 129
Holz, Hans Heinz, 118, 150
humanism, 185, 239; anti-, 211; of Man/men, 20, 186, 228–29
humanity, 24, 75, 84, 90, 170–71, 174–75, 178, 181, 228, 237, 256–57, 275–76; bourgeois, 171–73, 233; humane, 85; inhuman, 186, 202, 268; ipseity and, 206, 211; loss of, 254; of Man, 269–70; modern, 36, 171, 240; natural condition of, 83; Puerto Rican, 88, 91; redeemed, 26, 151; universal, 89; untarnished, 25–26
Humboldt, Wilhelm von, 115–16, 121, 128
humility, 30, 98
Hurricane María, 30, 288n13
Husserl, Edmund, 3, 7–8, 12, 48–49, 60, 105–6, 131, 172–74, 226, 284n6; being-in-itself, 140; genetic turn, 104, 300n12; *Ideen zu einer reinen Phänomenologie und phänomenologischen Philosophie*, 138; lifeworld, 166–67, 311nn31–32; "Origin of Geometry," 61–62, 284–85n13; sphere of ownness, 209, 316n118. See also *Abbau*; *epokhē*; geometry; *Rückfrage*; sedimentation; sense-configuration; tradition

Ibarbourou, Juana de, 69, 79
idealism, 116, 119, 121; German, 116, 118–19; historical, 48; narrative, 6, 166; of the self, 200; transcendental, 49–50, 211
ideology: aesthetic, 85, 160, 187; Albizuist, 72; of Creole intelligentsia, 320–21n187; of Generación del 30, 244; of male supremacy, 201–2; mestizaje, 257; Nationalist, 69, 76–77
illegibility, 1, 19; historical, 34, 58–59, 92–94, 103
image (Benjamin), 18, 39–40, 44–50, 52, 97, 100, 102, 107, 112–13, 179, 291n54; danger and, 141–44, 306–7n119; as historicist, 118; of the past, 51; as synthesis, 298–99n3. *See also* De Burgos, Julia: image of
imitatio Iuliæ, 17, 85
index, 45–46, 53; danger as, 143; fame as historical, 38–39, 42, 44; historical (Benjamin), 44–46, 48–49, 51, 53; minute-, 204, 229, 239–40; temporal, 45–46, 52
indexicality: of the dialectical image, 48; historical, 45–46, 52, 180; split, 100
industrialization, 14, 38
inheritance, 2, 59; De Burgos's, 247, 256; of filial genealogy, 101
intimacy, 143, 200, 206–7, 222, 226, 242, 246, 268, 315–16n110; "2. Íntima," and, 210, 218, 221, 227, 229; in "8. Amaneceres," 233–34; in "10. Nada," 236; enstatic movement of, 181; in *Poema en 20 surcos*, 19, 176, 180, 244, 255; poetics of, 174, 209, 266; time of, 244
ipseity, 5, 12–13, 16, 60, 112, 136–41, 147, 153, 167, 186, 192, 194, 202–3, 206–11, 216–17, 220–29, 231, 235, 238, 240, 242–43, 255, 266, 269, 273–76, 298, 299, 305n103, 305n106, 305–6nn108–9, 312n50, 319n158; danger and, 111, 277; de Burgos's, 18; embodied, 19, 175–76, 210, 226, 230, 239, 247, 265, 270; event of, 214–15, 218; feminine, 201; finite, 104, 106–7; flesh and, 241; gendered, 19, 176–78, 180–81, 185, 196, 246–47, 265, 270; of the historian, 48, 52, 55; historical, 20, 97–98, 107, 124, 152–53, 262, 275; intimacy and, 174; intimate, 232, 244, 247; kinaesthetic, 174; Levinas on, 304n100; metaphysics of, 122; modernist, 268; poetics of, 21, 181, 185, 208; sovereign,

ipseity (*continued*)
245–46; sovereignty and, 160, 276; worldification of, 234

Jackson, Zakiyyah Iman, 20, 177–78, 181, 243, 257, 256, 270. *See also* Black *mater*
Jimenes Grullón, Juan Isidro, 14–15, 74, 81, 260
Jiménez de Báez, Yvette, 66, 286n24, 294–95n96
Jones, Donna V., 208, 251
Jung, Carl, 36–37
justice, 27, 31, 136, 146, 159; divine, 183, 197; social, 87

Kant, Immanuel, 11, 46–49, 79, 145–46, 210–11, 235, 298–99n3; *Critique of Pure Reason*, 144–45, 231, 285n23, 291n53, 303n72
katabasis, 205, 234
Keller, Gottfried, 149, 152–53
Kimhi, Irad, 146, 308n139
Klages, Ludwig, 36–37
Kleinberg, Ethan, 7, 21, 45

labor, 157–58, 162, 191, 309–10n13; reproductive, 201
Lacan, Jacques, 226, 269
Lanauze Rolón, José, 15, 260
Lebensphilosophie, 36–37, 40, 42, 85, 168, 170, 174, 207, 209. *See also* Dilthey, Wilhelm von
legibility, 18–19, 21–22, 33–34, 39–40, 42, 53–54, 97, 164, 179; "1. A Julia de Burgos" and, 184; de Burgos's, 57, 91, 93; historical, 34, 50, 53, 93–94, 141–43; of history, 136; of the image, 44–45, 48–49, 52, 306–7n119; representation and, 117; specular, 17
letrados, 65, 79
lettered city: Puerto Rico's, 57, 63, 75, 80–81, 249; San Juan's, 14, 77
Levinas, Emmanuel, 103, 138, 186, 304n100
Levi-Strauss, Claude, 83, 89
lifeworld, 6, 19, 53, 57, 166–67, 172–73, 209, 220, 234, 309n11, 311n31; agricultural, 158; of the ancien régime, 199; capitalist, 159; feminism and traditional configuration of, 177; human, 5; patriarchal, 185; Puerto Rican, 208; Ur-historicity of, 311n32
literary history, 13, 20, 55, 96, 109, 144, 165; Benjaminian approach to, 92; modern, 34; nonhistoricist, 7, 19, 35, 44, 110, 114, 274

literary studies, 1–3
Lloréns Torres, Luis, 14–15, 79–80, 88, 161–62, 175, 210–11, 235, 249, 258
López Jiménez, Ivette, 184, 198, 249–51, 256
Lyotard, Jean-François, 146–47, 308n138, 311n29
lyric poetry, 34, 36, 39, 186, 191, 207

Malabou, Cathérine, 136, 181, 306n109
martyrdom, 64, 69, 74, 85; feminine, 295n102; logic of, 295–96n106
Marx, Karl, 86, 157–58
mastery, 10, 12–13, 21, 104, 107, 124, 131; attainment of, 98; desire for, 101; of the historian, 108; populism and, 199; possibility and, 137, 140; potentiality and, 5, 136
materialism, 286n26; dialectical, 141; historical, 53, 96, 113–14, 143, 149–50
memory, 28, 37, 40, 46, 58–59, 143, 150, 160; commodification of, 42; cultural, 14; historical, 58, 277; literary, 200; pure, 41–42; spontaneous, 38–39. *See also* Bergson, Henri; recollection
Méndez Ballester, Manuel, 159–60
messianic, the, 52–53, 151
mestizaje, 88, 249–50, 252, 259, 264–65, 270, 276; ideology, 257; whitening and, 178
metaphysics, 47, 88, 141, 291n53, 303n80; Bergson's racial, 208; Catholic, 71–72; closure of, 132; of historicism, 128, 152; history of, 129, 131, 133, 187; of ipseity, 112, 122; of life, 211; of modality, 11; of modernity, 245; of presence, 111, 132–33, 140, 278; racialist, 258; of racial life, 252; religious, 75; Western, 10, 110–11, 127, 146, 199. *See also* Ankersmit, Frank
Mistral, Gabriela, 13, 66, 69, 79
modernism: de Burgos's, 33, 44, 208, 275; literary, 15, 33
modernity, 19–20, 43, 166–67, 208, 211, 217, 253, 319n158; alternative histories of, 100; as catastrophe, 270; corrosive effects of, 206; critique of, 168, 175; dehumanizing forces of, 85; European, 34; gender and, 73; historicity of, 34–35, 53, 202; metaphysics of, 245; *Poema en 20 surcos*, and, 170, 179; violence of, 108. *See also* Echeverría, Bolívar
modernization, 43–44, 167, 221–22; capitalist, 41; colonial, 91; Puerto Rican, 19, 270

INDEX

Nancy, Jean-Luc, 138, 148
narcissism, 104–8; ethnonationalist, 16
narrative, 5–6, 10, 121; allegory as tropological, 213; contingency and, 21; cosmic, 166; cosmos 129; of feminist emancipation, 193; historical, 4, 122, 127; reading and, 185; self, 6, 12; of victimization, 84
nationalism, 64; Puerto Rican, 17, 82, 84–88, 93, 249
Négritude, 208, 251
New York City, 15, 25, 28–29, 83, 86, 260
Nietzsche, Friedrich, 3, 43, 95, 96, 147, 149. *See also* historians: critical
nonbeing, 11–12, 120, 146–47

objectivity, 48, 52, 113; historical, 47, 49, 51, 53, 141, 143, 152; nonhistoricist, 18
onto-epistemology, 89, 319n158
ontology, 136, 146–48; Blackness and, 284n7; closure of, 131; de Burgos's humanist, 242; of facticity, 210; fundamental (Heidegger), 11; historical, 21; historical time and, 10; of history, 5, 7, 11, 110–12, 118, 128, 131–32; ipseity and, 153, 306n109; of life (Bergson), 174; modern European, 245; modern humanity as temporal, 240; new (Wilderson), 251; political, 139, 288n14; realist, 6; Western, 153, 216; Whitened, 247–48
Ortega Y Gasset, José, 86, 168, 174, 258

Padilla de Sanz, Trina, 15, 190–92
Palés Matos, Luis, 161–62, 208, 249–52, 255, 320nn170–71
Partido Popular Democrático, 15, 87, 93
patriarchy, 29, 82, 140, 177, 184, 201
peasants, 14, 16; Whitened, 252–53
Pedreira, Antonio S., 87–88, 161–64, 167–68, 170, 174–75, 199, 252–55, 262–63; *Insularismo: Ensayos de interpretación puertorriqueña*, 87–88, 161, 163, 170, 249, 251, 253, 260; sexism of, 201; White supremacy of, 250, 252
Pereda, Clemente, 66–67, 71
Pérez Rosario, Vanessa, 84, 87, 184, 193, 250, 254, 256, 263; *Becoming Julia de Burgos*, 28, 56, 81
performativity, 30, 166
phenomenology, 137; classic, 103–4; deconstructive, 172; of embodied ipseity, 210; historical, 284–85n13, 309n11; Husserlian, 138, 172; of life, 174, 209, 248; material, 317n134. *See also* Henry, Michel
Plath, Sylvia, 27–29
Poema en 20 surcos (de Burgos), 14, 26, 32–34, 44, 64, 76–78, 81, 162–67, 170, 173–76, 179–82, 188–89, 202–4, 234–35, 245, 250, 255, 257–58, 261, 265, 268–71, 275, 288–89n19, 315–16n110; apostrophe in, 187; architectonics of, 236; erotic poetics in, 312n54; feminism of, 177; flesh/*carne* in, 247; historicity of, 194; intimacy and, 244; ipseity in, 19–20, 176, 178, 196, 201, 208–9, 246–47; phenomenology of life in, 248; poetics of presence and authority in, 184; raciality in, 266
poetics, 121; Afro-Caribbean, 256; antipatriarchal, 15; Aristotle's, 125, 129; of Blackness, 263; of bourgeois destruction, 172; de Burgos's, 44, 75–77, 86, 212; of empty and full time, 235; ergontology and, 126; erotic, 312n54; feminist, 176–78, 185; of *griferia*, 262; historical, 128; of historical writing, 122; of intimacy, 174, 209, 266; of ipseity, 21, 181, 185, 208, 276; Leibnizian, 127; metaphysical, 13, 22; modernist, 209, 212; of modern life, 208; of Nationalist glory, 72; nomadic, 87, 265; Palés Matos's, 250–51; of presence and authenticity, 184; of selfhood, 186; of sovereignty, 276; theologico-political, 69; transcendental cosmo-, 10, 111
positivism, 2–3, 20, 112–15, 118, 130, 152; historical, 4, 16, 116
possibility, 4–6, 11, 46–47, 57, 59, 94, 96, 104, 111, 121, 135–36, 144–45, 147–49, 152–53, 177, 285n23, 299n3, 303n72, 303n78, 304n98; of absolution, 85; danger and, 13; dangerous, 18, 62; *Dasein* and, 231, 241; of ergontology, 126; of historical appropriation, 98; of historical objectivity, 49, 143; historicism and, 12; of history, 53, 142–43, 146, 148, 150, 152; of intimacy, 19, 206; ipseity and, 137–40, 206, 246, 255; as ipseity, 124; necessary, 129, 133, 135–36; phenomenal event and, 123
potentiality: mastery and, 5, 136; sovereignty and, 139, 153
poverty, 13, 15–16, 74, 81

power, 121, 139–40, 245–46; coloniality as system of, 319n158; colonizing, 263; of historical constitution, 51; of historicity, 52; of historicization, 49; inequities, 1; of ipseity, 255; of labor, 309–10n13; of medical establishment, 26; poetic, 127; of poetics-cum-ergontology, 126; possibility and, 5, 12, 136–37; presentation and, 116, 133, 135; semantic, 131; of world-formation, 210
psychomachia/psychomachy, 183–84, 195–96, 200–1, 228; de Burgos's, 239. *See also* "1. A Julia de Burgos"
Puerto Rican Communist Party, 15, 26, 260
Puerto Rican diaspora, 26, 28–29, 87–88
Puerto Rican historicity, 54, 62, 265, 275; de Burgos and, 16–18, 55, 89, 91–92, 99, 102, 163–64, 184, 295–96n106; modernity of, 165, 175; modern life within, 167; readers of de Burgos and, 20; sameness and, 276
Puerto Rican history, 18, 65; as nomadology, 89
Puerto Rican independence, 65, 73, 77, 85, 258; de Burgos's support for, 16, 26, 31, 68, 81, 84, 287–88n9, 295n102; movement, 66, 72–73, 78
Puerto Rican Nationalist Party, 14, 64–67, 72, 75, 77–78, 93, 258, 293–94nn85–86; Catholicism and, 295n97
Puertoricanness, 161, 265, 276; Blackness in, 250; de Burgos and, 17–18, 20, 54, 57, 64, 88, 92–93, 164, 184, 275; de Burgos's heirs and, 85; *Insularismo* (Pedreira) and, 168, 174, 252; *mulataje* and, 249. *See also* Afro-Puertoricanness
Puerto Rican Socialist Party, 65, 86
Puerto Rican studies, 22, 273, 276, 279–80
Puerto Rico, 15, 23–26, 28, 55–56, 156, 201, 258, 260, 270, 287–88n9, 293n84; abolition of slavery in, 263; anti-Blackness in, 321n193; anti-colonial struggles in, 18; Blackening of, 254; coffee and, 308–9n2; colonial history of, 256; Gelpí, on, 88; independence movement, 66, 77–78, 258; Nationalist movement, 14, 16, 64, 66, 69, 73, 190, 295–96n106 (*see also* Puerto Rican Nationalist Party); relations with US, 29–31; speech patterns of, 219; statehood and, 65; US colonial rule of, 31, 65, 85, 87, 155, 157, 252, 320–21n187. *See also* sugarcane
Puerto Rico Ilustrado, 79, 81, 210, 230, 296n122, 316n122

Quine, W. V. O., 116, 134
Quintero Herencia, Juan Carlos, 94, 99, 276, 299n8

race, 169–70, 173, 254, 259, 261–62; Albizu Campos's conception of, 320–21n187; gender and, 295n102, 313n56; hierarchies, 288n18
raciality, 31, 178, 181, 245, 247–48, 256, 266
racism, 74, 90, 260; anti-Black, 256; cultural nationalism and, 249
Ramos Collado, Lilliana, 183, 185, 195, 201
Ranke, Ludwig von, 2, 115–16, 118, 152, 283n2
realism, 2–5, 11, 101, 109–10, 113; historical, 16, 46, 48; ontological, 7, 45–46
real subsumption, 157–58
recollection, 37, 123–24, 143
redemption, 52, 59, 150
remembrance, 58–59
Renovación, 14, 193
Ricoeur, Paul, 6, 138, 194
Riggs, Elisha Francis, 65, 72, 75
Rilke, Rainer Maria, 84–85
Rockefeller, Nelson, 15, 94
Rodríguez Beauchamp, Rubén, 66, 78–79
Rodríguez Pagán, Antonio, 28, 66, 71–72, 74, 259
Romano, Claude, 138, 305n103
Rorty, Richard, 117, 119
Rosado, Hiram, 65, 75
Rückfrage, 8, 60, 62

sainthood, 64, 69
Sartre, Jean-Paul, 137–38
schema of succession, 50, 59
Schmitt, Carl, 121, 182
Second Spanish Republic, 14, 77
sedimentation, 3, 8–9, 17, 20, 62, 64, 82, 284n5; catastrophic, 92; historical, 8, 156; tradition and, 60–61; uncritical, 113. *See also* sense-configuration
selfhood, 12, 111, 124, 137–38, 211, 216–17; de Burgos's poetics of, 186; historical, 52; ipseity and, 206; life as, 221; life of, 244; of life, 209; psychomachia and, 184, 195; social reification of, 194; sociopolitical modes of, 140
self-reading, 51, 54, 107
self-referentiality, 12, 104

self-reflection, 62, 270
sense-configuration, 8, 61, 130–33, 284–85n13, 303n78; de Burgos's image as, 164; historicism as, 4, 7, 10, 98; of Puerto Rican historicity, 265; within Puerto Rico's lettered city, 75
sexuality, 44, 80, 177
Silva, Denise Ferreira da, 31, 181, 217, 245, 256, 288n15
Sinnegebilde (sense-configuration), 7, 284–85n13. *See also* Husserl, Edmund
slavery, 177, 199, 257, 263–64; abolition of, 156; afterlife of, 22, 178, 250, 256–57
Solanas, Valerie, 27, 29
somnambulism, 2, 62, 283n4
Sotomayor, Aurea María, 91, 199, 256, 265
sovereignty, 12, 103–4, 111, 137, 139–40, 245–46, 262, 274; femininity and, 177, 185; of the historian and of history, 136; intimate, 270; ipseity and, 160, 177, 180; performativity and, 30; popular, 230; potentiality and, 153; Puerto Rican, 16, 78, 276
specularity, 102–3, 107, 191; idealistic, 249
Spengler, Oswald, 86, 168, 174, 258
Spillers, Hortense, 177–78, 185, 247, 276, 295n102, 317n130, 319n159
Spivak, Gayatri Chakravorty, 31, 303n78
Storni, Alfonsina, 69, 79
Suárez Díaz, Rafael, 67–69
subjectivity, 47, 136, 209; anthropo-centric, 274; of de Burgos, 190; de Burgos's nomadic, 163; historical, 53; ipseity and, 153; minoritarian, 18; modern, 174, 247, 305n103; Puerto Rican, 87, 276; transcendental, 138, 144–45
sugarcane, 157–60; industry, 65, 158. *See also* Méndez Ballester, Manuel; *tiempo muerto*

temporality, 181, 212, 229, 237, 239, 243, 268, 304n103; of agricultural lifeworld, 158–59; of *Dasein*, 231; without difference, 244; ecstatic, 205, 247; historical, 45; Husserlian, 180; metaphysics of presence and, 278; of tradition, 62
tiempo muerto, 158–61
Torres Santiago, José Manuel, 66, 93, 257; *Julia de Burgos: Poeta maldita*, 295–96n106
totem, 269; Freudian, 96; reactivation of, 60, 164, 315–16n110. *See also* De Burgos, Julia; traditionalization: totemic
totemic operators, 89–91
totemic tradition, 82–83, 162
totemism, 83, 89–91; de Burgos's theological-monumental, 64
traditionalization, 61, 88–89; catastrophic, 20, 58, 60, 64, 91–92, 164, 270; totemic, 162
tradition of the oppressed, 88, 101, 151, 163–64
transcendentality, 49, 111, 135, 144, 211, 213
Trujillo, Rafael Leonidas, 77–78

University of Puerto Rico: Association of Alumnae of, 81; Normal School of, 13, 66

Vasconcelos, José, 86, 258
Vientós Gastón, Nilita, 15, 81
violence, 22, 82, 295n102; in "1. A Julia de Burgos," 186, 201; in "2. Íntima," 211, 245–46; anti-Black, 276; counterviolence, 181, 185; history and, 1; intimacy and, 315–16n110; in *Poema en 20 surcos*, 20, 181, 245, 270, 275; threat of, 80; transcendental, 104–5

Weber, Samuel, 118, 298–99n3
Weheliye, Alexander, 20, 180, 247
Wells, Ida B., 27–29
White, Hayden, 3, 6, 16, 55–56, 115
Whiteness, 88, 252, 254, 258–59, 263, 266; US, 261
whitening, 178, 181, 253, 258–59, 263, 265, 320–21n187. See also *mestizaje*
white supremacy, 29, 252, 265–66; Hispanophilic, 179, 256; of Pedreira, 250
Wilderson, Frank, 31, 251, 288n14
Wittgenstein, Ludwig, 119, 146–47
writing, 134–35; arche-, 133–34; de Burgos's, 94; flesh and, 226; historical, 13, 102, 115–16, 120, 122, 128, 133, 135; of history, 126, 128–29; of life, 274; in neuter, 243; poetic, 128, 212
Wynter, Silvia, 89–91, 163, 178, 186, 199, 233, 246; canonism, 310–11n24; decipherment, 311n25

Zambrana, Rocío, 29, 73, 177, 200, 277, 288n18, 313n56, 319n166

Ronald Mendoza-de Jesús is Assistant Professor of Spanish and Comparative Literature at the University of Southern California.

IDIOM: INVENTING WRITING THEORY
Jacques Lezra and Paul North, series editors

Werner Hamacher, *Minima Philologica*. Translated by Catharine Diehl and Jason Groves

Michal Ben-Naftali, *Chronicle of Separation: On Deconstruction's Disillusioned Love*. Translated by Mirjam Hadar. Foreword by Avital Ronell

Daniel Hoffman-Schwartz, Barbara Natalie Nagel, and Lauren Shizuko Stone, eds., *Flirtations: Rhetoric and Aesthetics This Side of Seduction*

Jean-Luc Nancy, *Intoxication*. Translated by Philip Armstrong

Márton Dornbach, *Receptive Spirit: German Idealism and the Dynamics of Cultural Transmission*

Sean Alexander Gurd, *Dissonance: Auditory Aesthetics in Ancient Greece*

Anthony Curtis Adler, *Celebricities: Media Culture and the Phenomenology of Gadget Commodity Life*

Nathan Brown, *The Limits of Fabrication: Materials Science, Materialist Poetics*

Jay Bernstein, Adi Ophir, and Ann Laura Stoler, eds., *Political Concepts: A Critical Lexicon*

Willy Thayer, *Technologies of Critique*. Translated by John Kraniauskas

Julie Beth Napolin, *The Fact of Resonance: Modernist Acoustics and Narrative Form*

Ann Laura Stoler, Stathis Gourgouris, and Jacques Lezra, eds., *Thinking with Balibar: A Lexicon of Conceptual Practice*

Nathan Brown, *Rationalist Empiricism: A Theory of Speculative Critique*

Gerhard Richter, *Thinking with Adorno: The Uncoercive Gaze*

Kevin McLaughlin, *The Philology of Life: Walter Benjamin's Critical Program*

Alenka Zupančič, *Let Them Rot: Antigone's Parallax*

Adi M. Ophir, *In the Beginning Was the State: Divine Violence in the Hebrew Bible*

www.ingramcontent.com/pod-product-compliance
Lightning Source LLC
Chambersburg PA
CBHW020351080526
44584CB00014B/984